THE
MONEY
LAWYERS

*The No-Holds-Barred World
of Today's Richest and
Most Powerful Lawyers*

Joseph C. Goulden

T·T

TRUMAN TALLEY BOOKS
ST. MARTIN'S PRESS
New York

www.stmartins.com

Library of Congress Cataloging-in-Publication Data

Goulden, Joseph C.
    The money lawyers : the no-holds barred world of today's richest and most powerful lawyers / by Joseph C. Goulden.
        p. cm.
    Includes bibliographical references (p. 397) and index (p. 411).
    ISBN 0-312-20555-4
    EAN 978-0-312-20555-3
        1. Lawyers—United States—Biography. 2. Pratice of law—United States. 3. Class actions (Civil procedure)—United States. I. Title.

    KF372.G68   2006
    340'982'273—dc22

                                                                2005048657

First Edition: January 2006

10   9   8   7   6   5   4   3   2   1

For Truman M. Talley,
who started me on lawyers

For Leslie C. Smith,
wife and best friend

Contents

Introduction

Surely one cannot fault a single personal injury lawyer for the many problems besetting modern American law. Nonetheless, anyone seeking an answer to the question "What on Earth went wrong with an honored profession?" would do well to start in a modern office building in the Oak Lawn section just north of downtown Dallas. Here is the home of Baron & Budd, the epicenter of asbestos litigation, which can charitably be described as an out-of-control monster that has been gnawing chunks out of the U.S. economy for decades, with no surcease in sight.

I went to Baron & Budd one pleasant summer afternoon to talk with an engaging fellow named Fred Baron, who has earned millions from asbestos cases (he told me that his current caseload included 14,000 such clients) and who at the time was president-elect of the Association of Trial Lawyers of America, the trade group for the plaintiff bar. A graduate of the University of Texas law school, Baron did a stint with the Ralph Nader organization and then came to Dallas as a labor lawyer. He found himself, in the 1970s, representing workers in an East Texas plant who claimed injuries because of asphalt exposure. He seized upon what he recognized as a promising specialty, and the rest, shall we say, was very lucrative history. Baron and his firm have reaped millions of dollars from asbestos over the years.

But one thing puzzled me. Given that asbestos has been off

the market for decades, I asked Baron, how did he continue finding new claimants?

Baron set me straight in about ninety seconds. What was my
work history? I cited a boyhood grocery store job, and then mentioned the 1953 college summer I spent as a slusher operator and
high hangup man for the Climax Molybdenum Company, in Climax, Colorado. (In case you are interested, "molly denim," as we
mispronounced the term, is the stuff that makes stainless steel
stainless.)

Baron broke me off. "Heavy mining equipment," he said with
a triumphant smile. "Without a doubt the company had asbestos
on the brake bands. You probably have a case. Want to sign up
with us?"

He grinned but I got the idea he just might be serious. Climax
Molybdenum no longer exists, and I have the lung stamina of a
long-distance runner, so I gracefully declined Baron's offer.

But in that brief exchange, Baron made what was surely an
unintended point: If a shrewd lawyer really puts his mind to it, he
can find grounds—some would say a pretext—for a lawsuit in almost any given set of facts. And that ability, and a willingness to
use it, I concluded after several years of interviewing several hundred lawyers and lawyer watchers around the country, is the albatross that modern law has wrapped around its neck.

I do not fault Fred Baron; he plays under the rules as they are
written, he is a very skilled courtroom performer who does his
homework, and he has recovered handsome sums for many persons who suffered tremendous injury from exposure to asbestos.
Nonetheless, he epitomizes a system that has gone sorely awry.

To put it bluntly, Americans suffer from acute lawyer phobia.
All too many of our daily actions, personal and business, are
prefaced by the worrisome question "If I do this, is some lawyer
going to sue me? And even if I have a winning case, how much is
it going to cost me to avoid the trouble of fighting a suit?"

American law is light-years removed from the relatively se-
date profession described by Martin Mayer in his classic book
The Lawyers almost half a century ago. For the most part, the
lawyers of the generation that Mayer wrote about devoted them-

selves to solving problems, seldom resorting to litigation. To the average American, the lawyer was a distant but respected figure in the community, one with whom direct professional contact was limited to, say, writing a will or handling a real estate transaction. The thought of actually suing another person, or a corporation, was something that simply never came to most people's minds.

Let's commence with an important point: Lawyers have been an integral part of American life from the very beginning. Lawyers played distinguished roles in the founding of the great democratic experiment known as the United States. Our Declaration of Independence and Constitution were chiefly the product of lawyers. In the early days of the Republic, the legal profession was a sort of cultural glue that held the new society together. Hear the observations of a British naval officer, Capt. Frederick Marryat, who kept an extended diary as he traveled about America in the late 1830s. He was impressed with the lawyers he met, writing, "The lawyers are the real aristocracy of America; they comprehend nearly the whole of the gentility, charm, and liberal information of the Union."

Perhaps this is why lawyers long enjoyed an influence in most communities that was grossly disproportionate to their numbers. In my boyhood, they dominated local and state political offices, from the local school board to the state legislature. Along with clergymen, teachers, and physicians, they were likely the best educated men in town.

They bought (and read) books and wrote letters to the editor, and, as Martin Mayer observed, enjoyed an ex officio respectability as men who could be trusted with one's most intimate of secrets. (I write "men" deliberately, for in the Mayer era, women were just achieving a toehold in a profession that was predominantly male.)

The lawyer of the early 2000s, conversely, is a different fellow indeed, many seemingly interested only in finding new and interesting pretexts for suing someone else. Thus it has come to pass that the lawyer affects almost every one of us on a daily basis, through the indirect restrictions that their actions impose on our workaday lives. Here is a handful of examples:

✦   Because of the fear of lawsuits over injuries, Little League baseball players are no longer permitted to slide into bases, or await their turn at bat in the on-deck circle.

✦   Many churches formerly offered marital and other counseling services. No longer. The family of a man who committed suicide during counseling sued. The church won in court, but it and other congregations dropped the counseling because of the expense of defending against such suits.

✦   The swing sets and seesaws of playgrounds of generations past have vanished, to be replaced by spring-driven seats that can be used by one kid at a time. New York City even lops branches off trees in parks lest children be tempted to climb on them. Three-meter diving has vanished from schools in the Washington metropolitan area; too risky for young necks, and too expensive for school boards to defend in court.

✦   The ingenuity of lawyers in finding reasons for suing is seemingly boundless. In August 2002 lawyers for two Chicago men sued *Penthouse* in a class action, claiming that they and other readers suffered injuries because they bought copies of the magazine expecting to see nude photographs of the tennis star Anna Kournikova. The magazine had been hoaxed; the pictures actually were of another shapely naked blonde. A wise judge tossed the suit out of court.

✦   On a more serious level, fear of product-liability lawsuits caused the disturbing shortage of flu vaccine shots during the winter of 2004. In the 1960s and 1970s, America had as many as twenty-six vaccine manufacturers. Then came a flood of lawsuits, and the domestic production of vaccines essentially halted, with manufacturers fleeing abroad. In 2002, according to a study done for the Club for Growth, the vaccine industry worldwide had roughly $6 billion in sales. In that same year, plaintiff attorneys sought *$30 billion in damages in one lawsuit alone*. More than three hundred lawsuits were pending in various state and federal courts. Congress was warned in advance of the looming vaccine crisis, but a Democrat majority in both houses (well funded by the trial bar through campaign contributions) refused to permit a vote on a Vaccine Liability Protection Act.

But these lawyer-driven examples are trivial compared to the riches reaped in the past quarter century through class action litigation. And it is in this area that public disgust has veritably transformed the term "trial lawyer" into something akin to a barnyard epithet, in the minds of many persons.

As is true of many well-intended acts, class actions are a good cause that morphed into a monster. Changes in federal procedural rules in the 1980s, intended to strengthen consumer and civil rights laws, made it much simpler to bring class action cases in federal court, lumping thousands of individual plaintiffs into a single suit. Conventional tort lawyers quickly seized on the change to pursue a wide range of cases. On an individual basis, "damages" caused by a defective widget or credit practice might warrant only a few dollars of recovery. No lawyer is going to pursue a claim that results in damages of $10 or $20, or even less. But combining every person who ever purchased a widget into a single action can make such suits very profitable. And the most visible of today's high earners are men and women who specialize in class action suits—tobacco litigation, for instance, made billionaires out of at least a half dozen attorneys.

Eventually someone must pay the cost of class action litigation—and hence we come to the ultimate victim, the consumer. The amounts involved are serious money, hidden costs that boost the over-the-counter price of virtually every item that Americans purchase. A study published in 2003 by the Manhattan Institute, a conservative-libertarian think tank, found that settlements for litigation now exceed $200 billion annually in the United States. This works out to about 2 percent of the gross domestic product, far more than for any country in the world. Lawyers carry away about $40 billion of this pot of money—much of which they turn around and invest in new "liability areas"—that is, areas they can exploit for even more lawsuits, such as ubiquitous fast foods such as French fries and burgers, tap-water burns, and "cancer-causing cell phones." (My quotation marks are deliberate. No scientific linkage has been found between cell phones and cancer.)

The American consumer, of course, ends up paying for this litigation boodle in terms of higher prices. Consider Dow Chemical, a mammoth enterprise that has a supplier's role in the entire gamut of American commerce. John Scriven, a lawyer for Dow, is among the many defense attorneys who complain that "litigation expense is chilling business activity." As he states, "In the United States . . . Dow Chemical devotes one dollar in litigation to every $160 in sales, but in Europe, one dollar is devoted to litigation for every $40,000 in sales."

The Money Lawyers is an attempt to explain how the practice of law has become a dollar-driven enterprise in the past decades. A secondary theme is that the modern law firm has shed the old concepts of collegiality and loyalty that marked the generation written about by Martin Mayer. Time and again I found firms whose internal structure resembled that of their corporate clients, even down to "marketing departments" that used Madison Avenue advertising techniques to solicit new business.

In the Mayer era, a young lawyer joined a firm with the hope of making partner within seven or eight years, achieving the equivalent of academic tenure. He would stay with the firm for his professional life. No more. Salary wars that erupted in the winter of 2000–2001 saw fresh graduates being offered $125,000 annually (and often a $20,000 signing bonus as well) by major big-city firms. These new hires, mind you, were right out of school, with no on-the-job experience, and certainly no client base.

What was essentially a "money craze"—I first heard the term from an elder partner at one of Wall Street's premier securities firms—soon spread upward. In the Mayer era, it was unthinkable for a firm to try to hire away a partner from a rival office. No more, and indeed, firms set their sights on entire "practice groups," picking off dozens of lawyers in a single swoop. "Loyalty" became an outdated term, and lawyers also displayed the "follow the money" ethic of major league baseball in the era of free agents.

But *The Money Lawyers* is essentially a book about the

lawyers themselves, and how their careers illustrate what is still happening to their profession. Here are the personalities and firms that comprise the book.

In chapter 1, we meet David Boies, "the New Superlawyer," the man who became the best-known attorney in America because of his victory (albeit it a short-lived one) in the Microsoft antitrust case, and his role in the Florida election dispute of 2000.

Chapter 2, "Thomas Hale Boggs, Jr., Washington Superlobbyist," shows the nexus between money and politics in Washington, and reveals how a single law firm can channel millions of dollars of federal money to clients.

Chapter 3, "Breast Implants: The $10 Billion Rush to Judgment," shows how class action lawyers used bad science and a hysterical media to raid the coffers of manufacturers of devices that an overwhelming majority of affected American women desired.

Chapter 4, "The Diet Pill Wars," goes behind the closed doors of the so-called Class Action Club to show how a tight coterie of plaintiff lawyers control the largest cases in America's courts. You will witness how lawyers use both sharp elbows and bravado to gain dominant roles in these cases, and why one lawyer sighed, "I felt as if I had wandered into a dick-measuring contest."

In chapter 5, "Lerach and Weiss: The Class Action Scourges of West and East," we take an inside look at the money-machine firm created by attorneys Melvyn Weiss and William Lerach, which won an incredible $30 billion in suits against high-tech defendants. Many executives in Silicon Valley, and elsewhere, maintain that their loud and frequent charges of corporate fraud—more than a few of them with flimsy foundations, they argue—created an atmosphere of skepticism that resulted in serious misconduct being overlooked by regulators and corporate boards. Some of these critics stop just short of accusing the Milberg Weiss firm of being partially responsible for the high-tech stock collapse that shook the American economy in the late 1990s. The chapter also details how their partnership finally went on the shoals in mid-2004 because of an intense personal fight over a $50 million judgment against their firm.

Chapter 6 is a disturbing account of the ruthlessness a supposedly prestigious Wall Street firm used to drive away loyal partners so that newer persons in the firm could earn more money. The chapter vividly illustrates why American law has deteriorated from a distinguished profession to just another form of business. It details why a Florida judge, after reviewing the conduct of Cadwalader, Wickersham & Taft, declared that the firm was "up to its elbows in the dung heap."

During four-plus years of talking to lawyers and observers, I often despaired as to what could be done to restore the profession to its previous esteem. In a concluding section, I toss out some ideas on the subject. But first, the book.

THE
MONEY
LAWYERS

1 / David Boies: The New Superlawyer

The Smile. It never quite develops fully. Instead, his lips curl slightly, and his head tips a degree or so backward, usually to the right. His eyes flicker restlessly, as if seeking to find and acknowledge a friendly face. Then his neck straightens, and he makes a minute adjustment in the Smile, turning it up or down a perceptible degree. Nonetheless, never does it fully blossom.

I first noticed the Smile during the 1980s, when I dropped by David Boies's office at Cravath, Swaine & Moore in New York to ask him to help me make sense of the many antitrust suits against IBM Corporation, which he was helping defend. Cravath is a classy firm, with deep pile carpets and Portraits of Prominent Partners staring down from various walls, with a candelabrum out front to help the receptionist greet visitors. But going into Boies's office was akin to taking a stroll through a city dump. Discarded fast food containers under his desk and most everywhere else. Disorderly heaps of paper, both on his desk and the credenzas and the floor. Empty pop cans, a half-empty bag of pretzels, even a small bar of hotel soap. Someone else in the firm had told me, with a sad shake of his head, that among other foibles Boies was a dice freak who loved to take long weekends in the Las Vegas casinos, a most un-Cravath hobby which he went out of his way to flaunt. Gambling junk was scattered about in messy profusion—a miniature dice table and packets of casino chips. My hand went to my face to hide a smile when I realized that the desk itself was an old poker table.

Just how much Boies enlightened me on IBM and antitrust stuff long ago vanished into the crevices of my memory. I did conclude that Boies is one messy fellow and that he doesn't give a hoot about what other people think about him. But the main impression that remained with me was the Smile. I realized during our interview that in terms of understanding anything about antitrust law, Boies considered me perhaps one level above village duncedom. But he was kind about it, and after trying to explain an especially obtuse point, he would give me the Smile

But what was the man saying? Many lawyers speak in body language, but I am not always sure what they are saying. I spent many hours with Clark Clifford in the early 1970s; much of the time, the famed superlawyer sat with fingers spread and interlocked into a teepee at midriff level. By coincidence I read about the same time a book by body-language expert Julius Fast. Clifford was signaling superiority.

I saw the Smile again during the winter of 1998–99, in a federal courtroom in Washington, where Boies was cross-examining a minor witness in the Microsoft antitrust trial. The testimony was high-tech and tedious, so I decided to watch Boies rather than pay attention to words that I could download from a Web site at my leisure. Once again I found the Smile curious, and, for the moment, unfathomable. The Smile surely was not one of overt friendship. Instead, it seemed to be a convenient way for Boies to arrange his features as he performed for the judge hearing the case without a jury, more of a facial tic than an expression of any particular emotion. When he would momentarily turn away from the witness to examine a document, it would vanish altogether, as if not needed at the moment, then return quickly when he raised his head again.

Boies is interesting to watch. He is lank of frame, with sandy hair retreating beyond a domed forehead, a face of angles and gnarls. He is a fidgeter, even when on his feet; when he suddenly stands still, it is as if he wants his lack of emotion to focus attention on something he has just drawn from a reluctant witness. Born in Illinois, reared in California, schooled at Yale, Boies has a neutral voice that for the most part defies regionalization, although hints of the Midwest bounce up occasionally.

More than a year later I saw the Smile again on the television screen as Boies battled to gain Florida's electoral votes for Vice President Al Gore. And after several exposures I suddenly understood the Smile. What Boies was saying, through his facial expression, was "I'm smarter than you or anybody else, and I know it, and I'm going to prove it."

And indeed David Boies (rhymes with noise) might be smarter than the rest of us; at the dawn of the twenty-first century, he was arguably the most famous lawyer in America. As a special counsel to the Justice Department, he took on Microsoft and won a verdict that initially threatened to split the country's richest corporation into many parts. (A subsequent appellate court reversal led to direct negotiations that ended the case without significant damage to Microsoft.) Boies did the Microsoft case for peanuts, under a contract that averaged out to about $40 a working hour, perhaps one-twentieth of his hourly rate at his former corporate firm of Cravath, Swaine & Moore.

No matter. For publicity purposes, Microsoft was the ultimate loss leader in terms of attracting lucrative business for the firm of Boies, Schiller & Flexner, which he created shortly after leaving Cravath in 1997. His brand-new law office won a string of high-profile price-fixing cases that brought him and his partners tens of millions of dollars, plus more front-page publicity than most attorneys achieve in a lifetime. In concert with other plaintiff firms, Boies, Schiller & Flexner won a $1.05 billion settlement from vitamin manufacturers who fixed prices on sales to food-processing companies. His firm was lead counsel in an antitrust suit against the famed auction houses Sotheby's and Christie's that brought a $512 million settlement. The Boies firm reaped a fee of $26.7 million. There was the occasional loser—for instance, he could not persuade the federal courts to permit the online service Napster to provide copyrighted music to consumers.

But even this defeat had Boies on the front page of the *New York Times* six times in three weeks.

There were accolades from peers and the public alike. The *American Lawyer* dubbed him "the Lawyer of the Year" for 1999, based on his Microsoft victory. *Vanity Fair* put him in its portfolio of the most interesting persons of 1999. Even *People* magazine did a spread on his successes—as someone or another quipped, the first time in history that the celebrity-oriented *People* paid attention to antitrust law.

One thing I've learned after decades of lawyer watching is that the good ones are strong competitors. They are not unlike the NFL running back who wrestles out an extra yard or two on a run from scrimmage, or the NASCAR driver willing to steer through a paint-scraping opening at 195 miles an hour to move up a position. Boies summed up his attitude in an interview with Charlie Rose of PBS in late 1999, just after he won the Microsoft case. "Everybody's in the winning business," he said. "Everybody wants to win." Boies added a self-serving footnote: "But, when you're winning in the legal business, what you are doing is . . . you're creating justice." And, one might add, creating a good deal of personal wealth as well.

Boies's sudden prominence as a plaintiff lawyer is all the more remarkable because it came after he spent three decades doing the bidding of corporations at Cravath, Swaine & Moore, which is in the top rank of the nation's firms. Cravath is noted as an office that *defends* people who are sued by plaintiff lawyers. For a Cravath star to suddenly appear on the other side of the courtroom surprised many in and out of the legal profession.

Some, it did not. To people who have watched this extraordinarily complex man over his career, his decision to do a 180-degree career turn in his mid-fifties is part of a natural progression. One of his former Cravath partners sought to summarize Boise at the end of a long phone conversation. "David," he said, "is different from the rest of us. It is not just that he is smarter than a lot of people. He is different. That's all I can say." He repeated the sentence. "He is different."

SLOW STARTER WHO ACCELERATED

And, indeed, Boies was somewhat different at many stages of his life, starting in childhood. He gave full meaning to the term "late bloomer." One of five children of schoolteachers, Boies was born in 1941 in Sycamore, a northwest suburb of Chicago. The family moved to the Los Angeles suburb of Fullerton in 1954, where Boies earned spending money with a paper route. Boies's father supplemented his teaching income by working summers at a Sears, Roebuck store. (Years later, while toiling for the ultimate white-shoe law firm in Manhattan, Boies continued a preference for Sears' off-the-rack blue woolen suits.) Boies's early life was not easy. He suffered from dyslexia and did not learn to read until the third grade. As often happens with dyslexics, a keen memory compensates for the reading disability, and such proved the case for Boies. Even today he concedes that his "mental vocabulary" is twice that of his "spoken vocabulary," because there are words that he knows he cannot say.

Boies's life hit a detour soon after graduation from high school. His teen bride became pregnant, and the need to care for a family forced him to turn down a scholarship to Antioch College. Boies spent the next two years in nondescript jobs, including working as a construction worker for nine months. He realized he had to get his life on a productive track and enrolled in the University of Redlands. To support his family he held a medley of jobs, including editing a newspaper for a California mental hospital. He performed brilliantly, cramming three years' work into two, intending to follow his parents into teaching. A professor suggested that he reset his sights on law school. He took the Law School Admission Test and scored so high that the professor urged a friend at the Northwestern University School of Law to come interview him. Although Boies showed up in chinos and tennis shoes, the Northwestern emissary was so impressed that he offered a full scholarship. What especially drew Boies to Northwestern was a program that enabled students to enter law school after only three years of undergraduate work. The appeal was obvious: he was already years behind his contemporaries, and he wished to get on with his life.

Boies and the law were an immediate take. He scored the highest Northwestern marks since Arthur Goldberg, the future Supreme Court justice, who went through the school three decades earlier. By his second year he was editor of the *Northwestern University Law Review*. Much of the time he worked as an auditor six days a week from midnight to eight A.M. at a motel. He discovered a skill at tournament bridge, claiming to be winning more than his bookkeeper salary. Classmate Paul Rudnick would later tell author David Margolick for a *Vanity Fair* profile, "He was No. 1, and there was nobody close."

Then Boies did something that would come to typify his high-wire lifestyle. His early marriage had failed after producing two children. The unattached Boies struck up a romance with Judith Draynard, a student who served as his deputy editor on the law review. The discordant note in the affair was that Ms. Draynard happened to be married to a law professor. Academic life can be so barren, even at a major law school, that a minor sex scandal quickly becomes major gossip. The Boies-Draynard combination was no exception. Northwestern authorities dealt with the matter by suggesting that all three parties pursue their careers elsewhere.

Ms. Draynard went off to Columbia University; she and Boies eventually married, and they had twins, Christopher and Jonathan, born in 1968. (Both now practice with their father, as does his oldest child, Caryl, born in 1963.) Boies ended up at Yale Law, where he honed reputations both for brilliance and for being a man who did what he pleased. In 1966 he graduated second in his class, no mean achievement at highly competitive Yale. And he did not hesitate to accept an offer to join Cravath, Swaine & Moore.

WHITE SHOES AND BLACK NIKES

Let us pause to talk about Cravath, as the firm is known in lawyer shorthand. Founded in 1819, Cravath is the office that comes immediately to mind when one hears the phrase "white-shoe law firm." Cravath has long prided itself on preserving a distinctive culture, regardless of what is happening elsewhere in American law. It prides itself on doing things "the Cravath way," hiring top graduates from the top law schools and patiently schooling them in how senior partners feel work should be done. Cravath traditionally avoided hiring lateral partners, preferring men (and later women) who worked their way through the associate ranks.

Given the firm's reliance on blue-chip corporate clients, Cravath exudes conservatism. But it is also a tough litigation firm that gives clients muscle for their money. One man who worked there for half a decade during the 1990s told me, "To the casual observer, you'd think you had walked into a gentlemen's club, soft carpets and tasteful furniture and the right artwork on the walls. But when major litigation is under way, it's as tough as the Saturday night fights in Jersey City." Writing in the *New Yorker,* Renata Adler noted that Cravath prides itself "on the almost unremitting combativeness of its attorneys—who may be mild, kind, even poetic creatures outside their working lives." Not so at the office, however. She quoted a major client of Cravath's real estate department: "It's like having a pack of Dobermans, who are clamoring to be unleashed. I happen to prefer to avoid conflict, but it's reassuring to know that I have this pack I can unleash." In reading depositions, Adler was struck by the thought that such conduct were intended to "reflect the bullying standard, and to be read each night by other attorneys from Cravath."

Nonetheless, when Boies joined the firm he realized that he was going to be uncomfortable working in an environment inhabited chiefly by white males wearing pinstripes. His discontent was something that he kept to himself at first, for no associate with aspirations to partnership makes unseemly noises. Boies's rebellion was slow and subtle. He continued buying off-the-rack suits from Sears. Often as not, he wore tennis shoes to work. One trademark became a cheap watch worn over his sleeve. Boies argued that he could steal glances at the watch without letting jurors know he was checking the time. "A rather flimsy excuse," one of his detractors later told me, "given that the hours he actually spent before a jury were minimal. If that was the reason, why n't he slip the watch back under his sleeve when he left court? ut that is our David—he can find a reason to justify anything he does."

One man who came to Cravath about the same time as did Boies credited him for being a hard worker, but "on his own terms." During crunch times, partners and associates alike worked around the clock. "David would do his share of his work and then just drop out of sight for a day or so. He'd reappear and said he took some 'beach time.' He could drive you crazy, then turn around and do twice the amount of work you did in half the time." As he grew older, with more direct responsibility for cases, Boies would chide associates who griped about long hours, "Look, would you rather sleep, or would you rather win? Make your choice."

His politics moved leftward. The onetime president of the Young Republican Club at Redlands became a protester of the Vietnam War. During the 1968 Democratic presidential primaries he worked for Sen. Robert Kennedy. Cravath let him go to Jackson State College in Mississippi on a pro bono basis to represent students killed in clashes with police following the murder of the Reverend Dr. Martin Luther King, Jr. Occasionally, Boies's work on causes pushed the envelope at Cravath. One instance was his representation of students who seized administrative buildings at Columbia University late in the 1960s, vandalizing offices and shutting down the institution. One man groused about Boies's representing "a bunch of hoodlums who deserved jail time, not praise." Why did Cravath tolerate a rebel who was out of place almost from the very beginning? Put most directly, because the man was brilliant, a star among stars who delivered what clients wanted. He was voted a partnership after only six years, two years ahead of the Cravath career track. Samuel Butler, the firm's presiding partner, told the *New York Times Magazine* in 1986 (the article called Boies "the Wall Street lawyer everyone wants") that Boies "was kind of the eccentric genius here." And as a mentor he picked up one of the firm's top litigation guns, Thomas Barr, who was Cravath's point man when the Justice Department brought an antitrust action in 1969 intended to break up IBM. The government finally abandoned the case in 1982 after losing several rounds in court; nonetheless, the case proved enormously profitable for Cravath.

Boies's assignment was to defend parallel cases against IBM by customers who felt that they had been victimized. Barr said of his protégé, "The one talent of David's that stands out is his ability to lay out a course of action that would take into account any kind of complicated facts and develop a far-reaching scenario. It's a chess player's sense: If I do this, the following fifteen things are going to happen, and if step eleven goes so forth, I'll do this rather than that. It's a fantastic game-playing ability."

As a measure of Boies's discontent, he took a leave from the firm in 1977 to serve two years as counsel to the Antitrust Subcommittee of the Senate Judiciary Committee and then to the full committee. His second marriage had ended in divorce, and one person at Cravath told me, "David felt he should get out of Dodge City for a while. He had always talked about wanting to teach or do something outside of law. Although he was officially on leave, many of us never thought he would come back." He did, however, and with a new wife in tow, Mary McInnis, a lawyer in the Carter White House. A veteran of the Carter administration told me that Boies's name was bandied about as a potential attorney general had the president won reelection. The Reagan landslide halted such chatter.

For a lawyer with ego—the good ones invariably are so equipped—practicing at a firm such as Cravath can be frustrating. Cravath does not court publicity, either for its cases or for its lawyers. Its clients do not wish to see their legal troubles aired in the press. Of course, publicity cannot be avoided in such instances as the IBM antitrust case. Nonetheless, famed though he was in the legal community, the name David Boies still meant nothing to the average citizen.

All this changed abruptly because of a case entitled *Westmoreland v. CBS.*

BOIES VERSUS THE MILITARY

The case that gave David Boies wide exposure to the public began in January 1981 when Mike Wallace of CBS News leveled a grave accusation at Gen. William C. Westmoreland, who had commanded U.S. troops in Vietnam. Opening a ninety-minute documentary, *The Uncounted Enemy: A Vietnam Deception,* Wallace charged a "conspiracy at the highest levels of American military intelligence to suppress and alter critical evidence on the enemy," to deceive the American people, Congress, President Lyndon Johnson, and Pentagon leaders. Building its case chiefly through snippets of interviews conducted by Wallace, the program made heavy use of the phrase "CBS News has learned . . ." The camera focused tightly on the general's face, showing him nervously licking his lips as he struggled to answer Wallace's questions.

Supported by numerous military officers, Westmoreland demanded a retraction of "outrageous lies." CBS offered him fifteen minutes of interrupted airtime. He refused and sued.

Despite rote statements that "we stand by our story," CBS executives quickly realized that the network was in serious trouble. One problem was the provenance of the story. For years a resigned CIA officer named Samuel Adams had tried to peddle his story, but even an antiwar media dismissed him as a crank. In 1975 Adams persuaded a young *Harper's Magazine* editor, George Crile, to publish an article on the "conspiracy." When Crile moved to CBS as a producer, he hired Adams as a consultant and set about putting the material into documentary form.

That Crile had made up his mind before doing any reporting was reflected in what is known at CBS as a blue sheet, an outline for a program. In sixteen single-spaced pages, Crile used the word "conspiracy" twenty-four times and the word "conspirator" five times. Contrary to normal journalism, Crile started with a thesis that he tried to prove through selective interviews and use of material, rather than reporting a rounded story. Although CBS used Adams as an interviewee, his role as paid consultant was not revealed. An internal CBS investigation cast doubt on how Crile did his work—for instance, mismatching questions and answers to drive home points he wished to make. The sole pro-Westmoreland interviewee was edited down to a confused twenty-second sound bite.

Questionable journalism. An attack on a general who had served his country in three wars over forty years. A resurgence of American patriotism as reflected in the election of President Ronald Reagan. A general public unwillingness to reopen old war wounds. Collectively, these factors posed threats both to CBS's coffers and its reputation as a news organization.

Cravath is not known for expertise in libel law, but the firm wanted the Westmoreland case for several reasons. First, and foremost, CBS is a client that pays the firm millions annually in fees. The case would be high profile—the military versus the media. The firm's top litigator, Tom Barr, by coincidence was defending *Time* magazine against another military libel suit brought by Israeli general Ariel Sharon, so he was not available.

Boies happily stepped into the breach. As an antiwar activist, he relished the chance to take on the officials he felt had taken the United States into an unnecessary conflict. And some of the things he did during his self-appointed mission as scourge of the Johnson administration went beyond the scope of the suit. Boies immersed himself in the war. An outsized map of Vietnam went onto his wall, and he and other lawyers obtained thousands of pages of previously classified military and intelligence documents from the Johnson Presidential Library, seeking proof of the conspiracy.

Then Boies deposed the men who had run the war, often over their objections. Former Defense Secretary Robert McNamara started a two-day deposition by declaring, "I want it clear on the record that you are extracting these answers from me against my wishes. I told Crile that I had never spoken on Vietnam. I have no intention of doing so." That said, McNamara proceeded to talk in detail the about how he came to disagree with President Johnson over the conduct of the war.

Dean Rusk, the former secretary of state, was so adamant about testifying that he asked a judge to have his deposition kept under seal. He lost, and Boies toyed with him for two days. As Boies would admit to the journalists Bob Brewin and Sydney Shaw, "After the first day I must confess I had probably most of what I needed. The opportunity to sit with him and talk with him about the war and his role in the war and his perception of the war was just fascinating."

Westmoreland, concurrently, had the services of a lawyer with a vastly different professional background—Dan Burt, of Washington. Despite some successes in his legal career, Burt suffered several distinct disadvantages, foremost among them that he had never tried a case before a jury. After graduation from Yale Law School, Burt held a succession of jobs and teaching positions before finding his niche doing international tax work, chiefly for Saudi Arabians. He then ran the Capital Legal Foundation, a business-oriented public policy law firm in Washington funded by corporations and private benefactors such as Richard M. Scaife, the Pittsburgh multimillionaire. When friends of Westmoreland scouted for someone to take his case to court, Burt eagerly accepted. Burt's foundation had a legal staff of only five persons—Cravath could draw upon scores of lawyers—and nowhere near the money that CBS poured into the case. Dan Dorsen, formerly a New York federal prosecutor, signed on to help Burt. After the exchange of mountains of paperwork—one Cravath motion contained 1,487 pages—the case was ready for trial before Judge Pierre Leval, of the U.S. District Court for the Southern District of New York.

TRICKS OF THE TRIAL TRADE

Make no mistake about it. Boies is very good at his job, which involves persuading a dozen human beings to agree with him. The Westmoreland trial, which filled 9,745 pages of testimony, shows the elements a master litigator brings into play. Extensive preparation. A clear outline of what one wishes to prove, often through cross-examining witnesses from the other side—using the enemy to your advantage, in effect. Some elbow jabs and rabbit punches that you hope to sneak past the judge. The ability to be tough on witnesses without appearing to be a bully. And, finally, a flair for dramatic acts that inject emotion into the case.

Such is what Boies did at the very start of the trial. During his opening statement, he gave jurors the boilerplate admonition about keeping open minds until all evidence had been heard. Then came the first of several unusual ploys. To conclude, he began to play a video of a speech made by Sen. Robert Kennedy in 1968, less than a week after the Tet Offensive, challenging the Johnson administration's estimate of the number of enemy troops. Boies said, "While the Tet Offensive was still under way, while fighting was still going on, the same kinds of questions that were raised in the CBS documentary were being raised by the junior senator of New York." Judge Leval overrode Burt's objections and permitted the tape to be played.

As journalists Brewin and Shaw would write later, "The power of Kennedy's fiery Boston accent, condemning the war and the Johnson administration and questioning the accuracy of U.S. intelligence, silenced the court, achieving exactly the effect Boies wanted and Burt feared."

But the Kennedy gambit was a sideshow. The main event would be Boies's confrontation with General Westmoreland. The general had submitted to fourteen days of depositions with firm dignity. Could Boies break him?

Confronting the general was "the most difficult cross-examination I've ever had," Boies said. He continued:

General Westmoreland had many things going for him. First of all, he was well prepared. He had done his homework. He came across as thoughtful, and he was very very persuasive. On top of that, the man looked like a general—tall, white-haired, imposing in appearance, a man who had served his country all of his adult life, up against this young kid lawyer from New York. Somehow I had to manage to persuade the jury that the General had been less than truthful in his testimony.

But this was both difficult and dangerous—dangerous in the sense that if I failed on that cross-examination, CBS loses the case, and CBS pays out a heckuva' lot of money. If the jury decided I was beating up on Westmoreland, treating him unfairly or without the respect he deserved, we were in for trouble.

In direct testimony, Westmoreland proved effective. "He looked every inch the straight arrow," Connie Bruck wrote in the *American Lawyer*. "He was a man who loved his country, had served it in three wars, and was devoted to his troops." Westmoreland's demeanor contrasted sharply with his CBS appearance, when he nervously licked his lips while fumbling for answers about years-ago events. Burt's last question was whether Westmoreland had ever lied to a superior.

"Never," Westmoreland replied, and he got up and escorted his weeping wife, Kitsy, from the courtroom.

Boies knew he—and CBS—were in trouble. As Connie Bruck noted, during the early weeks of the trial Boies "had seemed the image of confidence, sporting a good-natured, even merry air." But as the impact of Westmoreland's testimony soaked in, "Boies became progressively more pale and somber. By the time he rose to face the general on cross-examination, all signs of Boies's habitual gaiety had fled." So Boies came at Westmoreland obliquely. As he stated,

In the beginning, I wanted to move very gently to show that regardless of his appearance and background, this was a man who did not always tell the truth. For instance, I asked Westmoreland, "Now, you said that you never talked with President Johnson about enemy troop strengths. Is that correct, General?" And he would say, "Yes, I am sure of that."

That's when I pull out a memo from Walt Rostow [President Johnson's national security advisor] in which he writes, "General Westmoreland was in to talk to the President and here is what he reported."* There it would be, in black and white—Westmoreland

---

*The memo was actually written by Assistant Secretary of Defense John McNaughton, who died in a plane crash in 1967. It pertained to a meeting which Rostow did not attend. Rostow contended, however, that given his knowledge of McNaughton, that "I assume this was an accurate set of notes."

in fact had talked to Johnson about troop strengths. That's when I would be entitled to go after the general, but not in a way that attacked him directly.

"General Westmoreland, you know Mr. Rostow, and you worked with him closely on the war, didn't you? You have a high regard for him? Now, General, can you tell me any reason that Walt Whitman Rostow would just make up what is contained in this memorandum?" Try as he could, Westmoreland wouldn't be able to make up a reason for Rostow to write a false memo.

I'd keep on going. "General Westmoreland, did you find that Mr. Rostow, as a senior assistant to President Johnson, that part of his job was to take things down when the President was talking with someone, and to do so accurately? You've read Mr. Rostow's memo. Now, does that refresh your memory? Is that what actually happened—that you in fact did talk with President Johnson about troop strengths?"

Now this is where you want, and you get, the "yes" answer. When he does, the jury sees that although General Westmoreland may be very articulate, he has said some things that are not truth. If he says "no"—which he did not, of course—the jury begins to think, "Well, I don't believe him. Walt Rostow would not have made that up. If he wrote it down, it happened."

Westmoreland's confident demeanor dissipated. Within fifteen minutes, Connie Bruck observed, he "seemed to undergo a metamorphosis, reverting to an earlier self." He began licking his lips nervously, just as he had done on TV. His left arm began twitching, apparently involuntarily. By the end of the day it was apparent to most persons in the courtroom that although Westmoreland had starred on direct examination by his own lawyers, who presumably had coached him well, he could not stand up to a vigorous cross-examination on the details.

Boies said of his cross-examination:

One of the issues was whether guerrillas who did not wear uniforms were not "fighters" in the traditional sense and therefore should not be included in troop strengths. I had the general repeat this statement, and asked him if he thought the issue was important. "Yes, I realize that's important," he told me. That's when I go into my magic box of documents again and pull out a cable signed by Westmoreland saying, "One-third of our casualties are caused by these irregular forces."

So I go after him. "Well, General, if these irregulars are causing one-third of our casualties, they are dangerous, aren't they? They could cause harm to your troops, couldn't they? And I know very well, General Westmoreland, that you are a commander who really cared about the well-being of your troops?"

What can Westmoreland say? The only honest answer, and the one he had to give, was "Yes." And then you get a "yes" to a question on whether the irregulars were really dangerous.

I spent more than a day going through this process, never attacking him directly, just using documents that showed the truth to be something other than what he had said on the witness stand. You build the pressure gradually in such a situation, because you want the jurors to be a step ahead of you. They are going to decide on their own, "This man was not totally truthful to us." That's when you have won your case.

The other side can argue some of the contradictions between a man's testimony and what the documents say is not all that important, because I am tripping him up on stuff that really isn't important. In these instances, though, we are talking about what a commanding general told the United States, and the safety of American soldiers. "It mattered what you told the President, didn't it? It mattered whether those irregulars were killing your men, didn't it?"

Connie Bruck would end her long *American Lawyer* article, "Committed then and now to his version of what was right, Westmoreland looked—by the time he left the stand—like a man willing to lie to prove his truth."

Boies had won the cross-examination. Now, could he win the rest of the case?

DOWN AND DIRTY

By the middle of the trial, Renata Adler of the *New Yorker* concluded that Boies was something of a legal charlatan, albeit an effective one. "It was Boies' style in bench conferences," she observed, "to argue fiercely and articulately for a position (often that he was 'entitled' to do something, or that it would be 'unfair' for opposing counsel to do it), and if the ruling went against him, to say that the whole question was 'not of enormous significance.' The phrase seemed a way of shrugging off the natural litigator's disappointment that *any* ruling should ever go against him, and of diminishing the importance of the ruling; it was also an instance of the Cravath style of having, in all discussions, and even after the judge himself has spoken, the last word."

Persons who followed the trial unanimously agreed that Boies outperformed the relatively inexperienced Dan Burt. Other problems plagued Burt. His absence from Washington troubled his marriage. The Capital Legal Foundation rapidly depleted its funds for the case, and the backers who had urged Westmoreland into the suit had second thoughts about posting more money. (Costs were later estimated at $800,000; Cravath spent eight to ten times that much.). Finally, Judge Leval wrote a draft instruction for the jury that Burt felt put him at a disadvantage. The judge also refused to admit into evidence an internal CBS study that found the documentary to be highly flawed, and in violation of network ethical standards.

In the end, Burt caved, and with Westmoreland's acquiescence, agreed to a settlement. CBS did not retract a single word. The key sentence of CBS's settlement statement read, "CBS respects General Westmoreland's long and faithful service to his country, and never intended to assert, and does not believe, that General Westmoreland was unpatriotic or disloyal in performing his duties as he saw them." As many observers pointed out, CBS had offered essentially the same statement long in advance of his suit.

The clear winner was Boies. The media hailed him as a hero who had fought off a case that threatened a "chilling effect" on

American journalism. (The same media seldom speak of the chilling effect that bad journalism can have on the subjects of its inquiries.) The media loved Boies, and he reciprocated the affection. He learned to pause outside the courthouse and face cameras and reporters and give pithy quotes about the strides he was making toward victory. A media star was born.

"A HORSE'S ASS"

The victory signaled the emergence of a new Boies—the Cravath lawyer as media figure. Yet despite his acknowledged brilliance Boies was not a universally popular fellow. One characteristic that particularly infuriated other partners was what they considered to be his love of publicity. Necessity drove him before the TV cameras during the Westmoreland trial, much of which was waged in the court of public opinion. But Boies had fully enjoyed star status, and retreating to the shadows of anonymous law was difficult. In 1987 the *American Lawyer* presented Boies what it called the Bruce Springsteen Media Darling Award. The magazine said, "Boies, like the Boss, is good at what he does, but the deification may have gotten out of hand." Boies thought the gibe was funny; other persons at the firm found it unpleasantly true.

There were other front-page cases. The Federal Deposit Insurance Corporation sued junk-bond king Michael Milken and his former employer. It hired Boies as special outside counsel, and he won a $1 billion settlement. On behalf of IBM, he helped overturn a $350 million antitrust verdict that Telex Corporation had won from an Oklahoma jury. By the 1990s his annual draw was in the $2 million range.

Although Boies continued to wear odd-fitting suits from Sears, his soaring income enabled him to indulge his liking for fine wines and food. He had personal quirks—for instance, he took fast trips to Las Vegas and Atlantic City, where he would shoot craps for hours. He also developed a reputation for volcanic eruptions of temper when things did not go just right at restaurants.

Even acknowledged genius can have its downside. Cravath, despite its size, is a clubby place, and some persons began to feel that Boies . . . well, *David just doesn't fit*. His most grievous defect, in the view of two persons in the firm who spoke under a promise of anonymity, was a lack of collegiality. "David wanted to run his own noisy one-man show without recognizing that he worked for a firm that was a partnership," one of these persons said. "Partnership meetings? Forget about it. David was too important to waste time on such matters. Firm social events? A chronic no-show. I was involved with him twice on cases where he would just disappear—fall off the face of the earth, out of telephone contact. Leaving a message with a secretary for David Boies was useless—you'd do better yelling out the window."

Another person, senior to Boies in the pecking order, was even harsher. "David behaved like a spoiled little brat his last years here. He was smarter than everyone else, none of the rules applied to him. . . . You might find interesting something that never got into the press when he finally left us. Four or five years earlier, there were serious discussions about *asking* him to go elsewhere. We knew we'd be kicking a lot of money out the door, but that shows what some of us felt about him.

"Let me give you my read on David. He came to Cravath knowing full well how we practiced law as a *partnership,* and you note that I emphasize that word. By doing so, he implicitly accepted the way we work. Over the years he changed. The decent thing for him to have done would be to recognize that he no longer fit in, and to take his ball and go play elsewhere. David did not have that decency. He ignored us and our culture, and behaved ignobly."

The man paused a long time. "You hear a lot about David's clever little eccentricities. I refer to some of the rude stunts he pulled both in and outside of the office. A client, for instance, would give David a small gift as a token at the end of a case. David would toss the unopened package over onto a credenza. The client would come in weeks later and see his gift sitting there in wrapping paper. Any person with a grain of decency would know that such behavior is boorish.

"I started to say that some of his more obnoxious stunts were what you'd expect from a small, ill-behaved child. But let me go further than that. At his core, David Boies was and is a horse's ass."

FROM PARTNER TO DEPARTEE

Perhaps appropriately, given the footwear he often donned for work, Boies ended his thirty-one-year career at Cravath in an argument over athletic shoes. The true issues, of course, were far more complex. His friend George Steinbrenner, the owner of the New York Yankees, signed a $95 million sponsorship deal with the shoe manufacturer Adidas USA, Inc. But Major League Properties, Inc., the marketing arm for Major League Baseball, objected, pointing to rules requiring that all endorsement revenues be divided equally among teams. Given the Yankees' popularity, Steinbrenner did not wish to share revenues with smaller teams. So he had Boies sue to challenge the rules.

Boies did so on May 6, 1997, a Friday. Exactly when Boies's partners at Cravath learned of the suit, and its implications, became a matter of dispute. Boies, who had been doing legal chores for Steinbrenner and the Yankees for eighteen months, is emphatic in stating that he submitted a "new business" memorandum about the shoe deal. But the memo omitted an important fact: One of the teams named as a defendant was the Atlanta Braves, which had become a subsidiary of Time Warner after its acquisition of the Ted Turner media empire. And Time Warner happened to be Cravath's largest client. Further, the partner overseeing the Time Warner account was a litigator named Robert Joffe, who was on track to become the firm's presiding partner (the term Cravath uses in lieu of managing partner) and thus a man of considerable influence. A lawyer who worked for Cravath at the time noted, "You'd have to be a blockhead not to know how important Time Warner was to Cravath. We'd frequently have twenty to thirty lawyers working on one of their deals. You could hear the cash register going clank-clank-clank."

Things got nasty quickly. Fay Vincent, the former commissioner of baseball, whom Steinbrenner detested both personally and professionally, served on the Time Warner board. When he learned of the suit, Vincent phoned Time Warner chief executive officer Gerald Levin. At first Levin had trouble believing that a Cravath lawyer would involve himself in such a suit. An in-house lawyer produced a copy of the complaint, and Levin exploded: "What the hell is going on here—we are being sued by our own damned law firm!"

The next call was to Cravath presiding partner Samuel Butler. In the words of a lawyer who was later told of the conversation, "Levin was in a hot rage, and when Jerry Levin is mad, the world hears it, and especially the person he thinks has screwed him." Levin's demand was simple: Either Boies and Cravath dropped the suit, or Time Warner would drop Cravath. Boies apparently realized that he had erred. He got Steinbrenner to offer to dismiss the Atlanta Braves as a defendant. Levin was not appeased; he wanted the entire action dismissed.

Had Boies in fact behaved improperly? Discussing the episode with Amy Singer of the *American Lawyer,* ethics expert Monroe H. Freedman of Hofstra University said that in a strict sense, conflict of interest rules do not make it unethical for a lawyer to sue a firm that is a subsidiary of another client. But Butler was in no mood for nitpicking over codes of ethics. To him, what Boies had done was intolerable from a business standpoint. He had put at risk Cravath's relationship with its most profitable client, and Butler knew Levin well enough to take his threats seriously. Butler gave Boies an ultimatum: Decide whether you want to work for Cravath or for Steinbrenner.

Boies spent the weekend hashing over the situation with his wife, Mary. He felt an obligation to stand by his client. He had thought for years about life outside Cravath—to teach, to spend more time with his younger children, to pursue cases that Cravath avoided.

He had already offended many partners by bringing a predatory pricing suit on behalf of Continental Airlines and Northwest Airlines against American Airlines in 1992. There were no direct conflicts, but Boies's suit risked upsetting some business rules useful to other clients. According to a partner, "To me, this suit was an 'in-your-face' act by David. He knew damned well that this was not the sort of action that Cravath handles. We heard some rumblings from some rather important general counsels about 'this wild man.' I could not argue with them." (In the end, American won the case. Boies has listed the case as his only loss during his Cravath career.) There were rumblings about Boies's prolonged representation of a Florida woman embroiled in litigation with her former husband over in a child custody dispute and also over control of a landscaping business. The case did not provide the sort of fees that Cravath expected; it did give Boies a reason to make trips south to "consult with his client." And ongoing complaining was heard about Boies's ego.

On Monday, May 12, Boies told Butler, "OK, I am resigning. Do the paperwork." In return for payments in succeeding years for work that he had brought into the firm, Boies agreed not to sue a sizable number of Cravath clients in any plaintiff actions he might bring. On Wednesday, May 14, Boies took a break from a deposition and walked down the corridor to Butler's office and signed what was tantamount to a divorce decree. In a week and one day, he had gone from Cravath partner to Cravath departee.

"MAKE SOME SERIOUS MONEY"

Boies is too wise to bail out of a $2-million-a-year job without knowing where he is going to land. As is true of many other corporate lawyers, he had long envied plaintiff lawyers who earned immense riches from class action suits. Hence one of his first conversations was with Melvyn Weiss, of Milberg, Weiss, Bershad, Hynes & Lerach, the New York–based firm that had long been the bane of the high-tech industry. (See chapter 5, "Lerach and Weiss: The Class Action Scourges of West and East.") As litigators—lawyers who actually try cases in court, rather than shuffle papers in the office—Weiss and Boies respected one another professionally. But the chemistry was not there. In addition to large talents, both men are endowed with large egos. Boies also worried about trying to fit his idiosyncratic style into another firm.

One intriguing offer came from Jonathan Schiller, a lean fifty-ish tennis buff who ran the Washington office of Kaye, Scholer, Fierman, Hays & Handler. They met during the 1980s when defending Westinghouse Electric Corporation against nuclear power contract suits brought abroad. "Come on over, you'll like it here," Schiller told Boies. Boies made a counteroffer: "Why don't you leave Kaye Scholer and come in with me on a new firm altogether? We can have a helluva' lot of fun, and make some serious money." Schiller's expertise was in international arbitration, and both men sensed the field would be increasingly profitable in the new global economy.

When Boies offered to advance the estimated $750,000 in start-up costs, Schiller accepted in a hurry. Boies would work from a corner of his wife's law office in Bedford, New York, in Westchester County, with a scenic view of a parking lot. (Boies & Schiller would later move to new offices in a business park in Armonk, several miles from Bedford.) Schiller opened a Washington outpost on Wisconsin Avenue, a short commute from his home in leafy Cleveland Park.

The original projection was for the firm to be operating in the black within six months, with Schiller reimbursing Boies for the seed money. Actual profits took a bit longer, but when they started flowing in, they were enormous. And the client list was impressive: CBS, which Boies lured away from Cravath, Georgia-Pacific Corporation, Philip Morris, Northwest Airlines. Within months they added another big-name partner, Donald Flexner, who had run the Justice Department's Antitrust Division and then practiced with the Washington firm of Crowell & Moring. The pitch to Flexner was simple and appealing: "Come with us, and you can make REALLY big money, on a scale you'll never approach in a firm."

From the outset, however, Boies told his new partners that there would come a time when he would not be able to devote his full attentions to work there. He had decided to take on the role of lead counsel for the Justice Department in an antitrust suit against mammoth Microsoft Corporation.

THE "MICROSOFT HIT MAN"

In a nutshell, the United States government decided to attack what is arguably one of the great success stories of American capitalism because of a Silicon Valley law firm named Wilson, Sonsini, Goodwin & Rosati. Arguably the premier high-tech firm in the country, Wilson Sonsini was responsible for doing initial public offerings for more dot-coms and related companies than are easily countable. The driving spirit against Microsoft was a combative young lawyer named Gary Reback.* Given that this chapter concerns David Boies, Reback's role must be perhaps unfairly summarized. But, in essence, he objected to the strong-arm tactics Microsoft used against other high-tech companies—many of them Wilson Sonsini clients—and he was instrumental in forcing the Justice Department to sue to force Microsoft to stop alleged anticompetitive practices.

Spend time with Reback, and you realize that he believes he waged a battle every bit as important as the trust-busting attacks on the Rockefeller oil empire in the early 1900s. Lean, dark-haired, and rather slight of stature, with a penchant for wire-rimmed glasses and sharp suits, he is messianic, even fanatic, about Microsoft.

"The major difference between Bill Gates [the founder of Microsoft] and John D. Rockefeller is that Rockefeller used dynamite against his competitors," he told me. "Well, Gates hasn't gone that far—not yet, anyway." Reback can rattle off his case against Microsoft at an ear-numbing pace; out of curiosity, I timed part of a taped interview against a transcript. At full throttle he clocked 281 words a minute—and this when discussing esoteric economics.

---

*The material on Reback's background and his strategy in stirring the Microsoft litigation to life when it was seemingly dead was recounted to me in interviews in Washington and many phone and e-mail exchanges.

Reback received degrees from Yale and Stanford Law, clerked for a federal appeals judge in New Orleans, and held jobs in Washington and elsewhere before landing at Wilson Sonsini in 1981.

As Reback settled into Wilson Sonsini he saw clients being shoved aside time and again by a rapacious Microsoft. "Put most simply," he said, "Microsoft did not play fair. They used a trick known in the industry as 'vaporware.' A competitor begins developing a new product. Microsoft right away says it is doing the same thing, and purchasers say, 'Well, let's wait and see what Gates does.' What happens is that they kill the market for the competitive product." Persons in the industry cite as examples Internet Explorer 3.0 for Unix, which was supposed to surpass Netscape, but which was never released; and Microsoft Exchange, a supposed equivalent of Lotus Notes, which was "announced" years before it went on the market.

Soon after joining Wilson Sonsini, Reback began pestering the Federal Trade Commission to move against what he felt to be monopolistic practices by Microsoft. He gathered a collection of horror stories from the firm's clients. But the FTC shoved him aside. Reback kept pressing, and a window of opportunity opened in late 1994. U.S. District Court Judge Stanley Sporkin of Washington, D.C., held a preliminary hearing concerning the Justice Department's proposed settlement of an antitrust action against Microsoft. Attorney General Janet Reno had announced the deal with fanfare, assuring the public that the decree would "save consumers money [and] enable them to have a choice when selecting operating systems."

Then Reback read a transcript of the hearing, and several statements raised his eyebrows. For instance, Judge Sporkin raised a question about Microsoft's claimed use of "vaporware" to persuade consumers not to buy competitors' products. What did Microsoft have to say on the point?

"Those charges, we believe, are totally false," replied Richard J. Urowsky of Sullivan & Cromwell, Microsoft's lead lawyer.

"In other words," Judge Sporkin continued, "the vaporware charge is false?"

"That's correct," Urowsky stated.

Reback knew otherwise, for he had seen documents in which Microsoft executives discussed vaporware schemes; some of the papers cited the personal knowledge of Bill Gates. When he returned to Palo Alto, Reback circulated copies of the transcript to Wilson Sonsini clients and asked if they wanted to attack the settlement. Three of these clients told Reback, *Go ahead, but do it without involving our names. We don't want to get into a public brawl with Microsoft.* (Citing confidentiality, Reback declined to tell me the names of these clients in an interview. The high-tech trade press has named the "covert clients" as Sybase Inc., Sun Microsystems, Inc., and Borland International, Inc. All are on a Wilson Sonsini client list.)

After hearing arguments from Reback and others, Judge Sporkin refused to approve the settlement. "It is clear to this court," Judge Sporkin wrote, "that if it signs the decree presented to it, the message will be that Microsoft is so powerful that neither the market nor the government is capable of dealing with all of its monopolistic practices."

The case would drag through the appeals process for several years. Eventually the U.S Court of Appeals for the District of Columbia would reverse Judge Sporkin, saying he had no authority to block the settlement. He was taken off the case and replaced by Judge Thomas Penfield Jackson. But Reback had caught the attention of the Justice Department, and especially its new antitrust chief, a lawyer named Joel Klein. Reback flooded the Antitrust Division with long memoranda outlining his theory of how Microsoft was using its economic muscle to dominate the market. Klein didn't like Reback, and he tried to ignore him. After all, Klein had been the Justice lawyer who defended the 1995 consent decree with Microsoft, only to have Reback snatch victory out of his hands. "A goddamn pest," he said of Reback.

But this time Reback had a specific deal to challenge: Microsoft's planned purchase of a rival named Intuit. Microsoft wanted control of an Intuit personal finance software program called Quicken, which commanded 70 to 85 percent of the market, versus only 5 percent for Microsoft Money. Microsoft was candid. Vice President Mike Mayless told the *Wall Street Journal* that if the deal did not succeed, "we were going to spend most of our energies dealing with existing competition."

To Reback, Mayless's candor was a smoking-gun admission. *Microsoft was saying in effect, If we can't beat them, we'll buy them.*

So again Reback cranked up his team of lawyers and economists to produce a documented argument as to why the Intuit acquisition would violate antitrust laws. The fifty-page paper was essentially an indictment of Microsoft's marketing schemes—a "better case against Microsoft than the government was able to do in four years of investigations."

But Reback chose his words carefully. He did not bash Bill Gates for being successful, only for violating the antitrust rules. He wrote, "The arguments in this white paper are neither populist-oriented nor are they based upon a 'big is bad' philosophy. Rather the arguments draw upon what has become an extensive and rigorous literature on increasing returns economics." He charged that Microsoft was willing to pay 100 percent of market price for Intuit so it could eventually "dominate home banking and eventually all home-to-business server products." Microsoft would be able to integrate "bank accounts, brokerage accounts, and credit information" and eventually dominate the home-sales market.

Reback kept gathering material. "I can't count the entrepreneurs and companies who brought me horror stories. I passed them on to the Justice Department." Even when speaking to the federal government, many businessmen insisted on anonymity. "That's how powerful Bill Gates and his monopoly are."

By now Reback had learned the value of networking. He formed a strong alliance with Sen. Orrin Hatch and the antitrust experts on the Judiciary Committee staff. He persuaded high-tech executives from Silicon Valley—many of them Wilson Sonsini clients—to give evidence. He also showed Klein he meant business. When Klein was nominated to succeed Anne Bingaman as heard of the Antitrust Division, Reback had a senator put a hold on the appointment.

Klein caved. The Justice Department used Reback's flow of new evidence as building blocks for a revived lawsuit. In October

1997 Attorney General Reno announced that Justice would seek an injunction against Microsoft for violating the 1995 decree, and a fine of $1 million a day.

Understandably, few persons are totally objective about Reback. Defenders of Gates detest him. Bob O'Regan, executive editor of *PC Week,* designated him as one of his "Turkeys of the Year" for 1996, calling him a "headline-seeking lawyer, currently peddling his wares to Netscape in its battle for world domination against Microsoft." Lawyers at the Justice Department and the Federal Trade Commission have denounced him to reporters as a "glory seeker," claiming that they would have sued Microsoft eventually even if Reback did not exist. Reback laughs. "The record, I think, is abundantly clear on that point."

Another line of criticism is that his campaign was "as much a promotional effort for Wilson Sonsini and Mr. Reback as it was an act on behalf of clients." Persons in Wilson Sonsini find this claim laughable. "We were doing a little bit of business before Gary joined the firm," a senior partner told me. "Sure, the publicity helps—but remember, we're also making a helluva' lot of money out of what he does, and most importantly, we are doing good things for clients. That's the bottom line."

Reback would leave Wilson Sonsini in 2001 to organize Voxeo Corporation, which is developing business software based on the telephone. He once mused to me that someone who practiced corporate law risked spending their years in anonymity. But this particular lawyer will not be remembered as "Gary Who?"

A HIRED GUN FOR JUSTICE

The ultimate hired gun, David Boies, would happily have toiled for Microsoft had anyone there had the wit to call him. (Bill Gates surely had interesting thoughts when he learned that his strategists could have preemptively hired the man who would humiliate him in court and before the world.) But as it happened, Joel Klein rang first, in November 1997, a few months after Boies

& Schiller opened for business. Boies knew Klein on several levels. Professionally, they had contacts during Boies's stint as counsel for the Senate Judiciary Committee. Personally, Mary Boies, his third (and current) wife, dated Klein when she lawyered in the Carter White House. With mock graciousness, Klein told David Margolick of *Vanity Fair,* "It shows me to be a man of exceptionally large spirit that I would hire someone who stole this woman from me."

Boies recognized the case's significance. "Anyone who is a trial lawyer, and especially an antitrust lawyer, would want to be involved in such a case of this importance," Boies told Charlie Rose of PBS after the trial. "You are going into new areas. You are testing whether the established antitrust rules apply to these new technologies. Well, they certainly do." He continued:

Over the years any number of industries have argued, "We are different, so these antiquated [antitrust] laws should not apply to us." Transportation, some of the service industries, broadcasting, even agriculture. They argue that they are "different." Well, that they well might be, but being "different" does not exempt you from the antitrust laws. Certain principles of economic life apply across the board. And the basic question, when you come down to it, is fairness for the consumer. So, I simply don't buy Microsoft's argument that "high-tech is a different business, so we should not be subject to the antitrust laws."

There was another reason why Boies was willing to step away from his new firm to work for a pittance. The Microsoft trial was sure to attract enormous publicity, giving Boies the chance to return to the limelight he enjoyed during the Westmoreland trial. As he assured Schiller and Flexner, he could not fail to attract new clients.

The government case rested on two broad allegations: that Microsoft charged nothing for its Internet browser in order to drive rival Netscape Communications Corporation out of business; and that Microsoft "bundled" the browser into its Windows operating system so that consumers would have no reason to buy the Netscape product.

Oddly, Boies was not convinced when he began his homework that Microsoft had violated antitrust laws. He told Klein, in effect, "If we get into this case and I decide there are no violations, I will so advise you." Boies had a reason for caution. In three decades of lawyering, he had learned to approach cases objectively and let the evidence determine the question of guilt or innocence. And contrary to what Gates and subordinates would charge, Boies firmly states that he was not out to destroy Microsoft, or to humiliate its creator. To Boies, the case was not about Microsoft per se, but Microsoft's course of conduct. He rejected Gates's self-portrayal as an innocent waif who did not intentionally violate antitrust laws. Gates was too smart, too objective not to realize that Microsoft's conduct went beyond the pale of acceptable business practices.

Boies walked on shaky legal ground. The core of the Sherman Antitrust Act lies in its first two sections, which are terse. Section One states, "Every contract, combination in the form of trust or otherwise, or conspiracy, in restraint of trade or commerce among the several States, or with foreign nations, is declared to be illegal." Section Two states, "Every person who shall monopolize, or attempt to monopolize, or combine or conspire with other person or persons, to monopolize any part of the trade or commerce among the several States . . . shall be deemed guilty of a felony." As critics were quick to point out, Boies worked on the Cravath team that defended IBM years earlier on markedly parallel antitrust charges. The government contended that IBM cut the prices of its mainframe computers to drive competitors out of business. Federal courts that had heard the case agreed with IBM when it argued that price cuts were good for consumers. The courts also rejected the government's claim that IBM designed its products so that its main-drive computers would not accept tape drives from other manufacturers. A Microsoft press officer called this dichotomy "blatant hypocrisy on the part of Mr. Boies." He might be correct. But whereas a court is bound by past decisions, a lawyer is free to plead the cause of his client of the moment, regardless of what he might have argued elsewhere.

Surely Microsoft felt antitrust laws were on its side, and indeed John Warden of Sullivan & Cromwell, its chief lawyer, had argued the specific case before the U.S. Court of Appeals for the Second Circuit that it felt was binding. Berkey Photo had attacked Eastman Kodak, claiming that the industry giant illegally required buyers of its Instamatic camera to buy Kodak film. Berkey won an $87 million verdict at trial level. On appeal, Kodak retained Warden, who convinced the court that what Kodak had done was legal. The court wrote, "Innovation is clearly tolerated by the antitrust laws." It was this language that Microsoft thought gave it a winning hand.

Boies prepared by spending weeks going though about 1,800 of the more than three million documents that Justice Department lawyers had obtained from Microsoft. Mark S. Popofsky, a young Antitrust Division lawyer, months later still marveled at Boies's ability to absorb so much material. "David would read through a stack of documents and Click! It was like they were embedded in his mind. He had a gift of recall that was almost uncanny. Once he saw what was on a piece of paper, he remembered it, and he could quote it virtually verbatim."

In his opening statement, Warden argued that the antitrust laws were "not a code of civility" and that the rough-and-tumble tactics Microsoft used were common in the competitive business world. Many business academicians and publications agreed. A *Wall Street Journal* editorial denounced the suit as "Microslop" and said, "If we were Bill Gates, we would set up an annuity to pay the lawyers and forget the whole thing." When Boies tried to stir British interest in a suit against Microsoft in Great Britain, columnist Robert D. Novak scoffed at him as a "transatlantic ambulance chaser."

In earlier cases Boies made himself an instant expert on the Vietnam War (for the Westmoreland/CBS trial) and on junk bonds (the Michael Milken case). When he got into Microsoft, his knowledge of computer technology was so meager that he didn't even know how to (or bother to) use his office e-mail. Now he had to go against persons who had spent much of their lives in a highly technical industry. Boies began by talking with people. His skills, which are many, include the art of picking experts' brains. And, given his dyslexia, he absorbs spoken information easier than documents. In time, he claimed, he perhaps knew "at least some things better than they did." Also helpful was the enormous documentary base that the Justice Department had compiled in previous Microsoft litigation. Many of the depositions had been reduced to summary form. Boies shoved them aside; he insisted on going back and "reading them in the raw," so that he could get a better feel for the people involved. He knew that he would be facing some of these persons in court; he wanted to know how they responded to lines of questioning—the same reconnaissance that a military commander would perform before battle.

As the case moved through the pretrial stages, including abortive settlement talks, the U.S. Circuit Court of Appeals for the District of Columbia issued a decision that at first glance did not bode well for the government. It struck down the preliminary injunction that Judge Jackson had issued in the consent decree case. The court held that Judge Jackson had not given Microsoft a fair day in court, and that he had misread antitrust laws. It wrote, "Antitrust scholars have long recognized the undesirability of having courts oversee product designs, and any dampening of technological innovation would be at cross-purposes with antitrust law. We suggest here only that the limited competence of courts to evaluate high-tech product designs and the high cost of error should make them wary of second-guessing the claimed benefits of a particular design decision." It sent the case back to Judge Jackson for further review.

At first blush the decision seemed fatal to Justice's case. Boies was flying from Chicago to the West Coast the day it came down. By the time he landed he realized that the appeals court had given him a road map on how to win. First, the court ruled that indeed Microsoft had a monopoly. Second, it said that if a company does not need to tie two products together to achieve any benefit, the tying violates the law. And, finally, if it could be proved that the tying was done for anticompetitive purposes, it was illegal. By no means had the appeals court given Microsoft a free pass. All Boies had to do now was to find evidence to support Justice's charges.

THE GAFFING OF GATES

When Boies went to Seattle in late summer 1998 to depose Gates, he expected to spend his time jousting with an executive who knew the nuances of his company's business. Boies knew that Sullivan & Cromwell litigators would have spent days, even weeks, coaching Gates on how to be an effective witness, one who would give direct but terse answers to questions. Every litigator dreads having a client suddenly become voluble in the witness chair, volunteering information for which he has not been asked, and playing a losing game of verbal one-upmanship with the opposing lawyer.

Boies guessed wrong. In a word, Gates was awful. He slouched in his chair and gave mumbling answers. He seemed bored. And even more damning, he professed to know little about how Microsoft had developed the marketing strategies that were at the heart of the government's case. If Microsoft had a monopoly on the PC market, Gates had a monopoly on ignorance of his company.

That Gates came across as a bumbler delighted Boies, who proceeded to make the most of the opportunity. Once he realized that Gates liked to say "I don't know" in response to questions, Boies happily gave him repeated opportunities to use those words. "For a man of Gates's stature to say 'I don't know' about his own company's activities a thousand times leaves his credibility in shreds."

Gates's decision to be evasive was evident to Boies during the very first minutes of questioning. He read Gates a quotation attributed to him in *Business Week*. "Did you say it, sir?" Boies asked.

"I don't remember saying that," Gates replied.

Boies came back, "That wasn't my question, sir. Did you say it?"

Overriding objections by a defense lawyer that he was "harassing" Gates, Boies asked, "Do you doubt that you said it?"

"You're sort of asking me to make some kind of guess," Gates complained.

When a defense lawyer broke in and said that Boies might "have to accept" an answer he did not like, Boies said emphatically, "Absolutely! Do you have any reason to believe that *Business Week* would make this quote up?"

At this point the video shows Gates more or less melting into his chair, eyes darting right to left, glancing down at his lap, and then staring into the distance. His silence lasted less than a minute, but to persons watching it seemed the proverbial eternity—and Boies was not about to encourage him to speak up. Gates's silence was making the point for him.

Boies worked over Gates for two days, then the depositions recessed for five days. Boies expected that Microsoft lawyers would use the hiatus to give Gates a crash course on deposition conduct and present a revived Gates when they returned. Such did not happen. Gates spend the interlude on a cruise to Alaska and returned to blunder through yet another day. "The Microsoft lawyers had to know that their boy had screwed up big-time," Boies said. "I can't understand why they did not try to rehabilitate him."

Microsoft offered a variety of excuses. Joseph E. diGenova, the former United States attorney for Washington, D.C., worked as a "legal spin doctor" for Microsoft during the trial. He contended that lawyers instruct clients to be as economical with answers during depositions, and to give only information that is specifically requested. For that reason, diGenova argued, Gates's pauses did not show a lack of knowledge, but a desire to hone his answers to the minimum. A lawyer for Sullivan & Cromwell would offer the argument that Microsoft did not expect the deposition tapes to be used in court, only the transcripts. Otherwise, the lawyer said, "Gates would have come across a lot differently." His excuse sounds hollow. Taped depositions are routinely used in federal trial courts, and Microsoft should have prepared for such an eventuality.

Persons not involved in the litigation got their first look at the Gates videotape during Boies's opening argument, when he played four segments to illustrate points he made. Further segments were played over the next three days. Although Microsoft lawyers complained that Boies was presenting isolated snippets of film out of context, nonetheless Gates came across looking stupid.

Incredibly, time and again America's richest executive claimed to be ignorant of major decisions made at Microsoft. That Gates had not even read the government complaint in a suit intended to dismember his own creation defied credulity. When he tried to deflect a Boies question with sarcasm, he sounded petulant. Microsoft lawyers realized after the first day that the clips showed Gates in a bad light, so they tried to persuade Judge Jackson to require Justice lawyers to play the entire tape, not selected bits. Judge Jackson refused. "If anything," he said, "I think the problem is with your witness, not the way his testimony is being presented."

Boies referred to a meeting mentioned in an e-mail, asking, "Who was at this executive staff meeting? he asked. Gates smirked. "Probably members of the executive staff," he replied.

Boies showed Gates an e-mail with the notation on the top: "Importance: High." He asked if Gates had typed in the notation.

"No," Gates said curtly.

"No?" Boies said, surprised.

"No, I didn't type that," Gates insisted. Well, who did? Boies asked.

Gates permitted a smug look to cross his face and said, "A computer."

Often the pauses between a question and his answer would last twenty seconds or more. At times Gates sounded Clintonesque. Even Judge Jackson shook his head in disbelief when Gates replied to a question about whether Microsoft competed with Apple Computer by responding, "depends on what you mean by compete."

Again, Boies read Gates a 1996 e-mail message that stated, "Winning Internet browser share is a very, very important goal for us."

GATES: I'm not getting your question. Are you trying to ask what I was thinking about when I wrote this sentence?
BOIES: Let me begin with that. "What were you thinking when you—"
GATES: I don't specifically remember writing that sentence.
BOIES: Does that mean you can't answer what you were thinking about when you wrote that sentence?
GATES: That's correct.

The fencing grew intense when Boies tried to pin down Gates on whether he was "concerned" about competition. Boies had produced an e-mail suggesting that was true. This exchange followed:

BOIES: So you don't remember what you were thinking about when you wrote it, and you don't remember what you meant when you wrote it; is that fair?
GATES: As well as not remember writing it.
BOIES: What non-Microsoft browsers were you concerned about it January of 1996?
GATES: I don't know what you mean by "concerned."
BOIES: What is it about the word "concerned" that you don't understand?
GATES: I'm not sure what you mean by it. . . . Is there a document where I use that term?
BOIES: Is the term "concerned" a term that you are familiar with in the English language?
GATES: Yes.
BOIES: Does it have a meaning that you're familiar with?
GATES: Yes.
BOIES: Using the word "concern" consistent with the normal meaning that it has in the English language, what Microsoft—

or what non-Microsoft browsers were you concerned about in January of 1996?

GATES: Well, I think I would have been concerned about Internet Explorer, what was going on with it. We would have been looking at other browsers that were in use at the time. Certainly Navigator was one of those. . . .

Joseph Nocera of *Fortune* was one of many journalists who gave Gates poor reviews. It "takes a good ten minutes" to get Gates to concede that the phrase "pissing on"—which appeared in an e-mail—is not "some [Microsoft] code word that means saying nice things."

THE SURGEON'S POSTMORTEM

Boies offered his analysis of Gates's testimony in an interview with Charlie Rose on PBS after the trial. "He was killing himself," Boies said. "He was coming across as deceptive, uncooperative— leave aside whether he was rude or not—but he was certainly coming across as someone who a judge or jury was gonna have a lot of trouble believing.

"What you wanted to do was to take him out and say, 'Look, I know that you're smart. I know that you're passionate. I know you're a salesman. Go in there and sell. Go in there and tell your story. Go in there and charm their pants off with your story.'"

Boies did concede that Gates was at a disadvantage. The examining lawyer controls the pace and the content. He moves the witness away from his strengths and concentrates on the weaknesses; he breaks the desired flow of presentation. Where Gates erred was in refusing to give any ground whatsoever. He felt that Microsoft was being subjected to an unfair suit, and he was not about to make things easier for his tormentors.

When a witness realizes that the time has come to yield ground, to concede that the other side has a point, he can do so to strategic advantage—for instance, Boies says, "The answer could be, 'Well, of course that's true, but you have to take into account so and so . . .' And then you add your point of view. If you are going to be forced to give a bad answer, give it and move on, don't drag your heels and let a lawyer like me keep dwelling on it. In the end, you are going to have to admit it anyway. What you are doing is inflating the importance of what you are conceding, and at the same time diminishing your credibility. You are losing both ways."

Boies pointed to Microsoft executive Paul Maritz, who as a witness gave ground when he knew he was being pressed, and did so quickly and naturally, without looking defensive. "And when he was not willing to give ground, Maritz was as firm as the proverbial rock. He might have done some things that were not permissible under the antitrust laws, but he still came across as a forceful, credible witness. Bill Gates could have learned much from him."

Watching Boies work his way through other witnesses resembled observing a cat tormenting listless and somewhat stupid mice. Time and again he baited traps for Microsoft witnesses with seemingly innocuous questions; repeatedly they snapped at his bait, only to find themselves forced to stammer out nonsensical answers.

David Ignatius, who observed the trial for the *Washington Post,* felt that Boies "has seemed to be shredding Microsoft's witnesses like a Vegematic—forcing embarrassing admissions from them, catching them with a doctored video and generally making them look like idiots. The atmospherics have been so potent that many observers are beginning to assume that Microsoft will lose and to speculate about how best to punish the giant company." But for all Boies's splash, Ignatius observed, "he did not introduce any convincing evidence that Microsoft's conduct harmed consumers." On this issue, William Neukom of Microsoft put into evidence about a thousand pages of Microsoft deposition testimony that essentially went unchallenged. Destruction of competition? Rival Netscape somehow had managed to distribute 150 million copies of its browser since 1995. One Microsoft lawyer said plaintively, "This is a strange antitrust case. Where are the customers who are complaining?"

After the trial, Boies shared some of his cross-examiner trade secrets with Karen Donovan of the *Record*,* a legal newspaper. He never begins a question with the "Isn't it true" declaration that TV audiences heard Perry Mason use for years. Asking a question in this form can let a witness slide away by claiming confusion. Boies avoids any ambiguity by making a statement and then asking, "Correct?" As he told Donovan, "I never want to leave an ambiguity in the record." This technique was especially important in the Microsoft case. The trial judge could use his judgment in deciding whether a witness was credible. But the appellate court would deal with the printed record only, where verbal nuances are not apparent.

Microsoft's clumsy witnesses did no better in trying to explain memos fished from their files. To antitrust lawyers, finding a document that contradicts what is said by a live witness is akin to opening a vein of gold. When the contest pits document against witness, the paper prevails, for reasons stated by Judge Learned Hand in a 1916 opinion involving a business accused of illegal monopolization. The evidence included typewritten memoranda between executives. Judge Hand wrote, "The documents were never intended to meet the eyes of anyone but the officers themselves, and were, as it were, cinematographic photographs of their purpose at the time they were written. A witness' attempt to contradict the validity of these memos served only to affect the general credibility of his testimony."

Boies made efficient use of the Microsoft papers. Every trial lawyer develops his own courtroom methodology. The late Louis Nizer, for instance, would plop a stack of legal pads on the lectern. He scrawled questions lengthwise across each page, and flicked through them one by one as he questioned a witness. Once the book was exhausted, he would flip it to his side—hopefully to be caught in midair by an associate, often as not to fall to the floor—and move on to the next pad. Boies's method is far simpler. He sketches out the territory he wishes to cover in

---

*Donovan's home paper is the *National Law Journal*; the version of the Boies interview that I read appeared in a sister publication, the *Record*.

scrawls on a manila folder. Each entry refers to the supporting documents. A former Cravath associate related, "When David wants a piece of paper, he simply stretches out his hand behind his back, and that is your signal to hand it up to him. And woe be to the associate who is slow in responding—or, God forbid, hands him the wrong thing."

But did Boies's performance cut to the heart of the case—that Microsoft's conduct harmed consumers—or did he use "the high jinks of courtroom tactics to try to obscure the evidentiary record," as William Neukom of Microsoft charged? Microsoft lawyers complained bitterly that reporters had "fallen under Mr. Boies's spell," reporting drama rather than facts that were more pertinent to the issues. For instance, Microsoft's leadoff witness was economist Dr. Richard Schmalensee, dean of the Sloan School of Management at Massachusetts Institute of Technology, who filed a 328-page statement as his testimony. Boies essentially ignored the paper. He depicted Dr. Schmalensee as a witness-for-hire by bringing out that Microsoft paid him $800 an hour, and that his 1998 income from the company was nearly $250,000. Then he poked at Dr. Schmalensee's past writings, seeking inconsistencies.

And as the day's proceedings wound down, Boies moved for what Microsoft bitingly called "the Boies Media Moment." A survey Schmalensee cited in his statement claimed that more than 80 percent of software developers felt Microsoft's integration of the Internet into Windows would help consumers. Did he know why Microsoft wanted him to conduct the survey? No, the dean replied.

Whereupon Boies read him a Gates e-mail: "It would HELP ME IMMENSELY [capitalization in the original] to have a survey showing that 90 percent of developers believe that putting the browser into the operating system makes sense. Ideally we would have a survey before I appear at the Senate on March 3rd."

Boies introduced other memos in rapid succession. One suggested that the survey was rigged to produce results favorable to Microsoft. Another concluded that most of the companies surveyed thought that Microsoft should be sued. In sum, even a "rigged poll" turned out to be unfavorable to Microsoft. At one point Dr. Schmalensee blurted to no one in particular, "What could I have been thinking?" When a Microsoft lawyer set out to restore the shattered credibility of the economic witness, Judge Jackson joked that he faced "a heroic endeavor."

Unsurprisingly, Boies walked out to the courthouse steps and waved copies of the memos for the TV cameras. He dominated the news coverage.

By midtrial the focus was on Boies's performance as much as the evidence. Dr. Schmalensee serves as a good case in point. Called later in the trial to present rebuttal testimony, he would not waver on a key point: Netscape had been so battered that the industry fight over browsers was over. Nonetheless, even in its dominant position, Microsoft had not raised prices. This statement received minimal press attention in contrast to his rough treatment by Boies.

Steve Lohr, of the *New York Times* team covering the trial, wrote of Boies, "He cross-examines like a jazz musician, starting with a few themes and mostly improvising. He constantly probes for embarrassing weaknesses." Jared Sandberg of *Newsweek* wrote, "The real story of the trial may turn out to be Boies, whose civility, flare for drama, and gift for making the other guy look bad is consistently scoring points against the software giant." Joe Nocera of *Fortune,* although giving Boies high marks as a performer, felt that Boies's treatment of Gates, good theater though it might be, "was a complete sideshow, utterly devoid of legal merit, whose only purpose is to influence the press. . . . Worse, the press has become increasingly inured to Microsoft's arguments, giving them short shrift in their accounts of the trial."

CRAVATH IS ANGERED

One group of lawyers irked at the media attention lavished on Boies consisted of his former partners at Cravath, Swaine & Moore. The media repeatedly overstated Boies's role in the IBM antitrust litigation. Typical was a sentence in a profile of Boies that David Segal of the *Washington Post* wrote on the eve of the trial: "Boies had led IBM Corp.'s triumphant twelve-year war of attrition, when in 1969 [he] accused the computer giant of antitrust violations that echo the government's allegations against Microsoft. . . . So who better to champion Justice's cause this time than the guy who wore them down in the last big brawl?" Another *Post* reporter, Rajiv Chandasekaban, wrote that Boies "successfully defended IBM against a similarly broad antitrust suit in the 1970s." John Wilke of the *Wall Street Journal* called Boies "the unpredictable maverick who successfully defended [IBM] in the government's last great antitrust showdown."

What finally caused Cravath to boil over was a *Fortune* article which stated that "Boies was the [IBM] company's chief litigator during its thirteen-year fight with the government." In a bristling three-page letter to *Fortune,* Samuel C. Butler, who ran Cravath when Boies left the firm, wrote that he felt "compelled" to set the record straight on a statement that "has appeared repeatedly in the media." When Cravath began representing IBM in January 1969, Butler wrote, Boies had been at the firm only two and a half years. Credit for the win rested with partner Thomas D. Barr, not Boies.

I offered a devil's advocate argument to a Cravath lawyer—that Boies should not be held responsible for what journalists wrote. The man responded with a horselaugh. "Boies reads his clips as closely as does a movie starlet. He was seeing these reporters on a daily basis. Have you seen any evidence that he tried to set the record straight?"

POINT, GAME, AND SET: BOIES

Midcourse in the trial Judge Jackson tried to nudge the parties toward settlement. His in-chambers remarks—the transcripts were released after the trial—demonstrated that he gave little credence to Microsoft witnesses. As the trial droned into its ninth month Judge Jackson made little attempt to conceal his uninterest in Microsoft's case. Microsoft lawyers had insisted all along that America Online's purchase of Netscape would make it a formidable competitor with Microsoft. But when Warden put into evidence what he considered to be key documents, Judge Jackson professed faint interest. "I'll admit it," he said of one paper. "I don't know what's probative in it; I really don't."

Unbeknown to lawyers, Judge Jackson was giving interviews during the trial to reporters Joel Brinkley and Steve Lohr of the *New York Times* and Ken Auletta of the *New Yorker* with the understanding that the material would not be used until he reached a decision. (These interviews would months later figured in an appeals court's reversal of Judge Jackson's decision in the case.) He had his own opinion of Gates's veracity: "Here is the guy who is the head of the organization, and his testimony is inherently without credibility. At the start, it makes you skeptical about the rest of the trial. You are saying, 'If you can't believe this guy, who else can you believe?' "

Judge Jackson's remarks in open court also disturbed Microsoft lawyers. Before court one morning, he said from the bench, in remarks that seemed directed at Microsoft, "The code of tribal wisdom says that when you discover you are riding a dead horse, the best strategy is to dismount." But some attorneys, he continued, "often try other strategies with dead horses, including the following: buying a strong whip; changing riders; saying things like 'This is the way we've always ridden this horse'; appointing a committee to study the horse . . . declaring the horse is better, faster, and cheaper dead; and, finally, harnessing several dead horses together for increased speed."

The Microsoft lawyers exchanged long looks. They knew the case was lost insofar as the trial before Judge Jackson was concerned. But he had given them grounds for appeal.

At trial's end the government moved for dismemberment of Microsoft. Joel Klein and other lawyers did not feel that the company would abide by any consent decree—that the only way to bring the company into conformity with the antitrust laws was to break it up. Boies played no role in this decision. His job had been to amass evidence that Microsoft had broken antitrust laws; what happened thereafter was "not my function," he stated.

Once the evidence was in, Judge Jackson issued a series of rulings that represented a total victory for the government. First, on November 4, 1999, he ruled that Microsoft was in fact a monopoly, writing, "Through its conduct, Microsoft has demonstrated that it will use its prodigious market power and immense profits to harm any firm that insists on pursuing initiatives that could intensify competition against one of Microsoft's core products." His order covered 207 pages and contained more than 400 paragraphs. As John Heilemann wrote in *Wired,* "Only one or two [paragraphs] were remotely favorable to Microsoft, while the remainder of the document could have been written by the [Department of Justice]." And despite the attention the media gave to Boies's evisceration of Gates, Judge Jackson did not mention the exchanges. Microsoft lawyers pointed to the omission as "proof" that the cross-examination was a noisy sideshow.

At a hearing on February 12, 2000—Microsoft was allocated only a single day to present countering arguments—Judge Jackson compared the company to John D. Rockefeller's Standard Oil monopoly, which the government broke up in the early 1900s in the nation's first major antitrust case. "I don't really see a distinction," he said. On April 3 he ruled that the fact that Microsoft had not overcharged customers was not relevant. Microsoft indeed had violated antitrust laws and kept "an oppressive thumb on the scale of competitive fortune." Gates commented, "This ruling turns on its head the reality that consumers know—that our software has helped make PCs more accessible and more affordable to millions."

And, finally, on June 7, Judge Jackson ordered that Microsoft be split into two parts, one for the Windows operating system, the other for other computer program and Internet businesses. By this time Microsoft stock had plunged nearly 50 percent, wiping out more than $200 billion of wealth.

David Boies had won a clear victory—albeit one that Microsoft challenged strongly on appeal. No matter. Boies's fame reached new heights, both in the legal profession and to the general public. The *American Lawyer* dubbed him "the Michael Jordan of the courtroom." Meanwhile, very profitable business was gushing into the firm of Boies, Schiller & Flexner.

But the victory did not long survive. Within weeks the U.S. Circuit Court of Appeals for the District of Columbia reversed Judge Jackson, holding that he misapplied antitrust law. It also cited his "improper" interviews with journalists while the case was being heard. And in a rebuke the court ordered that a jurist other than Judge Jackson hold new hearings on the case. And despite Boies's victory, the ultimate settlement was on terms highly favorable to Microsoft. No matter: David Boies had enjoyed another very warm day in the public eye, and by the time of the effective reversal of his courtroom victory, he had moved on to other matters.

A MONEY FLOW BECOMES A TORRENT

As Boies relished in telling the story, the first week of November 1999 will always hold fond memories. On November 3, a Wednesday, Boies, Schiller & Flexner settled a price-fixing scheme under which international vitamin makers agreed to pay customers $1.17 billion, one of the grander class action settlements in history. The firm's share of $121 million in legal fees was a shade more than $40 million.* Two days later, on Friday, Boies won a jury verdict in New York that awarded $11.6 million to a real estate developer in a contract dispute. That was in the morning. In the early afternoon came word from Alaska that two big petroleum companies, Atlantic Richfield and BP Amoco, would pay his client, the State of Alaska, millions of dollars in return for ending its opposition to their merger. Then came the late afternoon court session in Washington at which Judge Jackson ruled against Microsoft.

---

*The settlement did not satisfy all of the plaintiffs—153 different corporations, in fact, including such giants as Quaker Oats and Kraft Foods, Inc. They chose to opt out of the class action case and pursue individual suits. Their lead counsel was the Washington firm of Dickstein, Shapiro, Morin & Oshinsky. And in the spring of 2004 they won an out-of-court settlement of approximately $2 billion. Dickstein Shapiro's fee was estimated at $300 million.

Boies earned relative peanuts while working for the Justice Department in the Microsoft case—$114,000, plus out-of-pocket expenses. He computed that his hourly fee was around $40, less than experienced secretaries make at Cravath. No matter. Boies was suddenly the most famous lawyer in America, a status that gained valuable publicity for his firm. While Boies focused on Microsoft, partners Jonathan Schiller and Donald Flexner piled up millions of dollars elsewhere, notably a big win in the vitamin price-fixing case.

But Boies was by no means omnipotent, and he suffered a very public defeat in July 2000 in a case involving the Web music service Napster. To the delight of young music fans everywhere, Napster enabled the free downloading of thousands of pieces of music. Quite understandably, record companies objected to the distribution of copyrighted music that they preferred to sell as albums. On behalf of Napster, Boies offered the peculiar argument that the free downloads actually encouraged people to buy music, to the benefit of the record companies. A music industry lawyer laughed at this contention: "Perhaps Brother Boies can convince the Campbell Soup people that encouraging shoplifting will enhance their sales. Ridiculous!"

In any event, the Napster case was front-page news for weeks. An irony in the case was noted by persons who followed Microsoft. In that case, Boies prevailed in large part because of damning internal company documents. Boies learned that the documents game can be played both ways. Record industry lawyers found Napster documents stating that the company's main purpose was "pirating" music. U.S. District Court Judge Marilyn Hall Patel came down hard on Napster. What it was doing was clearly illegal, she ruled, and the people who ran Napster should have known it. She did concede that Napster had legitimate functions, such as posting music from new and unknown artists who agreed to online circulation of their work for promotional purposes. But these uses pale in comparison to Napster's illegal activities. As Judge Patel remarked, "Many of them [the legal uses] seemed to be thought of after this litigation started."

When Boies complained of the difficulties Napster would have in sorting out what music on its site was copyrighted, Judge Patel shot back, "That's their problem. They created this monster." The "clever" programmers who created the system could use the same wit to make it legal.

Should Napster be considered a loss for Boies? In a sense, yes, for Boies failed to gain the relief sought by his client. Once again, however, he enjoyed staggeringly favorable publicity, and especially among younger Americans who use the Internet to communicate with one another. Type the words "David Boies" into an Internet search vehicle, and the number of favorable articles concerning him and Napster is overwhelming.

And then came a representation that earned David Boies a permanent place in American history, even though in what ultimately proved to be a losing cause.

TO GORE'S RESCUE—WELL, NOT QUITE

Given Boies's stature as a lawyer and his close ties to prominent Democratic lawyers, it was no surprise that he was among the first big names summoned to Florida in November 2000 to try to salvage Vice President Al Gore's bid for the presidency. The call came the day after the election from fellow Yalie Walter Dellinger, a former solicitor general. Things were not going well for Gore. The elderly former secretary of state Warren Christopher was the Gore team's public face the first two days or so. Then Boies stepped forth, giving crisp sound bites, tossing his head to rearrange his straying strands of sandy hair.

Boies found instant fame in a Southern capital, Tallahassee, where residents perhaps had not followed closely such events as Microsoft. One woman sidled close to him after one of his innumerable press briefings and pleaded with him to autograph a copy of the local newspaper. Murmured ooohs signaled his entrance into a restaurant. Someone identified only as a "top Gore official" told Richard L. Berke of the *New York Times* that the campaign preferred that a lawyer, not a political operative, do the talking. "We see Boies as the public face—low-key, moderate, careful, not inflammatory. That's how we'd like to position this thing publicly." What was left unspoken was the chummy rapport Boies enjoys with the media, a legacy dating to the Westmoreland trial in 1984.

By Boies's account, the Microsoft case "never entered my mind" when he received Dellinger's urgent call. Why Boies? "I had been involved in voting rights cases for more than thirty years, in Mississippi and elsewhere, so I was grounded in the law." As did lawyers in both camps, he expected to be in Florida "three days, maybe four days, even a week." Events dictated otherwise: he was there a full month, breaking only for the Thanksgiving holiday—a short one, during which he worked on other pending cases. And even while scuttling around Florida, from court to court, Boies was on his cell phone many times daily, talking with clients and other lawyers in his office.

But Boies surely knew the risk that a victory for Governor George W. Bush would pose to his Microsoft verdict. Speaking in the spring of 2000 in Washington State, near the Microsoft offices, conservative candidate Bush said, "I stand on the side of innovation, not litigation. What I am worried about is if this company were to be broken up, this engine of change and this engine of growth . . . I am not sympathetic to lawsuits. . . . I worry about lawsuits on job creation. If you are looking for the kind of president I will be, I will be slow to litigate."

There was another factor, as noted by Kevin Sacks of *New York Times*: "[Boies] worked pro bono, paid only with relentless publicity." Indeed, the media tumult surrounding Boise led James V. Grimaldi, then the legal reporter for the *Washington Post,* to call reporters the "COB," meaning "the cult of Boies."

Unfortunately for Gore, Boies did not fare as well in court as he did with the media. His chief appearance in Florida was before Judge N. Sanders Sauls of Leon County Circuit Court in Tallahassee, in a bid to force recounts of ballots by election boards in selected counties. Those who attended the two days of hearings concluded rather early on that although some might consider Boies "the finest lawyer money can buy," Judge Sauls did not care for him. Indeed, reporters David Barstow and Dexter Filkins of the *New York Times,* wrote that Judge Sauls's "good humor seems to vanish each time Mr. Boies opens his mouth." (The same journalists noted that "Mr. Boies remains a favorite of reporters, who practically swarm him each time he sets foot in the hallway.") Columnist George F. Will observed that "many round-heeled journalists have a crush on Boies, who plays them as effortlessly as Paganini played a Stradivarius."

Boies got off to the wrong start with Judge Sauls by asking that the Florida Supreme Court force him to order that a ballot recount commence even before a scheduled hearing. The court summarily rejected his order. A lawyer friend commented at the time, "You know, the last thing a judge wants to hear is for some lawyer—and especially some hotshot from out of town—to try to get a higher court to tell him to hurry up. I realize that Boies was in a time bind [the deadline for certification of Florida's electors was rapidly approaching] but the most direct route to a good ol' boy's heart is not over his head."

Judge Sauls slouched behind the bench, eyes hooded, resembling nothing less than a venerable Florida gator crouching in the low waters of a stream, waiting for something edible to wander by. The unfortunate Boies felt the snap of his jaws several times. Judge Sauls didn't even pretend to be deferential, or even polite, for that matter. Late the first day of the hearing Boies spent hours cross-examining Judge Charles Burton, chairman of the Palm Beach County elections board. Judge Burton was a witness unfriendly to Gore, and Boies tried to establish that he and colleagues acted arbitrarily in refusing to extend time for voting recounts.

As Judge Burton stepped down from the witness chair, Judge Sauls beamed at him and called him "a great American." The pained expression on Boies's face showed that he surely realized he had lost the day, insofar as this witness was concerned.

Judge Sauls also gave Boies a rough time—perhaps more so than was warranted—in reining in his attempted cross-examination of opposing witnesses. Boies wanted to quiz a statistician, Laurentius Marais, about his past expert testimony in cases involving persons allegedly poisoned by lead paint. Judge Sauls abruptly shut him down, agreeing with Bush lawyers that the questioning was irrelevant. Time and again Judge Sauls instructed Boies to restate a question in acceptable form—an admonition tantamount to a slander of an experienced trial lawyer. As Barstow and Filkins wrote in the *New York Times,* it was "as if Mr. Boies were some fumbling rookie prosecutor trying his first shoplifting case."

Judge Sauls's rejection of the Gore position was so resounding that even Bush lawyers were confused. Republican political strategist Tony Blankley would write: "It was a *schadenfreudian* joy to watch Lawyer Boies manfully maintain that sickly smile on his ashen face as he listen to the judge dismiss as so much dross or bilgewater every last comma of Mr. Boies' lovingly crafted legal case. From the tone of his opinion Mr. Boies and his fellow Gore lawyers were lucky the judge didn't order them into leg irons and have them duck-walked straight into the basement jail of the courthouse." Nonetheless, Boies managed to smile as he suggested that something salvageable could be found in the wreckage of his case. "We appreciate the fact that the court has now ruled, and now we have an opportunity to take this issue directly up to the Florida Supreme Court," he told reporters outside court. He said it with a smile. As I watched Boies on television, I mentally composed a post-sinking statement for the captain of the *Titanic*: "We appreciate the fact that we now have an opportunity to test the efficacy of our lifeboats."

So what prompted the United States Supreme Court to issue two rulings whose net effect was to declare George W. Bush the winner of the White House? A torrent of legal analysis began within minutes of the court's December 12 ruling halting any further recounting of votes, with TV pundits scrambling to read the minds of nine justices. But in retrospect, lawyers on both sides agree that the turning point came late December 9, just after the Florida Supreme Court ordered a manual recount of some 43,000 ballots in selected precincts. The case was bounced back to Leon County Circuit Judge Terry P. Lewis, who convened an emergency hearing to determine what rules should govern the recount—for instance, how much would a chad have to be punched to demonstrate voter intent? Boies and other Gore lawyers wanted Judge Lewis to mandate a clear rule. He refused. Any recounts, he said, would be done under existing Florida law. He left it to individual canvassing boards to decide whether a dimple on a ballot, or varying degrees of chad punch-through, should be counted as a vote.

Litigator George Terwilliger, the White & Case partner who was one of the leaders of the Bush courtroom team, immediately saw the significance of Judge Lewis's ruling. Any recount done under such haphazard standards clearly violated the constitutional guarantee of equal protection under the laws. For days the Bush team had struggled to find a means of making a federal case out of the proceedings. Now, Terwilliger's side had been handed a blueprint for victory.

As Terwilliger walked out of the well of the court, gently pushing his way through a squirming mass of lawyers and media people, he came face to face with Boies. "David," he said, patting his adversary on the shoulder, "David, we just won this lawsuit." Boies smiled tightly. He knew what Terwilliger meant. "Don't break out the champagne just yet," Boies replied.

Terwilliger's confidence swelled during arguments before the U.S. Supreme Court. Given his hands-on knowledge of the Florida laws, and the varying court rulings there, Boies replaced Lawrence Tribe, the Harvard professor who had argued Gore's first appeal to the high court. Several justices immediately tried to pin Boies down on the standard for counting votes. There was this exchange with Justice Anthony M. Kennedy:

KENNEDY: Do you think that in the contest phase, there must be a uniform standard for counting the ballots?
BOIES: I do, Your Honor. I think there must be a uniform standard. I think there is a uniform standard. The question is whether the standard is too general or not. The standard is

whether or not the intent of the voter is reflected by the ballot. . . .

KENNEDY: That's very general. It runs throughout the law. Even a dog knows the difference in being stumbled over and being kicked. Now, in this case, what we're concerned with is an intent that focuses on this little piece of paper called a ballot. And you would say that from the standpoint of the equal protection clause—could each county then give their own interpretation to what intent means, so long as they are in good faith and with some reasonable basis finding intent?

BOIES: I think—

KENNEDY: Could that vary from county to county?

BOIES: *I think it can vary from individual to individual.*

A Bush lawyer who begged anonymity told me, "When I heard that exchange, I realized that Justice Kennedy had worked David into a box, and then slammed down the lid. Think about it—admitting in open court that two ballot counters could be sitting side by side, and applying different standards as to which ballots were valid. I felt kinda' sorry for David, even though I wanted Bush to win."

Even Justice David H. Souter, widely perceived as being friendly to the Gore cause, had trouble with Boies's argument. He asked, ". . . [I]f we were fashioning a response to the equal protection claim, and we assume as a fact that there may be variations, wouldn't those variations, from county to county, on objective standards, be an equal protection violation?"

Boies did not think so, for he felt "there are a lot of times in the law in which there can be these variations, from jury to jury, from public official to public official."

"Well," pressed Justice Souter, if the Florida officials needed guidance on uniform standards, "what would you tell them to do about it?"

"Well," Boies replied, "I think that's a very hard question."

The court the next evening ruled there should be no further counting of votes in Florida, effectively affirming Bush's victory.

BACK TO PROFITABLE BUSINESS

Even as Boies toiled for Gore in Florida, he busied himself by long distance and fast in-and-out trips back to New York in a case that epitomized why he abandoned Cravath: to earn super payouts from class action cases. In one of its first major cases, Boies Schiller capitalized on a decision by Judge Lewis Kaplan of the Southern District of New York to try a novel approach in choosing lead counsel for what portended to be a multimillion-dollar case. Critics of class actions frequently fret, with much justification, that lawyers who handle such cases often walk away with more money than the clients who ostensibly are the injured parties. Judges routinely approved attorney fees amounting to 25 to 30 percent of the settlement.

The case before Judge Kaplan concerned seamy conduct by executives of the supposedly classy auction houses Sotheby's and Christie's, which between them annually handled $4 billion worth of art and antiques for some of the world's biggest social names. In the mid-1990s the Justice Department heard that the houses colluded to set identical commission charges for buyers and sellers, denying sellers any chance to bargain for lower commissions.

The Justice lawyers got an unexpected break in January 2000. Under prosecution pressure, Christopher M. Davidge, Christie's former chief executive, produced documents detailing meetings at which the secret arrangements were made. He asserted that he and his counterpart at Sotheby's, Diana D. "Dede" Brooks, a Manhattan socialite and doyenne of the arts world, acted at the direction of their superiors. Both Davidge and Ms. Brooks pleaded guilty to criminal price-fixing charges in return for their testimony against their respective chairmen, A. Alfred Taubman of Sotheby's, and Sir Anthony Tennant of Christie's. Sotheby's paid a $45 million fine and Taubman was sent to prison for a year for fraud.

The Davidge documents, and the availability of him and Ms. Brooks as witnesses, meant that any class action antitrust action would be a slam dunk. Enter now Judge Kaplan and his unique approach to selecting the lawyers for the case. Essentially, he put it up for bids: Set the floor figure you think you can win, and you will receive 25 percent of anything over that amount. He wanted a firm that would work at a minimum cost to the class. The risk is that the lawyers would receive no fee if they did not recover their floor figure.

Ironically, Boies Schiller was not among the several firms that represented any of the bilked art patrons at the time. Nonetheless, when Judge Kaplan solicited bids, partner Jonathan Schiller saw his chance to edge aside other members of the class action club and win major business. Some twenty firms decided to enter bids, most of them setting settlement floors in the $100 million to $200 million range. After looking at what the available evidence, Schiller thought otherwise, as did Boies and partner Richard B. Drubel. "This case can top out at half a billion dollars," Schiller said. "Let's go high." So he and Boies submitted a settlement estimate of $405 million, twice again as large as that from any other office. Judge Kaplan designated Boies Schiller as lead counsel.

This was on May 26, 2000. On October 23, the two auction houses agreed to settle the case for $512 million, meaning that Boies Schiller had been counsel of record for less than four months. The firm's fee was $26.75 million—25 percent of $107 million, the difference between the $512 million settlement and the $405 million floor bid.

Seas of dollars now flowed through Boies Schiller—exactly the lucrative practice Boies envisioned when he took the gamble of leaving a $2-million-a-year partnership at Cravath, Swaine & Moore. The auction house settlement gave the firm a solid financial cushion. Although neither Boies nor anyone else at the firm will even whisper about partner incomes, anyone with a rudimentary knowledge of arithmetic could see that he and the other name partners surely exceeded the $2 million mark.* And given

---

*Although Boies's publicity flood had diminished somewhat as 2005 began, he took pains to let the world know he remained a busy lawyer. In March 2005 he helped negotiate the exit of Maurice Greenberg from the insurance giant American International Group. Boies told business reporter Jenny Anderson of the *New York Times* that he had to interrupt a weekend in which he was trying to engineer the departure of brothers Bob and Harvey Weinstein from Disney, and to support the New York Jets' bid to build a football stadium in Manhattan.

its growing reputation as a legal powerhouse, Boies Schiller could pick and choose among the literally hundreds of résumés that came into the office. By the end of 2004, the firm had more than two hundred lawyers spread around the country, with Washington being the largest operation. As at firms elsewhere, young associates were expected to work backbreaking hours— 2,200 to 2,800, persons around the office told me—and often under caustic supervision of whatever partner happened to be in charge. Top litigators are not known for even dispositions, and being chewed out is part of the price paid by an associate.

"THE SUPER BOWL OF LAW"

Many days after finality in Florida, Boies reflected on what happened there, and why. He was back to twelve- and fourteen-hour days, working weekends as well, preparing for a string of high-stake cases due to go to trial in coming months. He was named a special counsel to sort through the mess left by the collapse of Tyco, the communications giant, and to handle a massive class action case against officers accused of liability for shareholder losses. He and other plaintiff lawyers did the groundwork for potential bonanza cases against health care providers in many states.

To be sure, Boies's public visibility diminished drastically after the IBM trial and the Florida vote cases. His disappointment, even bitterness, about the Florida loss was obvious. "Let's just leave it at this: almost any lawsuit can go either way. In this one, I thought we had the law on our side. The court said otherwise." Nonetheless, he has no regrets about donating a month of his professional life to what proved to be a losing cause.

"I'm a litigator," he said, "so I like to win. But what lawyer would pass up the chance to play in the ultimate 'super bowl of law'—a case that essentially decided who would be the president of the United States?"

He paused. "Yeah, but I still prefer to be the winner."

A VICTORY CELEBRATION ELSEWHERE

But there was considerable irony to the outcome of the Florida vote. Boies surely dazzled the media and accumulated more publicity in four weeks than most lawyers do in a lifetime. But the day after the U.S. Supreme Court decision, celebratory red, white, and blue bunting flew not on his office, but at the Washington building housing the firm of Patton Boggs LLP. A partner there, Ben Ginsberg, served as campaign counsel for Gov. George W. Bush, and he was an unobtrusive legal presence throughout the Florida contest. That Patton Boggs triumphantly greeted the election of a Republican president was a matter of great irony, and more than a little amusement, because of the firm's reputation as a Democratic office. How it changed, and why, leads us to a man who epitomizes the term "Washington power broker."

2 / Thomas Hale Boggs, Jr., Washington Superlobbyist

As he entered his sixties, Thomas Hale Boggs, Jr., sported the girth of a man who has declared a permanent truce in a losing war with his waistline. Years of fine wines and rich Cajun cuisine from his native Louisiana have constructed a tummy that rolls out over his belt, the subject of an occasional pat when he is contemplating an issue. He is lodged deep in a leather chair in the Patton Boggs office in the West End of Washington, just across Rock Creek from Georgetown, with Sen. Trent Lott, then the Senate majority leader, speaking on the other end of a phone that is tucked between his shoulder and his ear. The thick cigar stuck between Boggs's clasped lips is unlit, and he has a little trick of using his tongue to make it twirl to and fro.

Boggs is listening. Indeed, he has sat in silence for almost five minutes now, absorbing whatever Lott is confiding. The four other lawyers present, seated across the room in a cluster of chairs, talk in subdued voices as they wait for Boggs to finish. From experience they realize that Boggs's Buddha-deep silence is a signal that he is seeking a solution for a problem—"Tommy running his traps, thinking through all the political ramifications of the problem, and how he can solve it," as partner Mark Cowan had told me.

Finally Boggs speaks. "Work on Bob Byrd," he says, in a voice that retains strong residues of a melodious Southern accent despite the fact that Boggs has spent most of his life inside the

Washington Beltway. "Get Byrd aboard, and he'll be good for two or three, maybe even four others." And he ticks off the names of senators, both Democratic and Republican, who could help Lott on whatever matter is at issue. A few final pleasantries with Lott, a deep chuckle at something the senator says, and he puts down the phone. One of the other lawyers asks a question by raising his eyebrows. "No problem," Boggs replies. "We got this one handled."

Just what "this one" involved was something that Boggs did not choose to discuss with a visitor, but no matter: the lawyer lobbyist who is arguably the most powerful private citizen in Washington had just worked magic on behalf of another client.

Thomas Hale Boggs, Jr., is an important figure in modern American law because he personifies the juxtaposition of money and politics. The media report at length on the influence of political contributions to the conduct of government at all levels. Boggs's firm, in essence, is the interface between money and the government. He and colleagues raise money for those persons who run Washington, and in turn go to them for help on matters benefitting the contributors.

Boggs is both product and king of the political aristocracy that rules modern Washington—a man who, in his three-decade career, has come to epitomize the awesome power that money exerts on government. He is a professional and political paradox. He professes to be a staunch liberal Democrat. He has raised uncounted millions of dollars for Democratic politicians at all levels. His father, Hale Boggs, served as Democratic majority leader in the House of Representatives when he died in an Alaska plane crash in 1972 while on a campaign trip. Mother Lindy succeeded him in Congress and then, during the Clinton years, he served as U.S. ambassador to the Vatican. Indeed, by Boggs's count, no fewer than seventeen Patton Boggs lawyers held high positions under President Clinton, including Lanny Davis, the chief White House spinmaster during the Monica Lewinsky scandal. And Boggs was among the Washington insiders the president called upon to save him from impeachment, plotting strategy in daily conference calls with the White House.

Yet: Patton Boggs concurrently boasts the largest aggregation of "name Republicans" of any single law firm in Washington. Further, these individual are not the "Rockefeller Republicans" whose political moderation and manners make them acceptable to the national media and Washington's liberal elite. When conservative Republicans won control of Congress in 1994, Patton Boggs went hard-core, hiring men such as Darryl D. Nirenberg, former chief of staff to Jesse Helms (R., N.C.), and Brian C. Lopina, who ran Washington operations for the Christian Coalition. Even the moderates are Republicans of note—for instance, Benjamin Ginsberg, onetime counsel for the Republican National Committee, who in 2000 became counsel for Gov. George W. Bush's presidential campaign. After the election Ginsberg headed the team of GOP lawyers who beat off challenges to Bush in Florida, working chiefly behind the scenes and leaving the TV mikes to more telegenic attorneys. And prominent in the firm's health care group is the nonlawyer lobbyist Willis Graddison, who crafted the "Harry and Louise" TV spots that smashed Hillary Rodham Clinton's attempt to reform the nation's health care system, the major legislative goal of her husband's first year in office.

With a straight face, Boggs argues that the firm always had a bipartisan cast—indeed, founding partner James Patton was a registered, if nonactive, Republican. Nonetheless, Boggs's office wall is festooned with photographs of Boggs shaking hands or standing alongside virtually every Democratic politician of note of the last two decades. There is another rare trophy as well: Boggs with Pope John Paul II and mother Lindy, the U.S. ambassador to the Vatican. Major wall space is devoted to a frame of pens—fifty or so—which President Lyndon B. Johnson used to sign the Great Society legislation that father Hale helped steer through Congress in the 1960s.

I joked with Boggs about the conception in the public and the media that Patton Boggs was a Democratic lobbying firm. He hoo-hahed. "Well," he said, "I kind of wish it was, 'cause I consider myself to be a Democrat." He paused. "A big-time Democrat!" In reality, he said, Patton Boggs has perhaps more

Republicans in its public policy practice (the firm's euphemism for lobbying) than any other firm in Washington. As if to buttress his contention that Patton Boggs is truly bipartisan, he notes that the firm had a strong presence at *both* the Democratic and Republican national conventions the summer of 2000 and 2004. Boggs rummaged around on a credenza and found a button distributed at a 2000 party the firm hosted for the Democrats in Los Angeles. It depicted a donkey wearing outsized sunglasses; the legend read, "Patton Boggs in LA: We're Lobbyists . . . We Just Look Like Movie Stars!!"

Nonetheless, one frequently hears a jest in Washington law offices that the Republican presence reflects a certain pragmatism on Boggs's part, if not outright cynicism. There is talk about a meeting Boggs convened the day after the Republican electoral tsunami of 1994: "It's time," Boggs supposedly said, "to wake up and smell the elephants." The Republican hires began in earnest within days.

Boggs watchers don't know quite what to make of the man. To David Segal, formerly the legal columnist for the *Washington Post,* Boggs is "an overdressed shark to enemies of the town's influence game, a godsend to scores of corporations in need of a legislative favor." To Louis Jacobson of the *National Journal,* Boggs is "the archetype of the ultra connected, backslapping, cigar-chomping Democratic lobbyist." But hear Carl Bernstein, of Watergate fame, who concluded a lengthy *Vanity Fair* profile dealing with Boggs's role in making lobbying a powerful force in Washington, "He has refashioned the town, helped build a hugely successful new industry, is renowned for his integrity, and he's a terrific guy. And that's the good news." Bernstein is not known for writing nice things about people.

One could argue, plausibly, that Tom Boggs now is the most influential lawyer in the nation's capital. Many of the super-lawyers I wrote about in the 1970s are now dead (Clark Clifford and Lloyd Cutler). During the Clinton scandals, the media blithely bestowed the title on such men as defense attorneys David Kendall and Robert Bennett and golfing pal Vernon Jordan. The designation was laughable. What, pray tell, is "super" about watching a client parlay a sexual harassment suit by a government clerk into impeachment, with the attendant personal and national humiliation? Surmise and hindsight are easy, but one can imagine a Clark Clifford extricating a client from such a mess without all the fuss.*

So who is Tom Boggs, and why does he stand imposingly tall among the nearly 100,000 attorneys in Washington? As is true of most attorneys whose practice is a blend of law and lobbying, Boggs seldom goes near a courtroom. His tools are, in random order, the telephone, a handshake, and—most important—an insider's knowledge of how things really work in Washington, and how to get people to do things that you desire.

Further, Boggs is not a man to leave fingerprints. He and lawyers at his firm are responsible for much of the major trade legislation of the last decade, from the North American Free Trade Agreement to the 2000 pact expanding economic relations with the People's Republic of China. Alaskan oil? Patton Boggs lawyers represented oil companies from the very beginning, when the North Slope was opened for exploration, to the early 2000s fight over further drilling. Communications? Patton Boggs lawyers hammered out the sweeping Telecommunications Act of 1995, which established rules for relations between long-distance carri-

---

*How could Clinton have escaped? Any number of lawyers, in Washington and elsewhere, wondered why Clinton's attorneys did not ignore the Paula Jones lawsuit as "unworthy of a response" and let the woman take a default judgment for what likely would have been token damages. Clinton could have projected the impression that her suit was beneath the dignity of his office and unworthy of an answer. Instead, Kendall's hard-nosed firm, Williams & Connolly, aided by the scorched-earth White House political staff, fought the Jones suit bitterly, and expensively, and in the end Clinton paid around $900,000 to Jones, plus millions more in legal bills and sanctions. As a final tribute to his "superlawyers," in addition to his impeachment, Clinton was suspended from the Arkansas bar for five years and resigned from the bar of the U.S. Supreme Court rather than face disciplinary action. Some argue, in defense of Kendall et al., that defense lawyers did not control legal strategy in the case, that the president and Mrs. Clinton dictated strategy. If so, I suggest that a stern Dutch uncle lecture from a Lloyd Cutler would have forced them to face reality.

ers, the cable industry, and the broadcast industry. The firm states that it participated in "the development of every piece of U.S. tax legislation" over three decades. The intricate scandal involving the collapse of the Bank of Commerce and Credit International, or BCCI? Patton Boggs got its banker clients through the ordeal relatively untouched. Of the three books I've read on the BCCI scandal, none mentioned Patton Boggs.

I mentioned this omission to founding partner James M. Patton, who worked on BCCI matters steadily for fourteen years, in courts both in the United States and many foreign countries. "That," Jim Patton said, "is just the way we like it. Do our job, keep our names out of the papers, and go do something else."

As is true at many Washington law firms, an aura of mystery helps business. The goal is to suggest, without ever saying so directly, that when you hire Patton Boggs, you are hiring people with special access, special knowledge, special skills. Several years ago Boggs gave an interview to a writer for the United States Information Agency on why foreign clients come to him for help in Washington. He said that these clients, even very sophisticated ones, "for the most part do not have much of an understanding of how the federal system works here between the Congress and the Executive" branch of government, nor do they understand the political relationship between the state and federal systems. He stresses to them the importance of dealing with Congress, because many of them think they can achieve their goals simply by approaching the White House." The USIA writer continued, "Boggs points out that a lot of time is spent telling the client what can and cannot be done, what obstacles must be overcome, and what costs will be incurred." Although he was speaking for an international audience, Boggs's comments are applicable to his domestic practice as well: When corporations have a problem involving Washington, he is the man who can help them. At any given time, Patton Boggs is the registered lobbyist for what it calls "approximately 225 entities, including Fortune 500 corporations, multinational corporations, trade associations, as well as state and local governments and agencies." In 2004, the firm reported $65.8 million in lobbying revenues, highest of the law-lobbying firms in Washington. Patton Boggs was trailed by Akin Gump, with $64.2 million, according to the Washington lobbying–watch group www.Influence.biz.

By lawyer count alone, Patton Boggs does not rank among the giants of Washington law. As of late 2004 it numbered 396 lawyers, 108 of whom were partners, making the firm ninth largest in the city. With more than $200 million in revenues, the firm boasted a comfortable per-partner profit of more than $535,000. How much money does Tommy Boggs take home each year? The people who know won't say; those in a position to make informed guesses say more than $3 million.

But Tommy Boggs's influence in Washington, and why he is such a key player in the nation's political process, cannot be measured by money alone. The Boggs story is a classic saga of an insider who was shrewd enough to grasp at every existing connection, familial or otherwise, to acquire enormous influence.

HOMETOWN BOY MAKES GOOD

When Boggs's father began his first term in the House of Representatives in 1941, he was twenty-six years old, the youngest member of Congress. He met a slender woman named Marie Corrine Morrison Claiborn at a dance while attending Tulane Law School in New Orleans and told her then that he intended to marry her. He did, and Hale and Lindy had three children: Barbara, Tom, Jr., and Mary Martha Corrine Morrison Claiborn Boggs, better known as the ABC News commentator Cokie Roberts. Hale Boggs took a break from Congress for navy service during the war, and was reelected in 1946.

Tommy Boggs made a minimal impression on other kids with whom he grew up in the tight Catholic community of postwar Washington. The family settled into a comfortable old house on Bradley Boulevard, and the chunky Tommy followed the route of many young men of his faith from elementary school at Blessed Sacrament in Chevy Chase to Georgetown Preparatory School to Georgetown University and its law school. "He was like a lot of us—he liked his beer, and he got along well with the girls, but as for any signs of future brilliance, I just didn't spot them," said one classmate who is now a lawyer lobbyist. Said another, now an investment broker, "A nice enough guy, nothing out of the ordinary. Congressional brats are always a dime a dozen in Washington, so who cares? If I had been asked to pick which of us would end up as one of the most powerful men in Washington, I'd be lying if I said I would have thought of Tommy." Indeed, sister Barbara seemed to be the "most brainy" of the three children. She married a professor at Princeton University and served as mayor of Princeton Borough, New Jersey, before succumbing to a prolonged bout with eye cancer in the 1990s.

But the young Boggs was constantly exposed to the men who ran political Washington. He often jokes that some families collect paintings and other objets d'art. The Boggs "specialized in people with names like Kennedy, Lyndon Johnson, and Sam Rayburn." Indeed, the latter, the longtime Speaker of the House, played a significant role in the elder Boggs's career. As Congressman Boggs related, "I was very close to Mr. Rayburn, very close to him. I felt a father-son relationship with him." Rayburn saw to it that Boggs rose swiftly in the House leadership, assigning him the job of majority whip (responsible for enforcing party loyalty) and giving him a seat on the powerful House Ways and Means Committee, which controls taxation. Further, a member of Ways and Means is uniquely situated to raise campaign funds, both for himself and other congressmen.

Boggs *père et fils* learned the importance of the Rayburn credo for a successful career in Congress: "You got to go along to get along." Never be afraid to compromise. Do not gratuitously offend someone with whom you have differences; he could be tomorrow's ally on another issue. Do what your party's leaders direct, but trust them not to force you to cast votes that could cost you reelection.

In Washington as is true in most towns in America, persons of power have friends willing to do nice things for their children. So young Boggs spent his high school summers with the somewhat cushy (for Washington) job of running elevators in the

House office buildings. "Hale's boy" got on a speaking basis with many members.

Boggs continued working around Congress while attending Georgetown University, and after graduation he went to Georgetown Law at night. He worked days for the vibrant liberal senator Paul Douglas of Illinois, for whom his admiration remains unabashed. "The closest thing I had to a mentor," Boggs stated. "He taught that there is room in politics for ideals." Through his father, Tom Boggs already had a wide range of acquaintances in the House of Representatives. Working for Douglas gave him an insight into the Senate as well—and especially to the majority leader, Sen. Lyndon Johnson of Texas. As Boggs related:

> Every evening around eight-thirty or nine o'clock, Lyndon would come over to one of those little hideaway rooms you find scattered through the Senate, where members can let their hair down after and kick back and talk and have a drink or two. As you know, Lyndon liked his Cutty Sark. He'd have a few drinks, and nine-thirty or so he'd decide it was time to go home, and he always wanted "one for the road." So he'd fill up a glass of scotch and hand it to me and say, "Come on, Tommy, carry this out to the car with me, I don't want to be seen running around Congress with a glass of whiskey in my hand." So I'd hold the glass as discreetly as possible, way down by my side, and go down to the parking garage with the senator and see him off for home.

These late evening tête-à-têtes with senators were a valuable learning experience. Political Washington is a peculiar culture, with methods and mores not always discernible to an outsider. Young Boggs was a good listener, and he learned from the masters how the legislative process really works—and forget the civics books. As is true of most closed societies, congressmen prefer to keep "civilians" at a polite distance; someone who aspires to be part of the process must learn the rules, and who makes the decisions.

After Johnson assumed the presidency, Boggs became a de facto political operative for the White House. "You couldn't tell it by my paycheck," he said. "I was on the payroll of the old Office of Emergency Preparedness, run by Buford Ellington, who had been governor of Tennessee. I had the title of 'liaison with state governors,' or something fancy like that." Boggs paused to laugh and slap his leg. "Ha! I may have talked to one, maybe two governors the whole time. I was doing political work for Lyndon." During the 1964 campaign, Boggs helped organize the celebrated campaign train that carried President Johnson on a whistle-stop tour of the South. (The media jibed at the train as "the Cornpone Express," but voters loved it.)

But did Boggs want to spend his formative years doing political scut work? Washington is littered with men (and women) who can accurately be identified as the "former so-and-so," low-echelon aides and assistants to the chairman who struggled to stay on the fringes of power and never acquired any usable clout of their own. During his time on the Hill Boggs saw his share of has-beens and never-weres, and he did not intend to squander his life pursuing a low-paid and potentially fruitless career in the political side of government. So he decided to go into law rather than continue in government.

Boggs went into Johnson's office to tell him of his decision. "I sort of expected that he would try to talk me out of it—that he would tell me how important I was in his political operation. Lyndon looked at me and said that I had made a wise decision, and he wished me 'all the luck in the world.' I realized that I was not as essential to the success of the United States government as I had assumed." So, law degree in hand, he went to the job market.

Boggs says up front that his father's prestige helped him obtain job interviews at "every law firm that I wanted to go to." He continued:

The first choice I had to make was what sort of practice I wanted to join. In that period, Washington had two broad kinds of firms. There were the large ones, such as Hogan & Hartson and Covington and Burling, and then a bunch of boutique outfits, run by guys who had been chairman of the Federal Trade Commission or the

Interstate Commerce Commission or whatever, and who did strictly regulatory work, usually before their former agency.

The one operation that really appealed to me was Clark Clifford's office.* He had a good reputation, both as a real lawyer and as a "public policy" man who could get things done, shall we say, in ways that were different and sometimes unusual. I spent quite a bit of time talking with Clifford, and then I made the rounds of the other lawyers in the office. Two things sort of took me aback. None of them, not even the senior people, referred to him as "Clark." It was always "Mr. Clifford." Second, several men told me that I'd spent more time with him during my interviews than they had in, say, the last year.

Then Clifford did something that really made an impression on me, although I'm not exactly sure how. He told me that he liked me, and that he could make good use of me. BUT. The "but" was that he liked to hire lawyers who had done things such as working as an assistant U.S. attorney, or gotten comparable practical experience. Here I was, with a good congressional background, low-level though it was, and some White House work as well, but nonetheless a novice just out of law school. Clifford told me that he wanted me to go to such-and-such a law firm for two years, and then he would hire me. One phone call, he said, and the firm would hire me, with the agreement that he could have me in two years. [Boggs declined to name the firm; someone else who had heard the story told me, Covington and Burling.]

Now think about this. Here is Clark Clifford, a man with so much power or whatever that he can use a major Washington law firm as a sort of farm club, a training school.

In the end, Boggs decided he would travel a more conventional route, and hence he accepted an invitation to talk with a

---

*Clifford began his public career as White House counsel for President Harry Truman, a fellow Missourian, in 1945; when he went into private practice in 1949, he quickly became one of Washington's most successful attorneys. Well-wired politically, he helped President Kennedy assemble his administration, and he ultimately served as secretary of defense during the last months of LBJ's presidency.

man named James M. Patton, who had left Covington & Burling three years earlier to start a firm with another Covington expatriate, George Blow.

FROM CIA SPOOK TO SUPERLAWYER: JAMES M. PATTON

Although his name remains on the firm he cofounded, James M. Patton, Jr., seldom visits the Patton Boggs office. He sold his home in suburban Virginia in 1998 and now splits his time between Snow Mass, Colorado, and Tucson, Arizona. Our seemingly endless game of telephone tag ended on a late summer Sunday evening when I picked up Patton at his hotel in the West End of Washington, a few blocks from his old law office. As we drove over to the Four Seasons for dinner I casually mentioned that I had talked with Tom Boggs two days earlier.

There was a silence from the passenger's seat, then an audible sniff. Patton laughed out loud. "I'll be curious to know his version of some things," he said. "I wager you are going to find some differences." One bone of contention arises from Boggs's repeated suggestions that he was a cofounder of the firm. "Actually," Patton said, "I had been in business for about three years when Tom came aboard. We had about six lawyers then. I was doing a considerable amount of work for Westinghouse, both in the States and abroad. The suggestion was made that I needed someone with political experience to handle Westinghouse's business on the Hill. That is why I decided to hire Tom." His tone made plain to my ear that he was not all that happy about what had been happening at Patton Boggs. And later, after a couple of glasses of wine, Patton told me something else: that he was "thinking seriously" about taking his name off the firm at the end of the year. (He did not; the structure housing the firm now bears the name "Patton Boggs Building." Patton did resign from the firm's executive committee some months later.)

One reason that Tom Boggs came to be the public face of the firm is that Patton shunned personal publicity. Much of the work he did over the years was for clients who did not want their affairs spread out in the media. Further, his background as an intelligence operative, as we shall see, also makes him reflexively secretive. Thus he told me that his first inclination had been to ignore my request for an interview. "I checked you out," he said, "and I decided to see how we would get along."

The *Washington Post* did not fare nearly so well. A secretary came into Patton's office one day and announced that a team of *Post* photographers had just arrived to do a photo spread on him and Boggs. Patton did not hesitate. "Tell them to leave," he instructed his secretary. She returned to report, "They apparently cleared this with Mr. Boggs."

"Well," Patton replied, "they did not 'clear it' with me. I told my secretary to call the police and tell them that we had trespassers here that we want out of the office." The photographers were leaving as the cops arrived. "As far as I know," Patton grinned, "there is not a photograph of me in any newspaper office in the country.

"So, anyway, now you've got me. What do you want to know?" And for the next four hours the courtly, white-haired Patton told me of the odyssey that led to his founding what would become one of the most powerful law firms in America.

A Carolinian, Patton spent considerable time as a youngster trying to decide what to do with his life. His first thought was to go to Duke Medical School, and to that end he entered the University of North Carolina at Chapel Hill as a pre-med major. But his interest soon shifted to literature, and his major became English, with a speciality in modern poetry. Afterward he fended off questions about why he changed career paths with the cryptic (and deliberately nonsensical) statement, "Because I fell out of a tree and broke my leg."

After graduation, Patton made an eleventh-hour decision to go to law school. He applied to Yale. Sorry, he was told, you are too late, and besides, you are not offering any LSATs to support your application. "So I tried Harvard, applying four days before classes began. They let me in, even without the LSATs." Patton did well, both in the law school and in an international studies program. There he acquired a mentor, a professor who was also a spotter for the Central Intelligence Agency—one of the many academics that the organization used in Ivy League schools and elsewhere to spot potential recruits. By this time Patton had married, to Mary Maughan, who was studying at the Rhode Island School of Design, an hour's commute from Harvard, and after graduation he needed a job. There was talk of his staying at Harvard, for $3,000 a year, an amount that was not enough to support the young couple. The mentor talked candidly with Patton about his career. Patton had no interest in joining a corporation or a law firm. The mentor could arrange for Patton to go to Europe as general counsel of the International Labor Organization. "I would have been the only noncommunist member of the staff had I accepted, so I decided against that one."

Then the mentor came up with another suggestion: "I would like for you to go to Washington," he told Patton, "and see some friends of mine." The "friends" turned out to be, first, Walter Pforzheimer, legislative counsel for the Central Intelligence Agency, and then Lawrence Houston, the agency's general counsel. Things went well, and to Patton's astonishment, he found himself summoned to the office of Allen Dulles, the director of Central Intelligence.

Puffing a pipe that never seemed to be totally afire, Dulles gave Patton a pitch on becoming a career intelligence officer. America needs men like you, he said; we are in a real war with people who wish to destroy us, and our way of life. "I was thrilled, completely blown away," Patton said. "I told Dulles, 'I'll do whatever you want me to do.'" Patton speaks of his CIA days with unabashed pride, even if he has the old spook's reluctance to speak freely of exactly what he did. "A generation of good men," he says of those days, "good men in a good cause."

Patton went through the agency's officer training program and then spent six weeks in Paris, meeting key figures in the French intelligence community. In February 1951, Jim and Mary Patton arrived in Saigon—and on that the very day communist guerrillas blew up a major public building, killing dozens of persons. Patton saw the scene. "Bodies were everywhere," he recollected. "I knew then that we were up against a very determined enemy, and that our work was cut out for us."

A French colonial government still clung to power to Indochina in 1951, and its control ostensibly extended to intelligence matters. At French insistence, the United States agreed not to mount any intelligence operations in the country. The French position was that whatever Washington learned would come through liaison with its intel officers. Hence there was no CIA station in the country, only a cluster of men (and a few women) working from the embassy with various nondescriptive titles. Patton's assignment was to work with French officers, and learn what he could, and send information and analyses back to Washington. And, the no-spying agreement notwithstanding, Patton and other officers developed their own sources among the Vietnamese. "We were what I would call quasi-covert," Patton said. Further, what they learned independently was not always shared with the French. "You must remember," Patton noted, "that France was going through a rapid succession of governments in those days, some of which were flat-out communist administrations, with a lot of leaks. So we were rather economical about sharing what we picked up on our own."

He was an eyewitness to the collapse of the French military. "I was the last American into Dien Bien Phu [a beleaguered French fortress that became a paradigm for that country's failure] and the last American out of Dien Bien Phu." Based on this ground-level view of Vietnamese reality, Patton deplored the decision by President Eisenhower in 1954 to come into South Vietnam to replace the French, and to attempt to prop up a new government. But such administration elders as Secretary of State John Foster Dulles and Douglas Dillon, the American ambassador in Paris, prevailed.

By 1955, through both talent and attrition, Patton had worked his way up to being the number-three spook in the embassy. He and wife Mary lived in a comfortable villa where they entertained a seemingly endless flow of military, diplomatic, and political figures, including Vice President Richard M. Nixon. "I pretty well got to know who's who in the national security establishment during those years, rather heady stuff for a guy in his late twenties."*

Patton's next CIA stint was with the Office of National Estimates, which did high-level strategic analyses of what was apt to happen in the world. ONE was run by the esteemed academic Sherman Kent. Among Patton's colleagues were William P. Bundy, a whip-smart young lawyer who would become assistant secretary of state during the Kennedy-Johnson years, and James Billington, a future librarian of Congress. "Because of my experience in Indochina, I found myself the Vietnam expert, and Bill Bundy and I were the guys who had go brief Eisenhower and the White House staff on what was happening out there."

But did Patton wish to spend the rest of his professional life as an intelligence officer? Despite a reputation for abrasiveness, his career track could have taken him to the upper echelons of the agency. He had a talent for cultivating older men of power, and without seeming obsequious. His interest in such arcane subjects as modern poetry, as well as a growing expertise in art, added a patina of culture—a man equally at home in a Georgetown drawing room and a Vietnamese rice paddy. Nonetheless, by 1956 he was ready to move on, to a new career in law. "Bill Bundy told me, 'You are a fool. You've got the job I've worked for all of my life. Why leave now?'" Once Bundy realized he was serious, he urged Patton to join his former firm of Covington & Burling, at the time the premier law operation in Washington.

So Bundy made the phone call, and in due course Patton met with Edward Burling, Jr., son of the firm's cofounder. "Ed offered me a position as a lateral associate at about twice what I

---

*Patton knew when to take things seriously and when to laugh. Soon after arrival in Indochina he paid a courtesy call on the French high commissioner, a debonair fellow who began the conversation by lighting up a cigar and deposing, "You know how these cigars are made? Beautiful young girls take the tobacco and roll it over their gorgeous thighs to shape the cigar. So every time I put one of these into my mouth, I think of those beautiful young girls and their gorgeous thighs." Patton came back, "Do you happen to have an extra cigar?"

was making. I turned him down. He came right back with an offer of three to four times my salary. I accepted. Gladly."

Patton joined Covington's international practice, dominated by the formidable Dean Acheson, the former secretary of state, and a fixture in Washington's power structure since the 1920s. His direct mentor was a grand old man of the Washington bar named John G. Laylin, and over the next years they enjoyed high excitement together. Patton's eyes danced with enthusiasm as he went through those years. He had a major role in negotiating a treaty concerning the river basin between Pakistan and India, "which well might have staved off a war." There was a deal involving the reimbursement of Danish shipowners for vessels which were turned over to the United States just before World War II, to be used for lend-lease shipments to the Soviet Union. "The Lend-Lease Act mandated the use of American bottoms [i.e., ships] for shipments. So the Roosevelt administration had to scrounge around to find enough American ships to do the job. The Danish government, in exile, told President Roosevelt, 'Our ships are yours.' German subs sank most of them. When the war ended, FDR was gone, of course, and since he had made the deal orally, no written record existed. The Federal Maritime Commission refused payment. Laylin and I sued and won cases for some of the owners, and we lobbied Congress for payments for the others."

Another case made use of skills he had learned at CIA. A Covington client, the Cuban American Sugar Company, burned waste from its sugar mills to generate electricity for the city of Santiago de Cuba and for its own operations. Rebels fighting under soon-to-be-dictator Fidel Castro regularly blew up the power plants as part of its economic warfare against President Fulgencio Batista. "The sugar people asked me, 'How can we stop this?'" Patton thought over the challenge and decided the only person who could halt the bombings was Castro himself. So Patton went to Havana, made discreet contact with the rebels, and soon found himself face to face with Castro in the Sierra Maestra.

Patton made his case in populist terms. Cutting off power harmed the poor people of Santiago, not just the rich American-owned power company. Why hurt the very persons who are supposed to be your own following?

Castro took a deep draw from his cigar, pondered awhile, and said, "Young man, I like your nerve." He halted the bombings.

Patton had a second brush with the Cuban government soon after Castro came to power. The Agency for International Development had purchased a shipload of Cuban sugar from Patton's client destined for Morocco. While the shipment was en route, Castro laid claim to it, saying that any deals made by the Batista government were void. He demanded that the ship turn around and sail back to Cuba. For whatever reason, AID officials chose not to get into a tiff with the new Cuban government, and the Cuban American Sugar Company faced the prospect of having to repay Morocco for the shipment. So Patton hastened to Havana for another face-to-face meeting with Castro.

At the outset, Castro seemed pleasant enough. He gave his visitor a cigar and a glass of cognac and listened as Patton argued that the sugar belonged to Morocco, since AID had already paid for it. Castro shook his head. "Oh, bullshit," he said. "I took this stuff over for the people."

Patton did not desist. He argued that legal title passed to Morocco once bills of lading were filed on the shipment, and such had been done.

Waving his omnipresent cigar in a wide arc, Castro replied, "You talk like a damned lawyer!"

"As a *learned* lawyer," Patton said, "I thought you would understand."

"I'll see you in hell before you get a grain of our sugar," Castro said. Meeting over.

A less determined lawyer might have abandoned the quest. "My client was outraged at what was happening and told me to do what I could. I got an order from the maritime court validating our claim. Then I flew out to Morocco. The new Cuban ambassador there was a very charming man; as did Castro, he gave me a good Cuban cigar and good cognac. He agreed that the law was on my side, but he shrugged and said, 'No matter, you are going to lose.'"

The ship, meanwhile, remained offshore, out of Moroccan territorial waters. To bolster his claim, Patton needed the actual bill of lading showing that the sugar now belonged to Morocco. So for three weeks he went on the local party circuit, courting local officials, "attending a lot of parties, gaining some minor local notoriety." He got an audience with the foreign minister and chided him, "You don't have much national sovereignty, do you? You have a court order and you can't force the ship to come into port with your sugar."

Were you trying to embarrass the minister? Patton smiled. "Take it anyway you want," he told me.

A day or so later a Moroccan prince offered Patton a ride home from a party at two A.M. "The prince had a Ferrari, and he drove me back to the hotel at a frightful speed. When he pulled up he said, 'Oh, I almost forgot,' and handed me an envelope. It contained the bill of lading. Within a few hours we had the ship ashore, and the sugar was in Moroccan hands, and our client got their money."

By the late 1950s Patton was an established figure at Covington. Although still an associate his earnings sometimes surpassed those of full partners—an accomplishment that, while financially beneficial, made for poor office politics. "I say it myself: I brought in a huge number of clients, the only associate who did so. In fact, I was known as a business getter."

The skein of events that led to Patton's departure—indirectly, at least—came when the federal government brought price-fixing cases against major electrical equipment manufacturers in the late 1950s, resulting in guilty pleas to criminal charges by many executives. Most, if not all, of the firms targeted belonged to the Electrical Industry Association (EIA), one of Covington's larger clients at the time. Patton had no role in the price-fixing litigation, but he heard from various industry sources that the companies felt that Covington's defense had not been aggressive enough, and that the firm assigned an inordinate number of associates to the case, with staggering fees. Soon after the case ended he found himself at the annual meeting of the EIA. A friend introduced him to the EIA president as a lawyer "with a thorough knowledge of our industry."

The EIA president looked at Patton and asked, "What law firm are you with?"

"Covington and Burling," Patton replied.

The president sniffed disdainfully. "You are fired." As Patton stood in stunned silence, the man continued, "On second thought, *you* are not fired. Go back and tell your partners that *they* are fired."

So it fell the lot of Patton—still an associate—to call senior partner Newell Ellison to announce that the firm had just lost a major client. Ellison took the bad news without visible reaction. "I thank you very much for the information," he told Patton, "I will take care of it." Then he hung up. The loss shook Covington, which in a matter of months shrank from one-hundred-plus size to around seventy lawyers.

Although he had no role in the antitrust cases, Patton chose this time to leave the firm. "Why? Well, I've always been a maverick. Let me tell you a story. A couple of years ago, some university business students did an interview with me on the subject of why I chose law as a profession. I told them, in all honesty, 'I don't know, and I still don't know what I intend to do with my life.'" (By this time, Patton was in his late sixties and had left any active role in Patton Boggs.)

Money was another factor. Although Patton generated much new business, he felt he did not receive proper credit, financially or otherwise. "Partners would walk all over you to take over a client you brought in," he said. "These were men who needed work to justify their high draws and they did not hesitate to take matters away from a lowly associate." If the associates complained of inequities, they risked offending persons who could deny them partnership. If they did not complain, they lost money. (Patton's displeasure with the Covington system was one reason he was instrumental in structuring a compensation system at Patton Boggs through which associates received proper credit for business they brought into the firm.)

Thus in 1962 Patton decided to create his own firm, along with another Covington veteran, George Blow.

AN INTERNATIONAL PRACTICE, DONE LOCALLY

Given his experience in the CIA, and his heavy international work at Covington and Burling, the natural thing for Patton to do in his new firm was to concentrate on foreign clients. He described Patton & Blow as "an international law firm that happened to be based in Washington." The first clients were American companies that needed advice on their foreign investments. As Patton points out, "In those days foreign investment was not all that welcome in many countries. United States businesses needed experienced lawyers who could counsel them on lawful ways to invest in environments that could be—well, just let me say, 'unwelcoming and even hostile.'

"All that has changed, of course; for the most part foreign countries beg for American investors. You have markets opening all over the world—the European Union, the World Trade Organization. You have democracy flourishing almost everywhere. From a legal point of view, investing abroad is now not all that different from investing at home."

Did his background in the CIA and the national security establishment help him get business? And were the links ever totally severed? "I did it on my own," Patton told me. "My work with the CIA certainly gave me a leg up, in the learning sense, but my law practice I did on my very own." And if Patton ever used his law firm as a cover for agency work overseas—and no evidence exists that he did—he surely is not going to talk about it.

ENTER THOMAS HALE BOGGS, JR.

Accounts of how Tom Boggs came to join the Patton firm vary. By Boggs's recollection, he met Patton when he came to Congress to lobby on a maritime issue. Although he had many big-firm offers, he decided he would be more comfortable in a smaller office, hence he took Patton's offer. By Patton's recollection, he met Boggs through an economist who did work in the machine tools industry, whose trade group he represented. Much of the group's work concerned strategic materials, which was always a sensitive issue with Congress. The economist told Patton, "You need political connections in this city. There's a guy named Tom Boggs who is just out of law school. You will like him, and he will like you." The introduction was made, and Patton offered the young lawyer $10,500 a year to join him as an associate. ("Tom says now it was eleven thousand. I still say ten-five.")

Congressman Boggs did not like his son's decision. For one thing, Patton had a CIA background, something that the elder Boggs thought was just awful. Perhaps even more grievous, Patton was a Republican, something totally anathema to the partisan Boggs. "But Tommy wanted to make some money. He got a lot of offers, but in the end he came with me."

Although hired for his political savvy, Boggs had a grander vision for his future. "Tom applied himself to becoming a good lawyer. He did not wish to be only a lobbyist. He wanted to learn what the practice of law was all about."

Boggs had his own ideas, which happily complemented those of the senior Patton. He argued that a law office whose core business was public policy could not succeed by lobbying alone, that it must be prepared to use other methods to gain what it wanted. "The best way to get the attention of some official," he told me, "is to sue him. Once they know that you are willing to go to court, they pay more mind to you when you ask them for something that your client deserves." So many partners described "the Patton Boggs approach" to me during two months of interviews that it came to be sort of a firm mantra: Persuade Congress to pass a law a client wants, then have the regulatory agency implement it your way. And if they don't, sue them.

Boggs got off to a fast start. Fortunately, Clark Clifford did not take umbrage when he declined to join his office. "Clark, bless his heart, sent me my first client. He told me the guy was going to pay about $25,000, which was below the minimum he required to represent someone. But that was a lot of money for me in 1967." Not all the business exuded glamour. Another early client was a "waste rags" company run by a brother of columnist William Safire of the *New York Times*. "Don't ask me to get too detailed, but essentially they hauled rags from one place to another and sold them, and made a lot of money in the process." Competitors reduced prices way below what Safire's company charged, intending to drive him out of business. He filed an antitrust suit that eventually drifted to famed litigator Joseph Alioto of San Francisco, who won a sizable verdict.

By design, Patton kept the firm compact the first years; when Boggs came in, for instance, the office had but four other lawyers. "I wanted it that way," he said, "a place where I could do hands-on law and not get caught up in all the big firm bureaucracy." For those first years Patton concentrated on such foreign clients as Indonesia and the Emirate states, with a smattering of sugar business that followed him over from Covington. But he came to realize the necessity of broadening the office's client base. "Governments come, governments go," he said. "And when one goes, the law firm can go, too." Thus he began hiring that bolstered the firm's domestic side.

Tom Boggs, meanwhile, dealt with issues outside the firm. First was the birth, and lightning-swift death, of his political aspirations. In 1968 he tried to follow his father into Congress, from a Maryland district. Boggs now shakes his head when he talks about the experience. "Had I won, it would have been a disaster. It was a mistake. I wouldn't be making all this money, for one thing.

"My Republican opponent was a very good guy, Gilbert Gude, who was finishing his second term. But I learned something very important, what it is for a politician to raise money. You have to get out of bed every day and go out to coffee klatches and meet people and shake their hands and listen to them and tell them what you intend to do. You get questions out of the blue on subjects you didn't even know existed." The constituency was three counties: Anne Arundel and Howard, which were rural, and Montgomery, a close-in and liberal Washington suburb. "I learned about perceptions being more important than reality. People out in the rural areas listened to me talk and decided I was a good ol' boy. I carried Anne Arundel and Howard, but I got my butt kicked in Montgomery. That was enough of politics." He waved his cigar as if still in disbelief about his folly.

During the same months, Boggs dealt with a personal matter that seared his family life: the near-indictment of his father on corruption charges. From this agony Boggs learned a hard lesson about political Washington. Anyone dealing with the volatile mix of money and politics must tread carefully lest the most innocuous of deals be mistaken for criminal misconduct. For that reason, new hires at Patton Boggs, regardless of their experience elsewhere, are made very aware of the boundaries between right and wrong when it comes to dealing with members of Congress or other government officials. Of the dozens of persons who spoke to me about Tom Boggs, including several who do not particularly like him, not a single one raised any questions about his ethics. One of these persons referred back to the corruption probe and said, "Tom never had the slightest doubt that his father was innocent; nonetheless, the episode scared the hell out of him."

The investigation of Hale Boggs, and the bitter feelings it spawned between the congressman and FBI director J. Edgar Hoover, are beyond the scope of this book. Briefly, Boggs was suspected, along with other political figures, of doing favors for a well-wired Maryland political figure, contractor Victor Frenkil. Boggs was said to have received a renovation project worth $42,000 on his Bethesda home, for which he paid Frenkil only $21,000. In return, Boggs was suspected of helping Frenkil receive several millions of dollars in cost overruns for renovation of a House of Representatives parking garage. No criminal charges were ever brought against Hale Boggs, although the U.S. attorney in Baltimore, Stephen Sachs, at one point prepared a draft indictment against him. The Justice Department (during the Nixon administration) refused to permit the case to go forward.

The probe spawned years of vituperation between Hale Boggs and Hoover. In floor speeches, Boggs accused the FBI of tapping his phone and of surveilling members of Congress—

"tactics of the Soviet Union and Hitler's Gestapo." Hoover strongly denied the allegations. Concurrently, Boggs developed a severe drinking problem, aggravated by a medical condition that required heavy medication. A string of informants sent Hoover reports of irrational behavior by the congressman. He got into a fight with another congressman in the men's room at a dinner. He showed up drunk at a Washington Senators baseball game. He had to be physically restrained by a deputy sheriff for unruly behavior at a fete for a fellow congressman in Florida. Hoover gleefully told one of his informants, Rep. Samuel L. Devine, an Ohio Republican, that "Boggs is an old drunk."

Hale Boggs's conduct became so erratic that Democratic elders considered stripping him of his leadership post. Realizing that his political life was at risk, Boggs backed away from further confrontations with the FBI. At the urging of family and friends, he consulted with physicians at Bethesda Naval Medical Center concerning what he finally acknowledged was a "drinking problem," discarding his excuse that his unruly behavior was caused by pills he took for a heart condition. Rather than go through the torment of a removal fight, Democratic elders let Boggs keep his majority leadership, but with a stern warning that any further outbursts would warrant punishment.

In the autumn of 1972 Boggs flew to Alaska to help colleague Nick Begich campaign. The plane vanished, and no trace of it was ever found. Tommy Boggs was now the senior male of his family. He was inconsolable for weeks, talking with law associates at one point of going back to Louisiana. Right after Christmas he perked up and helped persuade mother Lindy to seek "the Boggs seat" in Louisiana. She won, and an invigorated Tom Boggs set about helping Jim Patton build a legal powerhouse.

A frown burrowed Tom Boggs's face when I asked him about the Frenkil affair, and his father's battle with Hoover. I prefaced my questions by stating that the long-ago scandals were relevant only in that they could not have helped affect his career as a lawyer lobbyist. The memories obviously are painful, but after a pause to fiddle with his cigar, Boggs addressed them anyway. "There was a history of bad blood between the Sachs [referring to the prosecutor who wanted Hale Boggs indicted] and Frenkil families, both of which were prominent in Baltimore. It went back for a number of years, and I doubt that anybody can remember how it started. The bottom line is that this little garage deal was done on the up-and-up—heck, it was something my mother did, my father had nothing to do with it—and my father didn't do any favors for Frenkil."

Boggs managed a laugh. "You know," he said, "this whole mess happened right in the middle of my campaign for Congress. It didn't do me any help at all. A troubling time."

POLITICS, PORK, AND PUBLIC POLICY

To understand the success of Tom Boggs and his law firm, one must begin with one fact: despite the amount of "real law" done at Patton Boggs, the office is built on a bedrock of politics and pork. During the early years, to be sure, Jim Patton ran an international practice to rival anything found elsewhere in the city. Concurrently, Boggs was building the other side of the practice—in essence, an operation based more on know-who than know-how. The system in which Boggs and colleagues work is symbiotic. Clients give money (fees) to Patton Boggs to achieve a desired goal. Boggs plows some of this money into congressional political war chests, either directly or through political action committees over which he exerts influence. In turn, the members of Congress do what Boggs wishes, more or less, and the clients benefit. The process is ongoing, and no one will ever discover a specific quid pro quo, for none exists. Such directness is neither necessary nor desired. Boggs perhaps would not like, nor accept, the analogy, but what he does is akin to a missionary working to convert heathens. He cultivates trusting relations over a period of years so that, when he finally asks for something, the response is reflexively positive.

In his early sixties, Boggs is far too young a fellow to be

termed "a grand old man of Washington politics." But during his three-plus decades as a Washington wheeler, the politics of the city have undergone several sea changes, just why and how this happened is essential to understanding Boggs's success. One morning he slouched deep into his chair and, with cigar in constant motion from mouth to gesturing hand and back again, delivered a well-honed lecture on the realpolitik to Washington.

When I began practicing, things were a heckuva lot different, to understate. Let me give you a figure. The first year I registered [as a lobbyist] was 1968, and I was the sixty-first or sixty-second fella to do so. The number did not increase all that much the remainder of the year. Now, according to what I read, the number is well over fifteen thousand, and there's no sign of a slowdown.

So what happened? In the 1960s the number of lobbyists was in direct proportion to the number of people who actually ran Washington—ten or a dozen, in practical terms. You had the president, of course, and his chief of staff. There were one or two key cabinet officers. The leaders of both houses of Congress, and the chairs of the "money committees," Ways and Means and Appropriations, and the House Rules Committee, which controlled what legislation went to the floor for a vote. There were some other people who might not have an office or a title, but who helped make things work.

Now, each of these ten or twelve guys had about six friends they'd listen to—and by friends, of course, I mean lobbyists—and that is why you had sixty-something lobbyists. There was a fairly disciplined relationship between the White House and the Congress, even when they were run by different parties. Look at the stuff the Democratic Congress did during the Eisenhower years, when the Republicans had the White House. The interstate highway system, for instance, in which my daddy played a key role. It was his idea to create a trust fund to finance building of the interstate system—an idea that meant the funding was on a permanent basis, and that a particular Congress could not come along and stop the project.

The system began breaking down during the Vietnam War era, when Congress began taking back some of its clout via such things as the War Powers Act. Then came the financial scandals associated with Watergate and all the hollering about "reform" of just about everything that government does, including campaign fundraising. To me, the most important change was Congress's decision to abandon the seniority system in selecting committee chairman, and to have them elected by committee members.

Now, in my view, abandoning the seniority system is where Congress really screwed itself up, because it meant the death of any leadership. Under the old system, a committee or subcommittee chair could promise the leadership that something could be bottled up forever without a vote, or, conversely, that it would go through.

I've said this many times over the years, and I'll say it again. If Congress had set out to mess up things, they couldn't have done it any better. Getting rid of seniority destroyed the buddy system, which was a darned big thing in Congress.

The reformers make a lot of fuss about "doing things behind closed doors," but at least things got done that way. Sure, there was trading, but that's part of politics. For instance, I'm from Louisiana, and I want money for a levee project. You represent a potato district up on Maine. I vote for your potatoes, you vote for my levee, we do it in private. Now what happens? You've got the danged TV cameras and an audience, and I have to justify, as a Louisianan, why I'm voting for some potato patch deal up in New England. So nothing gets done.

In the old days, a man who got to be chairman ran his committee with an iron hand. Anybody from his party who crossed him was thrown out in the cold, not only in that committee but everywhere in Congress. You had discipline. Now guys come up here knowing that the chairman won't be around for more than six years, and they're not afraid to cross him.

Ten, twenty years ago, when I wanted something done for a client, I could deal directly with the chairman. Now I've got to pay attention even to junior members of a committee—and that, my friend, is why you have so many lobbyists in Washington. These junior members get out of control. It's no longer unusual for them to roll their own leaders. Can you imagine someone doing that to Sam Rayburn? He might as well leave the country, 'cause he's sure as hell dead in the Congress.

Let's talk about the money side of it. Say you were in a tight race in your district, and you needed fifty, a hundred thousand dollars. You could go to whoever ran [the House] Ways and Means [Committee] or [the Senate] Finance [Committee] and with one phone call he could get you that much from the oil people or the bankers or whoever. That doesn't cut [it] any more. Every member is out dredging for dollars, lot of dollars, all the time. You've seen the figures, about how guys need to raise ten, twenty thousand dollars every day of the year, counting Saturdays and Sundays, to finance a campaign.

Here is something else that has changed. Despite the public perception, Washington is no longer all that important as a source of political money. At one time, about fifty percent of the political money raised in the country came from Washington, or through people who worked from here.

Not any more. We've had a major shift out into the rest of the country, to areas with a large corporate presence, to Silicon Valley, to a lot of other places, the financial people, the trial lawyers, bless 'em every one. When you come down to it, Washington is not a major corporate city; our major industries are things like real estate and banking. Now I'd estimate that only ten, maybe fifteen percent of national political money comes out of Washington.

Boggs's value as a fund-raiser does not stem from his personal contributions to politicians, which seldom get past the high five figures in any given election year. It is Patton Boggs clients who cough up the serious bucks. When Boggs goes to a fund-raiser, the check he hands over more often than not bears the signature of a client, or the client's political action committee. Showing up in person benefits both the client and Patton Boggs. To John Zorack, who published a lobbying handbook in 1990, Boggs explained why contributions are vital to what he does. "Attending fund-raising activities increases access," he said. "If you expect a member of Congress to give you a few extra minutes, spend some time raising money for him. Members keep track of contributions, the companies that contribute, and the lobbyists who help. Lobbyists should not just mail money; they should attend fund-raising functions, even if they don't stay long."

Boggs amplified when we talked about money and politics. What does he gain by attending fund-raising events, rather than just mailing in a check? "It's not so much that you are noticed for being there, as you are noticed for *not* being there," he said. "When I go to one of these events, I am talking to other lawyers, to various people who work on public policy, to congressmen and senators. You have instant access. You don't have to go through a scheduling secretary, you walk over and say 'Howdy!' and start talking." Any lobbyist who declines to cough up money is a damned fool, in Boggs's opinion. As he told John Zorack, "Contributions are more a defensive than an offensive tool. In my case, if I don't give money to a member, his or her attitude is, 'Why did you contribute to Senator X and not to me?' You must contribute enough so that some members won't complain that you're not participating. Then, even if you don't give enough to be recognized as one of the inner circle, you won't be treated like an outcast, either."

Because of these one-on-one contacts, Boggs's presence can be persuasive even when he does not open his mouth. John Reistrup, who edits a legal newsletter from Washington, writes extensively about tort reform. He remembers covering hearings when Boggs would stroll into the room, find a seat at the back, and sit with legs crossed, nodding to congressmen and staff members but remaining mute. "Boggs," Reistrup said, "was just letting them know that he cared about the issue, and that he was keeping an eye on it." Intimidation? Perhaps, but Boggs would more likely consider his attendance a reminder that plaintiff lawyers who belong to the Association of Trial Lawyers of America, a Patton Boggs client, give politicians an estimated $4 million each election cycle.

Boggs can be sly when stroking a client such as ATLA. Just before the Democratic National Convention in 2000, the name of

John Edwards, an extraordinarily junior senator from South Carolina, suddenly appeared in media speculation about possible vice presidential candidates. The *Wall Street Journal* listed Boggs among his supporters. Given that Edwards had served for less than two years, and was a total unknown, his chances of being nominated ranged downward from none. I asked one of Boggs's partners why he involved himself in a transparent exercise in futility. He laughed. "Edwards was a trial lawyer, and the ATLA boys love him. Tommy is giving him the chance to sit out in the sun a few days. It can't hurt Tommy, making the folks at ATLA happy." Boggs's nudge helped. Perhaps because of the early "seal of approval" put on him by Boggs and other lawyers, in 2002, Edwards quickly jumped to a high ranking on the media's "hot prospects" list of potential Democratic candidates in 2004. He was the last competitor standing when Sen. John Kerry ultimately won the nomination, and became his running mate.

Tim May, who has worked with Boggs for thirty-five years, including a stint as managing partner of the firm, cites another lobbying talent that helps the firm enormously: "Tom is a great general. He is the mobilizer. A couple of lobbyists, no matter how good they are, are not about to change an issue on their own. Tom is a master at finding allies, people who might be affected indirectly by an issue, people who will be willing to work with you. Let me tell you something else about Tom: He does not embarrass a member when they can't give you a vote. He knows why they must do certain things, so he doesn't pressure them." Another partner, Mark Cowan, says, "There's a catchphrase in lobbying—'getting in the room,' that is, being able to see your target face-to-face. More important is having the credibility to ensure that the person hears and understands your message." Tom Boggs builds such credibility handshake by handshake, check by check.

The summer and early autumn of 2000, when I was in and out of Patton Boggs many times, happened to be the run-up to the election season, and catering trucks parked down on M Street NW late in the afternoon came to be part of the accepted scenery, as were handcarts of snack food on the elevators. People in the firm call such events meet and greets, but no one was willing to guess (even on an unattributed basis) how many are held each presidential season. Nor did Boggs care to tote up how many he personally attended, at the firm and elsewhere around town. During our chat I mentioned a neighbor couple who are prominent in Democratic money circles. "Ah, yes," Boggs said, "I know them well." He rummaged through a two-inch stack of paper on his desk, all invitations to various money events. "Here," he said, showing me a printed invitation to an event for a senate candidate in the Midwest. "I'll be over there next month." My eye estimated the stack as containing perhaps three dozen invitations, and the season was young.

Boggs has another value to politicians: he stands behind friends. He was among the strategists called upon for advice when President Clinton was going through the traumatizing Lewinsky affair, feeding the White House ideas in daily conference calls. Partner Lanny J. Davis, on leave to the White House staff, ran the overall Clinton political defense. Nonetheless, Boggs tends to take a realist's view on when to expend his political capital on behalf of a beleaguered officeholder. If the guy is beyond redemption, bury him, get him out of the way. Such was the verdict on House Speaker Jim Wright, who got into trouble in the late 1980s for, among other sins, a cheesy deal in which persons courting his favor bought crates of his privately published *Reflections of a Public Man*. The "book"—the quotation marks are deliberate—consisted of never-noted speeches Wright made on the floor of the House. He "sold" copies to avoid the limit on honoraria that a member might accept. The House Ethics Committee, citing this and other transgressions, charged him with sixty-nine violations of ethics rules.

As the besieged Wright fought for survival, his lawyer, William C. Oldaker, turned to Boggs for help. Boggs assembled more than a dozen of the town's leading Democratic lobbyists in the Patton Boggs conference room and told Oldaker, in effect, "OK, you have the floor, make your case on why we should help Jim." Oldaker's argument was that Wright's transgressions were not all that different from what other members did every day of the year, that he was being singled out for torment by Rep. Newt

Gingrich (R., Ga.) and other Republican hard-liners. The lobby-ists listened in stony-faced silence; they knew that the greedy Wright had, in fact, gone astray of the rules. After Oldaker left, Boggs sighed deeply and said, by one man's memory, "Jim is gone, there's no way in hell that the House is going to go against its own Ethics Committee. I am not wasting any time on this lost cause." Wright resigned a few days later.

Boggs said that this account—given to me by a participant in the meeting—"was not totally accurate," but he declined to be more specific. "I did tell Jim that he had to do a major mea culpa if he expected to stay on as Speaker. Jim's problem was that he was not as thick-skinned as some people you'll find on the Hill. What he was accused of doing, when you get down to it, was not all that awful or uncommon. The criticisms hurt Jim like hell. The man suffered."

BUT THERE'S A REASON . . .

Tom Boggs does not pay court to all these people just because he likes them (although he considers a good number of congressmen to be personal friends). To him, the stroking of politicians is busi-ness. Oddly, one seldom hears the word "lobbying" said out loud around Patton Boggs. People there prefer the higher-sounding euphemism "public policy" when they talk about what they do before the federal government.

Nonsense. The core of Patton Boggs's work is devoted to get-ting money, or a particular action, from the federal government for something their clients wish done. Pork barrel or public works? The venerable House Speaker Sam Rayburn, in his North Texas wisdom, once defined the issue this way: "A pork barrel project is something that goes to some other guy's district."

So exactly how does Patton Boggs go about delivering pork? The financial generosity of Boggs and his clients, and his bon-homie schmoozing with politicians in an Eastern Shore duck blind, certainly give the firm the desired entrée. But what hap-pens afterward, when a specific client wants something specific from the government?

A surprisingly candid insight is given in a massive loose-leaf binder that Patton Boggs circulates to attract new clients, a volume that is normally off-limits to curious writers. Most large firms prepare such material; they are widely known as brag books, for such works are by nature self-serving. What struck me about the Patton Boggs product was the specificity of its . . . well, what better word than *bragging*?

The cover page opens with a blunt declaration: "Patton Boggs was built on the idea that the law can be changed to achieve client objectives. Our decades of experience in Washington and our public policy roots impart a broader vision of what is possible. . . . We will work with you to develop solutions that are not limited by conventional legal concepts—in the belief that our wider focus will help you find answers others might overlook. . . . We see the law as a dynamic process, not as immutable rules and procedures." Indeed, it points out, "One of our attorneys may even have drafted the specific legislation or regulation involved in a client's dispute." And if an agency won't listen to reason (as defined by Patton Boggs) the brag book mentions another type of lobbying not taught in civics text books: "At our urging . . . Congress has been willing to preclude a recalcitrant agency from spending appropriated funds to enforce a rule or regulation harmful to our client's business interests."

Hire Patton Boggs, and you hire access: "Over fifty attorneys at the firm have either served in Congress or worked in senior positions in the Congress, at the White House, in the Executive Branch agencies, or at the national committees of the two major political parties. . . . We have developed solid relationships with the key House and Senate committees and federal agencies that are most closely involved with issues affecting municipalities. . . . We can marshal considerable bipartisan resources at the firm when needed." By spreading the work over many clients, Patton Boggs kept legal fees to a minimum.

One service provided is what Patton Boggs calls the Federal Funding Quick Alert System. Associates routinely go through the *Federal Register,* looking for available grant money, attend the weekly meetings of the U.S. Conference of Mayors, keep in touch with its "network of contacts" in Congress. The attention to detail pays: "Our clients . . . have received millions of dollars in grants and other assistance through this system. *We obtain important information for our clients well in advance of receiving it through normal channels, which gives them valuable lead time over their competition.*" (Emphasis added.)

By happenstance, I read that sentence the day before I interviewed an exuberant young partner named Ed Newberry, who had come to Patton Boggs from the staff of Rep. Frank Wolfe, a Virginia Republican. Newberry chairs the firm's development committee, i.e., the people responsible for finding new clients, and he was telling me about how the system works. Then he dropped a sentence into the conversation that made me straighten in my chair.

"You know," he said, "there are companies and other organizations that have needs that are not met, or who don't even realize they have needs."

Wait a minute—*"don't even realize they have needs"*—how can an outside law firm know more about a potential client's needs than the client? I felt that Newberry was acting overly prescient. Give me an example, I challenged.

"Easy," he said. "George Mason University [in the Virginia suburbs of Washington] is where I did my undergraduate work. Because of my work on the House Appropriations Committee, I knew of the competition among certain universities for federal research money. There is a certain prestige tied to how effective one is at winning research money. But lots of colleges didn't realize that hundreds of millions of dollars are up for grabs.

"So when I began practicing here in 1991, I went out to George Mason and told them, 'You are arguing that you want to be a tier-one research institution. Here you are, fifteen miles from Capitol Hill, and you're not doing any work to obtain earmarked federal grants.'

"They said, 'Can we really do that?' "

Yes, and Newberry became George Mason's point man, and the first year the college got $6 million in grants; in 2000 the figure reached almost $30 million. In the process, the university has established itself as a leader in developing what transit wonks call the Intelligent Transportation System, or ITS—essentially, ideas and assorted gadgetry that enable people to get around streets and highways easier. Newberry ticked off examples ranging from electric signs on freeways warning "Accident Ahead" to automated tollbooths that collect fees through a transponder inside the vehicle.

And, as Newberry made plain, loyalty to his alma mater does not extend to doing pro bono legal work: a good number of those federal transit dollars flow to Patton Boggs as fees. Millions of dollars in related transit projects have gone to such Patton Boggs clients as Cincinnati, the Ohio-Kentucky-Indiana Regional Council of Governments, Wayne County/Detroit, the New Orleans Regional Transportation Authority, and many others.

Money for airports, improvements to sewage systems, expansion of public libraries—Patton Boggs does an extraordinarily amount of work of this genre, nickel-and-dime stuff, when viewed on an individual basis, but collectively a good deal of fee income. After listening to a partner—not Newberry—describe these activities, I asked the obvious question: "People who live in these towns have someone in Washington who is elected to do this sort of thing. He's called the congressman. Why should they have to hire Patton Boggs to do what he or she should be doing?"

The fellow pursed his lips and fell silent a moment, as if deciding what, if anything, he cared to say. "Not for attribution?" he finally asked. Fire away, I said. His answer went something like this:

As far as I am concerned, the real downside of campaign finance is that members spend so damned much time rattling their tin cups that they aren't doing the right kind of constituent services. Getting funding for some of these projects takes years and years of detail work; you've got to keep coming back and pounding on the door. Members don't have the time, energy, or staff for this kind of sustained work. When they realize that someone like Patton Boggs is willing to step in and do the scut work, they are grateful.

Notice one thing, however: you will never, ever see Patton Boggs taking public credit for getting grant money for a city or a regional authority. The member of Congress makes the announcement and gets the picture in the paper and the slaps on the back.

Now let me go a step farther, and you'll realize why I don't want my name put on any of this stuff. We have all too many members of Congress these days who are either lazy or as dumb as a bale of hay that's been left out in the rain all afternoon. They have not the foggiest notion of how to get things done in this town, and they're not going to take the time to learn. I might not be any smarter, or more energetic, but Patton Boggs assigns me to this deal, and I give it all I've got, and I deliver.

Some day the folks who run local governments out beyond the Beltway are going to wake up and tell their member to get off his cotton-picking ass and go to work for them. Why should they have to pay some fancy Washington law firm to do the job they elected them to do? But until that day comes, we're happy.

One of the more difficult challenges of big-time law comes when an attorney must give a client unwelcome news. Here the lawyer faces a choice. If he sugarcoats a bad situation, the client might fall into even deeper trouble. Conversely, history is rife with accounts of messengers who bore bad news and suffered awful consequences.

In the late 1970s, the Chrysler Corporation found itself in such deep financial trouble that its executives pleaded for a federal bailout, rather than tumble into bankruptcy. Understandably, the proposal drew heated opposition from persons who argued that the occasional price of capitalism is failure, and that incompetent businessmen should pay the price, even if thousands of workers lost their jobs.

As Jim Patton relates, "Chrysler came to us for help, and we did a lot of work up on the Hill, trying to find out how we could persuade people to support this deal. The Chrysler CEO [John Riccardo] came to town for a strategy meeting. Of all places, we ended up on Tommy's eighteen-foot boat out on one of the rivers on the Maryland shore. The decision was that to get the federal money, Chrysler had to serve up a sacrificial lamb.

"The CEO said, 'Who do you have in mind?'

"We both looked at him, and I guess our silence spoke for us, and he said, 'Oh.' A few days later he resigned." The bailout went through.

RUSSIAN OIL, AFRICAN DICTATORS

The strength of its lobbying—sorry, "public policy"—operations notwithstanding, Patton Boggs still contains strong residues of what Jim Patton intended his creation to be, "an international law firm that happened to be based in Washington." One statistic suggests that Patton's legacy lives. In the early 2000s Patton Boggs represented more then two hundred clients with international business, from over seventy countries.

From a linguistic standpoint, the firm is a smorgasbord. Lawyers there are fluent in French, Spanish, Italian, Portuguese, German, Russian, Arabic, and Farsi. But Patton Boggs is somewhat of an anomaly in that it has no foreign offices. Over the years it experimented with foreign branch offices—in London, Tehran, Mexico City, and Saudi Arabia—and with formal affiliations with firms in other countries. But in time the firm decided to follow the strategy it uses in Washington: get the best people to do the job. As Patton explained, "The 'best people' in the context of, say, France, probably means the best firm of French lawyers to carry out an assignment. Just as we would not suggest hiring a German lawyer working in Washington to represent an interest before the American government, we would not recommend an American lawyer in Bonn." Thus Patton Boggs relies upon alliances with firms in major foreign cities.

Nonetheless, foreign travel by Washington-based lawyers is heavy. "On any given day," managing partner Stewart Pape said, "we have half a dozen—usually more—of our people out of the country." At what expense? "I know," he said, "but the amount is so staggering that it makes me uncomfortable saying it out loud." (Whatever the sum, it is charged back to clients as an expense item.)

Given the emergence of international trade during the last years of the twentieth century, Patton Boggs spends an inordinate amount of time helping clients with foreign import problems. The variety is staggeringly diverse: mushrooms from the People's Republic of China, golf carts from Poland, truck axles from Hungary, floppy disk drives from Japan and Korea, firearms from Brazil, beer from Mexico, chrome from Zimbabwe. Although it maintained a relatively low public profile, Patton Boggs was in the thick of one of the greater economic battles of the 1990s, passage of the North American Free Trade Agreement (NAFTA). Key sections of the final NAFTA legislation were written in a Patton Boggs conference room, and then the firm's lobbying stars—including Tom Boggs—worked hard in Congress to get it passed. The firm mounted a similar campaign in 2000 on behalf of obtaining Most Favored Nation status for the People's Republic of China, a key foreign policy goal of President Clinton.

Much of the foreign work involves high-tech deals, a Patton Boggs speciality. "Done deals" listed in firm printed material range from helping a Chinese internet service provider do an initial public offering to creating an electronic "business mall" and handling a $500 million deal for the Finnish national telecom company.

Patton Boggs has a client base large enough to enable it to turn away especially odious regimes that need help in Washington. Tom Boggs has boasted in interviews, for instance, that his firm refused to represent the pre-Mandela apartheid regime in South Africa. However, to his embarrassment, Patton Boggs during one period was the registered foreign agent for the notorious Haitian dictator Jean-Claude "Baby Doc" Duvalier. Boggs blames this glitch on partner Ron Brown, who left the firm to become secretary of commerce in the Clinton administration. "Baby Doc was strictly Ron Brown's client," Boggs told journalist Carl Bernstein in 1998. (Brown died in a plane crash in the Balkans in 1996.)

Then there are instances where clients get into trouble, such as the stormy failure of the notorious Bank of Credit and Commerce International (BCCI). Although he perhaps thought otherwise at the time, in reflection Patton volunteered BCCI as the most intriguing matter he handled during almost four decades of lawyering.

Patton swirled red wine around in his glass one autumn evening as we dawdled after dinner in the restaurant of Washington's Four Seasons Hotel. "A lot of the true villains," he said, "used to be found in this very place! This was the largest bank scandal in the history of the world, and I worked on the damned thing for fourteen years."

The head of the emirate states, including Abu Dhabi, was a longtime Patton Boggs client and also the major shareholder of the bank. "You know," Patton said, "for all the villains in the case, one that has escaped attention is the *venerable and respected* Bank of England." (His inflection reflected distaste.) When BCCI began sinking into trouble, it was the Bank of England that urged the head of the emirate states to pour many millions of dollars more into the bank, until his ownership share reached the 75 percent range. The bank failed anyway. Lawyers representing more than three million depositors worldwide descended upon the government of Abu Dhabi, with claims in the billions of dollars. BCCI liquidators went to work in England, Luxembourg, and elsewhere. There were grand jury and congressional investigations in the United States. On behalf of Abu Dhabi, Patton Boggs negotiated multibillion-dollar settlements that resolved issues with creditors in seventy-three countries. At one time the firm's lawyers were managing simultaneous litigation in five countries, directing a network of twelve law firms. "We were hiring lawyers all over the world and also shipping bodies out from Washington," Patton said. "A great big mess." Patton ran a command post in the Patton Boggs offices in Washington, but still found himself logging uncounted hours on international flights and in conference rooms and hotels around the world.

Although litigation still droned through various courts in 2000, Patton Boggs claimed to have diverted away from its clients, or eliminated altogether, what the firm calls "the regulatory and legislative thirst for blood that typically attends large institutional failures." Nonetheless, Patton said, "A lot of blame can be laid on the front steps of the *venerable Bank of England*." (Disgust figuratively dripped from his lips as he said those words.)

Not all cases, of course, contain such a patina of seedy glamour. But the work is varied, and interesting to the people who do it: advising Colombia and Peru on fighting money laundering and narcoterrorism; helping Guyana privatize its bauxite industry; drafting constitutions and organizing judiciaries for Latvia and Belarus; and helping the Northern Marianas on nuclear disposal and fishing rights.

Consider, for instance, a deal put together by a ginger-haired partner named Jeffrey T. Smith, who came to Patton Boggs in 1980. "I had gone through both business and law schools at Stanford, but I felt I wanted to involve myself in a practice that went beyond routine law—something that would let me combine both my business and legal training, someone who could be a strategic consultant as well as a lawyer. Well, I found such a niche here."

One major client Jim Patton had cultivated over the years was the Sultanate of Oman, a Kansas-sized monarchy on the Arabian Sea. Oman lived on an oil economy, with petroleum providing nearly all its export earnings, 70 percent of government revenues and more than 50 percent of the gross domestic product. But the government was eternally nervous at the prospect of its own reserves being exhausted, leaving no oil to be processed through its elaborate array of refineries.

Thus Oman was most interested in the early 1990s when Russia and Kazakhstan proposed a deal. Help us finance a pipeline from the Tengiz field in Kazakhstan across the north shore of the Caspian Sea to a terminal located on Russia's Black Sea coast

near a town called Novossyisk. The oil would then be shipped to
Oman for refining. The engineering challenge was enormous, for
the thousand-mile-plus line would cross twelve major streams
and canals, including the imposing Volga River.

"To understate," Smith said, "these first negotiations were
very difficult, considering the cultural and political disparities of
the three parties. There was also the costs, estimated at from two
to three billion dollars. Kazakhstan quite literally was sitting on
a pool of black gold, but did not have the resources to bring the
reserves to the international oil market. And, quite frankly, none
of the people involved at that stage had any experience in under-
taking such a project."

In due course, Omani officials turned to Patton Boggs for
help, and Smith was dispatched to the capital of Muscat to see
what he could structure. "It was apparent to me," he said, "that
outside help and expertise were needed, and that the people best
suited to provide it were oil companies themselves, and also the
people who had experience building pipelines and petroleum ter-
minals." The three governments agreed, and next commenced
what at times seemed to be an endless series of meetings, both in
Moscow and Muscat. Eventually eleven companies (construction as well as oil) from six different countries agreed to work on
the project, joined together as the Caspian Pipeline Consortium,
or CPC. But getting them aboard was not easy. "We'd be in
Moscow, at one of the ministries, and I'd count fifty people in the
room, at times all appearing to talk at once. We divided into
committees to handle different phases of the deal—finance, construction, whatever—and you'd find yourself running from meeting to meeting. The schedules were so open-ended that you were
afraid to make a plane reservation for home, or give up your hotel room. Something might happen that would keep you there an
extra week.

"Then came what I call my Oman phase. I left Washington in
January 1996 for Oman, expecting to be away from home a week
or so, 'just another business trip.' As it turned out, I didn't return
until late May. I can't count the number of times I found myself
on an Omani government plane, flying off to Moscow for yet an-

other meeting. I said to myself, 'This is crazy,' so I persuaded my wife to return with me, even though it was most inconvenient taking a four-year-old daughter halfway around the world to live. The government provided us a house, and she went into the American-British preschool, and things worked out quite well. At least I'm still married!*

"As a Washington lawyer, I was surprised to discover the folks elsewhere are not nearly so paper oriented as we are. They prefer to talk through a deal, rather than exchange proposals in writing. There was hard bargaining, on everything from how some of the revenues would pass through to various local governments on the pipeline route to environmental issues." In the end the deal was struck toward the end of 1996. The Russian Federation held the greater share of the CPC, 24 percent; Kazakhstan 19 percent, and Oman 7 percent. A medley of other companies, some of them Russian, held the remainder.

From curiosity in the next months, I found myself monitoring the progress of the Caspian pipeline on the CPC Internet site.† The trivia fascinated me—for instance, how workmen were astounded when they began unearthing the remains of soldiers killed in savage World War II fighting around Novossyisk. Eventually more than a hundred bodies were found—Russians, Germans, and Romanians—and afforded ceremonial reburial. Workmen steadily worked across the rough terrain. Simultaneously, the terminal took shape. And in November 2000 came the proud announcement of a "golden welding" ceremony marking the arrival of the pipeline at the Black Sea terminal. Once other work was completed, CPC estimated that the pipeline would carry 67 million tons of oil a year. I called Jeff Smith to offer congratulations.

"You know," Smith said, "if I do nothing else in my professional life, I have something to be proud of. Here is a Texas-sized

---

*Oman is not a pleasant place for Westerners. As the *CIA World Factbook* describes its environment, "summer winds often raise large sand storms and dust storms in interior; [there are] very limited natural fresh water resources."

†http://www.cpc.rus/

field being brought into the world market, and my fingerprints are on it. I'll admit there were times when I had had it up to here with Oman, but here you have it."

COUNSEL FOR THE WARTHOG

To state it gently, the affection that Tommy Boggs professes for the Democratic Party is not always reciprocated by key elements of the party, and most especially those persons concerned with environmental issues. Martin Lobel, perhaps the most vociferous foe of the oil and gas industries in the Washington legal community, calls Patton Boggs "a case study in hypocrisy where a new chapter is written almost every week." He avows, "No more striking example exists of how people who claim to be 'on the right side' sell out the public in return for lavish legal fees." The environmental left has detested Patton Boggs as an institution since the early 1970s, when its lobbying resulted in congressional approval of a pipeline that opened for development the North Slope oil deposits in Alaska. Detestation of Patton Boggs has grown in direct relation to the growth of the firm's "environmental practice."

The firm indeed is a power in the field. According to firm promotional materials, it represents "twenty of the nation's largest producers of metals, minerals, and building materials." And, to borrow a term from the criminal defense bar, Patton Boggs is adept at helping these clients "beat the rap" when they get into trouble with the law. In one year alone in the late 1990s it defended clients in more than a hundred enforcement actions, *"often without any penalties imposed."* (Emphasis added.) Patton Boggs's roster boasts lawyers who served as executive assistant to the secretaries of energy and the interior; two deputy assistants to the secretary of transportation, and an assistant administrator of the Environmental Protection Agency.

The irony is that all this business results from actions taken during the administrations of Republican presidents Richard M. Nixon and Gerald Ford. Former managing partner Tim May cannot suppress a chuckle when he notes that President Nixon created the Environmental Protection Agency, even though he was a conservative of the ilk reflexively detested by Tom Boggs and other Democrats. "I remember years ago when a young lawyer in the office asked if he could go down to Texas for a seminar on environmental law. We looked at one another and asked, *'Environmental law?* What in the dickens is that?' No one had ever heard of it. Then we had a case come in involving a gold mine in South Dakota. Residents would turn on the faucet in their house and mine trailings would come out with the tap water. We represented the mine owner, so we had to figure out how to take care of the problem, which we did, one way or another." May clucked his tongue. "I realized," he said, "that we were moving into a new era of law. And that we did, and we've had to find people with the skills to do very technical work—to create a 'skills bank,' if you would."

A key deposit in that skills bank is partner Mark N. Savit, an energy whiz with a well-tossed fizzy hairdo and beard—Jerry Garcia or Jerry Rubin doing big-time law. As counsel for big energy companies—mining, oil, whatever—he is in constant combat with environmental groups, and he seems to take wicked delight in poking fun at them even as he kicks them around in court. On the left-hand side of his desk is a collection of bumper stickers designed to make any Green see red:

Earth First—We'll Mine All the Planets Later
Mining: The Family Farm of the North
I Brake for Cooties
Save the Wells (illustrated with a silhouette of an oil well)
If It Doesn't Grow, Then You Must Mine It

Savit waves toward a striking wall hanging opposite his desk, something that looks like a misplaced five-foot length of cartilage. "Scrimshaw from a whale," he says with a grin. "I picked it up in Alaska. I think that every energy lawyer should have at least one relic from an endangered species." He grins again.

An hour deep into our conversation, a thought struck me. Persons in the environmental movement are not noted for humor, and especially when it is directed against them. Further, Greens make ample use of derogatory posters and bumper stickers directed at their foes, loosely defined as any activity that desires to use the outdoors for anything other than a postcard photo. By ridiculing the Greens, and baiting them, Savit was employing deft psychological warfare: Irritate one's opponent and he or she might make that fatal misstep that gives you victory.

Almost three decades of energy work—he had been at the firm since the 1970s—has left Savit cynical about environmental public interest groups. I sat in his office early in the summer of 2000, when rising gasoline prices had produced an uproar. He was not surprised. "Supply and demand," he said. "You don't let energy companies drill oil, the supplies get tight. You impose strict rules on refining, the supplies get tight. Why is everyone acting surprised? Economics 101."

Regardless, the environmental movement in the last three decades of the twentieth century created a vast new practice area for lawyers, and especially in Washington, from whence the most important regulations flow. Patton Boggs's multidimensional talents—before Congress, the regulatory agencies, the courts, even the White House—make it a natural powerhouse in the field.

I had asked Savit to give me a good case history of a contest that he thought typified the complexities of doing environmental law. First, however, we talked about his path to Patton Boggs. A native of Los Angeles, Savit began college at the University of Southern California thinking of a career in biology, an ambition dashed when a dean "invited me to find a different major." He switched to philosophy, working a sideline job in a TV studio making educational videos for the Federal Bureau of Mines. After graduation he came to Washington and continued making films while spending five years getting through Georgetown University Law School. After stints in a two-man firm, and then in the Washington office of a West Virginia firm, he joined Patton Boggs in 1995.

Why? "Freedom, foremost," Savit said. "The firm allows partners to do pretty much what they want, in terms of building a practice. You create your own practice. Second is the lack of formal structure. When you are working on an issue, no one at the top of the firm tells you who to use or how to organize your work. If there is someone in a specialty that you need, you go to that person, or he comes to you if he needs you. This doesn't happen at many firms." He can reach to the very top and ask Tom Boggs's help if he needs it. "Conversely, Tom will not gripe if you do not call him." And, finally, Savit felt he was at the stage of his career where it was time to enter a topflight firm, one that enjoyed a reputation "as a heavy hitter both in lobbying and in litigation."

Savit is archetypical of the gunfighter litigator who relishes a good courtroom brawl, and then talking about it later, even when victory in the courtroom does not bring the desired result. One of his prouder recent moments began in 1997, when petroleum giant Arco retained him to fight environmentalist attempts to block drilling of an oil well in the Beaufort Sea off the north coast of Alaska. The case was a natural follow-on to Patton Boggs's continuing work in North Slope oil development.* But given the *Exxon Valdez* oil-spill disaster, energy companies understandably walk gingerly when doing work in Alaska.

The Arco project was devilishly intricate. From a location viewpoint, the area was ticklish because the federal land on which the drilling ship—inelegantly named the *Warthog*—would operate abutted the Arctic National Wildlife Refuge. The actual drilling would be into hoped-for oil reserves under lands owned by the state of Alaska. Hence contracts had to be drafted to "unitize" royalty income from the wells, that is, split it equitably between Alaska and the federal government. "A mess of paperwork," Savit recalled.

But when Savit began reviewing work that had been done earlier by another firm, he spotted a potential deal-breaking er-

*Patton Boggs in the 1990s led the private-sector effort that eliminated a two-decade ban on exporting Alaskan North Slope crude oil to foreign countries.

ror. Arco had contracted with a non-U.S.-flag ship to drill the well. But as Savit pointed out, the arrangement did not take into account obscure restrictions on what a foreign ship could do when operating in state and federal waters. He hurried a memo to Arco outlining the problems, and "just prior to the payment of an eight-figure nonrefundable installment on the vessel, the contract was terminated, a partial refund was made on the monies already paid, and the project was postponed one season until the problem could be fixed." Had the oversight not been corrected, Arco could have been subjected to regulatory penalties "that would have become unacceptable."

As the next drilling season approached, Savit oversaw teams of attorneys, both from Patton Boggs and Arco's in-house staff, who did the tedious work of applying for permits, both for the drilling and for towing the *Warthog* from its mooring at Prudhoe Bay to the drilling site. "The *Warthog* was sitting there in the mud. Our first chore was to get the permits to take it to the drill site. I had been working energy issues in Alaska since the mid-1980s, and I knew that the key was to do everything on the assumption that you are going to be sued.

"Something else I learned over the years is that when courts review permit proceedings, all they can rely upon is the written record—what you have told the agency, and why. So I am meticulous when I make an application for a client. If you don't supply the supporting materials yourself, the challenge might be based on a record compiled by a government lawyer or a permit writer, who, at best, is a disinterested, and at worst, a reluctant participant in the project. You also have to be careful about not including language that you really don't need that might make the permit subject to attack."

So Savit was prepared when Greenpeace formed a coalition of environmental groups to fight the drilling. The war was fought on several fronts. Greenpeace lobbied Congress and began what Savit called a "massive letter-writing campaign" intended to turn public opinion against the drilling. But the main battle was a suit that Greenpeace brought under the Marine Mammal Protection Act, arguing that towing the *Warthog* to the drilling site endangered whales and other mammals in the Beaufort Sea.

"Time was against us," Savit said, "and Greenpeace knew it. The weather parameters are very restricted; towing was physically possible only a few months of the year. You also had to consider seasonal migration of the endangered species. In sum, Arco had a very limited amount of time to transport a large amount of equipment to the drill site. Greenpeace knew when the project would be most vulnerable, and it was not hard for us to figure out that is when they would file suit. And that is exactly what happened—they filed for a TRO [temporary restraining order] in federal court in Los Angeles, where Arco has its corporate headquarters, asking that the towing permit be canceled.

"Well, they made a mistake. They named Arco as the defendant. But under the Marine Mammal Protection Act, any challenge to the permit must be directed against the issuing agency, in this case the Department of Commerce. From the legal standpoint, Arco was a nonplayer, even though it had the permit. We knew the suit was coming, of course, and although it was filed over two thousand miles from the project location, we had our answers already drafted and ready to file. The judge heard our arguments, and in about six hours he ruled in our favor, denying the TRO on the grounds he did not have jurisdiction. He also suggested that if Greenpeace wanted to take their suit any further, that they do so in federal court in Alaska. He told them, 'If you want to go any further in this case, I really suggest that you buy some warm clothes.' "

Now came Savit's time to take the offensive. He had seen Greenpeace conduct protests in the past, dispatching small craft to drilling sites and physically interfering with the passage of tow boats and rigs. He filed for an injunction forbidding Greenpeace to tamper with the *Warthog*. "We feared that they would do something unsafe. If you cut a tow rope, you could kill someone. And hanging banners on a floating oil rig is not the safest thing in the world."

This action was filed in federal district court in Washington, and Savit by now acted as field marshal for an army of forty to fifty lawyers, from Arco, from Patton Boggs, from smaller firms on the West Coast and in Alaska. "Thank God for the fax machine and the four-hour time difference," he said. "For several days, all of us essentially forgot about sleep."

Some members of the team were selected because of their research skills—the ability to look for precedents that could be helpful. Savit would do the heavy litigating in court, the actual arguments. "We also needed what I call the 'two eyes versus the three eyes people.'" My blank look showed my ignorance, and Savit smiled and explained: "I'm talking about lawyers who know agency relations back and forth, so that when I get up in court and start talking about, say, 'Paragraph ii of section so-and-so,' he can lean over and say, 'No, no, you mean paragraph iii.' This is important because you don't want any errors, however trivial they might appear, to creep into the record. That is the sort of technicality which a smart opponent will seize upon."

Key to all this work was a concerted effort to anticipate what arguments Greenpeace would make against the injunction. And, again, someone on his staff was ready. "Greenpeace came up with an argument that I really thought was pretty cool," he said. "They maintained that a court could not enjoin someone from committing a criminal act, which would be the case if they ignored the injunction against going close to the *Warthog.*

"But luckily we had found a case on that very point—a Vietnam era decision where someone was enjoined from pouring blood on military records. He made the same argument—you can't enjoin criminal activity—and it was rejected. I simply handed our memorandum to the judge hearing the case, and we won."

Greenpeace was not finished. Next it sued the Commerce Department in an attempt to revoke the towing permit, again citing the Marine Mammal Protection Act, but this time in the proper jurisdiction, Washington, D.C. Here things got ticklish. Savit did not totally trust government lawyers to mount a vigorous defense of the permit. Yet he dared not intervene directly on behalf of Arco. As he stated, "Since we had contested jurisdiction in the first TRO action, we could not intervene in the second, as intervention would have given the court jurisdiction directly over Arco which it would not otherwise have." So Savit persuaded the judge to permit him to file an amicus curiae [friend of the court] brief presenting Arco's arguments.

Something caught Savit's eye as he went through Greenpeace's court filing. At the outset of the hearing, he told Judge Paul Friedman, "Your Honor, I want you to read Greenpeace's filing very carefully."

Understandably, Judge Friedman gave Savit a quizzical look. Why, he asked, was Savit directing special attention to his opponent's case?

Savit pounced. "Because," he said, "Greenpeace is saying they saw our boat causing bears to jump off ice floes. Their boat is right alongside our boat—and if our boat is scaring bears, so is theirs.' In other words, if Greenpeace was truly so concerned about the welfare of bears, what in the dickens was it doing running boats around the area?"

Judge Friedman looked to Greenpeace's counsel, Washington lawyer Abbe Lowell. "Do you [Greenpeace] own a boat?" Yes, Lowell replied, then added quickly, "But their boat is bigger than our boat."

The next day, Judge Friedman tossed Greenpeace out of court again. There was one final flurry, when Savit sought, and won, a further order directed against Greenpeace's protest tactics at the drill site.

"Arco four, Greenpeace zero," Savit related with some pride. "In twelve days, we were involved in four temporary restraining order proceedings in three separate federal district courts. In each case, we prevailed."

After the case was over, Savit walked over into Georgetown and had a specialty shop print up Polo shirts emblazoned with a warthog—more than four dozen of them for the team he directed. Arco gave him a framed color photograph of *Warthog* fending off the Greenpeace armada as it chugged toward the drill site.

"Now," Savit said, "let me tell you the rest of the story." He ducked down his head and his smile only could be called sheep-ish. "In a way, I love that story, because all the work in so short a period was what litigating is all about. But I've got to be honest with you, even if it takes the edge off the victory.

"After all that turmoil, all the legal work, Arco didn't find a single drop of oil at the site. It was a very, very dry hole."

REPUBLICANS REDUX: BOGGS UNDER BUSH

The return of the White House to Republican rule did not faze Tommy Boggs. The last days of 2000 he joined fellow Democrats in publicly lamenting the defeat of Vice President Al Gore. Pri-vately, he was not all that upset. As he told colleagues at Patton Boggs, "So what?" To him the loss "isn't all that big a deal." For one thing, in common with many Democrats in Washington—and elsewhere, for that matter—he thought little of Gore, either as a politician or as a person. The two men were never close so-cially, and when they did happen to encounter one another around town, there was none of the social chitchat that Boggs likes. Boggs once remarked to a man in his firm, "That guy is big-time boring. After three minutes I am looking for an exit." But such sentiments he kept to himself; Boggs has been around town long enough to realize the folly of criticizing putative allies.

Besides, Patton Boggs had carefully hedged its bets both dur-ing the election and in the postelection legal maneuvering. As noted earlier [see chapter 1] partner Benjamin Ginsberg was chief lawyer for the Bush campaign. And, although Ginsberg did not at-tract nearly the media attention as did the Democrats' David Boies, his presence meant that Patton Boggs now had a grateful friend in the White House. Managing partner Stewart Pape did grouse, "Well, the old swinging door is about to get active again, and we're going to be losing some people, at least temporarily," mean-ing that he expected persons from the firm to take positions in the new administration. But, conversely, he also foresaw an influx of former Clinton officials into the firm—shadow-government Democrats awaiting 2004.

A few days after the United States Supreme Court affirmed

Bush's victory, I strolled over to Patton Boggs to see what persons at the firm thought about the incoming administration, and to clear up some of the nagging detail work that always bedevils me when I am ending a book. "Tommy's over on the Eastern Shore killing ducks," the lady who runs his calendar told me, "try him again after the New Year." I didn't, but I did have a conversation with one of his colleagues, a senior man at the firm, who used anonymity to give me a candid assessment on what was in store for the firm.

> Right now, the country is about evenly divided politically as possible. The way this election came out shows that Tommy made a very wise decision earlier in the 1990s, when he made a conscious decision to bring some Republicans into the firm. Let's be realistic about politics. In this town, if you are in our kind of business, you've got to be willing to work with whoever is running the store.
>
> Sure, I have some political ideas of my own, and I have a strong preference for one of the parties. [The man is a Republican.] But do you think my ideology means anything to the people I represent? Clients don't give two hoots in hell about whether the country is run by Democrats or Republicans; they hire me to get something done for them. Corporate America is increasingly apolitical. We are in what I like to call "the Era of the Bottom Line." Well, if we can help improve a client's bottom line, so much the better for everyone.
>
> So what does a Bush administration mean for Patton Boggs? You've talked to our oil and gas people, and you know that we're going to be a major player in getting more of Alaska opened up for exploration. That's mega-buck stuff, and the energy scare means that we are going to be making our case to a very receptive Congress. That's one reason I think that deep down in his heart, Tom Boggs is damned relieved that Gore didn't win. The Greenies more or less own the man; he might go against them on some details, but on something major like Alaska, he would be a pain.
>
> The media are making a big fuss about "the government being paralyzed" because of the near-even split in Congress. Well, who gives a damn? Somehow it never occurs to editorial writers and

columnists that a good deal of the country—and certainly our clients, the boys who pay our bills—are perfectly content with gridlock. "If the government isn't doing anything, it isn't bothering us." That is what I hear.

In fact, having the neatly divided Congress works to our advantage, in many ways. We are going to have to spend more time getting what our clients want, or killing what they don't want. I've never objected to a situation that increases our billable hours, you know.

Playing devil's advocate for a moment, I suggested to the lawyer that what he was saying smacked of cynicism. "Damned right!" he exclaimed without hesitation. "Look at me as the engineer on a train. Someone hires me to take the train to a certain destination. They don't care about how I do it, the route I follow, the people who help me; they just want results.

"And that, my friend, is what Patton Boggs is all about: If you want results, come on in, we'll help you. If you want to discuss political philosophy, go hire yourself a professor. And if you are smart, don't ask too many questions about how we got the job done for you. OK?"

I suppose.

AN AFTERWORD: RICHES FROM IRAQ

Given its long ties to clients in the Middle East, especially Saudi Arabia, that Patton Boggs profited greatly from the Iraq war was no surprise. With more than $4 billion earmarked for "reconstruction projects" to be run by the Army Corps of Engineers and the Agency for International Development rebuilding projects, Patton Boggs geared up to grab as much as possible on behalf of clients. The firm even opened its first-ever foreign office, in Doha, Qatar, to handle the flood of Middle East business. Two partners, Dean M. Dilley and David E. Dunn, staffed the office on a rotating basis.

But the essential work was done back in Washington, where Patton Boggs put to good use its penchant for insider contacts. As the lead player, Patton Boggs hired a retired Marine Corps colonel, John Garrett, who "helps clients identify federal grants and contracting opportunities for government projects in the United States and abroad." Domestically, Garrett concentrated on homeland security issues. Abroad, the colonel "helps clients navigate the complex process of defining the government's specific program requirements and then developing comprehensive capability statements that communicate that the clients provides the best value and is best able to meet government requirements."

Such is the language that presents Colonel Garrett to potential clients on the Patton Boggs Web site. It continues: "In nearly thirty years of developing relationships throughout the United States government and defense industry, Col. Garrett has developed strong networks with policy and decision makers in the Congress, the Departments of State, Defense, and Energy, and the Department of Homeland Security. The access that comes with these relationships *allows Colonel Garrett to know in advance*—and in detail—how best to meet the needs of each agency's procurement program." [Emphasis added] He is said to be especially adept in dealing with a little known agency called the Directorate of Defense Trade Controls, helping "expedite clients' export license applications for defense and security related articles and technologies." He also "serves foreign sovereign governments and their embassies" in dealings with the government and private business.

To summarize: Any company wanting a share of the postwar rebuilding money would be well advised to seek the counsel of the colonel. And as the firm's Web site states, with the subtlety of an elbow-nudge to the ribs, "Colonel Garrett is a member of the Department of Defense Media Military Analysts Group, which receives weekly access and briefings with the Secretary of Defense; chairman of the Joint Chiefs of Staff, and other high level policymakers in the Administration."

To give its multiplicity of clients a one-stop brief on the available contracts, Patton Boggs was cohost of a two-day conference at Washington's Shoreham Hotel in October 2003, a sprawling hostelry on a bluff overlooking Rock Creek Park, about three miles upstream from the firm's office. The briefings, under the rubric "Rebuilding Afghanistan and Iraq," were organized for Patton Boggs by MFN Meetings, Inc., whose promotional materials noted, "Business opportunities continue to grow, as evidenced by recent pledges of United States and international aid. Billions of dollars have already been earmarked for the two countries."

A cynical observer could find considerable irony, given Tommy Boggs's political leanings, in his firm's representation of the construction company which got a contract to rebuild "the most difficult segment of the George W. Bush Kabul-Kandahar Highway in Afghanistan." In war or peace, Patton Boggs delivers.

3 / Breast Implants: The $10 Billion Rush to Judgment

I. Litigation: The First Ripples

One spring afternoon I sat in my basement in Washington, D.C., and watched famed trial lawyer John M. O'Quinn move into emotional overdrive as he asked a jury in Houston to give his client $61 million in damages because of breast implants she had received seventeen years earlier. O'Quinn had a problem—the question of any medical proof that the implants actually caused the many ailments of which the woman complained. So, instead, he asked that the jury consider what *might*—my emphasis—what *might* happen to other women with implants.

Give O'Quinn his due. The man knows how to play a jury. His voice shifting from anger to sadness within a single sentence, O'Quinn declared, "So many sick, diseased women whose bodies are infected with silicone for life, they're watching and they're praying for what happens in this case. You have the power to right a wrong. That's what this case is about: Righting a wrong, a wrong done to her and to thousands of other women. . . ."

I had seen enough. I knew that the jury would give O'Quinn's client, a forty-six-year-old secretary named Pamela Johnson, $25 million in damages, the largest jury verdict ever in an implant case. Forty percent of the money went to O'Quinn, meaning a $10 million payday for his work on a single lawsuit.

I turned off my VCR, put the videotape back into the Court

TV container, and mentally thanked entrepreneur Steve Brill for the innovative media technology that enabled a writer to "attend" a trial held four years earlier and 1,500 miles distant.

For the past year I had talked with lawyers who represented women in implant litigation, both in individual cases and in a massive class action, as well as lawyers defending the manufacturers. But not until I saw O'Quinn pounding on the emotions of a jury, his client weeping in the background, did I understand how he and other plaintiff lawyers were able to pull off one of the more startling legal feats in history: the removal of more than $10 billion dollars from the pockets of the manufacturers of breast implants without ever actually proving that they caused anything beyond local discomforts and, in a minute percentage of cases, disfigurement to one degree or another.

Hypocrisy abounded on both sides. I grew disgusted with plaintiff lawyers who cynically exploited women whose lives had gone astray, and who sought someone to blame. During the 1990s, any woman who developed, say, lupus—one of many ailments inaccurately attributed to implants—easily found a lawyer who would take her case to court and demand millions of dollars in damages. That the implant had nothing whatsoever to do with lupus was of no import.

I felt equal disgust as I read many documents making liars of manufacturers who refused to concede that their implants sometimes leaked or burst, spewing silicone into the bodies of the recipients. The manufacturers argued, accurately, that implants were an ongoing science and that they spent millions of research dollars improving the first devices that went on the market in 1962. True, but the fragility of the implants, and many of the possible side effects, were not shared with plastic surgeons or with the women whose bodies received the devices.

But did the shortcomings of implants warrant a widespread panic that resulted in their effective withdrawal from the market, and a perception that the lives of upward of two million women had been put at risk by callous manufacturers? I think not; hence I join medical people in wondering how many women chose not to undergo treatment for cancer because they feared what might happen to them should their breasts be replaced with implants.

To make one point clear at the outset. Many of the women who sought out lawyers to sue implant manufacturers are horribly ill and sincerely believe that the devices put into their bodies are responsible. In the 1990s implants came to be a catchall villain for any illness suffered by a woman who received the devices. At a Washington conference in July 1998, held under auspices of Institute of Medicine of the National Academy of Sciences, one woman, a person who was visibly ill, went so far as to claim that her implants caused measles, among other ailments. Even implant critics looked embarrassed at this remarkable claim. I have spoken with enough of these women, and read their depositions and court testimony, to realize that they truly suffered, both physically and mentally. Only a person with a heart far colder than mine would deny either their pain or their sincerity.

Nonetheless, one fact is indisputable: There is absolutely no medical proof that silicone gel breast implants are "chemical time bombs" threatening to "poison" recipients, as TV commentator Connie Chung would claim in a "news show" that helped start the implant panic. Indeed, even some of the shriller critics of implants have backed away from such exaggerated claims of silicone causing cancer.

Even as implant litigation progressed through the courts, reputable scientific studies—in the United States, in France, in the United Kingdom—refuted the notion that leaked silicone caused more than localized. What was considered the definitive statement came in June 1999 from the Institute of Medicine, an arm of the National Academy of Sciences, acting under a congressional mandate. The IOM concluded, "There is no convincing evidence to support suggested immunologic effects of silicone or silicone breast implants. . . . The committee finds no convincing evidence for atypical connective tissue or rheumatic disease or a novel constellation of signs and symptoms in women with silicone breast implants . . . such diseases or conditions are no more common in women with breast implants than in women without

implants." Concerning cancer, the IOM found that the incidence
is actually *lower* in women who have implants than in the general
population.

By exquisite irony, a week after the IOM report a federal
bankruptcy judge in Michigan announced a final hearing on a
plan whereby Dow Corning Corporation would pay $3.2 billion
to claimed victims of implants. Of this amount, up to $1 billion
would be shared by plaintiff lawyers.

How did the implant crisis come to pass? And how did our legal system handle one of the more dramatic litigation issues of
the closing years of the twentieth century?

"JUST LIKE A TITTY"

The first attempts to enhance the size of the human breast
came in the late 1880s and involved such materials as paraffin
injections, ivory, glass balls, ground rubber, ox cartilage, gutta
percha, and sponges. Unsurprisingly, none of these methods
matched nature. The modern era began in the early 1960s when
Dr. Frank Gerow, of the Baylor University Medical School in
Houston, noticed blood stored in plastic bags rather than glass
containers. Impulsively, he reached over and gave one of them
a squeeze, and as he told associates later, "It felt just like a
titty."

Gerow's interest was scientific, not prurient. He and colleague Dr. Thomas Cronin helped Dow Corning Corporation,
owned equally by the Corning Corporation and Dow Chemical
Corporation, develop an efficacious way of using silicone gel in
breast implants. Scientists developed silicone during the 1930s as
a caulking material to use as mortar between the glass blocks
popular with Art Deco architects. During the war a refined version served as a substitute for scarce rubber.

In postwar Japan, prostitutes discovered that American GIs
preferred women with breasts larger than the Asian norm. In the
name of commerce, the hookers injected their breasts with such
things as goat milk and paraffin, with minimal success. Then a
Japanese physician whose name is lost to history stumbled across

silicone, which is "rubbery" even in liquid form, and began injecting it into the breasts of willing prostitutes. Silicone fluid disappeared from docks all over Japan, stolen to supply unscrupulous surgeons with the raw material for implants. U.S. plastic surgeons copied the Japanese technique, injecting women with liquid silicone. Although many Hollywood stars and Las Vegas showgirls saw their careers enhanced along with their breasts, loose silicone tended to drift through the body. Many women ended up with grotesquely lumpy, ulcerated breasts. (A Nevada law passed in 1976 made direct silicone injections a felony.)

Enter Dr. Gerow, and his eureka squeeze of the blood container. Along with Cronin and a Dow researcher named Silas Braley, he developed an implant that was first put into a woman's body in March 1962. They had no fears about harmful effects other than localized irritations. Silicone is ubiquitous in nature; people are exposed to it when they brush their teeth, don a condom, spray their hair, or get a flu shot. Further, no medical study had ever shown that it is harmful to the human body. They knew that people have an understandable aversion to foreign substances being turned loose in their bodies. That problem, they felt, would be resolved by enclosing the silicone so that it would not stray from the breast area.

Essentially, what they made was a rubbery silicone bag containing about a cup of liquid silicone resembling clear jelly. The advantage was that the silicone supposedly would not "migrate" through the body, as happened with direct injections. Full production started the next year. Dow soon commanded 88 percent of the market.

And the market was both vast and profitable. During 1979–1992 from 100,000 to 150,000 women annually had implants. Perhaps 80 percent of these went to replace breasts lost through mastectomies. The others were cosmetic. Big money was involved. Surgeons' fees were estimated at $300 million to $450 million (based on a $3,000 fee) and manufacturers took in $50 million to $75 million ($500 per set of implants).

Nonetheless, there were problems. The first models had relatively thick shells, intended to prevent the silicone from leaking.

Scar tissue tended to form around the implants, enclosing it in a "capsule" which sometimes would contract. Often this scar tissue would squeeze against the implant so tightly that it became hard and unnaturally rounded. Women complained that the highly visible bulges at the top of their breasts were not only unsightly but also painful. Surgeons tried to solve this problem by massaging the implants to break up the scar tissue—a procedure that often ruptured the bag. Manufacturers tried to solve the problem by using progressively thinner shells, which in turn led to increased gel leakage.

More than 90 percent of American women with implants expressed satisfaction, but nonetheless, disquieting sounds were heard from others.

"KID LAWYERS IN A WAREHOUSE"

Nancy Hersh was stunned one day in 1982 when a frail woman named Maria Stern hobbled into the office of her San Francisco firm, Hersh & Hersh. Although still in her early thirties, as a medical malpractice specialist Hersh was accustomed to seeing sick women. But Ms. Stern was especially pathetic. She sat slumped in a chair, struggling to find the energy to speak. The slightest movement caused her to gasp with pain. She explained what had happened.

After a mastectomy, she had double implants. She felt that silicone gel was leaking into her body, causing pain in the joints, arthritis, and chronic fatigue. After being rebuffed by several law firms that could find no medical literature supporting her contention, she sought out Hersh because of her expertise in product liability cases involving women. Could Hersh help her? She pleaded. She could no longer pay her medical bills, even for the pills she needed to ease her pain.

Ms. Stern had come to the right lawyer. Nancy Hersh and her father, Leroy, had just finished a round of cases involving hundreds of women who suffered a rare type of vaginal cancer. These cases began with a mystery: Exactly what caused the cancers? The story is too complex to pursue here, but through involved epidemiological detective work, Hersh found a common factor: The mothers of each of the women had taken an antimiscarriage drug named DES. When fears about the drug's safety arose in 1971, manufacturers took it off the market. "We had a dickens of a time establishing causation—that a specific drug made by a specific manufacturer caused the cancers," Hersh recollected. "After the passage of twenty years, records were scanty, to put it mildly." But Hersh and her father amassed enough evidence on causation that the manufacturers paid substantial settlements.

Although not an archetypical feminist, Hersh feels strongly that most medical products for women are designed by males who give short shrift to how they affect the body. With three daughters, she is passionate on the issue. "Rather than do adequate testing, they put the stuff on the market and use the buyers as guinea pigs," she argues. "My blood comes to a fast boil when I see women who literally have trouble walking into my office because their lives have been ruined. If they [the medical device manufacturers] do test, and get bad results, they hide them. They are making a killing—literally and metaphorically. And what was happening to poor Maria Stern? She was going from doctor to doctor, and all they'd tell her was, 'Take more Valium.'" So now Hersh would put her talents to work trying to find why Maria Stern was ailing—and if her implants truly were the cause.

Hersh knew through the lawyer grapevine that earlier implant cases had gone nowhere. "There was talk about settlements of $20,000 to $30,000, but always under seal. The lawyers who handled them couldn't talk about the evidence. The manufacturers were keeping a tight wrap of things. I talked to my father, and we agreed, 'What the heck—let's see what we can find, even if we invest money we'll never see again.'"

Risk does not deter Nancy Hersh. A petite, hyperenergetic woman who sports a just-off-the-beach tan even in the depths of a San Francisco winter, she was among the pioneers who opened law to American women. She was but one of twelve women of a starting class of 220 students at Boalt Hall, the law school of the University of California Berkeley. Even her own father, a good San Francisco liberal, didn't like the idea of Hersh becoming a lawyer. "Girls," he told her, "don't do this kind of thing."

"There was a lot of prejudice against us," she said. "The men, including some of the professors, would say, 'I don't know why you are here—get married, get pregnant, and get out of here.'" One professor quizzed her every class day for two weeks, trying to harass her into quitting. She didn't. She went to him and asked, "Why are you doing this to me?" He desisted. When she qualified for the law review, several males urged her to reject the honor, saying, "You don't really need it, let a man have the position." (She turned down the offer, but for other reasons: "I decided I'd rather spend the year skiing.") Soon after graduation she was in a judge's chambers for a conference. The judge repeatedly called her "Miss" and asked her to make and serve coffee to him and the male lawyers. She refused, and she suggested, politely but firmly, that she preferred to be addressed as "counsel," as were the men.

Ms. Stern's situation intrigued Hersh. She retained an immunologist connected with Stanford University who maintained that the lymphatic system could drain the escaped silicone throughout the body, causing an autoimmune disease, which in turn caused Maria Stern's problems. No proof existed that the silicone caused Ms. Stern's medical problems. But the fact that the implants had leaked seemed grounds for a products liability case against the manufacturer, Dow Corning. So she sued, charging that Dow Corning had manufactured a defective product.

The task of wheedling documents out of Dow Corning fell to associate Dan Bolton, then twenty-six years of age and only a year out of Hastings College of Law. More than a decade later, Bolton shuddered as he recounted what happened:

Dow Corning took the position that they had tested the implants, and that nothing was amiss. Nonetheless, they absolutely refused to turn over any documents. We argued back and forth for months. We had to threaten sanctions even to make them respond. At one point they offered us about $75,000 just to go away. At first I thought that they were correct—that their internal studies would show no problems, because we could find nothing to the contrary in the medical literature. Dow Corning finally offered to pay to fly me and another associate, Patricia Szumowski, out to their facility in Michigan to inspect what they had. This made me feel even stronger that they had nothing to hide.

So, in the dead of winter, they escorted me and Patricia into the huge storage room—*brrr,* real chilly—and showed us a couple of hundred boxes, and a single table where we could work, and then locked the door and left. Patricia and I looked at one another and pulled down the boxes and got at it. The only telephone was on the floor. We had to call for someone to let us out to go to lunch or use the bathroom.

Well, Dow Corning made a big mistake. My first theory was that they felt that these two kid lawyers weren't smart enough to understand medical test results. But even a child could figure out the quality control records, which showed that the implants fell apart almost immediately, leaking silicone into the recipients. They had hundreds of complaints about implants rupturing. You've got to remember that the shell is mighty thin, only three one-thousandths of an inch or thereabout.

The second day or so Patty and I found even better stuff—tests done by the company showing that the leaking silicone gel could cause inflammatory reactions. Of course, that was the sort of thing we were claiming happened to Paula Stern. That night, when I got back to the hotel and thawed out, I called Nancy and said, 'We've got a smoking gun for you. In fact, we have so many smoking guns we don't know what to do.'

Why did Dow Corning make a such a mistake? I've wondered about that. It's more than just a head-in-the-sand attitude. These devices had been on the market for almost twenty years, and I doubt that people in management even knew what was in the papers stuck off in a warehouse. They'd paid off claims for a few thousand bucks over the years. They didn't see any reason to fear these two young lawyers.

"KILL DOGS—FORGET ORGANS"

The most damning documents that Bolton found pertained to myriad leakage problems Dow Corning had with its implants. Here is where Dow Corning—and other manufacturers—got themselves into deep legal trouble, in terms of what plaintiff lawyers could brandish to juries as evidence of sloppy manufacturing procedures and a lackadaisical attitude toward correcting problems. The documents contained the language that makes a plaintiff trial lawyer's heart quicken, and defense attorneys want to crawl under the table. It was these papers, defense lawyers now concede, that made winning cases in the courtroom nigh impossible.

The seepage problem was recognized in 1961, when the implants were being developed, and a year before they went on the market. Dr. Ethel Mullison, of Dow Corning's Center for Aid to Medical Research, wrote to another researcher, "If enclosed within a silicone bag, the fluids would tend to diffuse out through the walls of the silicone rubber and be absorbed into the tissues." That was the first of scores of such papers. Here is a sampling:

✦ In 1976, the head of Dow Corning's breast implant division wrote top management: "I have proposed again and again that we must begin an in-depth study of our gel envelope and bleed phenomenon. . . . Time is going to run out for us if we don't get under way."

✦ In 1977, a Dow Corning representative, Chuck Leach, attended a meeting of the International Society of Clinical Plastic Surgeons. Physicians asked whether Dow was doing studies to determine if silicone gel was leaking and "migrating" from breasts to vital organs. Leach reported, "I assured them, with crossed fingers, that Dow Corning too had an active 'contracture/gel migration' study underway." His memo concluded, "the black clouds are ominous and should be given more attention." (When publication of this memo brought criticism, Leach replied that his reference to "crossed fingers" had been misconstrued as a lie; what he meant was that he was hopeful that what he said was true.)

✦   In 1975 a concerned Dow Corning salesman wrote about the implants being unstable and prone to burst: "To put a questionable lot of mammaries on the market is inexcusable. I don't know who is responsible for this decision, but it has to rank right up there with the Pinto gas tank." A sales executive responded with a memo entitled, "Oily Phenomenon With New Mammary Prostheses." He advised, "You should make plans to change demonstration samples often. Also, be sure your samples are clean and dry—wash with soap and water in nearest washroom, dry with hand towels."

✦   In 1983, Dow Corning's head of biomaterial safety wrote management, "I want to emphasize that to my knowledge, we have no valid long-term implant data to substantiate the safety of gel for long-term implant use."

During the same years, Dow Corning distributed to implant recipients a brochure entitled, "Facts You Should Know About Your New Look." It stated, "Based on laboratory findings and human experiences to date, *a gel-filled breast implant should last a lifetime.*" (Emphasis added.)

There was also numerous warnings, mostly ignored, from plastic surgeons about implants that ruptured prematurely, sometimes even during surgery. Dr. Charles Vinnik, of Los Angeles, wrote Dow Corning in 1985 that "your company has both a moral and legal obligation" to warn patients about the dangers of ruptured implants, adding that he was "loath to publish my series of cases as I feel that it may open Pandora's box."

Dow Corning constantly changed manufacturing techniques but the problems persisted. On December 15, 1977, a Dow Corning employee wrote to a superior, ". . . as you know, we have discussed the rupture problem twice in the past month, and as of this date, the problem is still recurring at an inordinate rate." In 1975, a video was made of implant surgery; to the chagrin of everyone present, the silicone bags kept bursting during the filming. But as a Dow Corning executive wrote, with apparent relief, "Fortunately, these were edited from the tape."

In fairness to Dow Corning, other manufacturers were also tucking unwelcome findings safely out of sight. A classic memorandum that later circulated among plaintiff lawyers concerned beagle tests done by Medical Engineering Corporation that showed such adverse reaction to implants as hemorrhage, possible pneumonia of the lungs, and hyperplasia* of lymphoid tissue in the large intestines. The MEC president ordered, "sacrifice dogs ASAP" and "no organs of dogs in freezer." This was in 1978. A year later, when an underling wrote the president complaining of animal maintenance costs, he replied, "I thought we wiped out all dogs. My rec[commendation]—kill dogs; forget organs; just dispose of them."

Dow Corning's in-house lawyers chose not to grant me any interviews for this book, but the strong circumstantial evidence is that someone belatedly realized what sort of dynamite that Bolton and Szumowski had found. They did not simply stick the papers in their briefcases and take them back to San Francisco. What they wanted, they marked, and Dow Corning made copies, and it was at this point, presumably, that the lawyers recognized that the company could be in deep trouble. So Dow Corning exacted a price for its cooperation. Hersh, Bolton, and Szumowski had to sign nondisclosure agreements barring them from sharing the documents with anyone else, including other plaintiff lawyers. Nonetheless, as Hersh said, "the documents were a plaintiff lawyer's dream come true." The major missing element was any study showing that the leaked gel actually harmed anyone. But the fact that the implants leaked, and that recipients were not warned, was enough to encourage her to put the case before a jury.

Hersh did not yield totally on the issue of whether implants caused Ms. Stern's ailments. She found a scientist named Marc A. Lappe, formerly a staff toxicologist for the California Department of Health Services who had joined the Stanford University faculty as professor of health policy and ethics. The Stern case

---

*Hyperplasia is an abnormal increase in the number of cells in an organ or tissue; the condition is often pre-cancerous.

was his first as an expert witness, and he had problems arguing that the silicone leaks caused her illness. He could not cite a single study stating that the incidence of her ailments was greater among implant recipients than among women who had not received them. Dow Corning took the position that she could have become sick even without the implants.

But Dow Corning got into trouble on the issue of fraud. Had Dow Corning told plastic surgeons all they should have known about implants? When Lappe was testifying, Nancy Hersh handed him an unpublished 1971 Dow Corning study concerning test implantations of silicone into dogs. One died; two others had inflammation symptoms of the sort suffered by Ms. Stern. Dow Corning lawyers rebutted with a 1973 study, which had been published, showing the dogs to be healthy. Something did not ring true with Lappe; he recollected seeing contrary material. After a grueling day on the witness stand, Lappe spread dozens of documents out in his hotel room, and found what he needed. The study which Dow Corning used in court was published in 1973 but it had actually been completed in 1970 and was based on the dogs' condition six months after they received implants. But another study, done eighteen months after they received the implants, showed all of the dogs to have serious medical problems.

To Hersh, the discrepancy was critical, because it enabled her to persuade U.S. District Judge Marilyn Hall Patel to admit it as evidence of fraud and leave the company liable for punitive damages. At the end of a month-long trial, the jury awarded Stern $211,000 in compensatory damages and $1.5 million in punitive damages, exactly what Hersh requested. Dow Corning appealed—and then something happened that both Hersh and Bolton still regret. Ms. Stern's condition abruptly deteriorated, and she asked that the case be settled as rapidly as possible: she needed the money. So, with much reluctance, they settled out of court. Further, the judgment was expunged from the court record—legally, it no longer existed—and documentary evidence was returned to Dow Corning. "It was a disappointing climax," Nancy Hersh said. "But we had no choice. We had to consider the best interests of our client. Unfortunately, we don't live in a perfect world."

Outside San Francisco, the Stern case received minimal attention, although the *Wall Street Journal* did carry a brief United Press International article. The gag order prevented Hersh and Bolton from telling other lawyers about the documents they had found. The result was that lawyers receiving complaints from women who claimed that their implants caused trouble did not know how to sustain a case in court. During this period Dow Corning bought off many complaining women by offering them $600 for "replacement expenses" if they would release Dow Corning and the surgeon from further liability. Hersh and Bolton felt that these pittance payments were outrageous, but they could do nothing.

Then Bolton saw an opening: an announcement that the Food and Drug Administration was to conduct public hearings concerning breast implants. Could he use these proceedings as a forum to publicize what he had learned from the Dow Corning files?

REGULATORY RUMBLINGS

Although hundreds of thousands of American women had received breast implants by the late 1980s, the devices effectively fell outside the purview of any regulatory agency. When Congress passed a law regulating the sale of so-called medical devices in 1976, items already on the market, including breast implants, were assumed to be safe, and their continued sale was permitted. In 1982, the FDA did recognize implants as potentially risky and started the process of requiring manufacturers to prove their safety. But not until 1988 did the FDA advance to public hearings. In the intervening years, manufacturers gave the agency tens of thousands of documents concerning implants.

But were manufacturers telling the truth to the FDA? Bolton doubted it. He thought back to the tenacity with which Dow Corning lawyers had resisted giving documents in the Stern case. Bolton bridled. He wanted to tell the FDA what he knew, but the secrecy agreement sealed his lips. "I had information the FDA needed, and from what I read I realized that Dow Corning was not sharing what we had seen in their files." So Bolton flew to Washington and testified before the FDA review panel. He stated that he had seen documents in Dow Corning files about the damage silicone can cause. He added, "I am prevented from discussing these documents under the terms of a protective order requested by Dow Corning. I can tell you, however, that the jury saw many of these documents and determined that Dow had committed fraud, misled the public, and disregarded the safety of women in marketing silicone breast implants."

Panel members scoffed. Dr. Norman Anderson, of the Johns Hopkins University Medical School, told him that his evidence was "anecdotal, not scientific," and demanded, "Do you have any hard data? Do you have any evidence of fraud, falsehood, and misrepresentation?"

The question stung Bolton. He briefly considered blurting out what he had seen. But doing so could result in Dow Corning voiding the settlement and demanding that Ms. Stern return the money that had been given to her. Given that she had already spent the sum on medical care, Bolton's law firm would in all likelihood have had to come up with the money. Bolton would also subject himself to bar disciplinary action.

Bolton flew home angered. The panel had treated him like one of the noisy cranks who infest Washington. What he did not know was that the exchange between him and Dr. Anderson had been in a TV news clip—and that it was seen by a suburban San Francisco woman named Mariann Hopkins.

THE LITIGATION FLOW STRENGTHENS

Mariann Hopkins's situation was markedly parallel to that of Maria Stern. In 1976, Ms. Hopkins, who suffered from severe fibrocystic disease, underwent a mastectomy. The physician, Dr. Karl Bollinger, did reconstructive surgery with silicone gel implants. There were complications, and the next month Bollinger removed the left implant; later he inserted a replacement implant in the left breast and replaced the right implant in the interest of symmetry.

Ms. Hopkins's health remained poor; eventually, in 1979 another physician diagnosed her with mixed connective tissue disease (MCTD), a rheumatological disorder which includes symptoms such as extreme fatigue, weakness, muscle aches, myalgia, and arthritis, for which there is no known cure. In 1986 Dr. Bollinger removed the implants and discovered that they had ruptured. He spent four hours removing silicone gel that had spread through her body. Bollinger sent the implants to Dow Corning. The company responded that "examination and testing of both envelopes found no evidence to indicate that any of the damage was manufacture related." Dr. Bollinger told Ms. Hopkins of the letter, and she thought nothing further of the matter. Two physicians she consulted had never heard of any causal connection between implants and MCTD.

Then Ms. Hopkins saw the televised exchange between Bolton and Dr. Anderson. She telephoned the law firm of Hersh & Hersh. Come on in, Nancy Hersh told her, we just might be able to help you. And in a few days Hersh and Bolton sued Dow Corning.

So once again Bolton delved into the Dow Corning documents repository, his work easier this time because he could retrace what he had done in the Maria Stern case. (He left Hersh & Hersh soon after the suit commenced, taking the case with him.)

The papers that Bolton produced showed how Dow Corning rushed a new gel implant to market in five months despite warnings sounded by several members of a Mammary Task Force that oversaw the project. One potential problem spotted early on was the possibility of a "gel bleed situation." The suggested solution was to use a "double dip" manufacturing process to increase the bags' strength. But Dow Corning opted for a "single dip" method because it was "easier" and "cheaper." Salesmen were instructed to wash the bags with soap and water to remove gel seepage before making presentations to doctors and to "dry with hand towels" if they bled on showcase velvet.

Perhaps the most damning evidence was that Dow Corning

did no long-range research on possible adverse health effects. The only premarketing study lasted only eighty days and "revealed evidence of inflammatory immune response caused by the gel." Dow Corning put them on the market anyway. Dow Corning did not release this study for several years, and even then "omitted the negative findings and implied that the implants were safe," as an appeals court later stated.

But was there proof that the implants actually caused Ms. Hopkins's MCTD? Her original physician, Dr. Louis Pelfini, had tested her for autoimmune disease in 1975—a year before the implants—but the results were inconclusive. Her rheumatologist, Dr. Stephen Gospe, who made the MCTD diagnosis in 1979, believed her symptoms began before the implants.

Dow Corning lawyer Frank Woodside III strongly challenged the credentials of Ms. Hopkins's three expert witnesses. Neither of the two physicians, Dr. Nir Kossovsky and Dr. Frank Vasey, actually examined Ms. Hopkins, although the former did examine tissue specimens from her body. The third expert, Dr. Marc Lappe, was not a medical doctor, although Hopkins's lawyers maintained that he was "a recognized expert on the immunological effects of silicone in the human body."

So how much medical expertise did these three men bring to the courtroom? Dr. Marcia Angell, editor of the *New England Journal of Medicine,* did a literature check of the man's writings. Of the fifty-odd papers by Lappe in the computerized index at the National Library of Medicine, only one dealt with breast implants. He advanced a theory about implants causing autoimmune disease in a journal called *Medical Hypotheses.* As Dr. Angell bitingly observed, "As a hypothesis, it contributed no new evidence."

Dr. Angell also found fault with Dr. Kossovsky, of the UCLA Medical Center, whose specialty is anatomic pathology, or the study of diseased tissues. His thesis was that the silicone causes such changes in tissue that the body no longer recognizes them as natural, and mounts an autoimmune reaction that leads to connective tissue disease. Dr. Angell states, "Despite Kossovsky's long-standing attachment to this theory, there is still no good evidence for it." Nonetheless, Kossovsky was a witness who charmed jurors: in his midthirties at the time of the Hopkins trial, but much younger in appearance, he gave "the impression of wanting nothing more than to explain the immune system to the jury," as Dr. Angell tartly noted.

The third expert, Dr. Frank Vasey, was a rheumatologist who taught at the University of South Florida College of Medicine. He testified about a study of women who "felt better" after having implants removed. But as Dr. Angell pointed out, Vasey did not do a study with controls and a valid population sample. "In medical practice," she wrote, "it is not unusual for a specialist who attracts patients with a certain type of problem to gain erroneous impressions about its frequency or its association with other conditions." Indeed, she said, not a single epidemiologist testified, even though "this is the only kind of specialist who could authoritatively speak to the issue of a possible line between breast implants and connective tissue disease." Nonetheless, the trial judge permitted their testimony.

Dow Corning's punishment, the jury ruled, should be $840,000 in compensatory damages for Ms. Hopkins, and $6.5 million in punitive damages. When Dow Corning claimed the punitive damages were excessive, the appeals court slapped it down with harsh language.

Dow's conduct in exposing thousands of women to a painful and debilitating disease, and the evidence that Dow gained financially from its conduct, may properly be considered in imposing an award for punitive damages. Moreover, given the facts that Dow was aware of possible defects in its implants, that Dow knew long-term studies of the implants' safety were needed, that Dow concealed this information as well as the negative results of the few short-term laboratory tests performed, and that Dow continued for several years to market its implants as safe despite this knowledge, a substantial punitive damages award is justified. Coupled with the facts that Dow is a wealthy corporation and that Dow made a considerable amount of money from the sale of its implants, the jury's award of $6.5 million is reasonable. . . .

For Dan Bolton, his success in the Hopkins case was doubly important. Not only had he beaten Dow Corning in court, he now had the documents with which he could goad the Food and Drug Administration into action. "I wanted to get the damned things off the market," he said years later. "Sure, winning a lawsuit makes any lawyer feel good. But what was being done to these implant women was a helluva lot more important to me." He got queries from more than a thousand women claiming bad effects from implants. He winnowed through them, taking "about 125 of the best." Even of these few, "some turned out not to be so good."

But even as he signed on dozens of new clients, Bolton moved to transform breast implants into a volatile political issue—one that would engage scores of thousands of American women over the next decade.

A THREE-FRONT ASSAULT

One of the undiscussable secrets in political Washington is the existence of a three-pronged network that is as effective, in its own way, as the old baseball double play combination of Tinkers-to-Evers-to-Chance. The triangle goes from plaintiff lawyers, who want publicity for their cases (so that more clients can be signed), to self-styled public interest groups, which long ago recognized the potency of fear in raising money, and thence to the media, who never ignore a "good story," regardless of whether it has even remote resemblance to the truth.

The breast implant triangle began when Dan Bolton, fresh from his San Francisco trial victory, chatted up Dr. Sidney Wolfe, the head of an activist organization named Public Citizen Health Research, part of Ralph Nader's umbrella group entitled Public Citizen.*

---

*Although Nader keeps the amounts secret, Public Citizen and his myriad other subgroups receive substantial funding from plaintiff lawyers. The love flows both ways. I once watched Nader at a convention of the Association of Trial Lawyers of America (ATLA), where he received the adulation usually accorded a sports star or a movie starlet.

Wolfe is something of an anomaly. He bleats incessantly for the need for strict government regulation of industry but is perpetually critical of the way bureaucrats do their jobs. The man is seemingly convinced that his smallish think tank, whose young scientists and medical people seem to value zealotry more than hard science, is better qualified to oversee industry than are such agencies at the Food and Drug Administration. If FDA tries to work with industry to resolve a problem, Wolfe is quick to scream "collaboration." Wolfe spent the Reagan years (1981–1989) in a condition of permanent agitation, and breast implants seemed an issue ripe for exploitation.

Wolfe's interest in breast implants commenced at about the time of the Stern verdict in San Francisco. Wolfe fished around among Nader's friends at FDA who might help him make the case that implants harmed women. The manufacturers, as noted, had given heaps of scientific data to FDA in their attempt to get approval for the continued sale of implants. Included in the Dow Corning materials was a study in which dabs of silicone gel were implanted under the skin of two hundred lab rats. About one-fourth of them developed fibrosarcoma, a form of cancer, at the site. Similar studies (and findings) dated back to 1941. But persons who did the study said the reaction was "rodent-unique," a form of tumor which does not occur in humans. An FDA reviewer disagreed, saying that the malignant tumors found in some of the rats were "large and had extensive necrosis . . . more than half of these tumors are fatal." The reviewer quoted scientists who said that such tumors had been detected in humans. The review concluded, "It would be irresponsible to disregard the possibility of malignant development of permanent implants in humans."

The excitable Wolfe held a press conference, charging that the study proved implants were possible sources of cancer and that they should be banned. Actually, as several scientists quickly noted, fibrosarcoma "occurs in rodents in response to the implantation of any large smooth object." The FDA concluded that "the types of tumors seen in the rats would be extremely unlikely to occur in humans, and that, if a human cancer risk does exist, it would be small."

No credible science existed, then or now, to support Wolfe's claim that implants cause cancer; nonetheless, his charge was widely publicized. The germ of truth in Wolfe's assertions is that, yes, some women with implants suffer cancer. But, as was noted by Dr. Jack Fisher, then a professor at the University of California San Diego, and a plastic surgeon, given that breast malignancies occur in more than one hundred thousand "new" patients each year, and that some 2 million women have received implants, "an overlap between the populations is to be expected." And as scientists writing in the medical journal *Diseases of the Breast,* reported, "The incidence of breast carcinoma following silicone implantation is actually less than that found in the general population." (In 1999, a scientific panel assembled by the Institute of Medicine reached the same conclusion, writing, "If anything, evidence (though limited) suggests a lower risk of breast cancer in women with silicone breast implants."*

But the outburst had the desired effect. As stated by David E. Bernstein, a law professor at George Mason University School of Law in Arlington, Virginia, "Public Citizen's nascent crusade against implants gave anti-implant litigators a respected 'neutral' source to help shift public opinion against implants." The next step in the triangle called for involvement of the media, but in a fashion trial lawyers and Sidney Wolfe could tightly orchestrate.

Let me state my premise directly. What the television networks pass off as "news departments" are staffed by persons who, for whatever reason (gullibility and sheer intellectual dishonesty come immediately to mind) regularly peddle unsubstan-

---

*Experts such as Dr. Fisher give Wolfe little credence. He said, Public Citizen "conducts no scientific research of its own, yet offers scientific judgments." Fisher gave an example. In 1998 Wolfe served on a panel convened by the Institute of Medicine, an adjunct of the National Academy of Sciences, to hold hearings on breast implants. As Fisher said with disgust, Wolfe gave his presentation in the first few minutes, again charging that implants caused cancer, then immediately walked out. "Wolfe has no interest in sitting and listening to people who happen to know what they are talking about," Fisher stated.

tiated nonsense to the American public. The TV "news magazine" shows such as CBS's *60 Minutes* and NBC's *Dateline* are especially egregious. A person pushing a cause—someone such as Wolfe or colleagues in the Nader conglomerate—seeks out a producer and gives him or her the outline of a sensational story, a carefully selected stack of documents, and an offer to provide persons for on-camera interviews. Rather than doing original reportorial work, the producer takes the package and converts it into a segment for the magazine show. "Research" is devoted to finding materials to develop the working thesis, rather than objective reporting aimed at presenting both sides of the issue. The "other side" is presented in brief sound bites edited to present the designated spokesman as callous or ignorant.

It was through such a route that the breast implant story reached a national audience, via a segment on NBC's *Face to Face with Connie Chung* in December 1990. Chung called silicone gel "an ooze of slimy gelatin that could be poisoning women." She interviewed three of them, including a woman who let the network air a photo of her chest to show how multiple surgeries disfigured her body. The woman indeed had a valid complaint: Her implants failed, horribly, and forced a series of operations. But where Chung overstepped was in making sweeping assertions about leaked gel "poisoning" any woman who had implants. Here no scientific proof existed.

Chung interviewed two doctors whose comments about the dangers of implants were interspersed throughout the segment. One of them, Dr. Douglas Shanklin, a pathologist at the University of Tennessee, said flatly, "Silicone gets right into the heart of the immune response system and is processed in a way that causes the formation of abnormal antibodies." But Chung's audience was denied two bits of pertinent information. Both doctors served frequently as paid medical experts for lawyers suing manufacturers. At the time neither had published peer-reviewed articles on implants in any major medical journal. What they stated was opinion, not scientific fact.

As is often the instance when the media are planning such exposé stories, the target—in this instance, the implant manufacturers—faced a choice. If they gave on-camera interviews, they risked having what they said being taken out of context to buttress the anti-implant viewpoint. If they refused, they appeared afraid to defend their products. Given the pending lawsuits, industry lawyers dictated silence; they did not wish to expose executives or scientists to hostile questioning in an uncontrolled situation. The highly emotional segment thus contained no challenges to the accuracy of the charges.

Nonetheless, Chung's report infuriated thousands of American women. Rep. Ted Weiss, who represented the Upper West Side of Manhattan, took the next step. Weiss was correctly viewed as among the most liberal Democrats in Congress. On December 18, 1990—eight days after the Chung broadcast— Weiss convened a peculiar hearing of a House subcommittee (he was the only congressman present). The witnesses provided the desired negative answer to the question posed by the title of the hearings, "Is the FDA Protecting Patients from the Dangers of Silicone Breast Implants?" Weiss gave top billing to three well-traveled expert witnesses for plaintiff lawyers—Dr. Pierre Blais, Dr. Frank Vasey, and Dr. Nir Kossovsky. In their oral testimony none mentioned their pecuniary stake in implant litigation.

Weiss now moved against the FDA. The agency had just acquired a new director, Dr. David A. Kessler, and he soon received a Weiss letter charging (with no proof) that "the cancer risks [from implants] may be more than 100 times the level reported by FDA. . . ."

Kessler is an interesting fellow. Among other characteristics, he is a whiz-bang at finding a favorable political wind and riding with it. He got the FDA post at the insistence of Sen. Orrin Hatch, a Utah Republican, on whose staff he had served. Much of his career had been spent as a bureaucrat and academic. Other than Hatch's support, he had scant credentials qualifying him to run the FDA in the last years of the first Bush Administration.

Kessler's craving for being "politically correct" was voracious. He recognized that his media image would be far more favorable if he got along with critics such as Wolfe and Weiss, who had roundly abused his predecessor. Kessler decided to trans-

form FDA to their liking. As he would remark later to a conference of the Food and Drug Law Institute (lawyers who do FDA
work), "we needed to get things done quickly. We needed to send
out a message that, ultimately, it was in no one's interest to dereg-
ulate a public health regulatory agency." Unfortunately for implant manufacturers, Kessler made them his first target.

Following the dictates of Weiss, on April 10, 1991, Kessler ordered manufacturers to submit scientific data demonstrating that
they were safe. A similar notice later went to makers of saline implants. He also set up an FDA panel to review the submissions
and take public testimony about implants.

By any standard, the panel was a stacked deck. One member
was writer Rita Freedman, who argued in her 1986 book *Beauty
Bound,* "Having been taught that feminine beauty means having
full, softly rounded breasts, women judge themselves against this
standard. Missing the mark, they put on padded bras or suffer
silicone implants." Unsurprisingly, after her supposedly "objective" examination of the scientific evidence, she called for an implant ban.

Organizations such as the American Medical Society and the
American Cancer Society urged the panel not to support a ban
on implants. To the surgeons' surprise, the panel agreed, saying
that action should await further review of documents which the
manufacturers were supplying to the FDA.

Then came what was a public relations disaster for the industry. Seth Rosenfeld, a reporter for the *San Francisco Chronicle,*
obtained a set of the Dow Corning documents that Bolton had
used in the Maria Stern case, and which were still under seal. Just
how Rosenfeld got the papers remains a mystery; citing "confidentiality of sources," he has declined to say. Bolton, the most
obvious suspect, says, "It wasn't me." In turn, Rosenfeld passed
the documents to Dr. Norman Anderson, the Johns Hopkins
professor and panel member who had criticized Bolton at the
1988 hearings.

In Anderson's view, the papers confirmed what Bolton had
been saying—that Dow Corning knew the implants routinely

burst open, and that the company had done no systematic studies of the effects of silicone on the human body. He hand-carried them to Kessler's home over the Christmas holidays in late 1991. Copies went to such papers as the *New York Times* and *Washington Post.*

Thus for the first time the public read the Dow Corning documents that Bolton had found in a Michigan warehouse years earlier—including the internal warning that the company's conduct on implants "has to rank right up there with the Pinto gas tank."

Kessler responded quickly. On January 6, 1992, the first post-holiday Monday, he announced a forty-five-day "voluntary" moratorium on the sale and use of silicone implants, citing the leaked documents as justification. Several weeks later, the FDA advisory panel recommended limiting implants to women requiring reconstruction due to mastectomy, under controlled clinical protocols. Saline implants could continue. "A sop to the breast-cancer crowd," one person called this concession.

The FDA process deeply disturbed panel member Dr. John S. Sargent of the Vanderbilt University Medical School. The panel contained only two rheumatologists, he and Dr. Nate Zvaifler. There was but one epidemiologist (a scientist who specializes in determining the incidence of an ailment in the general population versus the incidence among persons who have been exposed to the object of a study). And even this epidemiologist "had no apparent familiarity with the diagnostic difficulties involved in complex rheumatic diseases, as was also true of the panel's only immunologist." Bias in the FDA process also disturbed Dr. Sargent. "For example," he said, "one panel member, in explaining her vote to restrict implants, stated that she decided to change her vote after a confrontation by the director of women's studies at her university." In his view, the FDA relied heavily on "junk evidence of poorly designed and unconfirmed laboratory tests, and anecdotal reports from doctors whose practice consists largely of women referred by plaintiff lawyers."

THE "NINETIES DOCUMENTS"—WHOSE FRAUD?

But how valid was Dr. Kessler's public declaration that the Dow Corning documents were "startling new information?" A task force created by the Plastic Surgery Educational Foundation (research arm of the plastic surgeons association) analyzed them in a study issued in February 1992. When he announced the moratorium, Kessler "conveyed the impression . . . that these documents represented newly discovered evidence." In fact, the surgeons found, "more than half of the scientific documents were previously known to us and also to the FDA," which received them in July 1991 as part of Dow Corning's Pre-Market Approval Application (PMAA).

One example, among many cited by the surgeons, was a 1978 study concerning gel "leakage" or "bleeding." The study indeed found that silicone got into women's bodies after implants, but in quantities so small that it could be detected only with a sophisticated scanning electron microscope. But Kessler and Wolfe did not mention the paper's conclusion: "namely, that no correlation was found between the presence of silicone and capsular contracture [breast hardness]." In any event, the issue had been rendered irrelevant by 1992. Gel bleed had concerned both surgeons and manufacturers during the 1970s. But the 1978 study, which had been reported earlier in *Science Magazine* and later the journal *Plastic and Reconstructive Surgery,* put the problem "into clinical perspective"—i.e., what bleed existed posed no medical problems. Meanwhile, manufacturers were producing a "new era of low-bleed implants. . . . A 1970s implant placed on a paper towel soon leaves a stain but a 1990s implant takes several months to leave a stain."

The surgeons concluded their review that the documents released with such fanfare "include no scientific surprises, no hidden answers that reflect unsuspected risk." Kessler and his FDA ignored a vast volume of scientific literature which failed to substantial the charges against implants. They wrote, "Dr. Kessler's field staff, who have devoted countless hours rifling the file drawers of the implant manufacturers at great expense to the taxpayer, should be called back to the National Library of Medicine in Bethesda to read the pertinent published literature on silicone-related issues." Scientific submissions by the American Society of Plastic and Reproductive Surgeons went unanswered by the FDA. Instead, the FDA was letting the process be dominated "by advocacy groups without scientific scruples."

Criticisms by the plastic surgeons could be dismissed as coming from parties with a financial interest in continuing implants. But there were other critics whose objectivity could not be impugned. The most devastating indictment of Kessler came from Dr. Marcia Angell, a physician who describes her as both a feminist and a liberal Democrat, and as a person who is "is alert to discriminatory practices against women." Dr. Angell then served as executive editor of the *New England Journal of Medicine*. She had paid little attention to implants until Kessler effectively banned them. Shortly afterward, Kessler sent Dr. Angell an article explaining his reasons. That many women wanted the implants and were comfortable with the results was of no import to him. Although this argument might be "fashionable," he wrote, "to argue that people ought to be able to choose their own risks, that government should not intervene, even in the face of inadequate information, is to impose an unrealistic burden on people when they are most vulnerable to manufacturers' assertions."

Dr. Angell was not impressed. "In reviewing the manuscript," she wrote later, "I began to realize that the matter was more complicated than I had suspected. Kessler's decision involved not just science, but public opinion, politics, and the law." She thought the consequences of the decision would go beyond what Kessler anticipated. She published Kessler's article but she also wrote an editorial expressing her skepticism about the ban, calling it "overly paternalistic and unnecessarily alarming."

She questioned Dr. Kessler's decision on several grounds. "Demonstrating the safety and effectiveness of a drug or device does not, of course, mean showing that there are no side effects or risks. If there were the standard, we would have no drugs or devices, since nearly all of them have possible adverse effects. The issue is the balance between risks and benefits."

Although Kessler claimed that 4 to 6 percent of implants ruptured, he did not address the consequences except to say that "the link, if any, between these implants and immune-related disorders and other systemic diseases is . . . unknown." Dr. Kessler simply ignored the fact that more than 90 percent of women with implants expressed satisfaction. And, finally, Kessler's decision "ignores the social context. Targeting a device used only by women raises the specter of sexism—either in having permitted the use of implants in the first place or in withdrawing them." (Several commentators noted that Kessler stood mute on testicular implants, many of which contain silicone.)

Dr. Angell continued, "The view that it is sexist to withdraw implants is exacerbated by the fact that people are regularly permitted to take risks that are probably much greater than the likely risk from breast implants; they do so when they smoke cigarettes, for example, or drink alcohol to excess. The argument that many of these other risks lie outside the purview of the FDA may be seen by many as a legalism."

Finally, whatever Dr. Kessler's reasoning, "The fact is that the FDA's decision is widely seen as official confirmation that breast implants are dangerous, despite Kessler's assertion that it simply reflects a lack of evidence."

As events turned out, Dr. Angell was absolutely on target.

To Richard Hazleton, chairman and CEO of Dow Corning, the loophole for cancer patients was meaningless because "the fear of lawsuits has driven many physicians and hospitals away from using [implants]." For the same reason, physicians and hospitals turned away women wanting saline implants. So women were left with the choice of going overseas for implants, prohibitively expensive, or of a form of plastic surgery involving the creation of breasts from other tissues.

At one point in 1992, the Dow Corning press office counted no less than five thousand media stories monthly, both print and electronic, charging that implants caused immune system diseases. In Hazleton's words, these stories were "conjuring up images of women terrified by these diseases. The stories driving this concern were anecdotal case reports. At that time, not a single peer-reviewed epidemiology study showed a link between implants and these diseases, but there were also no epidemiology studies that disproved that link. As a result, the mere possibility— not the probability—that implants might cause immune diseases drove the product off the market."

Silicone implants essentially were dead. Weiss and Wolfe halted their criticisms of Kessler. But the demise created another industry: the rush by plaintiff lawyers to take the manufacturers to court.

The litigation rush was on. And the epicenter soon became Houston, a plaintiff lawyer heaven in south Texas.

II. A Litigation Tsunami in Houston

In no other city did plaintiff lawyers profit more from breast implant suits—and provoke more industry rage—than in Houston. A juxtaposition of medical research and law made Houston what *Texas Monthly* called "Silicon City." As noted, the first implants grew from research by Drs. Frank Gerow and Thomas Cronin and other physicians at the Baylor University Medical School there, and were marketed by hometown industry Dow Corning.

For plaintiff lawyers—they populate Houston in abundance— that Dow Corning was a local corporation (via its partial ownership by Dow Chemical) meant that it could be sued in local courts. This element is important for the implant litigation. Harris County, Texas, has long been notorious (to defense lawyers, in any event) for courts that were slam-dunk jurisdictions for personal injury suits. The reasons are several. Despite a surfeit of oil-rich businessmen, Houston is essentially a working-class city. Its petroleum refineries and chemical complexes are operated by persons who flocked in from neighboring farm country in southeast Texas, an area with a populist mind-set. Unions are strong; the black and Latino populations are a minority, but a significant one. Mix these elements together in a jury, and dollar signs dance through the minds of plaintiff lawyers.

Then there are the judges, who are elected, not appointed. Even plaintiff lawyers will acknowledge that the Harris County bench is not of sterling quality. One of these critics told me, "The basic problem is that Houston has too damned many lawyers. The ones who aren't making it in private practice decide their lives would be a lot easier if they became judges. The plaintiff bar kicks in the campaign money, and when they put on those black robes, they remember where they came from, and how they got there." The lawyer continued, "Of course, I ain't bitchin'—I make a lot of money down in Houston. But don't put my name on any of this stuff or I'll be kicked out of the lodge."

Mimi Schwartz, who became somewhat of an expert on implants for *Texas Monthly,* attributed the popularity of implants to the sixties era "when a big bust was the prevailing symbol of femininity." She wrote, "A new generation of Baylor residents, trained by Frank Gerow, perfected their talents on homemakers and secretaries, psychologists and elementary schoolteachers. It particularly appealed to young white women who worked among powerful white males: on airplanes, in hospitals, in law firms, and in courthouses. Though most women asked to be made 'normal,' what came to be normal in Houston was larger than the national average—a C cup." The cost for starlet-quality breasts was about $4,000 during the period. One plastic surgeon, Dr. Gerald Johnson, reputedly did as many as seventeen implants a day. Some of his earnings bought a breast-shaped swimming pool, with a nipple-shaped hot tub at the tip.

The significance of all the Houston implants was that when questions arose about their safety, the town had a deep pool of potential plaintiffs. A lawyer named Richard Mithoff, who worked as an associate for Joe Jamail—famed for winning a $12 billion verdict for client Pennzoil against Texaco Corporation—brought the first suit on behalf of a woman whose implants ruptured, causing her pain and mental anguish. Mithoff won a $170,000 verdict, then the largest in the nation, but the national media ignored him.

A full decade passed before the Houston plaintiff bar realized the profit potential of implants. Richard Laminack, of the
firm O'Quinn & Laminack, heard a woman who complained
that implants made by Bristol-Myers had broken open, causing
her severe pain. Laminack first saw the case as medical malpractice, but when he interviewed the plastic surgeon his strategy
changed abruptly. The surgeon said, "I know you're suing me,
but I could be your best witness." He gave Laminack a short
course in what he felt to be the flaws of implant designs, and the
case became one of product liability—against a corporate defendant with infinitely deeper pockets than a single Houston plastic
surgeon.

Bristol-Myers chose to settle out of court for an undisclosed
amount, but Laminack deducted that he had stumbled into
something truly big. If only a fraction of women who received
implants suffered ill effects, he could hit the industry for millions
of dollars. Laminack went to work. Aligning himself with activist groups working for implant bans, he became an ever-visible
TV talk-show guest, sounding the scare tocsin to anyone who
would listen. Women responded by the hundreds. And when they
did, they found their cases under the direction of a man who is
arguably one of the better trial lawyers in the Southwest—but at
the same time one of the most controversial.

John M. O'Quinn grew from rough roots. The son of a Houston man who ran a gas station, he considered becoming an engineer before turning to law. He ranked first in a class of thirty that
graduated from the University of Houston Law School in 1967.
To put it gently, the school in those days did not carry much of a
reputation; many Texas lawyers considered it a thin cut above a
night school. But the brash O'Quinn was brainy enough to get a
job with Baker & Botts, a top Houston firm. He did two years of
corporate work, often defending clients in personal injury cases,
and his courtroom abilities impressed the opposition. In 1969, on
the eve of a major trial, two partners in the city's leading plaintiff
firm died in an air crash, and O'Quinn was persuaded to leave
Baker & Botts and, figuratively, move to the other side of the
courtroom. He never regretted the move.

O'Quinn proved himself a master of plaintiff law, and he won some interesting verdicts along the way. One case that delighted the state was on behalf of a farmer whose prize bull, Superman, died after being sprayed with an insecticide. Other lawyers laughed at him, asking, "What do you think you can get for a dead bull?" Just watch, O'Quinn said. By happenstance, a lawyer pal was going to trial concurrently in a case involving a man who was left paraplegic in an industrial accident.

"I'll get more for my dead bull than you'll get for your paraplegic," O'Quinn replied. During the trial he referred to the bull as "Superman," rather than "it" or "he." He asked a man from the insemination clinic where the accident occurred, "Did he have a personality?" The man replied, "He was dog gentle and liked to have his picture taken." Juries nodded sympathetically, and they gave O'Quinn the requested $8.5 million.

The size of some O'Quinn verdicts was staggering even in a state noted for generous juries. He sued Tenneco, the pipeline company, for reneging on a contract to buy natural gas from a small producer. Tenneco argued that every pipeline company in the country did the same thing when natural gas prices collapsed in the 1980s and offered to negotiate a settlement. No way, retorted O'Quinn, you're going to trial. He found a transcript of a business conference at which the Tenneco chairman had said, "Business thinking, not the law, must guide our decisions." O'Quinn pounded that statement home to a rural jury in Wharton County, outside of Houston, and he got a verdict of $650 million—far more than the value of the gas involved.

Another case, against Monsanto, the chemical manufacturer, brought a $108 million verdict for a worker who died after exposure to benzene. Afterward, a judge asked if the amount did not trouble O'Quinn's conscience. No, he said, he would feel no remorse until the amount hit $500 million, Monsanto's profits for a year. All he had asked was three months' income—and that is what he got.

The downside for O'Quinn was a congeries of personal problems. Even friends considered him a rambunctious fellow. Despite being one of the best trial lawyers in a state noted for plaintiff talent, O'Quinn spent an inordinate amount of his time contending with an alcohol problem, and in fending off ethics charges. He acknowledged publicly that he was an alcoholic. Several times, former partners and associates sued him for allegedly not giving them agreed-upon shares of fees. The cases were reportedly settled. But these demons did not deter O'Quinn from wreaking merry havoc on the implant industry. And, once the breast litigation slacked off, O'Quinn got a lead role on the Texas team of lawyers that won a multibillion-dollar settlement from the tobacco industry.

A Houston lawyer who is a longtime friend of O'Quinn lamented to me, "If John had kept his personal life in order, and learned when to put the cork back in the damned whiskey bottle at night, no telling what he could have done. Look what he did when he was working at half or three-quarters speed. A real pity."

Partner Richard Laminack's victory in the Bristol-Myers Squibb trial convinced O'Quinn that major money could be made in that sort of case, so he went to trial on behalf of Pamela Johnson, then a forty-six-year-old administrator. The case didn't look all that good. Although Ms. Johnson's implant had ruptured, releasing silicone gel into her body, the medical evidence of any damage was scanty. She (and O'Quinn) claimed she suffered from "autoimmune disorder," with constant flu-like symptoms. No matter. As stated at the start of this chapter, O'Quinn chose to argue that she *might* become ill in the future. Once again Bristol-Myers Squibb was the defendant.

The climactic moment came during O'Quinn's cross-examination of Bristol-Myers Squibb's star witness, an immunologist from the Johns Hopkins University Medical School named Dr. Noel Rose. The doctor got himself (and the defense) into deep trouble by admitting that more research was needed to determine what silicone actually did to the body. O'Quinn, through a series of skilful questions, asked Rose whether he understood why women who had silicone in their bodies might feel scared.

"I can imagine how they feel," Rose replied. "Of course, I'm not in that position myself."

"You're lucky," O'Quinn said.

"I am indeed," Rose said in a quiet voice, head slumping to his chest.

Lawyers and almost everyone else in the courtroom felt that Rose's statement was a stunning admission. He would later argue to the *New England Journal of Medicine* that such was not the case, that he was simply stating his "sympathy for all of the women who have had breast implants and had been told that they had silicone 'time bombs' in their bodies." No matter; in the eyes of the jurors, the damage was done.

In his closing argument O'Quinn described Mrs. Johnson as typical of women who did not receive adequate warning about the consequences of breast implants. "So many sick, diseased women whose bodies are infected with silicone for life, they're watching and they're praying for what happens in this case. You have the power to right a wrong. That's what this case is about: Righting a wrong, a wrong done to her and to thousands of other women."

Defense lawyer William Mays, of Akin, Gump, Strauss, Hauer & Feld, argued that no scientific evidence linked silicone to the ailments about which Mrs. Johnson complained, and that poor surgical techniques could have caused the implants to rupture. He and colleague Mitchell Rosenheim also stressed that Mrs. Johnson got the implants solely to improve her personal appearance.

The defense did not work. The jury awarded Mrs. Johnson $25 million, $20 million of which was for punitive damages. O'Quinn had asked for vastly more, $61 million total—$1 million for past damages, $3 million for future damages, and $57 million in punitive damages, the latter being the amount remaining to Medical Engineering Corporation, a subsidiary of Bristol-Myers, when it closed down its implant operation and sold off its assets in 1992.

The Johnson case was a public relations breakthrough, and phones began ringing loudly and often at O'Quinn & Laminack. Laminack and O'Quinn had such a rush of business they started being selective in taking on clients. For instance, the firm would not represent strippers or topless dancers, on the theory that juries didn't have sympathy for women who made a living from displaying their breasts in public.

The O'Quinn implant factory ran with production-line speed, if not always with industrial efficiency. Much of its medical work was done by a local physician named Dr. David Burns, who told the CBS news magazine show *60 Minutes* that he had examined more than fifteen hundred women. When he testified for plaintiff lawyers, which was often, Burns charged $500 an hour.

O'Quinn's policy was that any accepted client had to have their implants removed. So the next stop for his clients was surgeon Dr. L. Fabian Worthing III, who testified he did removals for at least a thousand women. Once extracted, the implants were stored in containers resembling Tupperware stacked in a standup cooler in the O'Quinn office. A defense lawyer who glanced into the cooler was appalled. "It looked like a chamber of horrors, all those horrid gray things sitting there, with a keen chemical smell coming out."

Also, volume causes problems, which leads to a convoluted case involving a Houston woman named Mary Klager. Max Boot of the *Wall Street Journal*—a sort of one-man watch-O'Quinn squad—told her remarkable story in 1995. Mrs. Klager had implants in 1979, and when the scare stories erupted in the early 1990s, she went to the O'Quinn office to ask what she should do. Richard Laminack took her in hand. In due course her implants were removed, and tissue samples sent to a clinic in Syracuse, for testing. The doctor there could detect no "foreign materials" in the tissue, meaning that chances for winning a suit were minimal. So Laminack sought another opinion, this one from Dr. Saul Puszkin, a pathologist at Mount Sinai Medical Center in Manhattan, another expert witness who shows up frequently for plaintiff lawyers. His finding was startlingly different. He reported that the tissue contained "intraductal carcinoma"— breast cancer, in other words. Back in Houston, Dr. Worthing recommended that Mrs. Klager undergo a double mastectomy, even though a mammogram showed no evidence of cancer. She agreed, a surgeon removed both her breasts, and the biopsy came back negative—she had no cancer.

Predictably mad, she sued the O'Quinn firm and two of the doctors involved in her case. But she never got to trial. State District Judge Carolyn Marks Johnson granted the O'Quinn firm's motion for summary judgment.

Who is Carolyn Marks Johnson? Jon Opelt, of Citizens Against Lawsuit Abuse in Houston, has tracked her career. She is the wife of Jake Johnson, like O'Quinn a noted personal injury lawyer. The then-governor of Texas, Ann Richards, appointed her to the bench in 1993. Opelt notes that O'Quinn donated more than $150,000 to Richards over the years. When Mrs. Johnson ran for election on her own in 1994 she amassed a campaign war chest of $402,768.73, most of it from trial lawyers. The largest single amount, $6,250, came from O'Quinn, contributed in November 1993 when Judge Johnson was gearing up for the campaign. Four months later, she presided in an O'Quinn suit against three implant manufacturers. He won $27.9 million.

In the 1994 elections Judge Johnson was the only Democratic judge to survive a Republican sweep, winning by half a percentage point over David J. Willis, the GOP challenger. Willis is now pleased to pass along the information that according to an 1995 survey by the Houston Bar Association, Judge Johnson received the second highest "poor" rating of the nineteen state civil court judges in Harris County.

Soon after her election the *Houston Chronicle* recorded a peculiar outcome in two implant cases against Baxter Healthcare. To the surprise of the plaintiff lawyers, the jury deliberated for ten days, a sign that they were not going to win the slam-dunk verdict to which they had become accustomed in Houston courts. Judge Johnson came to their rescue. She called in the jurors and declared a mistrial on grounds they had not been able to reach a verdict. Eleven of the jurors were so mad that they issued a statement lambasting Judge Johnson. They had already decided in favor of the implant manufacturer in one case and were within reach of a verdict on the other. The statement added, "We are appalled at not being asked if we were making progress during the latter days of the deliberations." One juror told the *Houston Post,* "I think when the plaintiffs saw it wasn't going in their favor, they decided to pull out." (Never before in Harris County had an implant manufacturer won at trial.) Judge Johnson lamented to the *Houston Chronicle* that the jurors "did not fully understand the court process." The cases were retried before another judge; this time the implant manufacturers won.

Forbes Magazine documented the fantastic financial success enjoyed by O'Quinn. In 1988, the magazine put him on its list of America's highest-earning lawyers, with an annual income of $8 million. Then he began a siege of success in implant cases, and in 1994, *Forbes* said, his annual income was up to $40 million, chiefly from breast implants—the second highest of any lawyer in the country. The *National Law Journal* ranked him one of the nation's ten top litigators.

Success made little physical impression on O'Quinn. He came into court with rumpled clothes and hair that was weeks overdue at the barbershop. His appearance was no accident. Texas juries, even in a big city such as Houston, like their lawyers to be folksy and plain-spun.

By gross irony, even as O'Quinn, Laminack, and other implant lawyers prospered, credible studies attested to the safety of implants. Dow Corning and other manufacturers nursed the hope that pure science would prevail over what they decried as "junk science." But O'Quinn and others were not about to let the medical establishment stem the flow of implant riches. Their response to the new pro-implant studies was to attack the persons who did them.

"JUNK SCIENCE" JUNKED?

The medical people in Dow Corning management are trained in the scientific method: Anecdotal instances are worthless in determining whether a particular device or medication causes harm. The only studies of value cover a wide enough range of the general population to determine whether the material at hand increases the incidence of a particular ailment. Thus these scientists sat in angry frustration as O'Quinn and other lawyers used what they considered to be junk science to sway juries. From progress reports on various studies, Dow Corning knew that the hard evidence was on its side, and that implants would eventually be proven harmless. But would Dow Corning be driven into bankruptcy in the interim?

What was the first of many exculpatory studies concerning implants and connective diseases appeared in 1994. It drew upon an extraordinary database maintained by the Mayo Clinic—the medical records of 749 women living in Olmsted County in southern Minnesota who had had breast implants but no obvious excess medical problems. In a program run in conjunction with the clinic, Olmsted County keeps computerized medical records of all its residents dating back for decades. Dr. Sherine E. Gabriel of Mayo compared records of 1,498 implant recipients with those of an equal number without implants. She found absolutely no evidence that silicone implants caused connective tissue disease or other illnesses. (The records ranged from 1964 to 1991, just before the FDA ban.) As Dr. Gabriel told Gina Kolata of the *New York Times,* she did not prove that there were no ill effects from implants; establishing a negative is virtually impossible. But she asserted, "What I hope is that these results can reduce some of the anxiety that many women with implants feel." To Dr. Gabriel, in determining whether implants cause connective tissue diseases, it was not enough to note that some women with implants developed these conditions. "Instead," she said, "it is necessary to determine whether women with implants are developing these conditions at a higher rate than women of the same age and health who do not have implants."

When the *New England Journal of Medicine* published Dr. Gabriel's debunking study (on June 14, 1994) executive editor Marcia Angell could not resist repeating the cautionary note she had sounded two years earlier, at the time of FDA Director Kessler's ban. She wrote another editorial, declaring: "The accumulated weight of anecdotes was taken by judges and juries as tantamount to proof of causation. Multimillion-dollar settlements followed, along with poignant stories in the media and appearances by plaintiffs on talk shows. All this added to the weight of the anecdotes, which in a circular way became accepted by the courts and the public as nearly incontrovertible evidence."

The Gabriel study, and Dr. Angell's biting editorial, stung plaintiff lawyers. Dr. Gabriel was attacked as a "hired gun" because her study had partial funding from the Plastic Surgery Educational Foundation, the educational arm of the American Society of Plastic and Reconstructive Surgeons. Dr. Gabriel told Gina Kolata of the *New York Times* that she conducted the study with an open mind concerning implants, and that the work had been conceived and designed by Mayo Clinic investigators months before the grant money was offered. Nonetheless, she received what she considered to be an unduly harsh subpoena demand from Charles E. Houssiere, a Houston lawyer who represented two to three thousand women who were suing implant manufacturers. According to Dr. Gabriel, "They [Houssiere and associates] want over 800 manuscripts from researchers that were here, they want hundreds of data bases, dozens of file cabinets, and the entire medical records of all Olmsted County women, whether or not they were in the study." She fought the discovery requests for more than a year, at what she described as "an enormous cost." She also said that colleagues told her they would do no more implant research for fear of legal harassment. Houssiere told the *New York Times* that he wanted the documents so he could establish the basis of Dr. Gabriel's opinion, and that he found information that would be useful to him in court.

The attack on Dr. Angell also implied that she and her journal were tools of the plastic surgeons and implant manufacturers. One subpoena by O'Quinn demanded "all documents reflecting or relating to any payments made by [a long list of implant manufacturers and their parent companies] to [Angell] or the *New England Journal of Medicine*" concerning Dr. Gabriel's study. There were requests for numerous other documents, "most of which did not exist," according to Dr. Angell. The Massachusetts Medical Society, publisher of the journal, denounced the subpoenas as a "blatant fishing expedition" and got them dismissed.

But the message was clear to the implant manufacturers: science meant nothing to the lawyers earning millions of dollars from implant cases. Executives realized they faced a crisis of mammoth proportion. Given that they had hundreds of cases, O'Quinn and other lawyers needed only to win a handful of boxcar-sized verdicts to drive the companies out of business. And in addition to the individual cases—Dow Corning alone faced 12,359 by December 1993—an attempt to resolve implant litigation through a class action settlement was in jeopardy. O'Quinn's success at trial threatened to derail a strategy through which Dow Corning and other manufacturers were trying to resolve the implant litigation: a class action settlement that would pay billions of dollars to plaintiffs.

CLASS ACTION CHAOS

Here we must backtrack in our chronology just a bit. On January 24, 1992, as juries were beginning to hit manufacturers with expensive verdicts, Cincinnati attorney Stanley Chesley stunned the plaintiff bar by filing a class action on behalf of every woman who had received an implant. Chesley, who likes to call himself "the Master of Disaster," had been involved in more than thirty class actions since 1977, ranging from air crashes to hotel fires, tobacco, and orthopedic bone screw products.

But Chesley was a fringe player in implant litigation. He got his first such client in late 1991, only weeks before filing the class action. In an interview with Alison Frankel of the *American Lawyer* later, he thought that "only two" implant cases had been litigated to a verdict—he was off by about 300 percent—and argued that his knowledge of case management would prevent clogging of courts nationwide.

Other implant lawyers angrily accused Chesley of jumping ahead of attorneys who actually knew something about the field, and who had done the scut work of discovery. They also charged that he had done some astute forum shopping by filing the case before U.S. District Judge Carl Rubin. A few years earlier Rubin had given swift approval to a similar class action involving the anti–morning sickness drug Bendectin for $120 million.* At the insistence of the manufacturer, the deal was structured so that women could not opt out and pursue individual claims. Many lawyers argue that such a requirement is grossly unfair to persons who do not want to be lumped unwillingly into a class. Further, the Bendectin lawyer was Frank Woodside III of Cincinnati, who, by coincidence (other plaintiff attorneys used a different word), also represented the implant manufacturers. Just a bit too cozy for comfort, the aggrieved lawyers complained. Woodside seemed to have found a means to get Dow Corning out of the implant mess relatively cheaply.

Their rage was intensified when Judge Rubin, although aware of the wide opposition to the deal, gave the required certification without even holding a hearing. The implant committee of the Association of Trial Lawyers of America, voice of the plaintiff bar, voted unanimously to demand a further hearing, which Judge Rubin reluctantly granted a month later.

He heard and read language that lawyers normally do not dare direct toward a federal judge. For instance, David Gold of San Francisco (now deceased) argued in court papers why he felt that the Chesley-Rubin-Woodside combine should be broken up: "We note that the . . . plaintiffs' counsel, Stanley Chesley, and Dow Corning's counsel, Frank Woodside, all reside in Cincinnati. When viewed together with the expected certification of a class . . . one can fairly draw an inference that what has already transpired there is motivated by considerations other than the fair and adequate 'protection of the interests of the class.' . . . Counsel is aware that attorneys throughout the country have expressed concern over the Ohio court's motives. Some questioned whether there exists a pact between friends to provide defendants

---

*The Bendectin deal fell through, and manufacturer Richardson-Merrell, Inc. lost several jury trials. However, an appeals court found that no link between Bendectin and birth defects was supported by scientific evidence. The company has not paid a penny in judgments, although it has spent more than $100 million defending itself.

with a friendly forum, or to give local counsel an opportunity to earn money."*

Rubin has said that this conspiracy theory is nonsense—that he got the case because the original judge to whom it was assigned was preparing to try an individual implant case and wished to avoid any conflict. Woodside had fought Chesley "tooth and nail" for twenty years and that any idea that they were working together was nonsense.

Nonetheless, the complaints caused a federal judges' panel on multidistrict litigation to take the case from Judge Rubin and assign it to Judge Sam C. Pointer in Alabama. Even so, Stan Chesley maintained his position as dominant counsel. After a raucous beginning—chiefly among plaintiff lawyers—Judge Pointer seized control of the case and it began heading toward resolution.

But a significant barrier threatened a settlement: the opposition of John O'Quinn. Another player was Houston lawyer Mike Gallagher, who had a thousand or so implant clients in his portfolio, enough for him to demand, and receive, a seat on the steering committee set up to run the class action litigation. Gallagher did not like Chesley. They worked together on the class action involving Agent Orange, the defoliant used in the Vietnam War, and Gallagher later would fuss to colleagues that Chesley got a fee of more than half a million dollars, while the most a disabled veteran could receive was around $12,000. He complained to several lawyers that he feared Chesley "will settle on the cheap just to get a fee."

In the implant negotiations, Gallagher also made what defense lawyers considered to be peculiar demands. He wanted to preserve the opt-out opportunity if a client decided that he or she did not receive enough money. The manufacturers, of course, wanted all the cases out of the way. He did not want the women to be required to prove that breast implants actually caused their

---

*Although the motion bore Gold's signature, the language was that of an associate, Reed Kathrein, later a partner in the San Francisco office of Milberg Weiss. Kathrein mentioned his authorship when I was interviewing him on another subject in 1999.

ailments, a request which one defense lawyer called "staggering in its audacity—causation was what the cases were all about." And, finally, he wanted implant recipients to be able to recover even if they had not developed discernible symptoms of ailments. He badgered the defense lawyers into accepting settlement language referring to "breast adjuvancy disease." (Don't look for that phrase in any dictionary of accepted medical terms; it does not exist.)

Defense lawyers argued futilely against the causation issue. According to Joseph Nocera of *Fortune,* Gallagher ended this discussion by slapping the table angrily and shouting, "I worked out a claims process where the claim goes in one end and a check comes out the other. And we're not going to change that!"

The lawyers dickered for months on how much the manufacturers had to pay to escape the crushing litigation burden. In September 1993 the four major implant manufacturers—Dow Corning, Bristol-Myers Squibb, Baxter International, and Minnesota Mining & Manufacturing Company, now known as 3M— tentatively agreed to pay $4.75 billion. Dow Corning threw in the largest amount, $2 billion. The anticipated payout was from $200,000 to $2 million per claimant.

"Even its proponents do not claim that this settlement is perfect or without problems," Judge Pointer acknowledged in his opinion. "In approving this settlement, this court is heading the admonition of Voltaire . . . 'The best is the enemy of the good.'" About 5 percent of the claimants told the court that they would opt out of the settlement in the belief they could recover more through individual litigation.

But numbers quickly upset the deal, putting it into jeopardy. The lawyers' working assumption was that less than 100,000 women would file claims—one early estimate had the number as low as 6,000, even through three to four times that many had already filed suits. The worst-case estimate was for 60,000 claimants. But wide publicity given the negotiations, and the prospect of any woman with implants receiving hundreds of thousands of dollars—ill or not—sent the number of claimants skyrocketing to 480,000. "Without the causation factor," stated a defense lawyer, "even women without any symptoms whatsoever wanted to get their hands into the pot of money. Their theory was that they 'might' develop an illness years later."

In Houston, meanwhile, John O'Quinn and Rick Laminack lawyered on, thumbing their noses at the class action negotiations, preparing cases for trial, and muscling multidigit settlements out of manufacturers. They piled up very large verdicts: $19.2 million for one woman, $10 million for another. Of the latter, O'Quinn told reporters, "Frankly, it may not be strong enough. The whole attitude of the corporations has been to write these women off as crazy. That is not so. These women are genuinely sick from this product. They ought to stop it."

Other lawyers warned O'Quinn that his opt-outs would kill the class action—that Dow Corning and other manufacturers would lose their incentive to settle if they would still face a plethora of individual suits. O'Quinn could have cared less. A lawyer friendly to him quoted him as saying, "The reason we build courthouses is to try lawsuits. The people trying to do these settlements on the cheap can take a running jump up my wild Irish ass."

So what could Dow Corning do to prevent itself from being bled dry? The decision was made: O'Quinn must be beaten in a major case, and in a Houston courthouse. Once he was shown that the days of outsize verdicts had ended, he would have no choice but to go along with the class settlement. And Dow Corning thought it knew just the lawyer to beat O'Quinn.

III. The Litigation Dikes Crumble

To combat what in-house lawyers called "the O'Quinn menace," Dow Corning put its fate in the hands of a slightly built, intense lawyer named David Bernick, from the Chicago firm of Kirkland & Ellis. (Bernick has the self-confidence that enables him to joke about his height in court. As he told a Houston jury, "I have to confess to you that I have moved the podium out of vanity. When I stand behind a podium, there's not as much of me that sticks above the podium as some of the other people that have spoken.")

Bernick was but thirty-eight years old in 1991 when he began work on implant litigation, yet in his thirteen years at Kirkland he had assembled an impressive record in corporate defense work. To call Kirkland a "hardball firm" is as fully descriptive as saying that Gen. Douglas MacArthur served in the army. Kirkland attorneys pride themselves on being what one observer called "rough-and-tumble," and the general consensus in the legal community puts it in the top flight of litigation firms. Kirkland has the sort of lawyers that corporate America enlists when it is in grave legal trouble, and despite his comparative youth Bernick was recognized as one of the best.

Bernick typifies a new breed of lawyer who, despite not having a technical background, possesses the intellectual acumen to master complex materials. We sat in his office high above the Chicago Loop on a summer afternoon, Lake Michigan alive below us with reflected sunlight, as Bernick told me how he goes about defending a case involving technical information. "First," he said, "I have to educate Dave Bernick." This means wheedling essential information out of expert witnesses—scientists, doctors, and other professionals who tend to speak their own versions of English. "Next, I have to be able to teach these experts to pass this information on to jurors in intelligible form, and to get the heads of twelve laymen nodding in my favor." In the instance of implants, "educating jurors" also meant purging them of misinformation circulated by the media for years.

Much of Bernick's pre-implant litigation had been for Dow Chemical Corporation, half owner of Dow Corning, and he gets high marks from executives there. Thomas Creswell, a Dow Chemical executive who worked closely with Bernick on several megabuck cases, says quite simply, "To call Dave Bernick brilliant is an understatement. He is a lawyer whose intelligence at times seems almost superhuman."

Bernick did not set out to be a lawyer. A native of Glencoe, a northern suburb of Chicago, he studied philosophy as the University of Chicago, graduating with Phi Beta Kappa honors in three years, and thought about getting a doctorate at Yale. "I was a pretty young squirt, trying to decide what to do with myself. But once I got to Yale, I didn't like the idea of doing more philosophy. So I returned to Chicago and the law school. Although I found it exciting, I had no particular desire to practice law. My feeling was that an education in law would help me regardless of what I did."

When he joined Kirkland in 1978, "my ambition was to become involved in 'big picture' cases—cases with complex political problems as well as legal issues." He had hoped to do antitrust work, but the Reagan administration's laissez-faire attitude toward mergers and acquisitions essentially killed this area of practice for the next eight years.

Kirkland & Ellis dropped the young lawyer into deep water in a hurry. Dow Chemical and other manufacturers of a grain pesticide were being sued in Milwaukee by persons claiming neurological damages. Other defendants settled out of the case. Bernick chose to go to trial. The plaintiffs demanded $24 million. The jury found for Dow Chemical. A parallel case in North Dakota was dismissed. Another Dow Chemical case involved a magnesium explosion. Along with three other defendants, Dow Chemical settled with five of six plaintiffs before trial; although Dow was the primary target, it had to contribute only 8 percent of the settlement package. The remaining plaintiff went to trial and settled out for what Bernick calls "nuisance value."

But the case that made lawyers elsewhere pay serious attention to Bernick involved a Dow Chemical product called Sarabond. It was claimed that Sarabond, an additive to mortar, weakened brick and stone structures and corroded steel. The first two cases that went to trial resulted in victories for plaintiff lawyers. Dow Chemical paid more than $100 million to settle these and other claims. With a long string of cases pending nationwide, executives at Dow Chemical worried about payouts in the billions of dollars. Enough, someone from Dow Chemical finally said: Let's put someone else on these cases.

That someone else was Bernick, who took two cases to trial

in Denver in 1993. The plaintiffs demanded $32 million in actual damages and treble that amount in punitive damages. Representing them was one of the nation's premier plaintiff firms, Robins, Kaplan, Miller & Ciresi, of Minnesota, best known nationally for winning a $4 billion settlement in the State of Minnesota's suit against the tobacco industry. After a seven-week trial involving thousands of documents, the jury found that Sarabond was not defective and that no fraud had been committed. The trial value of the remaining cases quickly evaporated, and they were settled on what Bernick called "very favorable terms." He said, "The company did a very smart thing. It found a way to achieve resolution."

Dow Chemical executives realized Bernick had a unique talent for making science comprehensible to jurors, and casting corporate behavior in the best possible light. "He stands out because his mind is so incredible," according to Mark Tucker, a senior counsel at Dow Chemical. "He can take a complex scientific conception and distill it and explain it like nobody else." In 1995 the *American Lawyer* dubbed him one of the top "forty-five [lawyers] under forty-five" years old in the county.

As did other lawyers at Kirkland & Ellis, Bernick had followed the implant saga as it developed in the media. Given Dow Chemical's partial ownership of Dow Corning, his suspicion was that eventually plaintiff lawyers would try to draw the larger, richer company into litigation as a defendant. One evening in 1991 Bernick watched a *MacNeil/Lehrer NewsHour* segment on PBS featuring the verdict in the Mariann Hopkins case in San Francisco. He thought, "This situation seems to be getting out of control; perhaps I can help." The next morning, he rang a lawyer acquaintance at Dow Corning and more or less asked if he could become involved in defending implant cases.

Dow Corning accepted, and Bernick during the next four to five months immersed himself in Dow Corning documents. He found nothing showing that silicone caused any of the illnesses claimed by plaintiffs. With science on Dow Corning's side, why, then, had a jury found against the company in the Hopkins case?

"The science was there [for Dow Corning], but the jurors were not listening," Bernick said. "It was essential to show that my client had behaved properly." He felt he had a story that, if properly presented, would impress jurors. He delved into the history of silicone, which "biologically, had some very friendly qualities." For instance, one of its first uses in medical devices was in a shunt designed to drain liquid from the heads of hydrocephalic children. "Silicone was tolerated by the body, and the shunts gave rise to its use in any number of medical products. That's one of the things I had to demonstrate to the jury." Another factor was that women felt implants were beneficial physically and psychically.

Bernick also felt he had found a way to explain seepage from and ruptures of the implants. In the Hopkins trial, the plaintiff lawyers claimed that these defects reflected reckless conduct. Bernick differed. The technology of breast implants evolved over more than a decade, with scientists tinkering with the thickness of the container and the chemical content of the gel. "We are talking 'state of the art,' and what Dow Corning was doing at any given time reflected what was known." These ongoing studies were reported in the professional journals read by plastic and reconstructive surgeons.

Eventually, Bernick knew, "we were going to have to go to Houston and beat O'Quinn on his home turf. We had to show O'Quinn that we were going to fight these cases, and fight them hard, and win them. The more I got into implants, the more I felt that science was on our side, and that the manufacturers had been level with everyone."

As matters worked out, the first case Bernick tried turned out to be in Denver, a non-O'Quinn case brought by a sometime topless dancer named Tammy Turner-McCartney. Bernick made three decisions:

✦   "I intended to stand squarely behind the company's [Dow Corning's] conduct. I was not going to shy away. I looked forward to putting the documents before the jury, and explaining them.

✦   "I knew I had to isolate the important elements for the jury, and put them forth in a manner that someone of average intelligence could understand them. I made extensive use of graphics. I wanted to show the jury that we were not afraid of the scientific evidence in the case. In essence, I ran a science tutorial for the jury.

✦   "I put on Dow Corning's story with company witnesses, live people who took the stand and explained the science and the products. I urged that they be good communicators, and that they stress that we had nothing to hide."

Bernick displayed another quality in the Colorado trial: his ability to use cross-examination to attack the credibility of the opposing party's expert witness, and by doing so, cause the jury to doubt anything he or she says. In this instance the target was Houston physician Dr. Andrew W. Campbell, who was among the cadre of medical witnesses being used in implant cases. What Bernick did to Campbell in a Denver courtroom illustrated why he and other Kirkland litigators are considered dangerous adversaries. An expert witness who shows up in court to testify against a Kirkland client ipso facto puts himself in harm's way. And if there are any questions about his or her claimed background, the Kirkland lawyer is going to know about it, for the firm does intensive investigation in advance.

Bernick began by exploring Dr. Campbell's explanation of his educational background. Dr. Campbell was born in Beirut, where his father worked for an American oil company. By his account, when he tried to enter medical school in the United States, he was told that "I'd have to show that I was an American citizen." He went to the State Department, where he said he was told, "It's going to take about two years." So he attended medical school in Guadalajara, Mexico, and eventually studied at the University of Georgia Medical School, earning certification in family practice.

Such was his testimony during a pretrial deposition. Bernick felt the claim sounded suspicious, for he knew any number of foreign doctors who had studied medicine in Chicago. After the deposition, Bernick had an associate do some library work. At trial, Bernick simply handed Campbell issues of the *Journal of the American Medical Association* for the years 1968 through

1972, when he was in medical school in Mexico. The issues showed that more than four hundred foreign students enrolled in U.S. medical schools those years. Did he still claim that the only reason that he could not get into a U.S. medical school was his lack of proof of citizenship? Correct, Campbell said. Bernick simply looked at the jury with an expression on his face that said, "OK, if you want to believe that yarn, go ahead."

There was also a problem with Dr. Campbell's résumés. As Bernick brought out in excruciating detail, Dr. Campbell had once claimed membership in three prestigious professional groups—the Society of Toxicology, the Society of Clinical Immunology, and the American Society of Immunologists. These listings disappeared from subsequent résumés.

Bernick posed the issue. "That's because, is it not, Dr. Campbell, that you have never been a member of these societies of immunologists?"

Campbell responded, "Yes, sir." He had an explanation. He had skimmed the résumés for typographical and spelling errors but not for accuracy. He relied on his office staff to stay current on his memberships. "Someone in my office goofed," he said. Again, Bernick simply looked over at the jury.

Then Bernick turned to the thoroughness of his examination of Ms. Turner-McCartney. Dr. Campbell testified that he spent four hours with her and gave her various tests. He concluded that her complaints stemmed from the implants. But did he know her full medical history? In 1983—months before she received the implants—she had an auto accident. Soon thereafter she complained to her physician that she had a medley of complaints, including back spasms, cramps, joint and chest pains, weakness, anemia, and depression, among other ailments. For whatever reason, the lawyers handling her implant case did not give records concerning this accident and its aftermath to Dr. Campbell before he examined the woman. At trial he testified that she told him of the accident, and her 1983 condition. No such discussion was mentioned in his notes because "I just didn't feel it was significant in any way."

As Bernick carefully noted for the jury, Ms. Turner-

McCartney based her implant case on the same ailments about which she had complained before receiving the devices. "Are we in agreement," he asked, "that according to her 1983 medical records, in this particular case, she had many of these symptoms even before she had implants?"

"Yes," Dr. Campbell replied.

Next came the nature of Dr. Campbell's practice. Although he admitted to Bernick that he was not a board-certified immunologist, he had chosen to name his practice the Chronic Fatigue and Immune Center, and that "the great majority" of his practice concerned the immune system and toxicology. "I see patients usually that are quite ill. They have been to see many other physicians without getting any answers, and they eventually come and see me." He had examined many women with breast implants— "getting close to 600 now," he said.

So was Dr. Campbell a true expert on implants—or a hired gun who would give the testimony that plaintiff lawyers needed to win a case? Bernick put into evidence two documents pertaining to his fees. One was a letter concerning scheduling of his deposition. It read, "Dr. Campbell normally requires that the date and time for his appearance at a deposition be reserved in writing 30 days or more in advance. He also normally requires that a nonrefundable appearance fee of $4,000 for each half day be paid at least 30 days prior to his deposition." A subsequent court filing defending this amount stated, "Plaintiff was examined by Alexander Campbell on or about February 17, 1993. Dr. Campbell's charge for examination and testing was $4,000. According to Plaintiff's best information, Dr. Campbell sees three patients per day and each is charged a similar amount."

Dr. Campbell protested that his business manager (his brother) handled billings and "determines . . . what is the appropriate fee." He received only a $400 "consultation fee"; the "rest is lab." He danced around questions about the $4,000 deposition fee.

Bernick aimed for the jugular. He brought out that Ms. Turner-McCartney had seen many physicians, some referred by her lawyers, who would not say that implants caused her problems. He asked, "Now, is it true that another reason they come to see you [is] because you are a person who will testify as an expert on their behalf at trial?"

"No," Dr. Campbell replied.

Bernick persisted. "Isn't it a fact, Dr. Campbell, that as we sit here today, you've been retained by lawyers in other states such as Houston, Texas, to act as an expert with respect to literally hundreds of cases brought by plaintiffs? Isn't that correct?"

Dr. Campbell demurred. "Sir, I had one case in Houston on one of my patients . . . and this is number two." He denied knowing that plaintiff lawyers attended his depositions to see how he performed. And he denied having any "relationships" with plaintiff attorneys.

It took the jury about an hour to find in favor of Dow Corning.

Afterward, in an interview with the *Rocky Mountain News,* a juror made disparaging remarks about Ms. Turner-McCartney's lifestyle. Her lawyers complained that the verdict went against the woman because she danced seminude, not because of the evidence. The jury foreman, Chuck VanDevander, wrote a rebuttal: The juror's "disparaging remarks about McCartney's life history . . . were her personal opinion only, not the opinions of the rest of the jury. McCartney's history was never an issue in determining the outcome of the case. Abortion, adoption, nose surgery and topless dancing were never discussed. . . ." What was wrong with her case, VanDevander wrote, was that her attorneys could not prove implants caused any illnesses. "The easiest way to explain the result is to put it bluntly: The plaintiff had very little evidence, and the evidence which was presented was effectively rebutted by the defense."

"That was the last time," Bernick said, "that Dr. Campbell ever showed up as an expert witness in a breast implant case."

But Bernick—and Dow Corning—recognized that the Denver case was a warm-up. What was needed was a jury victory over John O'Quinn in a state court in Houston. The consequences of failure were grave. O'Quinn's continuing victories threatened to kill the class action settlement that Dow Corning desperately sought. Executives were discussing filing for bankruptcy so that implant claims would not put it out of business.

A SHOWDOWN IN HOUSTON

In the autumn of 1994 Bernick went to Houston to be lead counsel (of seven lawyers) representing both Dow Corning and Dow Chemical, the latter because of its partial ownership of the implant manufacturer. O'Quinn chose his plaintiffs well (although not from his own 2,500-client pool but from those represented by another lawyer, Edward Blizzard). One was a fifty-seven-year-old nurse, Gladys Laas, who had implants after an operation to remove cysts. Deeply religious, grandmotherly in appearance, Mrs. Laas could not be accused of getting implants out of vanity. Nor could the other plaintiff, an army doctor named Jenny Ladner, the mother of three children, who claimed she developed lupus after having implants.

O'Quinn pulled out all existing oratorical stops in denouncing Dow Corning. In his opening statement O'Quinn painted a villainous picture of the manufacturer. "Dow Corning," he said, "violated the sacred rules that you don't sell a product to be put in the human body until he have first done the testing and proven it to be safe." Realizing that Bernick was prepared to demolish his scientific witnesses, O'Quinn built a firewall: "This case is not that much about science and chemistry. This case is about ethics. We will see whether . . . Dow Corning . . . blames Ms. Laas and Ms. Ladner for their problems."

Bernick immediately disposed of this straw man, telling the jurors, "Ain't gonna happen. No one is pointing the finger at Ms. Laas and Ms. Ladner. That will not be part of our case." Nonetheless, "we will talk about the medical history of Ms. Laas and Ms. Ladner, because we think it is important. All right?"

To get around the "impersonal corporation" label used by O'Quinn, Bernick noted that eight thousand persons work for Dow Corning. He had one of them sitting in court, a woman named Lois Duel, who had worked on implants. "That's what Dow Corning Corporation is, it's all those people. Within that eight thousand, there is a smaller group which has worked in the area of medical products. And within that group, there is an even smaller group of people, including Lois Duel, who have worked on research relating to breast implants." Eventually, he said, the jurors would be "asked to judge what is going on in the minds of people like Lois Duel." He continued, "They are people. They have things on their minds. They have jobs. They have hopes, aspirations, obligation." And they were entitled to be treated "the same way as you treat Ms. Laas and Ms. Ladner."

Bernick explained why he felt it vital to "personalize" the case. "Human beings were making decisions over the years. For Dow Corning to knowingly market faulty implants would involve a conspiracy throughout the company. Jurors look at the people involved, and they say to themselves, 'These are ordinary people—I just don't believe they could do such a thing.'"

As a key witness, O'Quinn relied heavily upon Dr. Thomas M. Biggs of Houston, who had dual roles: He did the implant surgery on Mrs. Laas in 1977, and he was a protégé of Dr. Thomas Cronin, one of the implant inventors. During thirty years of practice he did an estimated seven thousand implants. O'Quinn clearly wanted to heap all the blame on Dow Corning by showing that the company deceived surgeons as well at patients.

The thrust of Dr. Biggs's testimony was that Dow Corning was not candid with surgeons about the fragility of implants, and the fact that they "bled" silicone gel. He relied solely on Dow Corning to vouch that implants were safe. He was distressed at having to deal with patients who were "tremendously apprehensive and worried and concerned," nothing that he was being sued by about 150 of them.

O'Quinn wound up Dr. Biggs's testimony by having him demonstrate how he would open a box containing implants in the operating room, and the need to maintain sterility. Clearly he would not have the opportunity to read the package insert containing various warnings about the implants. He asked, "Dr.

Biggs, you are here as a witness. Are you charging anything for your time or has anyone promised to pay you anything for being here?"

"No, sir," Dr. Biggs replied.

What Bernick sought to establish through his cross-examination was that the technology of implants was an ongoing art, with Dow Corning working constantly to improve them. He reminded Dr. Biggs of his deposition testimony that "talking about the implants back in the sixties is like talking about the Wright Brothers' first airplane."

Bernick began roughing up the physician. Bernick baited his trap by putting Dr. Biggs on the defensive. "Is it too much for a patient," he asked, "to expect of a plastic surgeon that he spend fifteen or twenty minutes, at least when the new product comes out, to read the package? Is it too much to expect?"

Dr. Biggs protested, "You are making it sound as if you are derelict if you are not reading these package inserts every time you open one of these boxes." Ultimately Dr. Biggs gave Bernick the answer he wanted: "No. I don't think the package insert carries that much importance . . . it's more important for me . . . to hear from the company what they are doing than it is to read one of . . . these long documents that's struck inside." Bernick got Dr. Biggs to agree that a balance must be struck on any sort of surgery, with the patient making the final decision after consultation with the physician.

Then Bernick moved in for the kill. He got Dr. Biggs to state that he used his specialized knowledge to decide what information should be given to the patient. Then he asked, "When did you start telling your patients who were getting silicone-gel-filled implants that [they] have been shown to cause immune disease? When did you start telling your patients that."

Dr. Biggs replied, "I haven't told my patients that."

Bernick did not want the admission to go unnoted by the jury. He had heard the answer, but he asked, "I am sorry?"

"I have not told my patients that," Dr. Biggs repeated. Only in 1991 or 1992 did he tell patients that questions had been raised, at the FDA and elsewhere, about whether implants caused immune diseases. But he did not revise his patient-consent form.

Bernick again: "Isn't it a fact that if we focus on breast implants, pure medical-grade silicones, there were no case reports of immune disease associated with those implants?"

"I don't know of any," Dr. Biggs replied. As of 1977, when he did Mrs. Laas's implants, the reported experience was almost uniformly favorable. There were no reports of immune reactions.

Bernick also reminded Dr. Biggs of an interview he gave in 1992 in which he was quoted as saying that there was "not a lick of good science which substantiates a connection between breast implants and diseases." (Dr. Biggs said the phrase "not a lick of good science" was not his exact words but he did not dispute the thought it expressed.)

Bernick had used O'Quinn's own witness to tell the jury that implants were not harmful to women, even when they leaked or burst.

A good cross-examiner wants an opposing witness's last impression to the jury to be unfavorable. So Bernick ended his questioning by asking Dr. Biggs just how he came to be a witness for Mrs. Laas, given that he was appearing voluntarily and without a fee. The physician related that he originally had been named as a defendant in her suit.

Bernick: "Isn't it . . . true, that almost at exactly the same time as you gave your deposition, a notice was filed saying . . . that the plaintiffs no longer want to proceed against you? They decided to drop you from the case, right?"

Biggs: "Yes."

Bernick: "Mr. O'Quinn's firm still has a lot of lawsuits pending against you, don't they?"

Biggs: "Yes."

Bernick: "And isn't it true that as other cases have come up to trial, the same thing has happened? You have been voluntarily dismissed, you have been identified as a witness for the plaintiffs, correct?"

Dr. Biggs said he had been dismissed as a plaintiff in some cases "but I don't recall that I have been asked to testify for any of them." More than a hundred cases were still pending against him.

Bernick ended at that point. O'Quinn's first question tried to repair the damage. "Dr. Biggs," he asked, "do you feel like you have been put on trial today?" Dr. Biggs replied "yes" before Bernick could get in his objection, which the judge sustained. But Bernick had made his point: He had raised, in the minds of jurors, the suggestion that Dr. Biggs was testifying to save his own hide.

Bernick gave similarly rough treatment to other medical witnesses. One fellow said during his deposition that as far back as 1988 he felt that implants caused autoimmune diseases. But he never told any patients that implants harmed them. This physician testified that he had examined upward of a thousand women sent to him by plaintiff lawyers.

Bernick heaped scorn on the medical testimony in his closing statement. "In all the closing arguments that you have heard today from the plaintiffs," he said, "where did you hear reference to the study where they said, 'Let me tell you about this piece of data?' Not once. Why? I guess because this case is about ethics, not science and chemistry," he said sarcastically.

The jury's verdict stunned almost everyone in the courtroom. Neither defendant was found to have done any wrong in the case of Mrs. Ladner. Concerning Mrs. Laas, the jury ruled that Dow Corning has not acted negligently, had not made a defective product, had not misrepresented the implants, and had not acted with "conscious indifference." Nonetheless, it found Dow Corning guilty of a "deceptive trade practice" and awarded Mrs. Laas $5.2 million. And although the jury found that Dow Chemical* had not conspired with Dow Corning, it was ordered to pay 20 percent of the verdict.

O'Quinn leaned over and said to Bernick, "Dave, it don't make any sense." For one of the few times in the trial the two lawyers agreed.

Given that the verdict against Dow Corning was nonsensical, based on the jury's other findings, Bernick was confident the case

---

*As noted, Dow Chemical was co-owner of Dow Corning.

would be overturned on appeal. The judge tossed out the 20 percent holding against Dow Chemical immediately.

But Dow Corning had had enough. On May 15, 1995, it filed for bankruptcy, thus freezing all litigation. The company's president, Gary Anderson, lamented that Dow Corning had already spent more than $400 million in "costs and legal liabilities," in addition to committing $2 billion to the class action settlement. Anderson said, "As we enter the summer, we will face 75 cases, with other 200 plaintiffs represented. It is going to be physically impossible for our corporation to deal with that." Anderson found it ironic that Dow Corning was forced into such a capitulation just when "the science we talked about is beginning to come in and beginning to say there is no connection between the implants and the immune-system diseases that are alleged here."

Why did Dow Corning agree to the $4.25 billion settlement and then go into bankruptcy—a decision which *Forbes Magazine* characterized as "a splendid act of corporate cowardice"? Anderson's successor as chairman and chief executive officer, Richard A. Hazleton, told a House committee later that he did not consider either action to be an admission that Dow Corning had sold an unsafe product. "Believe me," he said, "our every instinct was to stand and fight for our principles, and we've had considerable success doing that in individual cases. But when our legal system has been distorted from one which seeks justice based on sound scientific evidence to a business driven by billion-dollar economic incentives, in our case resulting in nearly 20,000 lawsuits, then CEOs like me have no choice. We must make business judgments for the survival of our companies, regardless of our instincts."

Hazleton noted that even after the class action settlement, plaintiff lawyers persuaded many women to proceed with individual suits, leaving Dow Corning facing some seven thousand suits. "By mid-1995," he said, "we faced 75 trials involving 200 plaintiffs over the next six months. Even if we had gone to trial and won the majority of these cases, the enormous resource drain represented by this number of trials risked permanently damaging our business. Without an ongoing, financially stable business, Dow Corning would not have had the funds to participate in a global settlement."

The person who was wrong throughout the affair—it turned out to be dreadfully wrong—was Dr. David Kessler of the FDA. As other scientific studies attested to the safety of implants, he would admit to Congress in August 1995, "We now have, for the first time, a reasonable assurance that silicone-gel implants do not cause a large increase in traditional connective-tissue disease in women." He still expressed concern about other complications such as leakage, ruptures, and contractures. But he had not a word of apology for his role in the implant scare.

By this time, of course, the damage was done. Dow Corning was in bankruptcy, and hundreds of thousands of women had been unnecessarily terrorized. And as of late 2004 an uncountable number of companies involved in implants, in one fashion or another, remained enmeshed in litigation or bankruptcy proceedings.

The total cost was above $6 billion and rising.

NANCY HERSH OPTS OUT

One person not around for the finale was Nancy Hersh of San Francisco, who had litigated the first implant case to go before a jury. She viewed with disgust the class action. "I don't like the other people who live off us," she told me, speaking of herself and other implant pioneers. "They are making an industry out of women's injuries. It's unfair." Class actions "attract the wrong people—women who really haven't been harmed by implants. I might sound sanctimonious, but I try to take cases where I am ethically and morally right. I can make a living that way."

Out of curiosity, Hersh attended a hearing on whether implant litigation should be made a class action. "I saw lawyers from all over the country clawing themselves to death, fighting over fees. I didn't like it. . . . I go to sleep at night and feel good about myself.

"Once they became mass production affairs," she continued, "I lost interest. Scores, even hundreds of women contacted our office. It was apparent that some of them had not suffered any ill effects from implants; they just wanted money." She sighed. "Well, this is one lawyer who was not going to get involved in that kind of stuff."

Did she have any regrets about her role in starting the skein of litigation that toppled Dow Corning and other manufacturers? Ms. Hersh's bright eyes flashed. "Not in the least," she said. "Mariann Hopkins was a very sick woman when she walked into her office. I helped someone who had been hurt—after all, that is what a lawyer is for."

The implant litigation also disgusted Marcia Angell of the *New England Journal of Medicine*. As she complained later, "Our tort system enables lawyers to prey on people's fears, to destroy thriving companies, and, in the breast implant case, even to threaten an entire industry [medical devices] and an important area of medicine [epidemiologic studies]—and at the time to make huge amounts of money in fees. The legal system virtually invites this sort of abuse. The practice of paying lawyers contingency fees in court cases, along with the easy electronic exchange of information about lawsuits all over the country, means that plaintiffs' attorneys can mass-produce lawsuits of very little merit with almost no risk to themselves. If they win only one out of every ten or twenty, they can still do very well."

What is the solution? Executives such as Richard Hazleton of Dow Corning asked whether plaintiff attorneys "who stand to gain billions of dollars by the mass marketing of fear" should have the power to determine whether a product is safe—or whether the determination should be left to institutes such as the FDA, the National Institutes of Health, Harvard, Mayo, and Johns Hopkins. "The answer," he told a House subcommittee in the 1990s, "should be obvious, but our experience would suggest otherwise."

A plastic surgeon who was of enormous help to me in tracing the development of implants, and the litigation they spawned, was Dr. Jack Fisher, of La Jolla, California, formerly on the faculty of the University of California San Diego Medical School and the staff of the Veterans Administration Hospital. Soon after our talks, Dr. Fisher embarked on a new career as a writer of history, and, in his midsixties, entered graduate school at UC. He called in 2001 to report publication of his first book, on medical aspects of the assassination of President William McKinley. Eventually we got around to implants.

"The irony," Dr. Fisher said, "is that despite all the media scare stories, and the litigation, and the fearmongering plaintiff lawyers, the volume of breast implants is right back where it was before, or even higher. The moral, I think, is that the average American woman has more common sense than a courtroom of lawyers. What pleases me is that a woman who wants implants after a mastectomy is not going to be burdened with needless fears the rest of her life.

"Now, of course, if industry had been able to put that $10 billion into research and development, we'd have even better implants. But, of course, we'd also have poorer lawyers, and that would never do, would it?"

4 / The Diet Pill Wars: Meet the Class Action Club

O ne afternoon in the late spring of 1998, Dallas lawyer Kip Petroff picked up his phone to hear a man speaking in a nigh-unintelligible New Jersey accent that could have come from the sound track of the TV show *The Sopranos*. The man rasped, "I just drove down from Philadelphia in this tractor trailer, and I got a whole bunch of stuff for you. Boxes of paper, some kinda documents. Where you wanna put 'em?"

What the man said took a few moments to absorb. "An entire eighteen-wheeler of documents?" Petroff asked.

"Yeah, I got 'em, pal," the man said. "So where do you want me to go?"

That phone call propelled a relatively obscure Dallas attorney in a two-man firm—Petroff had a single partner, Robert Kisselburgh—to the forefront of the hundreds of plaintiff lawyers scrambling for a share of what portended to be the most lucrative litigation of the late twentieth century, lawsuits against the manufacturers of a combination of diet pills commonly known as "fen-phen."

The previous autumn, in 1997, the U.S. Food and Drug Administration had ordered the drugs off the market after reports that they caused heart damage—sometimes fatal—to persons who took them. Predictably, trial lawyers rushed to courthouses with lawsuits aimed at manufacturers and distributors of the pills, as well as the physicians who prescribed them. As many as six million people, chiefly women, were estimated to have suffered either immediate or potential long-term harm.

The fen-phen litigation shows both the bright and dark sides of today's plaintiff bar.

Skeptics who criticize "avaricious, money-hungry, sue-crazy plaintiff lawyers" should look closely at those attorneys' white-hat role in the sordid story of fen-phen. Villains are many, and it took the lawyers to ferret out their misdeeds.

✦   It was plaintiff lawyers who demonstrated that drug manufacturers ignored warning bells that their pills were damaging the hearts of women both in the United States and in Europe, and kept on selling them anyway, earning hundreds of millions of dollars a year.

✦   It was plaintiff lawyers who documented that politicians such as Sen. Edward Kennedy pressured the FDA to approve for the market one of the more controversial drugs, Redux, in the face of warnings by agency scientists of the pill's potential dangers.

✦   It was plaintiff lawyers who discovered that, for fees, physicians signed articles ghostwritten by pharmaceutical companies that endorsed the use of diet pills far beyond what the FDA considered a safe period of time.

✦   It was plaintiff lawyers who discovered that the FDA itself put the economic health of the manufacturers above that of the health of Americans who would ultimately take the pills. When FDA staff people urged that an application for approval of Redux be withdrawn, Dr. Bobby Sandage, an official of Interneuron Pharmaceuticals, Inc., the manufacturer, argued that "withdrawal, from a financial standpoint, was really out of the question because the company would be ruined." A complaisant FDA let Redux go to market.

Kip Petroff is one of the lawyers who came out of the litigation wearing, in my judgment, a white hat. In terms of class action numbers, he did not approach such attorneys as Paul Rheingold of New York, a slim, sixtyish baron of the tort bar who signed on more than three thousand fen-phen clients via an intensive advertising campaign in such publications as *TV Guide,* required reading for overweight couch potatoes, and *Newsday,* the Long Island tabloid. Nor was Petroff part of the high-powered consortium of lawyers—the Class Action Club, as they are called—that chose to lump thousands of cases into a single action in U.S. district court in Philadelphia. The class action group eventually won a settlement from American Home Products, the primary fen-phen manufacturer, of $3.8 billion—more than $400 million of which they kept as fees. In due course, we shall meet Rheingold and the lawyers who ran the class action suits.

Two factors make Petroff sui generis. First was the audacity with which he went after the manufacturers, and the damning evidence that he rooted from their files, and from their executives' mouths on deposition, at a very early stage of the litigation. Within the space of a very few months Petroff established himself as arguably the major player in the fen-phen saga. (Stanley Chesley of Cincinnati, a charter member of the Class Action Club, nonetheless dismissed Petroff with sneering references to "that boy.")

Second, Petroff was the first lawyer to actually try a fen-phen case "to verdict"—that is, to convince a jury that a manufacturer had marketed a product that caused harm to someone, and to win an award. It was $23.3 million. The punitive-damage part of the award far exceeded the cap set by Texas law, and the ultimate settlement was in the $2 million range. Nonetheless, his victory was what another lawyer conceded was "the final incentive" to persuade American Home Products to move for a national settlement of all remaining cases.

The fen-phen case shows a darker side of the plaintiff bar as well. Once the class action settlement was announced, in late 1999, plaintiff lawyers fell into a nasty intramural fight. Many argued that justice would be better served if they could continue to pursue cases individually rather than lump their clients into a group.

In January 2000, with the acrimony at its height, Paul Rheingold permitted himself a moment of astounding candor. We were sitting in his townhouse office in the Murray Hill section of Manhattan, a few blocks below Grand Central Terminal. Rheingold was relating various alleged sins of the Class Action Club and telling me why he and other lawyers intended to opt out of the settlement and continue cases on their own. He was especially peeved that the class action lawyers would get not only fees set by the court, but 9 percent of any fees he might earn on his own on fen-phen cases. This Rheingold did not like.

"You know," Rheingold said, "at the heart of it, this is an economic battle, although everyone sees it as something of high principle. The [class action] lawyers want to make money even though they have no real cases themselves. I'm not going to let them get away with it."

SO, WHAT IS FEN-PHEN?

Before we go further, let us pause briefly to discuss the craze that swept the "fatty industry" in the early 1990s. (I do not claim authorship of the term; I heard it used in lawyers' corridor talk at the federal courthouse in Philadelphia during hearings on the class action.) For four decades, researchers specializing in weight reduction had sought the magic pill that would enable humans to shed weight with ease, without resort to the discomfort of exercise or sensible eating. Most involved amphetamines or other speed drugs, long the favorites of students cramming for exams. But most doctors shied away from these drugs because of their propensity to become addictive or to cause psychiatric or physical problems. Both European and American drug companies toyed with various pills going back to the 1960s without signal success.

Then along came a researcher named Dr. Michael Weintraub, who in the early 1990s was an associate professor at the University of Rochester School of Medicine and Dentistry. Weintraub had been working on a weight-loss study sponsored by A. H. Robins Company, Inc., which manufactured a diet drug known as fenfluramine, sold since 1973 under the trade name Pondimin. (European versions were sold under various names.) The downside of the drug, a big one, was that it tended to make users drowsy.

En route to a conference one wintry day, Dr. Weintraub found himself stranded by a blizzard in an airport. He whiled away his time going over a paper he was to present, and a thought kept bobbing through his mind. How could he overcome the drowsiness problem that kept Pondimin from becoming a big commercial success?

In what he would later describe to colleagues as a eureka moment, Weintraub thought of another drug, phentermine, which acts as a stimulant. Why not put them into a single pill—fen-phen, incorporating the first syllable of each component drug—so that they could counter one another'side effects?

Dr. Weintraub did clinical tests, the startling results of which were published in May 1992 in the journal *Clinical Pharmacology and Therapeutics*. He claimed that subjects who took fen-phen lost an average of thirty pounds in thirty-four weeks. The magic pill seemed at hand. (The next year Dr. Weintraub would move to the FDA as head of the office that evaluates over-the-counter drugs and thence to Rutgers University.)*

Meanwhile, a New Jersey company named American Home Products (AHP) acquired A. H. Robins, and with it control of Pondimin. Dr. Weintraub's work excited AHP, as did further clinical tests. AHP worked closely with a Massachusetts firm called Interneuron Pharmaceuticals, Inc., which wanted to mar-

---

*But this and other Weintraub studies had flaws, plaintiff lawyers would later charge. David Terry, of the Dallas firm the Law Offices of Vic Terry, P.C., commented in October 1998 at a seminar run by the Association of Trail Lawyers of America, "While Weintraub and his colleagues did perform some follow-up testing on participants in various trials with fen-phen, this testing was not done on participants who dropped out of the study, and almost 15 percent dropped out because of cardiovascular or central nervous system complaints." Nor did the follow-up testing include echocardiograms, a sophisticated test that is the rough equivalent of a cat-scan of the heart. Terry stated, "The medical and pharmaceutical community appears to have been so content with the drastically increased sales that they overlooked serious questions concerning safety."

ket phentermine under the brand name of Redux. Analysts predicted that the drugs could have annual sales of half a billion dollars.

But Redux had problems. European reports told of heart problems associated with use of similar drugs there. An FDA advisory committee initially voted 5–3 in September 1995 to withhold the drug from the market because of concerns about both the heart problems and evidence of brain cell damage in animal experiments. After an intense sub rosa lobbying campaign by AHP, details of which would not become known for years until Kip Petroff and other lawyers got into the company's files, the panel reversed itself and decided, by a 6–5 vote, that the benefits for the clinically obese outweighed health risks. The full FDA gave final approval to market the drug in April 1996.

Driven by a heavy ad campaign and wide publicity, the pills set off a diet pill craze. AHP's official line was that the pills should be used for only thirty days to avoid harmful side effects. In less than two years, physicians wrote an estimated 18 million prescriptions for the drugs. Many were prescribed by physicians concerned about grossly obese patients, the majority of them women. Many went to people who were not clinically obese, but simply wanted a painless way to peel off pounds. And then there were charlatans.

At the height of the frenzy, unscrupulous promoters set up storefront "pill mills" that doled out fen-phen indiscriminately. Prospective patients sat on folding chairs and watched a video touting the benefits of fen-phen without a word being said about downside effects. No physician would appear to answer questions, although one's name might be rubber-stamped on prescription forms. One clinic claimed that the pills were "proven safe for up to four years," far beyond the safe usage period accepted by manufacturers and the FDA.

Weight-loss companies gave fen-phen free to those who signed up for their exercise and diet programs. There were careful disclaimers that the programs were not practicing medicine, and some clinics urged that persons undergo an EKG before taking the pills. There was also language about an "important but rare" association between the pills and a heart condition known as primary pulmonary hypertension (PPH), a potentially fatal condition.

As American Home Products would later stipulate in court proceedings, approximately four million people took Pondimin from 1995 to September 1997, and two million people took Redux from June 1996 to September 1997. Earnings soared for both AHP and Interneuron. But the glory days of diet pills were to be short-lived.

TELLTALE VIDEO IMAGES

Fen-phen's fall from grace came swiftly, chiefly because of the curiosity of a laboratory technician named Pam Ruff, at MeritCare Medical Center in Fargo, North Dakota. One day she saw something extraordinarily curious as she viewed, on a video screen, echocardiograms taken of two women who had been referred by separate physicians. (Essentially, an echocardiogram produces the equivalent of a multidimensional photograph of the heart.) Each of the images displayed heart valves deformed in a manner she had never seen before. Mrs. Ruff is not a physician, but she does hold a bachelor's degree in biology, and she had learned much about the heart during her six years at MeritCare. "Curiosity got the best of me," Mrs. Ruff said some years later. "There had to be a reason. So I talked with the women when the procedure was finished and asked what sort of commonalties they might have had, and if they were taking the same medicine." Both women had taken Pondimin.

Mrs. Ruff reported the deformities to Dr. Bruce Pitts, MeritCare's medical director for quality management. He shared her puzzlement and suggested that she begin keeping a record of similar deformities that appeared. Mrs. Ruff and other sonographers did so for two years, and by 1996 they counted almost two dozen cases of heart valve abnormalities, all of them in women who had taken diet pills.

Dr. Pitts and other physicians turned the data over to researchers at the Mayo Clinic. By happenstance, doctors there in May 1996 had admitted a forty-one-year-old woman complaining of shortness of breath. Surgeons noted that valves in her heart were "white and shiny," suggesting an adverse reaction to a drug. Mayo began its own analysis. And in August, the *New England Journal of Medicine* published a study suggesting that anorexic drugs—chiefly derivatives of fenfluramine—were associated with primary pulmonary hypertension.

These alarms caught the attention of the Wyeth-Ayerst division of American Home Products, the actual manufacturer of fen-phen. Wyeth-Ayerst issued a warning that phentermine and fenfluramine should not be used concurrently, and that Pondimin should not be prescribed for more than a few weeks. But was this warning serious? Kip Petroff and other lawyers would find reason to suspect otherwise in coming months.

The pace quickened in 1997. In March, Mayo researchers called AHP to Minnesota to discuss further disturbing clinical findings about diet pills and heart disease. And in July, Mayo held a press conference to report on a study of twenty-four young women who had taken fen-phen for periods of one to sixteen months, and who developed bad heart valves. As many as 30 percent of the women studied had abnormal heartbeats. Dr. Heidi Connolly of Mayo, the chief researcher, noted that the study had been scheduled to be published in the fall by the *New England Journal of Medicine*. In an unusual move, the journal decided to waive its usual embargo on prepublication publicity because "of the immediate danger posed by fen-phen."

A series of further blows followed. The FDA issued warnings to physicians to check fen-phen patients for heart defects. IMS America, which monitors sales of the pharmaceutical industry, reported that fen-phen prescriptions dropped about 40 percent literally overnight. The *New York Times* reported on August 28 yet another fifty-six cases of heart valve damage linked to diet drugs had been found in addition to the twenty-four cited by Mayo. And on September 15, the FDA announced that Wyeth-Ayerst was voluntarily withdrawing Pondimin and Redux from the market. Notices went to 450,000 physicians and pharmacists instructing them to no longer distribute the drugs.

Now commenced the Time of the Lawyers.

THE EDUCATION OF A PLAINTIFF LAWYER

The experience of Kip Petroff illustrates a financial fact of life for the modern plaintiff lawyer. Becoming anything approaching the status of "a player" in big-bucks litigation requires a sizable nest egg. In the instance of Petroff, he was able to go into fen-phen work with no immediate prospect of the recovery of a single dollar—perhaps never—because of his past success in breast implant cases. Even in that area he was by no means prominent: The cases he won were individual local verdicts, and in terms of money earned he fell light-years shy of such attorneys as John O'Quinn of Houston.

Kip Petroff (a younger brother mangled his birth name of Clifford into Kip) is an intense man with an athlete's build and energy—"the original workaholic," as he describes himself, and the days I spent around him confirmed what he said. An admiring female journalist wrote that he "resembles a young Tommy Lee Jones," the actor. A native of Ohio, he studied law at Notre Dame, graduating in 1983. "When you come out of a school like Notre Dame, you don't look for a job, they [the firms] look for you." He went to Dallas as an associate at Strasburger & Price, a big defense firm, but after a couple of years decided to try plaintiff law. "Frankly," he says, "the defense work bored me, and I wanted to make some serious money."

The first years were tough. He did workmen's compensation and car-wreck work, "the pots and pans that a personal injury lawyer washes to pay the bill." But there was a handful of biggies. In 1990 he picked up the sort of case that other lawyers refer to as a "well-traveled dog," a suit alleging that a Dallas blood bank had sold blood contaminated with the AIDS virus. Several attorneys had worked the case without success, and one gave it to Petroff in frustration. Petroff persuaded a jury that the blood bank should have asked donors whether they were homosexuals or drug users, categories that are high-risk for AIDS, and, if so, had they tested the blood before putting it out for transfusions. Petroff won $800,000. There was another notable case for a man who came out of a Dallas saloon tipsy and fell over a ledge while waiting for a valet to bring his car. The sealed settlement that Petroff obtained for the widow contained an impressive number of zeros.

Then along came breast implants, and as is true of innumerable lawyers, Petroff made a good amount of money.

But the arduous hours contributed to the breakup of his marriage, leaving him even more time to work. "If I'm not with my three kids, I'm working," he told me.

But "by the mid-1990s, these [breast implant] cases were becoming essentially unwinnable. Jurors weren't giving the kind of verdicts they had earlier; they were beginning to doubt whether implants caused real damage to women. I disagree with them, but what the hell, I'm not a juror, I don't have a vote."

Just at the right time, a woman for whom Petroff had won a sizable implant verdict called to ask a favor. She had a friend with a bad back who was told to take fen-phen to shed twenty to thirty pounds or face corrective surgery. A doctor kept her on the pills for two or three months, rather than the six weeks considered safe. The woman had seen media stories about their dangerous side effects, and she was scared. Her heart "just didn't feel right," and she thought the pills were responsible. Would Petroff talk with her?

"Send her over," Petroff said, and within forty-eight hours he had a new specialty. He filed suits on behalf of that woman and one of her friends. He also did something else important. "Having done the breast implant circuit, I knew the value of publicity. So I wrote a memo describing the cases and faxed it to the *Dallas Morning News* and several of the local TV stations, saying, 'If you are interested, call me.' Well, when I looked up, I had two camera crews and a *Dallas News* reporter in my office. The stories ran, and the clients came in droves. I knew exactly what I was doing, and it worked."

AN AUTHOR'S INTERLUDE

When I first spoke with Petroff, in April of 1999, he had been working more than a year on fen-phen and had settled only two cases. His investment in out-of-pocket expenses, not to mention time, was what he estimated "in the high six figures, so high that I don't want to think about it." He faced the risk of his individual suits somehow being lumped into the federal class action in Philadelphia, which meant that his reimbursement could be minuscule. There was also the danger that he would not be able to prove that any of the drug manufacturers misbehaved, and hence see a wholesale dismissal of the cases.

Petroff decided to gamble. He laid out for me exactly what he intended to prove should the cases ever go to a jury—and what evidence he would be presenting to defense lawyers if he tried to negotiate out-of-court settlements. He also outlined what defenses he expected to be presented. His level of candor—and trust—was extraordinarily high for any lawyer, and especially one who was risking every cent he had earned in his lifetime on tricky scientific litigation. He knew I was concurrently interviewing lawyers involved in the class action case in Philadelphia, both for the plaintiffs and the defense. The one requirement he imposed on me was that I not tell them specifics about the talks we had.

Why did Petroff take an outsider into his confidence? Ego? Surely, to some degree, but I think that a better term is bravado. Petroff is a man with confidence in his ability as a lawyer. Other better-known, and far wealthier, plaintiff lawyers would scoff at him as a blowhard and a novice. But, in the end, as we shall explore, Kip Petroff beat the odds—and the manufacturers—in overwhelming fashion.

FIRST OUT OF THE GATE

In any event, the defendant in Petroff's first round of cases was American Home Products and its subsidiary that actually made the pills, Wyeth-Ayerst Laboratories, located outside Philadelphia. To ensure that he could keep the cases in Texas state courts, rather than have AHP move it to federal court, Petroff also sued the physicians who prescribed the pills. Ironically, the woman's health improved once she got off the diet pills, and Petroff eventually dropped the suit. No problem; by this time, he had more than a dozen other cases. Keeping the suits in state court also meant that Petroff could fend off attempts to fold them into a multiplaintiff class action, as was done with thousands of other cases, as we shall explore.

Petroff also decided on an audacious gamble. "We had not gotten even into the first phases of discovery, but we put our hands on letters to physicians that had been written by a fellow named Dr. Marc Deitch, who was the senior medical officer for Wyeth labs. We decided to go ahead and depose him without the documents I knew we would eventually receive. Why? Well, we wanted to get to him before the defense lawyers had their game plan in place. We thought at that point that they [AHP] might even resort to telling the truth, which would be a novel thing to do.

"Deitch was also a senior guy. Whatever he said would be on behalf of the company. I wanted to get him on the record so that AHP would be stuck with what he said. The defense lawyers shook their heads and said, in effect, 'You guys are crazy, going into this without the documents.'"

Petroff heard some snickers from other plaintiff lawyers. As he states, "Some big-name plaintiff lawyers were accusing me of being a 'cowboy who doesn't know what he is doing.' By the time we finished, they were saying, 'Well, you guys are not as dumb as you looked.'"

Texas court rules helped. Petroff's lead suit was before Judge Fred Davis, who sits in Fort Worth, thirty miles west of Dallas, and who believes in running his docket at green-flag speed. Whenever Wyeth lawyers tried to stall the Deitch deposition, Judge Davis slapped them down.

Deitch was also an important figure because Wyeth had used him as a public spokesman, on television and elsewhere, when the FDA cracked down on diet pills. In a statement posted on the Wyeth Web site after the first critical *New England Journal of Medicine* article in 1997, Deitch commented, "From the beginning, we have been educating health care providers and their patients that Redux is serious medicine for a serious condition—obesity. It is not to be used for cosmetic weight loss." Deitch also maintained that since the FDA had approved the drugs, Wyeth had done nothing wrong.

But under strong questioning by Petroff over two days in March 1998, Deitch was forced to admit that medical people in the company had worries about the health effects of the pills, but that these fears were pushed aside because of their profitability. This admission proved to be a key element in the litigation.

Petroff came away happy. "We cracked the case open right there," he said. He also got another welcome decision from the Fort Worth court in October when Wyeth was ordered to surrender essentially all the files it had on diet pills—scientific, promotional, financial, whatever. Under the Texas rules of civil procedure, Petroff could have rushed other Wyeth executives into depositions, as he had done with Dr. Deitch. This time he chose to wait—to see what the documents contained before he began further questioning.

Wyeth went along with his plan. On March 27, 1998, its lead Texas lawyer at the time, Kenneth J. Ferguson, of the Austin firm of Clark, Thomas & Winters, agreed to produce documents beginning on May 1. In return, Petroff would delay depositions until the summer. Ferguson wrote, "Defendants will not object to you being the attorney having the first opportunity to question each of the witnesses."

That single sentence sent Petroff and partner Bob Kisselburgh bounding ahead of other fen-phen lawyers around the country. They would not only have first look at Wyeth documents, they also had the first chance to interrogate the executives and scientists who developed and marketed the diet pills.

Thus the day late in the spring of 1998 when Petroff heard a New Jersey truck driver's thick voice announcing the arrival of the first of two eighteen-wheelers laden with Wyeth documents—papers that lawyers like to call "hot docs," or hot documents, meaning evidence of special value in litigation because they came from files of the other sides. In brief, trial lawyers can use such "hot docs" to prove what their adversaries knew, and when.

A DELUGE OF DOCUMENTS

Luckily, in preparation for litigation, Petroff had rented two floors of off-premise office space near the Tarrant County Courthouse in Fort Worth. He told the driver to dump the documents there. He and Kisselburgh, after opening a few random boxes, shook their heads in amazement. "Just imagine hundreds of thousands of pieces of paper, dumped into boxes. No code, no index, no system [of organization] that we could discern." And the driver remarked that an equal quantity would be arriving within several weeks.

So what could be done? Obviously, Petroff and Kisselburgh did not have time to examine each document personally. Then, an inspiration. Dallas law schools were breaking for summer vacation. So the partners recruited students to do the drudge work of examining what they hoped would be a treasure trove of evidence. In due course, hundreds of thousands of other documents arrived from the manufacturer Interneuron, which worked closely with American Home Products in product development. And Interneuron would be added to many of the suits as a codefendant.

According to Petroff, "At any given time, we had ten to fourteen students going through papers, pulling out each page and analyzing what it covered. We ran seminars in the office, telling them what to look for—for instance, reports of adverse reactions to the drugs, and what they were telling physicians about their use."

Kisselburgh acted as on-site supervisor for much of the summer. He remembers those weeks as a blur. His home is in the rural community of Rowlett, east of Dallas, meaning his days began and ended with a fifty-mile drive to Fort Worth. "Bob didn't complain," Petroff said. "He realized we were doing something no other lawyers were doing—we were the first to get our hands on these papers, and we were itching to find out what they contained."

What followed was the scut work of litigation—the painstaking task of going through an endless maze of paper, establishing who was responsible for what activity in the company, and what they said to one another, the potential significance of a phrase or sentence in a poorly reproduced piece of e-mail. Ultimately, far more than a million documents came into the warehouse. Of these, Petroff and Kisselburgh winnowed out perhaps 1,200 for use as trial exhibits. And, in due course, these key documents were scanned onto CDs and made available to plaintiff lawyers all over the country, contributing significantly to American Home Product's legal woes.

"WHAT DID THEY KNOW, AND WHEN?"

After frantic weeks of work on the documents, Petroff and Kisselburgh moved into depositions. "Vinson & Elkins, [one of] Wyeth's local counsel, agreed to let us have eighteen people, one day each, here in Dallas," Petroff said. "Giving us the home field advantage was in exchange for us ceasing fire for five months. Bringing in defense witnesses from as far away as Philadelphia is unheard-of in this sort of litigation. You never do that. As the plaintiff lawyer, you are always forced to go where they are. Now, of course, this is very expensive for me. So we got a big break. We started depositions in the middle of July, at the Vinson & Elkins offices here in Dallas. We had both a physical and psychological advantage. All of their witnesses, they had to fly in and stay in hotels. We were sleeping in our own beds."

There was another factor as well, which Petroff related with a smile. "There is something about being in a room with fifty other lawyers and you are the only one asking the questions." Petroff would interrogate fifteen witnesses that summer; three others were excused for various reasons. Using the hot documents as a foundation, Petroff and Kisselburgh walked the Wyeth witnesses through the story of how the company failed to give notice to the FDA, the physicians who prescribed the pills, and the patients who took them.

The process was often frustrating. One witness said at the outset that he spent fifteen hours preparing for his deposition.

"What documents did you examine?" Petroff asked.

"I don't remember," the man replied.

As Petroff would later complain at a fen-phen conference sponsored by the Association of Trial Lawyers of America, the three answers he heard time and again were, "I don't recall. I don't know. It's not my job." He spent hours trying to find someone who would acknowledge responsibility for the labels and package inserts that went with Wyeth products. The company supposedly had a "labeling committee," but only one person had ever heard of it, and no documents could be found about its work.

In essence, what trial lawyers try to determine during discovery parallels the famous Watergate questions, "What did they know, and when did they know it?" From this starting point, Petroff and Kisselburgh went in several directions, using the documents as they questioned various Wyeth witnesses. The most damning areas turned out to be early warnings that the diet pills were hurting patients, Wyeth-Ayerst's failure to pass along these warnings to physicians, and not so subtle attempts by sales people to skirt the two-month limit on their safe use.

The value of a paper trail was vividly illustrated when Petroff deposed a physician named Dr. Frederick Wilson, who was a "medical monitor" for Wyeth from 1989 to 1995. One of his duties was analyzing so-called adverse events that doctors reported to the company after prescribing Pondimin or other of its drugs. Some of what Dr. Wilson saw concerning Pondimin worried him. By law, manufacturers are obliged to include on their labels and in package inserts any information about the harmful side effects of drugs.

On June 27, 1994, Wilson wrote to a colleague: "Thank you for providing the printout on Pondimin and the increased number of pulmonary hypertension cases reported. As I mentioned to you last week, I have been concerned that our approved labeling contained only four cases when in fact, we have a total of 37 reports in addition to those mentioned in the labeling. I will draft a suggested labeling revision for approval."

Wilson did as promised, but the revised label languished on the desk of Dr. Marc Deitch, Wyeth's director of medical affairs. Deitch scrawled a note on the bottom of the form that there was a "need to discuss implications [relating] to dexfenfluramine before proceeding." The label was not changed.

In February 1995, the documents showed, Wyeth received another cluster of ten reports of damage to heart valves from doctors prescribing Pondimin. Petroff asked Wilson if he ever considered whether the heart problems stemmed from Pondimin.

"No, I guess I didn't," Wilson replied.

Did he do any research to see if there was a relationship?

"I guess it never occurred to me to do that."

"The tragedy is that a cardiologist is sitting in an office three doors down the hallway from Wilson," Petroff complained. "But he never walked down to ask the fellow whether these cases might have anything to do with the diet pills. Those reports were a wake-up call for Wyeth, and they dropped the ball."

In 1997 Dr. Wilson was in the process of retiring, to be replaced by a woman named Dr. Kelly Davis, who had joined Wyeth in January. Petroff described her as "young and smart, and ready to do her job." Among other things, she went through the adverse event reports, and some three months into her new job she expressed doubts about the adequacy of the Pondimin package insert. On April 9, she sent a memo to colleague Patricia M. Acri stating, "Under adverse reactions, I am concerned that the list seems to be very brief, certainly much less extensive than the Redux label. Has this section been updated as safety . . . data has come in over the years? At the very least, it should include CHF, cardiac valvular disease, but I'm sure there are others."

Dr. Davis then searched the adverse reaction database and found no fewer than ninety-three reports, most of them from Europe, that she felt should be added to the Pondimin package insert. Most of these had been reported years earlier. Wyeth's position was that since pulmonary hypertension was listed on the label as a possible side effect, it had no obligation to report the non-U.S. cases.

Two physicians who prescribed Pondimin would tell Petroff and Kisselburgh during depositions that they would not have given the pills to patients if these ninety-three adverse reactions had been listed on the package insert.

Petroff asked Dr. Wilson directly, "Do you agree with me that these were adverse reactions that under the federal regulations were required to be listed in the product labeling?"

"Yes," Dr. Wilson replied.

As Petroff commented, "There you have negligent failure to warn, right out of his own mouth." But twenty-five months would pass between Dr. Wilson's first warning, in June 1994, and the actual change of the label. During that period, Petroff estimated that "at least three million people had taken the drug, with Wyeth running up profits of more than $50 million."

Why did Wyeth resist changing the label? From 1994 to 1996, another manufacturer, Interneuron Pharmaceuticals, of Lexington, Massachusetts, was attempting to obtain FDA approval of a pill, dexfenfluramine, that would form the "fen" portion of the fen-phen combination. American Home Products intended to market the drug under the name Redux. Petroff postulates—and offers considerable circumstantial supporting evidence—that Wyeth did not want to change the Pondimin label to show increased health risks because of concerns that doing so might cause the FDA to give closer attention to Redux. As Petroff notes, "the Pondimin label was not changed until *after* the FDA approved Redux."

There was considerable unease among Interneuron officials when they took Redux to the FDA for approval. Many papers obtained by Petroff suggest that an overriding concern was to be stingy with information given to the agency. The application listed 132 PPH cases associated with the drug. People in the company clearly were edgy. One memo stated, "Now that a steady flow (stream? river?) of international serious reports has begun . . . we've been talking about [the] reportability of them."

Several FDA scientists had so many qualms about safety that they proposed a Draconian measure: requiring what is known as a "black box" label stressing the risks of PPH. As Petroff explains, "The black box is literally just that—a box intended to focus your attention on something that is important. Physicians and pharmacists know that they should pay serious attention to anything put in a black box."

Wyeth-Ayerst lawyer Sheila Connor, perhaps mindful that women used most of the pills, urged superiors to accept the FDA's black box recommendation. One of these persons, Joseph Sonk, who ran Wyeth's women's health division, wrote a memo stating "SC [Sheila Connor] strongly favors black box." Connor was ignored.

Wyeth did not get around to modifying the label until June 1996. By that time, the FDA had approved Redux, so a crisis was averted. Petroff commented, "There was a note, one of those yellow stickum things on an internal paper, we found going to May 1995. Marc Deitch had written that they needed 'answer to discuss implications re: dexfenfluramine before proceeding.' That told the whole story. Deitch would claim later in his deposition that they wanted to have the Pondimin and Redux labels read the same. My point is that if Wyeth had changed the label, as its own people were urging, the FDA panel studying Redux would have been put on notice that something was amiss. The bottom line is that Wyeth did not want the FDA to start asking questions about all these new cases of pulmonary hypertension while the jury was still out on Redux."

There was further circumstantial evidence that Wyeth-Ayerst lawyers were wary of the company making statements that could not be supported by science. Petroff found a paper headed, "Standby Statement and Q and A for Wyeth-Ayerst Laboratories," to be given to physicians who prescribed Pondimin. One sentence read, "Pondimin has been used safely and effectively . . ." A slash of the attorney's pen removed the word "safely." Elsewhere, the lawyer objected to the word "safe," scrawling in the margin, "Can't say this. . . . Don't use the word safe or safely in an unqualified fashion."

Interneuron officials on occasion were candid in telling the FDA the importance of Redux. An FDA memo summarized a phone conversation in which Interneuron told an agency safety officer that "withdrawal, from a financial standpoint, was really out of question because the company would be ruined." Still later, according to yet another FDA memo, the same person stated that Interneuron had "nothing to lose and would stop at nothing to get dexfenfluramine [Redux] approved." The position of both Wyeth and Interneuron, according to internal memos, was that a stronger warning label would cause "public panic" and hurt sales.

The discovery documents show that Interneuron's concerns caused the company to turn to powerful friends for help. One ally was Sen. Edward M. Kennedy who persuaded seven colleagues to join him in writing a letter urging the FDA to let the pills made by his home-state company be sold. Kennedy's role miffed lawyers at Public Citizen, the public interest law group founded by Ralph Nader, which was working to block FDA approval of Redux. One of these lawyers told me, "We expected more of Teddy Kennedy. His office's excuse was that Interneuron was a Massachusetts company. Well, a helluva lot of women hurt by fen-phen live in Massachusetts also."

Interneuron also sought the help of Rep. Tom Lantos (D., Calif.)—specifically, to force the FDA to bar public health advocates from an FDA meeting where the black box label would be discussed. Interneuron wanted the issue to be discussed only by friendly witnesses, not by outside experts who might ask tough questions. Lantos set up a meeting in his office in February 1997, and the pesky outsiders were banned. Why Lantos's interest? Alicia Mundy wrote in *U.S. News & World Report,* "A review of political contributions show that officials of Interneuron, including its board chairman, CEO, and some of their wives, contributed to Lantos and his son-in-law former Rep. Dick Swett, for whom Lantos was raising funds in 1996 and 1997." Lantos's press agent told Mundy that the congressman "did not remember" the event.

Whatever the role of political clout, the companies won, and an internal Wyeth memo boasted the next day, "The meeting with FDA yesterday was a tremendous success! No black box!" (The political maneuvering was for naught. Within months, the FDA ordered a recall of the drugs, and the manufacturers faced a tidal wave of litigation.)

From the legal standpoint, in Petroff's view, these documents were "very useful to help prove that failure to warn resulted in the client receiving a dangerous drug. The package insert or product label is probably the most critical subject area for debate in a pharmaceutical product liability case. The manufacturer can frequently win a case by proving that it gave full, complete, and thorough warnings concerning the very illness, injury, or disease that the plaintiff suffers from as a result of the drugs."

Wyeth's dilemma, and that of Interneuron as well, was that they were reaping millions of dollars of profits from fen-phen. And in terms of sheer corporate dishonesty, little can be found to rival Wyeth's use of medical journals to encourage use of fen-phen for periods far beyond what regulatory authorities—and the company's own scientists—considered to be safe.

"A PROFESSIONAL COURTESY"

One of Wyeth-Ayerst's defenses, when the FDA pressured fen-phen off the market, was that physicians who prescribed the drugs ignored warnings about use for more than two months. In other words, the doctors, not the manufacturer, were to blame for any women who were harmed. But Petroff discovered that this contention stopped considerably short of the truth. One covey of documents showed how Wyeth used winks and nods to encourage long-term use of the pills, regardless of warnings on the labeling.

Two of these documents were letters written by Dr. Jennifer Beamish, Wyeth's manager for drug information. These ostensibly were letters to weight-control specialists "in response to your request for information regarding Pondimin. . . . We understand you are particularly interested in studies on the long-term use of fenfluramine for weight control." Petroff and other lawyers found many physicians who said they never requested such information, but received the letter anyway. Dr. Beamish continued, "As Pondimin is not indicated for long-term use in weight control, we cannot recommend such use."

But Dr. Beamish's next sentence began with the word "however"—"a damned big 'however,'" Petroff raged—and went on to summarize research papers on use of the pills for as long as twelve months. She enclosed eleven of the papers—seven of them written by the same researcher, Dr. Michael Weintraub, published in 1992. Dr. Beamish concluded, "The enclosed information is supplied as a professional courtesy *in response to your inquiry.* [*sic,* emphasis added.] It is intended to provide pertinent data to assist you in forming your own conclusions and making decisions. The information is not intended to advocate any indication, dosage or other claim that is not covered in the enclosed package insert material."

Petroff read these lines to me and underlined them with an angry stroke of his pen. "What hypocrisy!" he exclaimed. "What they are saying is although we can't recommend usage beyond two months, here are studies saying you can do just that! Why the hell else would Wyeth send out such a letter?"

The sub rosa campaign apparently succeeded. Dr. JoAlene Dolan (a nonphysician) of Wyeth acknowledged that the studies done by Dr. Weintraub helped in marketing Pondimin. On July 12, 1995, she wrote a memo commenting on a "Prelaunch Marketing Plan" for Redux, which still awaited FDA approval. Dr. Dolan commented, "Sales of Pondimin are already much higher in 1995 than they were in 1994, showing the increasing trend based on the results of the Weintraub study."

Another series of documents showed how AHP and Wyeth-Ayerst inspired favorable publicity for the pills in publications directed at physicians. Consider the provenance of an article entitled "Current Views on Obesity," which appeared in the February 1996 issue of the *American Journal of Medicine* (not to be confused with the *Journal of the American Medical Association*). Wyeth distributed the article widely during the pill craze. It bore the byline of Dr. Albert J. Stunkard, of the Weight and Eating Disorders Program at the University of Pennsylvania Medical School in Philadelphia. Readers did not know the full story.

In the article, Dr. Stunkard noted that one objection to diet pills was that once the patient stopped using them, "weight rebounds to pretreatment levels." He continued, "Newer findings . . . suggest that appetite-suppressant medication should be used on a long-term basis or not at all." In the same paragraph, Dr. Stunkard repeated the argument, citing studies "reinforcing the view that medication should be used on a long-term basis or not at all." One of the drugs he listed was Wyeth's Pondimin.

"Where do you think this 'objective' article came from?" Petroff asked me. "When we got into the Wyeth documents, we discovered it was prepared by an outfit named Excerpta Medica, which owns the *American Journal of Medicine*. Wyeth pays $20,000 to have the article written, and then Excerpta Medica finds a physician who will sign off on it and gives him a $1,500 honorarium. Nowhere in the article is it revealed that Wyeth paid money for it to be written. For Wyeth's purposes, the article is golden because it is not connected to Wyeth. So, if they are challenged, they can say, 'What the hell—we had nothing to do with it.' A doctor on the street reads this and he says, 'Hmmm, this is a reputable doctor at the University of Pennsylvania; this isn't a guy at a one-doctor diet clinic down in Tyler, Texas."

Petroff elicited the story of Excerpta Medica from Dr. Dolan, the Wyeth executive. Dr. Dolan said she first encountered the company when she worked with another pharmaceutical manufacturer, Lederle.

"You used that company to ghostwrite articles that would be published in medical literature under someone else's name, right?" Petroff asked.

"That is correct," Dr. Dolan replied. But she quickly denied any deception. "When articles are written with, for instance, an opinion leader as the author, that opinion leader has the opportunity to review the outline, the content, the full manuscript, the references . . . the author whose name appears on the paper can be as involved as that individual wants to be in the writing of the article."

Doctors who signed other articles apparently were pleased with what was done in their names. One physician, an obesity specialist, wrote to Excerpta Medica, "Let me congratulate you and your writer on an excellent and thorough review of the literature. Clearly written. I am impressed at the level of understanding of the topic. Perhaps I can get you to write all my papers for me." The doctor did comment, "My only general comment is that this piece may make dexfenfluramine sound better than it really is."

Wyeth also commissioned—and edited—an article entitled "Treatment of Obesity in Patient with Non-Insulin-Dependent Diabetes Mellitus," signed by Drs. John W. Kennedy and Edward S. Horton, of the Joslin Diabetes Clinic in Boston. It contained the statement "Studies of obese patients treated with dexfenfluramine for as little as three months *or as long as six to twelve months* confirm the efficacy of this drug in inducing weight loss." (Emphasis added.)

Nancy J. Vobecky, Excerpta Medica's director of clinical communications, sent the Kennedy-Horton manuscript to two Wyeth-Ayerst staff members—Dr. Dolan (who is not a medical doctor) and Dr. Kelly Davis—on May 14, 1997, for review. (Copies also went to the putative authors.) Vobecky wrote that a "final draft and the submission package for *Archives of Internal Medicine*" hopefully would be ready in June.

One sentence stated that persons taking the drug "for more than three months were 23 times more likely" to develop primary pulmonary hypertension, or PPH, "a potentially fatal disorder." A swipe of the editorial pen, and the sentence was changed to read that "23 to 46 out of a million" people risk PPH by taking the pills. The incidence of PPH in the general population is one person in a million—a fact not stated in the article. Another sentence in the draft read, "Individual case reports also suggest a link between dexfenfluramine and primary pulmonary hypertension." Wyeth-Ayerst editors deleted this sentence. It is unclear whether the authors knew of the editing changes.

American Home Products earned enormous sums from diet pills—$178 million in the peak year. Since Wyeth had acquired the patents when AHP absorbed another drug company, Robbins, production costs were negligible. One Wyeth document boasted of a "97 percent profit" on sales and suggested ways of increasing even this figure. Petroff deposed the woman who wrote the memo. Isn't 97 percent a rather good rate of return? he asked.

"Oh, I don't know," she replied, "some of our drugs do even better."

READY FOR ACTION

The evidentiary record that Petroff and Kisselburgh amassed—both the depositions and the documents—could be used in repeated fen-phen trials around the country, both in their cases and in those brought by other plaintiff lawyers.

And, indeed, the first case that Petroff prepared for trial was referred by a Little Rock lawyer whom he met while speaking at a seminar on how to prepare a fen-phen case. The Arkansan related a sad case. He had a client, Mary Perez, a day care center operator who took Pondimin for three months in an effort to lose twenty-five pounds. Now she was dying of primary pulmonary hypertension, or PPH. Petroff met the woman and her family. What especially distressed him was that she had a daughter the same age as one of his children. Petroff signed on as co-counsel.

Mrs. Perez's condition worsened over the months. Eventually, her medications bill reached $500 a day, with a catheter constantly feeding drugs into her heart. She and her husband had to declare bankruptcy and close their day care center. A doctor specializing in PPH wrote an affidavit declaring, "She is currently at risk of dying suddenly without warning. . . . It is my opinion that she is at significant risk to die the next year."

Wyeth lawyers had reason to worry about the Perez case.

They knew what documents Petroff had obtained, and the often-damaging deposition testimony he had elicited from its executives. They also were acutely aware of Petroff's ability to churn up favorable publicity for his clients. In February 1999, with the trial date a bit more than a month away, he and Mrs. Perez went on the CBS newsmagazine show *60 Minutes II* and discussed her case. Having this wheezing, gasping woman tell her story to a jury could be financially deadly.

So Wyeth folded. Six days before the trial was to open, Wyeth made a settlement offer that the Perez family felt they could not refuse. Wyeth, however, did exact a price: The agreement forbade anyone to disclose the terms. Bloomberg News Service in a matter of days reported that the amount was in the neighborhood of $4.5 million.

A month later, one of Petroff's Fort Worth cases was ready for trial; this one, too, settled, a few weeks before my first visit with Petroff in Dallas in April 1999. The *Dallas Morning News* put the amount at half a million dollars. Was that figure, and the one reported in the Perez case, anywhere near the truth? Petroff threw up his arms in frustration. "Look," he said, "I can't talk about the money, but if you consider Bloomberg and the *Dallas News* to be reliable sources, I can't stop you." I shan't speculate on how the figures became public. But the "disclosure," even if unofficial, did serve the purpose of setting a "market price" for future fen-phen cases.

As is true of most trial lawyers, Petroff did not like settling cases under a seal of confidentiality. Potential jurors read newspapers and watch television, and revelations about corporate misconduct have a cumulative effect upon their judgments. Petroff also feels that companies such as Wyeth should be held publicly accountable for their actions. Realize also that much of the material in the preceding pages had not been publicly disclosed at the time of the initial settlements. Petroff also had other nasty stuff tucked away in his sleeve, ready to be used if and when he came to an actual trial. And, of course, publicity brings in clients, who are, after all, the lifeblood of a trial lawyer.

Petroff's position of strength was that the defendant corporations and their lawyers knew he was ready for trial. During our first visit he ticked off his schedule for the summer of 1999—four cases on track for trial, at six-week intervals. He had a hundred or so cases in his inventory, all, in his estimate, "big-bucks cases, not junk." He did not want the thousands that are claimed by such fen-phen specialists as Paul Rheingold of New York. "We are ready to try these cases, one after another. Other lawyers can have their hundreds or thousands of cases. That number is impossible to manage. We have cases we can handle, and the judges know it—and more importantly, so do the defense lawyers."

I played devil's advocate. What kind of defenses did Petroff expect if he ever got into a courtroom? Lawyers for AHP had been telling me that fen-phen was "breast implants revisited," a few scattered cases of harm blown totally out of proportion by attorneys and the media. Come on, I told Petroff, are not some of these fatties prone to sickness and heart disease because of their obesity? How do you intend to answer that?

Petroff rejoined, "No proof exists that being obese causes valvular heart disease. Period. Let me tell you what makes these damned pills even worse. The company's own literature says that weight loss would be less than a pound a week. Assume that you lose nine-tenths of pound for twelve weeks—that's less than eleven pounds. So what do you get in return? A twenty-three-fold increase in the risk of developing primary pulmonary hypertension. I am not saying *23 percent,* mind you, but *twenty-three times the risk!"*

Based on what defense lawyers had been arguing in preliminary hearings, and in their court filings, Petroff expected to hear claims that diseases such as PPH occur in high percentages of the general population, regardless of whether the person took diet pills. His voice dropped several octaves as he mimicked their argument: "Eight out of ten of you in this room have some degree of heart regurgitation. . . . This lady with mild valvular regurgitation could pass a physical for an NCAA college basketball team or for a navy fighter pilot.

"They are claiming that, A, there is basically nothing wrong with her, and, B, that valvular regurgitation [a symptom of PPH] had been out there forever but was not detected until the development a few years ago of a new screening test called the Doppler echocardiogram. Nonsense. I say it again—use the stuff for more than two months, and your risk of PPH increases twenty-three-fold."

Petroff was pacing the floor now, and I could hear him summoning the rage that makes for a good closing argument as he went through the other anticipated defenses.

"They say, 'Well, the FDA approved the diet pills.' Yeah, the FDA did just that. But we now know that Wyeth withheld information about the adverse effects of these pills.

"They say, 'Look at our packaging notices. They make plain that these pills are for short-term use.' That's not the whole story. Look at all the other stuff they put out about long-term use—those letters telling doctors 'Here is some other literature, make up your own mind. Ignore what the government requires us to tell you.' "

So how was American Home Products going to succeed in getting Petroff off the back of its Wyeth-Ayerst subsidiary?

"Pay me," he said. "There is talk about striking a deal. The problem is that they can't make a deal with me that says I will never take another case, that I won't keep coming back at them time and again every time some woman injured by their pills comes to me. It's not legally enforceable."

Petroff knew that I had also been interviewing lawyers handling the separate class action case in federal court in Philadelphia. As I gathered up my tape recorder and notepads and a thick stack of documents he was giving to me, Petroff showed a mischievous grin.

"Do me a favor," he said. "Tell those yo-yos in Philadelphia to get off their comfortable, well-padded asses and try a case in court. Some of their claimed clients are dying without receiving a dime. Let them come to Texas and I'll teach them how to run a lawsuit."

I did as requested, and the reaction was what I expected: up-turned noses and sneers at the upstart. But there was also a strong undercurrent of resentment, for Petroff and other lawyers push-ing individual cases threatened to scuttle any hopes for a negoti-ated settlement that would put hundreds of millions of dollars into these attorneys' pockets. Let us now shift to Philadelphia, the other front of the fen-phen wars.

The Class Action Club

The fifteenth of January 1998, a Thursday, was one of those es-pecially nasty days that make many people avoid Philadelphia in the wintertime. A gusty wet wind swirled up Market Street from the Delaware River, half a dozen blocks to the east, strong enough to stir the sodden rubbish on the curbs. Dirty remnants of a days-ago snowstorm clung to the fringes of the sidewalk outside the United States Courthouse.

The limousines and rented town cars began arriving about 9:30 A.M., discharging a seemingly endless procession of men and women with briefcases. Most were well coiffed and well shod and, on the part of the men, well fed, all past their fortieth birthdays, protected from the biting cold by an array of expensive coats— camel hair, fur collars, the occasional rebel in a thigh-length parka. The distinctive aura of affluence seemed to form around them as they walked the few feet to the revolving doors, joshing and exchanging greetings. Behind them trailed much younger men and women whose arms strained under the weight of the outsized briefcases known to law firm associates everywhere as "hernia bags"—cases large enough to hold a two-foot stack of legal briefs.

The elite of America's class action bar, along with numerous wannabes, were assembling for the first round of what many of them were saying could be the "biggest one ever," the fen-phen class action case. Jostling for position in line and exchanging friendly jibes, the dozens of lawyers filtered through the security gate and rode the elevators upstairs.

By ten A.M. more than a hundred lawyers had trailed into the undistinguished eighth-floor courtroom of U.S. District Judge Louis Bechtle, sloughing off overcoats and stowing their brief-cases under the benches. A relative handful of defense lawyers sat in their own side of the court, their role today that of observers rather than active participants.

Underlying the disorder was a feeling of tension—big-money tension. Today's business was for lawyers to request appointment to what is called the Plaintiffs Management Committee, or PMC, the group that would oversee the litigation. As one lawyer would comment to me later, "Being named to the PMC is equivalent to being given a license to print your own money. These people are going to walk away with millions and millions of dollars for a relatively short period of work." As John Coffee, the Columbia law professor, has commented, "Predictably, an attorney who is granted membership on the steering committee that runs the plaintiffs' side of the action will be more highly compensated than an attorney who simply conducts discovery for the plain-tiffs' team—even in the unlikely event that both work an equiva-lent number of billable hours. In effect, plaintiff attorneys engage in a two-front career battle: they wish both to be recog-nized and respected by their adversaries (because this affects set-tlement negotiations) and to achieve status within the fluid world of the plaintiffs' bar (because this predictably enables them to a more senior position on the plaintiffs' team.) Winning a publi-cized victory can be the best route to both ends."

What happened Philadelphia that day, and in subsequent proceedings, highlighted several important developments in American law in recent decades. First is the sharp cleavage in the plaintiff bar between lawyers such as Kip Petroff, who prefer to pursue cases on an individual basis, and those who prefer the class action route. Second is the development of a coterie of in-sider lawyers—the Class Action Club, as they informally call themselves—who dominate class action litigation. The fen-phen case illustrates the reluctance of an American corporation, re-gardless of the wealth in its coffers, to risk its very survival by de-fending products that its executives insist are safe. David Bernick, of the big Chicago defense firm of Kirkland & Ellis, is known as a lawyer who plays hardball when it comes to defending clients he feels have done no wrong; he is not a man who bails out of cases. But even Bernick states, "There comes a time when a corporation is foolish to 'bet the store' in a courtroom. If you look down the road and see a potential disaster awaiting you, get out of the case. Whether you are in the right is irrelevant."

Finally, fen-phen calls into question whether the supposed victims of an imperfect product are given proper financial relief—or whether a disproportionate share goes to lawyers, many of whom never meet an actual plaintiff face-to-face.

I began watching fen-phen with as open a mind as I could muster. And what I saw in succeeding months, as the dual-track litigation progressed, left me with grave doubts about the efficacy of the judicial system. One of my early qualms—it proved a continuing one—concerned Judge Bechtle.

"A MINIMUM OF SIX MILLION PRESCRIPTIONS"

After introducing his clerks, Judge Bechtle opened by doing something that lawyers would grouse about for months. He exercised his authority to name Philadelphia lawyer Arnold Levin, of Levin, Fishbein, Sedran & Berman, as "liaison counsel" with the other attorneys, essentially putting the hearing in his hands, and implicitly signaling that at least one Plaintiffs' Management Committee member would not be forced to audition for his seat.

Levin has an interesting approach to occupying a chair. He sprawls, rather than sits, ample belly thrust skyward, suit jacket hanging from his shoulders, his face locked in a permanent, somewhat petulant scowl. Invariably he was alongside Stanley Chesley of Cincinnati; at first glance the men are near twins in physical appearance, although the latter's hair is a bit whiter.

Permanently established to their right was Elizabeth Cabraser of San Francisco, an elfin woman in her fifties with a penchant for short black skirts and black tights. She stands a shade less than five feet tall and is far less than half the weight of either Levin or Chesley. Gender alone makes Cabraser's presence unusual, for women remain relatively rare among the big-name class action attorneys.

But my thoughts came back to Levin and Judge Bechtle, and some history between the men that was already the subject of corridor gossip. Levin was on the PMC of another massive class action that was winding down in Judge Bechtle's court, one involving medical screws used in facial surgery. Levin negotiated a settlement that was happily accepted by the defendant company, even if it left some of his critics in the plaintiff bar most unhappy. Their complaint was that he had permitted the defendant, a company called Acromed, to get away with a claim that it had borrowing power of about $100 million and thus its ability to pay damages beyond that amount was limited. Acromed got its settlement, and within months was sold for $325 million. Although none would speak on the record, two lawyers suggested that Levin goofed. "Arnie blew it," one of them insisted. "He should have gotten deeper into Acromed's books. Sure, he had witnesses who supported Acromed's financial claims."

Judge Bechtle's role in the case also drew criticism, perhaps unjustifiably so. Some lawyers felt that the judge pressed overly hard for a settlement, however flawed it might be. One of the many unspoken secrets of the federal judicial system is the degree of pressure put on trial judges—meaning those at the district court level—to dispose of multiplaintiff class action cases. From whence does the pressure come? A federal judge brought up the question himself during a discussion of class actions, and proceeded to answer it. "We're talking [Chief Justice William] Rehnquist," the judge said. "The Chief doesn't like seeing the system clogged up with cases where you have thousands and thousands of plaintiffs. When you attend judicial conferences you get the message. Bechtle's strength is that he will push these cases along to settlement. He knows how to handle them. And it goes without saying that if he can work with a plaintiff lawyer who is experienced, he is much happier." Thus Bechtle was happy to give the leadership role to Levin, whom he trusted.

Against this backdrop, there were both grins and hushed

murmurs of dissent when Levin arose to speak. He recognized that dozens of lawyers were hoping to get into the case. They "have been told that this is not a beauty contest. If you don't have to speak, nobody will think less of you." He added, "They are not bashful, and they know, at least, what they think they want." Levin was properly deferential to the judge. He had become liaison counsel simply so that the plaintiff lawyers could "share our views with you. This in no way is intended to tell an experienced multidistrict litigation federal judge how to run a case or what to do."

"It should be," Bechtle agreed.

Roger Brosnahan of Minneapolis gave the background on how the plaintiff bar had come together to pursue the class action. "Your Honor, over the last months, and indeed, in some cases over several years, a group of traditional plaintiff lawyers have met and corresponded concerning this diet pill litigation, and more recently have had several meetings involving representatives of over thirty-five law firms throughout the country. In that process, we have been sharing our research with regard to the scientific and medical literature, the nature of the injuries, the liability issues, the potential defendants, and the procedural issues."

What Brosnahan did not mention was the relatively limited group of lawyers included in these discussions. Put most directly, the coalition paid no attention to lawyers such as Kip Petroff, who intended to litigate their cases one at a time. Nor did the group include Paul Rheingold, whose advertising campaign that enabled him to obtain hundreds of clients had been featured in a front-page article in the *Wall Street Journal* less than three months earlier. Rheingold felt that he was being unjustifiably excluded. "They knew what I had been doing; they simply wanted to grab control of the entire litigation," Rheingold would tell me later.

Rheingold did not like the idea of lumping cases into a class action, but, as he said of that January morning, "It didn't take a lot of brains to see which way the wind was blowing." In court, he began by acknowledging, correctly, that he was not a member of the inner club of the class action bar. Nonetheless, he felt he deserved a seat at the table. "I have quite a stake in this litigation by virtue of having approximately three thousand cases, which is not unusual, having talked to some other lawyers out there. By virtue of that stake, I'd like to actively see these cases prepared in a way that those lawyers who have a stake in it do this work."

Rheingold worried that "eventually we'll go to American Home Products and get them to give us a lump sum of money. There will be a global settlement. Global settlement means that the severely injured people, those with PPH and other fatal diseases, will get fifty cents on a dollar because there's only so much money to go around, and the other fifty cents are going to pay people with trivial injuries. . . . [W]e have a large number of plaintiffs who have a fifty-fifty chance of dying in a relatively short period of time from this . . . disease." Rheingold urged that the litigation focus on American Home Products, the major manufacturer, and resolve the cases in short order to benefit persons who were dying.

So how many persons are involved? Judge Bechtle asked.

Stanley Chesley replied, "There are a minimum of six million prescriptions, and that's debatable. . . . So that's a reality that we need to think about."

Gayle Troutwine, who made millions in breast implant cases with husband Mike Williams in Portland (they later divorced and she quit law), saw a feminist issue. Of the two and a half to four million persons she estimated took diet pills, 85 percent were women. "So once again," she said, "we have a mass disaster that has substantially affected women substantially more than men."

But how were some of the second-tier defendants to be located? J. Michael Rediker of Birmingham said that some of his clients obtained pills by a prescription. "There are thousands of women, we believe, that never got a prescription. They just got a bottle with a label on it that had their name, didn't say what was in it."

But was too much being made out of the cases? Peter L. Zimroth, of the New York office of Arnold & Porter, was one of several lawyers in court to defend American Home Products. Zimroth challenged the assumption that thousands of persons suffered serious injuries. He said, "Your Honor, the pleadings that we've seen so far just don't bear it out. . . . Most of the pleadings are pretty much 'notice pleadings,' people who say they are afraid of this or that."

As the day wore to a close Judge Bechtle invited lawyers who wanted to be on the Plaintiffs' Management Committee to send him a résumé. He warned, "It should be understood that whether we like it or not, the persons who will be serving will be expected to commit a considerable amount of time. . . . And that can get to be a problem of resources, financial and otherwise, because usually such persons are not compensated for this work on a committee, if they are going to be compensated. It's likely in this case that they will be, in a fair and equitable way."

On February 5 Bechtle appointed the committee, with Arnold Levin, Stanley Chesley, and John Cummings as coliaison counsel. The others were all seasoned veterans of massive class actions: Roger Brosnahan; Elizabeth Cabraser; Michael D. Hausfeld of Washington, D.C.; Will Kemp of Las Vegas; Dianne M. Nast of Lancaster, Pennsylvania; and Darryl Tschin of La Jolla, California. In his formal order, Bechtle said:

> The court has appointed the named persons because of the expectation of their personal contribution to the work of the PMC and to the furtherance of the MDL portion of the litigation. For this reason, the court will look to the individual members to satisfy the goals that the court expects the PMC to achieve. The court will likewise consider the contribution of each of the PMC members when the court is called upon to distribute appropriate compensation for service on the PMC.

Judge Bechtle's order covered some areas that are frequently contentious. He ordered that "counsel are expected to cooperate with, and be courteous to, each other and deponents." He warned against "unnecessary attendance by counsel" at deposition. He expected periodic—and detailed—reports of what the

Plaintiffs' Management Committee was spending on the litigation. He gave the lawyers thirty days to decide on how the work would be divided, and ordered monthly status hearings, either in his court or by conference calls.

The litigation now was on two tracks: the individual cases being waged by such lawyers as Petroff, and the class action. But what intrigued me at the moment was why certain lawyers were given control of the class action phase.

SOCCER MOM—SUPER LITIGATOR

So how does one become a member of the Class Action Club and share in the largest pools of money available to lawyers in the United States? For a tutorial on the select group, I drove north from Washington into the Pennsylvania Dutch Country, to the Lancaster offices of Dianne Nast. Both the woman and her offices are unique. For months I had been interviewing lawyers in high-rise buildings in New York, Chicago, Dallas, San Diego, and elsewhere. The firm of Roda & Nast, conversely, occupies a stand-alone two-story building in a small office park opposite a shopping center on the outskirts of a town with a population of perhaps 85,000.

The differences extend to Nast physically. The first time I saw her in person, in federal court in Philadelphia, the thought flickered through my mind, "She looks like a soccer mom." Indeed she does. She is a pleasant woman with dark hair, with none of the excessive confidence—arrogance, even—of the post-fifties males who were also in court. She has the ability to poke fun at herself, something rather rare among trial lawyers. Her body language exudes energy. She is seemingly incapable of remaining still, even when munching a salad at the Lancaster Country Club. Her memory is strikingly precise. Several times when I chatted with her in Lancaster, she would hark back to something we had discussed earlier in Philadelphia and say, in effect, "I know we dealt with this earlier, but something else important came to mind." And she would proceed to give details on some subject that had fallen into the crevices of my memory.

Further, Nast is a woman who achieved her rating as one of America's top lawyers—female or otherwise—while at the same time raising five children. How did she do it? "Well," she said, "let's just say that I had a darned good support system."

AN AUTHOR'S INTERLUDE

Given that a dozen or so other plaintiff lawyers played seminal roles in the fen-phen class action, why do I choose to focus on Dianne Nast? My reasons are several. But paramount among them is Nast's demonstration of how the role of women in American lawyering has undergone a sea change the last quarter century.

How far have women come in gaining acceptance in the practice of law? Given that Nast resides in Pennsylvania, and does much of her work there, a local anecdote is illustrative. In 1871 a woman named Carrie Burnham applied to the University of Pennsylvania law school. Dean E. Spencer Miller venomously rejected her, writing, "I do not know what the Board of Trustees will do, but as for me, if they admit a woman I will resign for I will neither lecture to niggers nor women." A few years earlier, another dean, George Templeton Strong, of Columbia University, stormed, "No woman shall degrade herself by practicing law, in N.Y. especially, if I can save her."

The turnaround has been staggering. Women now make up almost 30 percent of all U.S. lawyers; some 40 percent of law school graduates are women. More than half the students entering American law schools the autumn of 2004 were women, according to the National Association of Law Placements. And women as of this writing were managing partners of such firms as Pillsbury, Madison & Sutro, in San Francisco; Baker & McKenzie and Mayer, Brown & Platt, of Chicago; and Hughes, Hubbard & Reed of New York. Although discriminatory glitches still exist, as witness sex bias cases that bedevil both large and small firms, the profession has made truly awesome strides toward sexual equality. To me, Nast epitomizes how the change has come about. The original outline for this book called for a chapter on women in law. I changed my mind. Lumping certain lawyers into a chapter simply because of their sex perpetuates discrimination.

I have yet another reason for focusing on Nast. She was the most personal, and human, member of the Plaintiffs' Management Committee. Egos can bother me, especially when they are not supported by commensurate talent. Suffice it to say that when speaking with certain PMC members, pomposity often had me grinding my teeth. Nast posed no such problem.

THE BLUEBERRY PICKER

Things did not come easy for Dianne Nast. Her mother, the daughter of Polish immigrants, was one of eighteen children, fourteen of whom lived to adulthood. Her father was of mixed Polish and German ancestry. His father died when he was eighteen months old, and his mother, who could not speak English, took him to Poland, where they lived outside Warsaw. When he was twelve she was kicked by a horse and died; his grandparents took over his rearing. Dianne's father was in the fifth grade when soldiers walked into the school and, for reasons he could never explain, shot his teacher dead. His education ended. Thereafter he worked as a fisherman. When war neared, Polish authorities gave him two choices: Either join the Polish army, or take advantage of his U.S. citizenship and leave the country. Her father wisely opted for the latter, although he knew no English and had no family in the United States. But he did know the family of the woman who was to become his wife. Her brother met him when his ship docked, and he went to live on their farm.

The family settled in the Mount Holly area of southern New Jersey. Her father, essentially illiterate, became an ironworker. Her mother, who dropped out of school in the eleventh grade, worked as a telephone operator. (Years later, while Nast herself was in college, her mother received her high school equivalency certificate and entered college. She died before she was graduated.)

Times were tough. "When you come down to it, we were very poor. There were meatless meals. We [Nast and two younger siblings] started picking blueberries when we were eight, and when those were out of season, we did something else. We always worked." But the upside was loving parents. Her mother loved music and reading, interests she passed on to her daughter. She was close to her father. "I was supposed to be a boy. After a while, my father gave up waiting for one, and so he did all the boy things with me, such as fishing and repairing cars." When she was fifteen, her mother said she could have only one Christmas present. She asked for what was called a "visible V-8," a miniature replica of an automobile engine, the working parts visible beneath plastic. She assembled it, and her father proudly put it on the wall.

College was Pennsylvania State University, financed by student loans. That she was female, and that the women's movement was just beginning to stir, did not bother her. "I just never thought of myself being constrained because I was a woman. My father did not raise me that way." She was active on the college newspaper, and in her junior year she put in for the job of business manager. "The reply was like, 'Hey, come on, you're a woman!'" She was selected anyway, the first female to hold the job, and oversaw a budget of more than $1 million. And she was also selected as Miss Pennsylvania in the contest for "national college queen," based on brains and beauty. "One of my happiest memories of college is going to New York with some of the other state queens and appearing on the *Ed Sullivan Show*."

Nast spoke gingerly when recounting her harsh early life, and especially what happened at the next juncture, nervous about saying anything that might reflect unfavorably on her father. I got the idea that I was hearing her talk about some painful family history, for she commented, "I want my children to have the picture of this well-adjusted woman, and not this lunatic."

The sensitive point arose after graduation, when she accepted a job in Philadelphia with Bell Atlantic, one of the first women to hold a management position there. She commuted from the family home in Mount Holly, an hour drive each way. Her mother had died, and her father expected her to be the "woman of the house," and do such things as to prepare dinner every night. "I did it," she said. "I quit Bell and started taking care of him. I've often thought about what might have happened to me had I stayed with Bell—probably ended up as a corporate executive." She got a teaching job in New Jersey and thought about what to do with her life.

On college aptitude tests, she showed an affinity for law. "But I didn't perceive myself as going to law school. People from . . . my environment, just didn't do such things." Nonetheless, she decided to enter the Rutgers University School of Law and see what she could make of herself.

There was a marriage now, one that was to produce her two oldest children (and Nast made plain to me the subject was off limits). She juggled work, school, and family things for three years. Her first year she estimates that she attended only about 35 percent of her classes. She taught two and a half days a week, and there were also pickup jobs as a student law clerk for a judge and as a researcher for a professor. "I alternated cutting classes. I'd go to some courses one week, ignore them the next, switching back and forth all the time." She was graduated magna cum laude, fifth in her class.

She wanted to work in Philadelphia, but white-shoe firms there were still wary of graduates of Rutgers, which was not then in the top flight of law schools. Dechert, Price & Rhoads wouldn't let her in the door. The hiring partner at Schnader, Harrison, Segal & Lewis would be interested only if she spent a year as clerk to a federal judge, telling her, "We want all of our newcomers to clerk for a judge. So, go find a clerkship, and after a year we'll hire you."

As Nast recounts, "I couldn't afford to be a clerk, I had bills and college loans to pay off." Eventually she ended up being interviewed by a lawyer named Harold Kohn, who was in the process of revolutionizing class action litigation. (Kohn's firm would undergo many name changes over the years; at this particular time, it was known as Dilworth, Paxon, Kohn & Dilks.)

Kohn could be a foreboding man, and things did not augur well when Nast spoke with him. He gave her an appraising look across the desk and said, shaking his head, "I'm concerned about the fact that you have a family, and that you are a single parent. I don't know if you can do this job."

Nast lost it. "It was like the breaking point, after being smiley and polite during all of these interviews. I said to him, 'Mr. Kohn, I have raised two children. I have worked three jobs. I graduated fifth in my class. I think I can handle your job." Once the flash of anger passed, Nast thought to myself, "Oh, my God!"

Kohn arose and said, without a trace of a smile, "Thanks for coming in." Nast left.

A few minutes after she got back to New Jersey, Kohn telephoned. "I want you to work for me. When can you start?" he asked. Later he would tell Nast that her outburst got her hired—that if she could speak up so vigorously on her own behalf, she would do the same for clients. "That is the kind of lawyer I want around here," he said.

A CLASS ACTION TITAN—
AND A FIRST-CLASS MENTOR

Given the seminal role that Harold Kohn played in Nast's career, and indeed in the development of class action litigation, let us pause a moment to discuss Harold Kohn, who had earned a reputation as a tough antitrust litigator. His fame became national in the 1960s when he capitalized on the Justice Department's prosecution of major electrical equipment manufacturers— General Electric, Allis Chalmers, Westinghouse, and lesser lights for price-fixing. As executives went to jail, Kohn went for the corporation's pocketbooks. On behalf of three Philadelphia area utilities, he won a treble-damages award of $28.9 million, an enormous figure for the time, and sizable verdicts elsewhere. Kohn never talked about his fees, but years later several lawyers involved told Connie Bruck of *American Lawyer* that his fees were about $10 million. Nationwide, the manufacturers paid out about half a billion—and antitrust lawyers saw a profitable new world lying before them, that of class action litigation.

Kohn was an immediate leader. He besieged manufacturers all over the country, looking for price-fixing cases in other areas, and soon he was earning untold millions as the uncrowned king of class actions.

Nast was hired specifically to do communications law on behalf of a major Kohn client, Triangle Publications, Inc., owner of *TV Guide,* the *Philadelphia Inquirer,* and other publications. She couldn't begin work until the autumn, so "I spent the entire summer studying First Amendment law," she recollected with a sigh. "I showed up at Harold's office right after Labor Day. And the first thing he said to me was. 'Well, young lady, we need you for some antitrust work. Here's what I want you to do . . .' It was baptism by fire in the truest sense. My first month, I found myself on a plane going to Chicago with Harold—the second time I'd even flown—for one of the paper antitrust cases. I was scared to death—not only from the flying, but from sitting there with the country's best antitrust lawyer. A wonderful opportunity. Learning antitrust law with Harold Kohn was like taking art lessons from Michelangelo."

Although he was a good (if tough) teacher, Kohn kept a tight rein on Nast and other associates. But the sheer magnitude of work meant that the entire office got involved in cases. "You've got to remember," Nast said, "that some of these cases dragged on for years." Her apprenticeship lasted seven to eight years, with responsibility gradually increasing. But she never felt restrained. "He never held anybody back. When you were ready to fly, you flew." Another thing touched Nast. "Harold was absolutely gender blind. This was an era when women were a rarity in law. It was a mostly male culture. He assumed that I could do anything [that a man could] until I showed him I couldn't."

So, I asked, when did he give you your first case on your own? Nast stiffened perceptibly. "No, I *got* them," she said, with emphasis. "I wasn't *given* them." She explained how this happens. "Once people find you have a reputation, and especially in class actions, you get calls. There are also referrals from other lawyers who have clients with class action problems and don't know how to handle them on their own. And finally, there are calls from aggrieved people who think they were defrauded or duped."

So Nast found herself pitted against trash haulers—the so-called waste management litigation, which lasted for years and marked her as a rising star in class action cases. She went after Chrysler Corporation for tampering with the odometers of cars, and won $16 million, a small amount when compared to some of the price-fixing cases, but big for a consumer case. There were numerous other cases, and Nast slowly became a recognized figure in the class action community.

She also married a lawyer in the firm, Joseph Roda, with whom she would have three more children. Once the family started growing, Roda's father persuaded him to return to his native Lancaster to take over his law practice. Nast moved there also, and now her life was further complicated by a daily commute to Philadelphia.

By 1995 she had had enough of Route 30. "When you begin to think you can make a drive in your sleep, it's time to stop unless you do just that and kill yourself. I made a realistic judgment. Most of my time was spent out of town, and I could travel just as easily from Harrisburg. So I decided to come to Lancaster and work with Joe in his firm. Right away my quality of life improved dramatically. No longer did I have that awful commute. There was another factor. Kohn was aging and withdrawing from an active role in the firm. So that emotional bond was no longer there.

"Harold used to tell me, 'You know, young lady, I taught you everything you know. But by no means did I teach you everything that I know.' Maybe so. But those years with Harold were most important in getting me where I am today."

JOINING THE CLASS ACTION CLUB

I had come to Lancaster specifically to talk with Dianne Nast about how one becomes a member of the inner circle of plaintiff lawyers who dominate class action cases. She had thought about the subject, and she started her attempt at an answer with a sigh.

"Well," she said, "the truth is, I guess I don't know the answer, because if one exists, it is a multidimensional answer. It's not like filling out an application and getting approved. To be honest, a lot depends also on whether you are a male or a female, for the requirements are different." She stopped and looked up at the ceiling, and corrected herself. "No, 'requirement' is not the right word. Say that the 'entry mechanism' is quite a bit different.

"I think repeated appearance is one factor. There are certain people who tend to show up early and often who get to know one another, and take the measure of what their abilities are, and their drawbacks. The familiarity factor is very important. And there definitely is an ability component. There are definitely enough people who want to be a member of the club that you don't have to have dead weight. You need to have people who can make a contribution.

"There is the success factor. Success fosters success. If you are successful in fen-phen litigation, for instance, then the next drug case that comes along, you have entrée."

Socialization also plays a role, although not a deciding one. Nast sighed and shook her head as if she was reliving a horrible memory, but one she decided not to share. "I live with these people, you must understand, and among other things they read books. Being social sure helps. Although, I must say, we do put up with ill-tempered, ill-mannered people. But even they have to have something important to bring to the table. I suppose it's that way in any profession; there are people you don't want to work with."

She ticked through the strengths of the various lawyers. When essentially the same group was thrown together in breast implant class actions, "nobody knew what anybody else could do. By the time we got to fen-phen, we had worked together four or five cases, and people knew what other people did well, or didn't do as well as other things. Some people, like Stan Chesley, don't do anything [in the courtroom]. Stan is the bargainer. He talks. He gets involved in settlement negotiations, but you rarely hear Stan make an oral argument or a presentation in court, or write a brief. It's not that he is incapable; he is very capable. But he knows what his assignment is going to be, and he does it."

"Stan and Wendell Gauthier [of New Orleans] have an extraordinary ability to see the big picture and not get bogged down in details. They leave that to other people. They can conceptualize and visualize settlement in a way other people can't. Elizabeth Cabraser is good on her feet; we find ourselves doing many of the oral arguments.

"What do I bring to the table? What I am generally asked to do is to tend to a lot of the strategy, decision making, the legal maneuvers. If I say so myself, I am good at making oral arguments when we are doing the motions—for instance, during the class certification in tobacco. And I've been involved in settlement negotiations as well."

There is one major barrier that keeps many lawyers, especially younger ones, from getting into the Class Action Club: money. As Nast put it, "You always have to cough up in advance; you don't come in free, unless you have really something of value that is not available anywhere else.

"You go into these things open-ended, not knowing how much you are eventually going to have to put up. In breast implants, the initial payment was something on the order of $300,000 each. This went into the common fund to pay common expenses, plus you gotta pay your own expenses." At one point she had another $900,000 in out-of-pocket expenses, for a total investment of $1.4 million. "You must travel all over the country, spending a thousand dollars every time you get on a plane, because you are not getting those stay-over-Saturday cut fares.

"It runs up in a hurry. Copying expenses, daily office expenses, Lexis [the legal online search service], you can spend $300,000 or $400,000 on Lexis alone over the course of five or six years. That's just the actual cash expenditures. You are also looking at many millions of dollars more in time—three or four millions." Her firm took out a bank loan to finance their share of the fen-phen costs.

Eventually, breast implant fees awarded by the court were for an hourly rate averaging around $200, which Nast and others felt was abysmally low. "Nobody in their right mind," she said, "would put up a million four and just leave it on the table for seven years, knowing that I am going to earn seven percent, plus of course the time. These have not been rich cases." By contrast, antitrust cases were moneymakers. "They were not expensive to litigate. And they are usually quicker. They are also much less emotional. They only involve a pocketbook."

Watching the members of the Class Action Club in court I sensed a certain reserve between several of the lawyers. Elizabeth Cabraser, for instance, seemed to deliberately avoid being around Stanley Chesley. There was no overt hostility or impoliteness, just a suggestion that she did not want to occupy the same space with him. But Nast says that by and large, the member lawyers get along tolerably well.

"Look at the realities," she said. "You have a big group of people who come to a hearing from out of town, and they are thrown together two, three, even four nights a week. You quit working at six or seven in the evening, so you have drinks together, you go to dinner together. You are most likely discussing the case—the work never ends when you are in one of these cases—but you are in a social situation. It's good, because you have more camaraderie than if you went to the library and read law books all evening."

THE FEN-PHEN LAWYERS

Two groups initially sparred for control of fen-phen. One centered on Roger Brosnahan of San Francisco, the other on Stan Chesley. Each held strategy meetings for months, trying to decide where to file the main suit, and how to divvy up the work. It was Nast who finally brought suit in Philadelphia, and in a series of meetings the factions more or less agreed on who would be the main contenders for the Plaintiffs' Management Committee. Nast would not go so far as to say that lawyers dictated Judge Bechtle's selections for the PMC.

Nast has little patience with the individual litigators such as Kip Petroff and Paul Rheingold. "The bottom line, as always, is money, regardless of what anybody tells you," she says. "Trial lawyers advertise, and sign up plaintiffs in return for fifty percent of the recovery. Against this you have those of us who do class actions, and who have their fees set by the court.

"The trial lawyers, for lack of a better term, wanted to keep them in their backyard, before their own judges, their own juries. Their fear of federal jurisdiction is almost irrational. I don't fault them—any lawyer prefers to work in a friendly environment—but you've got to think of what is best for the client."

I quoted to Nast a statement that Paul Rheingold had made to a legal journal a few years ago—that 90 percent of the persons who ended up as plaintiffs in class actions did not have strong cases. "That's not too far off track," she conceded. But there are reasons. "Persons who don't want to spend the rest of their life in court, these will settle." Conversely, many persons with legitimate complaints "don't have the stomach for litigation, and all that it entails." A prime example was the tobacco litigation. "When the tobacco company lawyers take your deposition, your entire life is opened up—starting with your grammar school grades and conduct. They'll come up with bad stuff that really has nothing to do with your claim, stuff that makes a plaintiff look like a degenerate." She shook her head. "You can make anybody look like a degenerate if you try really hard."

I digested for Nast a phone conversation I had had several weeks earlier with Elizabeth Cabraser. Despite the sharp difference in lifestyles—the San Francisco lawyer who plays drums in the office to blow off steam and the Dutch Country mother of five kids—the women have a bond. To watch them, standing to the side of a courtroom and talking, is a study in affectionate body language, as if two sisters are meeting for the first time in weeks.

In any event, what Cabraser had said to me was that she was displeased with the "star" approach that writers take toward lawyers. She complained that she receives the publicity for everything done by her firm, "although there are fourteen equity partners in Lief, Cabraser, Heimann and Bernstein who are of equal importance." So, too, with class action litigation: the media seize upon a name lawyer and do not give proper credit to persons of equal ability, who do equal work.

"The day of the great individual lawyer who wins by persuasion is over. There is never going to be another Melvin Belli," Cabraser said.

Class action litigation, in Cabraser's view, compels plaintiff lawyers to cooperate. "Sometimes the lawyers don't particularly like each other, and they do not always see eye to eye on how to handle a case. But it is effective." And necessary. Plaintiff firms tend to be lean. The committee system in class action litigation enables lawyers to pool their resources and spread around the work, especially depositions and other laborious discovery. Much of this work is done by persons who go unnoted. "The essential effort," Cabraser told me, "is going on beneath the waterline."

Nast endorsed Cabraser's "no star" theory, and the necessity for plaintiff lawyers to pool their resources. Defense firms have an advantage that goes beyond resources. Because they are defending parallel litigation all over the country, they "know the global picture" of a case. By contrast, a plaintiff lawyer who has a case about a defective auto part in Illinois might not know that similar cases are being heard in Louisiana and Colorado. But the defense lawyers know the full scope of these cases, and how to go about minimizing the disclosure of damaging evidence. (Given the skill with which the Association of Trial Lawyers of America and such private companies as Mealey's Reports speed information to plaintiff lawyers, I feel that this claimed "isolation" is much overstated.)

Dianne Nast is a lawyer who made a lifestyle decision—to live in and work from a small town in Pennsylvania. Yes, she misses the cultural life of Philadelphia, and as a reminder of the city she keeps on her office wall a large photographic aerial view of the downtown business district, as she used to see it daily from her desk at Harold Kohn's firm. But, no, nothing could persuade her to return to big-city living, or lawyering. "My life," she said, "is right here."

AN ANGRY RHEINGOLD

Months after the "beauty contest" hearing at which he was denied a role on the Plaintiffs' Management Committee, New York attorney Paul Rheingold remained in a foul mood. Given the harsh words directed at him in court about amassing more cases than he could handle, I called on him to solicit a response. Rheingold has a sense of history, and the walls of his office are decorated with turn-of-the-century photographs of New York City. He proceeded to explain to me why he felt he deserved a role in the class action, regardless of what Judge Bechtle held.

A rangy man in his sixties, Rheingold has terrorized the pharmaceutical industry for decades. In the 1960s he sued over a drug named Mer/29, which lowered cholesterol levels. Rheingold proved that it caused serious ailments to thousands of persons, and the manufacturer was slapped with punitive as well as actual damages. His other coups included a leadership role in a suit against a Japanese company for making a botched batch of a dietary supplement called L-tryptophan. The error caused persons to come down with a rare blood ailment, and the Japanese firm paid more than a billion dollars in damages.

Rheingold had read of the Mayo study concerning fen-phen dangers while vacationing in July 1997; upon his return to New York he began running ads noting his medical expertise, and the clients came in by the dozen. Later that summer he went to San Diego for the annual meeting of the Association of Trial Lawyers of America.

At the convention hotel, Rheingold surveyed friends who did medical cases and found interest in making fen-phen a major target. So he printed up signs announcing an informal meeting. "ATLA, of course, had already booked all the conference rooms, so all the hotel could provide for us was one of the bars," Rheingold recollected. More than one hundred lawyers attended and agreed to start an informal fen-phen steering group and exchange information.

Rheingold is a fiddler, and he gave sharp attention to a paper clip as he talked about what happened in Judge Bechtle's court. I soon realized that he was not about to say nasty things about a federal judge, for jurists form a clan with a deserved reputation for fraternal protection—criticize one of them, and others are apt to make a little mental note to wreak revenge in the future.

He finally sighed and said, "Well, it certainly didn't go the way I thought it should . . ."

But Rheingold did not waste time crying over the rebuff. With other excluded lawyers, he quickly set about organizing state-level class actions in New York and New Jersey. In each state hundreds of cases were consolidated before a single judge, with shared discovery. Other lawyers did the same thing in Pennsylvania.

"Actually," Rheingold said, "I think we are light-years ahead of the Philadelphia group. We have lawyers in our state consortium who grew up in the computer age. Each of the firms involved in the state cases put up $6,000. We worked out an arrangement with Wyeth [a subsidiary of American Home Products] to put more than a million documents on CD-ROMs. These were optically scanned and coded so they could be easily retrieved. By comparison, what the lawyers did in the MDL is an age back. Their committee, a very large one, demanded hard copy from the defendants, and then proceeded to read them all, and select those which seem most interesting. Allowing for a little hyperbole, that can be done at the press of a button on the state court cases."

The electronic format of the documents makes it easy for them to be shown in court if a case gets to a jury trial. "You put the document up on the screen and highlight the quotation you want to emphasize. Jurors love it because they can see it, rather than listen to someone read it." ("Paper" documents can also be electronically displayed, but doing so requires a cumbersome overhead viewer.)

Rheingold was also miffed that the MDL lawyers put a price tag on their documents. "They say, 'If you want to use them, you must pay nine percent of any recovery you make, in every case you have.' That we are not about to do."

He left me with a parting message: "Whatever is happening in Philadelphia, just remember that those of us doing the individual cases—me, Kip Petroff, and others—are away ahead of the pack."

A DEFENSE DILEMMA

As discovery proceeded in the dual-track litigation—the class action in Philadelphia, and individual cases elsewhere—lawyers for American Home Products, and the company's own executives, found themselves in a troubling situation. On the one hand, AHP became more and more convinced that claimed damages from fen-phen were grossly overstated; that a relative handful of women might have suffered heart damage, but nowhere near the number claimed by various lawyers. AHP even published new studies purporting to show that adverse side effects from the pills were relatively rare, and that chronic obesity among the supposed victims was to blame.

AHP's confidence was bolstered during an unusual hearing in February 1999 before Judge Bechtle. Critics were plaguing the judge. Lawyers for several plaintiffs who had been lumped into the class action against their wishes wanted the cases severed for individual trial so that their clients, many of them severely ill, could collect damages while they were still alive. Almost reflexively, in these lawyers' view, Judge Bechtle denied their requests. Further, he paid no heed to state court judges who pleaded with him for better coordination. "Bechtle simply would not listen to reason," one of the protesting lawyers told me. "He can be a hardheaded Dutchman when he sets his mind to something. I got the idea that he wasn't even reading the pleadings that we were sending to him."

Finally, in an attempt to hush the dissidence, Judge Bechtle asked the class action lawyers to tell him how many persons were claiming *diagnosed* injuries, rather than conditions that *could develop* in the future.

After a laborious review of some eight thousand files, the Plaintiff's Management Committee came up with an answer that surprised even AHP attorneys: *no more than eleven plaintiffs.* Judge Bechtle told the lawyers for these persons that he would entertain motions to put their cases on a separate fast track.

Here is an anomaly. By now the class action lawyers had gathered essentially the same documentation that Kip Petroff and others had acquired for their individual cases—millions upon millions of pages, all of which were laboriously indexed and filed in a separate locked room in the Philadelphia courthouse, as well as being stored on CDs. The various legal motions alone generated a stack of paper that one of several court clerks working exclusively on fen-phen estimated "would make a stack higher than this courthouse." The building has eight stories.

Yet all this churning had produced not a dime of recovery for a single fen-phen plaintiff. Such is the nature of a class action: Lawyers who handle such cases learn to think in the aggregate, and to work for years with no immediate payout in the expectation—or hope—of a bonanza payday when the matter is negotiated to an end. (Not a single member of the PMC with whom I spoke over more than two years ever gave serious thought to the idea that the action might actually result in a trial.)

Regardless of what was happening in Philadelphia, however, AHP realized that enough "serious" cases existed elsewhere, in state courts, to threaten the company's survival. As quietly as possible, AHP began settling these cases. Although the precise amounts AHP paid supposedly were secret, under a confidentiality agreement, gossip on the fen-phen circuit spoke in terms of millions of dollars.

Essentially, several lawyers working for AHP told me in 1998 and 1999, the company was playing for time. "We know we have exposure, the question is, 'how much?'" The question hanging over all the litigation, class action and otherwise, was how well the fen-phen cases would play before a jury. I kept thinking of the "fatties got sick on their own" defense that Petroff had predicted to me months ago. AHP chose to tread carefully, choosing to settle what it considered to be the worst cases rather than risk a trial. As one of the defense lawyers told me, "The hope was that we could hold off going to trial and wrap up everything with the class action, under terms that would be acceptable to the Petroffs and their individual cases as well. I'll admit that our overriding fear was that someone would actually get to a jury trial and win so damned much money that other plaintiff lawyers would say, 'Whoa! Why should we settle? We'll take our chances with a jury.'"

Conversely, the plaintiff lawyers had good reason to force AHP to trial. "In these sorts of deals," Petroff told me, "you need a jury verdict to set a true market price. How much are the cases actually worth? How much exposure will AHP realize it has?" And, ironically, at the very time the Class Action Club derided Petroff as an amateur intruder—"a cowboy"—several of these lawyers were quietly praying, as they told me, that he would succeed in getting one of his many cases into a courthouse and before a jury.

As events worked out, a nonlegal factor came into play that nudged AHP into settlement negotiations. The drug industry was going through a period of consolidation, and AHP was desperately seeking a merger partner. In recent months AHP had tried to arrange marriages, first with Smith-Kline Beecham, and when those talks failed, with Monsanto. As a lawyer working for AHP would explain, "One underlying problem in both those proposed deals was the uncertain outcome of the fen-phen litigation. Of course, you could structure a deal where the core liability remained AHP's problem. But would AHP be so weakened that it would not be a good merger partner? I wouldn't go so far as to call fen-phen the ultimate deal buster, but it certainly was on everyone's mind." The litigation also served as an albatross on AHP's stock price—and in the late 1990s no corporate management could afford to ignore growth-happy Wall Street. So, in early 1999, when another potential merger partner appeared, in the form of Warner-Lambert, AHP decided to sue for peace in the class action.

The first concrete move came in April, when Peter Zimroth of Arnold & Porter, AHP's chief outside counsel for the class action, sent letters to "many plaintiff lawyers" asking them to come to his office "to begin this process." Even some of the industry lawyers who been talking about a "to the death" defense seemed relieved. As one of them told me, "We were dealing with cases with highly emotional overtones. My gut feeling was—and it continues to be—that the diet pills didn't cause nearly as much harm as claimed. But who wanted to go into court week after week and face gasping women who couldn't get out of their chairs without help? What management said, in effect, was 'Make a deal.'"

So lawyers began trooping to the Arnold & Porter offices in Manhattan. A former partner named Ellen Reisman had just become in-house counsel for Wyeth-Ayerst, the AHP division that actually manufactured the questioned drugs. The plaintiff contingent was headed by Michael Fishbein, one of Arnold Levin's partners.

The talks were frustrating, and several times appeared on the brink of collapse. Judge Bechtle imposed a gag order on the participants, and formerly voluble lawyers on both sides suddenly fell mute. The periodic updates I managed to wheedle from attorneys were vague—in effect, "We're still talking . . . fifty-fifty chance this week, up from forty-sixty last week." Wall Street analysts, meanwhile, bandied around their own estimates of what a settlement might cost AHP. One sum mentioned was $15 billion, an amount that an AHP lawyer would later state "was totally unrealistic, a figure that was never on the table, one that never could have been paid."

But even to an informed outsider, the plaintiff strategy was clear: No settlement was going to be possible until something happened in court to convince American Home Products that it was at risk of financial disaster. Thus we return to Dallas, and Kip Petroff.

AND FINALLY, A TRIAL TO VERDICT

By the summer of 1999, the Dallas office of Vinson & Elkins, which led American Home Products' Texas defense team, had had its fill of Kip Petroff. The brash lawyer had bludgeoned AHP into settling out of court a number of cases where medical damage attributable to fen-phen arguably existed. A further aggravation was Petroff's ability to generate media attention to his fen-phen wins. But lead partner Bill Sims and colleagues felt that Petroff was overreaching—that if he could be bested in an actual trial, he would lose much of his zest for fen-phen. One lawyer in the firm suggested to me that Petroff was cherry-picking, that is, concentrating on a few strong cases and using settlements to drive up the value of weaker cases.

Just as Petroff had predicted months earlier, AHP lawyers felt strongly that juries would not look kindly upon fen-phen plaintiffs if the cases actually got to trial. Choosing his words very carefully, a lawyer working for AHP said, "I don't want to sound unkind, but most of these plaintiffs were women who had been grossly obese for most of their lives. Smokers, awful eating habits, no exercise—and they try to blame all their problems on fen-phen. Defending a case against such a plaintiff would have to be done very, very carefully; you slip, and the case blows up in your hand. But we felt that it could be done."

Indeed, a case in Houston in June suggested to company lawyers that they had not been aggressive enough. The trial had been under way for several days when the order came from AHP corporate headquarters: Settle the case. So the woman walked away with $6.7 million. Then came the stunning aftermath. Reporters who interviewed jurors later found that most of them would not have awarded the plaintiff a cent—a clear defense victory had been in AHP's grasp, and the company blew it. (Petroff was not involved in this case.)

But Vinson & Elkins looked to another case that seemed to qualify as a "tide-turner," a chance to maneuver Petroff into a corner with a can't-win case.

Ironically, Petroff found himself in a dilemma of his own making. Through referrals he had several plaintiffs in Van Zandt County, a rural area an hour east of Dallas. Judge Tommy W. Wallace, who presides over the 294th Judicial District Court, prides himself on running a fast docket, and the Petroff cases were ready for trial by the summer of 1999. The first to proceed was on behalf of Debby Lovett, who worked as a manicurist.

Even Petroff concedes that his client was not an ideal fen-phen plaintiff. At age thirty-six, Mrs. Lovett was a grossly over-weight smoker who had first been diagnosed with a heart abnor-mality in 1989. When her weight neared two hundred pounds in 1995 she went to a physician who prescribed Pondimin. She took the pills off and on for six months between October 1995 and January 1997, losing forty-five pounds. Her prescription was for twenty milligrams a day, rather than the recommended dosage of sixty milligrams. By AHP's computations, she took the equiva-lent of only two months of the full regular dosage.

In March 1997 an EKG showed moderate to severe damage to two of her heart valves, but even her own physician said that fen-phen was not to blame. Her medical bills were only $2,000, and although she complained of shortness of breath and fatigue—the two-hundred-foot walk to her mailbox exhausted her—she lost no time from work. After one frightening heart experience, she declined to seek medical treatment, choosing instead to carry out plans to go to the riverboat casinos in Shreveport, Louisiana, several days later and gamble until three A.M. Nor was the trial venue particularly attractive. The county seat, Canton, has 3,521 residents, and juries there tend to be conservative when returning civil verdicts.

Petroff said, "One of the reasons American Home Products was eager to go to trial on Lovett was that they felt even if they lost, they wouldn't have to pay much, because her damages were so small. I felt really, though, that I was in a win-win situation. Let me explain. I was willing to go to trial with a case a lot of lawyers said they would have never tried. No, this wasn't my choice of cases. I wished I could have tried some of the earlier ones first, because they were better, in terms of damages and the medical stuff. That's why AHP settled them. Now, if I hadn't taken Lovett to trial, AHP would have thought that I was weak, that I was afraid to go into a courtroom with them on a tough case. AHP certainly was not going to let me try a *good* case, those are the ones they settled.

"Do a balance sheet. If I lost, all they could say was that I was a gutsy guy who lost a bad case. If I win, I am a gutsy guy who won a bad case. So, I had it both ways, win or lose."

So how did the case look from the viewpoint of American Home Products? "This was one where we thought we were going to give Petroff a kick in the ass that he would remember," a member of the Sims trial team told me. "There was another case set for trial immediately afterward that was about as weak, or so we thought. We looked forward to a one-two punch."

Petroff kept the case simple. "My story was that American Home Products was a bad company that had bad documents that concealed the fact that it sold bad products that hurt a lot of people." He put before the jury the documents and deposition testimony he had acquired beginning the spring of 1998, and thus panel members heard how AHP knew of problems caused by fen-phen but did not share the information with physicians. The adverse reaction reports, an inch-and-a-half stack of paper, covered a broad range of ailments, ranging from headaches to constipation to sudden death in a few instances. All the reports went to the jurors for study, but Petroff kept his focus on heart disease. "I didn't want to pile on with the other stuff—this wasn't a case about constipation, for god's sake. But as it turned out, the jurors said later that they read the other stuff, and that it hurt AHP."

Petroff realized he would have difficulty on the issue of causation—that is, that Mrs. Lovett's condition resulted from fen-phen. So he focused on what he charged was corporate misconduct and deception.

In Petroff's view, the AHP legal team erred by bringing too many lawyers to court. As many as five attorneys sat at the defense table at any given time, with more in the spectator area. "One lawyer would be standing up objecting, while another was whispering in his ear or trying to pass him a note. Keep in mind that this is a small East Texas town where the words 'Dallas lawyer' don't sit too well." By contrast, Petroff and Kisselburgh sat alone at the plaintiff table.

In court, Mrs. Lovett's own physician pooh-poohed the notion that fen-phen damaged her heart. Her condition was a "natural progression" of her earlier problems, specifically a prolapsed heart value diagnosed years before she began talking the pills. (A prolapsed valve, Petroff explained, "is like a door that doesn't totally close.") Her valvular heart disease, the physician testified, was "so minor I wouldn't even call it a disease."

The AHP team responded by attacking Petroff's expert doctors as "medical mercenaries," one of whom charged $8,000 a day for his work. In closing arguments AHP lawyers focused on the lack of any medical proof that fen-phen caused Mrs. Lovett's troubles. They also attacked Petroff for waiting until the trial to present testimony that she faced potentially fatal heart surgery. Brian P. Johnson, of the Houston firm Hanson, Alexander, Johnson & Spalding, said of Mrs. Lovett: "I'm sorry that she's been dragged through a lawsuit by some people and has been used and misled. I think it leaves a stain on my profession that I'm not very proud of."

Further, Mrs. Lovett made only one trip to the doctor the last six months of 1998. "Where is the medical evidence?" Ray asked. "What medical evidence have you heard to support some serious damages to her physically? I may be wrong, but I think I saw her carrying some boxes into the courthouse the first day of trial."

Petroff seethed as he listened to the attacks, both on him and his clients, and the defense use of such terms as "litigation lotto" to describe his case. Partner Bob Kisselburgh several times reached out with a restraining arm, muttering, "Let them alone. They're overdoing it with this personal stuff. They're hanging themselves."

The jury was out for about three days, returning at noon on August 6 with a verdict of $23.4 million against AHP—$3.4 million for pain and future medical bills, $20 million in punitive damages.

So why and how did Petroff win? His strategy of making corporate deception the issue proved sound, according to media juror interviews after the trial. Kathryn Culver of the *Tyler Morning Telegraph* quoted juror Ronnie Jones: "Three people who worked for the company testified they knew of thirty-seven cases of heart valve damage possibly back to 1994. It took roughly two and a half years before they put it on the label as a warning. There were two cases of hair loss and that warning went on the label within six months." Foreman Diane Welsh commented, "I'm not against the company making a profit, but it has to be done ethically. I don't have a lot of confidence in their ethics now." But Robert Allen, one of two jurors who voted to absolve AHP of blame, claimed that the panel was swayed by emotion, not fact, and that seven of the twelve "had closed minds."

Petroff's feelings after the first-ever fen-phen victory? "Vindication. I had said that I could win that case; very few people agreed with me. I felt validated." Even after his victory, he would admit, "I don't think that the jury believed she had that strong of a case, but their [AHP's] conduct was so bad that they should pay."

And the publicity. Petroff counted ten TV camera trucks in the street outside the courthouse the day of his victory. He gave interviews there, then went to his local counsel's office. "Diane Sawyer was on one line, The *Today* show on the other. I was putting one on hold to talk to the other." In New York on Monday he was a most busy fellow: ABC's *Good Morning America* to start the day, then the Fox News Network, next CNN's *Burden of Proof,* plus more local TV stuff than he can remember. Petroff is not devoid of ego. But by his calculations, the media attention was valuable for a far more important reason: "People who are going to be on juries watch television. And in a seventy-two-hour period, you had millions of Americans learning that fen-phen was a bad product, and that a company lied to keep it on the market, and that a jury had sent them a message with a multimillion-dollar verdict."

AHP got the message. Defense lawyers who had been baiting Petroff with bold talk about "fighting to the finish" now phoned to see if he'd care to enter settlement talks on his inventory of several hundred cases. "By now," he said, "they have basically gone away, in terms of wanting to fight."

In the year following the trial he settled thirty-five cases. A

few days before our April 2000 visit, Petroff had put together settlement packages on eleven cases. "By three in the afternoon," he
said, "we settled all eleven." How much? Petroff again graced me
with his none-of-your-business grin. "Come on," he said, "you
know these settlements are under seal. Let's just say that it's a
damned big check that we are going to get." He finally put the
amount at "over $10 million."

And, again, he laughed derisively at the pace of the class action. "As we sit here right now, in April of 2000, how much
money has that crowd actually put into the hands of a single
woman whose heart was damaged by fen-phen. You know the
answer as well as I do. Not a damned thin dime!"

THE PRESSURES MOUNT

Wire services reported the Canton verdict at midday on August
7, and the impact on Wall Street was immediate. American
Home Products shares dropped 11.9 percent, causing stockholders a paper loss of $8 billion. The stock now had slid some 40
percent since April, when the settlement negotiations began.
AHP clearly had a mess on its hands.

The Plaintiffs' Management Committee now played a much
stronger hand, one reflected in a cryptic e-mail message I received at our August retreat at the Delaware shore. "Bastards are
on the run," the communiqué stated. "Suggest you stand on
beach and enjoy spectacle of mass drowning suicide of all levels
AHP." Another PMC attorney would tell me, "In August, we
went into what I would call our 'why hurry?' mode. The pressure
was on AHP; we weren't about to make it easier for them."

AHP's situation deteriorated even further in August in a
courtroom in New Brunswick, New Jersey. Sol Weiss, of the
Philadelphia firm of Anapol, Schwartz, Weiss, Cohan, Feldman
& Smalley, P.C., began trying a case that would require AHP
to pay for medical monitoring of every women who had taken
fen-phen—another potential multibillion-dollar problem for
AHP. "I was taking a unique approach," Weiss related. "I wasn't

asking for a dime in monetary damages for an individual. What I
wanted was a requirement that people who took fen-phen, most
of them women, get an echocardiogram examination so that they
would know for a certainty whether their hearts had been damaged. If damage was found, well, there was another issue for another lawsuit.

"AHP screamed bloody murder about the cost, which would
be around a thousand bucks a person. Call me cynical, but I got
a feeling that AHP was not so much concerned about the cost as
they were about what the tests would show. What if we turned up
hundreds, even thousands of women with primary pulmonary
hypertension? Their liability would be out of sight."

Over a period of weeks, in August and September 1999,
Weiss built a damning documentary case against AHP. As did
Petroff in the Texas trial, he focused on the company's deception
and sloppy reporting. Weiss kept his focus on the period during
the first six months of 1996 when adverse reaction reports about
fen-phen soared. The most serious ones went into red folders,
prompting a memo from a harried AHP administrator, "Will this
flood of red folders never end? We are in need of a lull." At one
point, according to AHP documents, about 40 percent of the
safety division—the people responsible for monitoring the adverse reports—were temporary employees; more experienced
permanent workers spent much of their time training them.

Dr. Marc Deitch, the Wyeth-Ayerst senior vice president for
medical affairs who had been Kip Petroff's first deposition witness years earlier, took the stand in a court for the first time, and
Weiss treated him roughly. He produced a 1997 memo that Dr.
Deitch wrote to a colleague in the United Kingdom soon after
the critical Mayo Clinic study. Discussing his duties at Wyeth-
Ayerst, Dr. Deitch claimed he had been successful by "questioning everything we do on an R.O.I. basis, that is, if it does not add
value, it does not get done."

What do those initials mean? Weiss asked.

"Return on investment," Dr. Deitch replied.

Then Weiss brought up comments Dr. Deitch had made at a
1995 FDA hearing on approval of Redux. Professing that the

company wanted to be a "good public citizen," Dr. Deitch continued, "We certainly want to protect equity just as well."

"Profits over safety," Weiss told me. "Right there, in black and white, the guy's own words." Dr. Deitch and his attorneys tried to establish that the remarks were taken out of context and that the company indeed was concerned with safety.

Several weeks into the trial, Superior Court Judge Maria Corodemus seemingly had heard enough. She summoned lawyers into her chambers and, in so many words, told AHP that the wisdom of the ages cried out for the case to be settled, that the evidence against the company was so overwhelming that it would be well advised to surrender. AHP capitulated. Its lawyers told Weiss they would fold his medical monitoring claims into the overall settlement. And he suddenly found himself a member of the PMC negotiating team.

THE WAR IS OVER—PARTIALLY

But could a deal be struck that would pass scrutiny by Judge Louis Bechtle? Some months earlier a minor player in the litigation, Interneuron Pharmaceuticals, had agreed to pay about $100 million to settle all claims. With its main product off the market, Interneuron was essentially out of business, and legal fees of about $1 million a month, plus operating costs of $3 million monthly, were fast draining its remaining assets. The company had new products for which it was ready to seek FDA approval, but the fen-phen litigation made it impossible for Interneuron to raise money in the capital market. But Judge Bechtle in September 1999 stunned both sides when he turned down the settlement, ruling that it did not adequately protect the rights of individual claimants who wished to pursue their cases on their own. (Judge Bechtle had no choice. The U.S. Supreme Court in the summer of 1999 threw out a proposed settlement of an asbestos class action on grounds it did not give individual plaintiffs the right to opt out and proceed on their own. The court held that a settlement must insure that all claimants are "treated equitably among themselves.")

So the next months were spent crafting a settlement that would protect the so-called opt-outs, with negotiators well aware that Petroff, Rheingold, and other lawyers would oppose any deal that did not protect their clients' right to continue individual suits.

The deal that was finally struck, on October 7, 1999, contained more than one hundred pages of dense legalese; even the lay language "explanatory material" distributed to claimants, potential and otherwise, is unfathomable in spots. But the salient points can be summarized as follows.

Anyone who had taken Pondimin or Redux or both, regardless of whether they had filed a suit or suffered any claimed injury, could file for payments, the total of which were capped at $3.75 billion, over fifteen years.* The only exclusions were persons diagnosed with primary pulmonary hypertension, the most serious illness attributed to fen-phen. These cases, an estimated one hundred of them, would be litigated separately. The settlement created two funds, to be administered by the AHP Trust:

Fund A, $1 billion, would pay for echocardiograms for persons who took fen-phen for sixty-one or more days (at an estimated $1,000 each). Those who took the pills for a lesser period could ask for payment on "compassionate and humanitarian reasons and/or true financial hardship." Anyone who bought fen-phen could seek refunds, with a cap of $500. This fund would finance a registry of persons who took fen-phen and devote $25 million to research on heart problems linked with the pills. Lawyers would receive, with judicial approval, $200 million from Fund A.

Fund B, at an estimated "maximum present value of $2.55 billion," would compensate persons with "significant heart valve disease." The amounts varied according to the severity of the claimed damage. News accounts differed on the high end of the payment scale—"as much as $1.4 million a person," according to the *Wall Street Journal,* "as much as $1.5 million," according to

---

*As AHP stated, the exact amount the company would eventually pay depended "on actual claims experience." Several PMC members felt that AHP would pay 15 percent less than the $3.75 billion over the payout period.

the *New York Times*. Both newspapers missed the exact mark of $1,485,000. And not mentioned in press reports were payments at the low end of the scale, which ranged as low as $500 to a maximum of $10,000. Further, the number of persons at the high end of the scale, as we shall see, was a handful. Lawyers would receive "an amount not to exceed" $229 million from Fund B, or 9 percent of the $2.55 billion.

MILLIONS OF MISSING "VICTIMS"

The settlement plan was formally offered to Judge Bechtle at a hearing on January 13. Bechtle had been criticized in the legal press for not paying sufficient attention to state court judges who had their own fen-phen matters, so for the occasion he brought in five of them, from Chicago; New York; Philadelphia; Conroe, Texas; and Spokane, Washington.

Other lawyers had let Mike Fishbein, Arnold Levin's partner, do what Levin jokingly called the heavy lifting during negotiations with AHP. So it fell to Fishbein to explain the deal. Fishbein made interesting assertions. He called the settlement "an almost unprecedented effort of coordination between the state courts and the federal court in trying to reach a resolution for the victims, millions of people who have taken the diet drugs Pondimin and Redux"—a statement that surely surprised the state judges.

But where were all the victims? The settlement announcements spoke of some six million persons being eligible for recovery. But only 100,000 to 300,000 were known to the lawyers or manufacturers, by virtue of filing lawsuits or registering for benefits under the Interneuron settlement. "We are certainly missing about five and a half million names," Fishbein conceded. "So we have to devise a way to get word out to the public. . . ." Thirty-second spot commercials had begun running on network and cable television, and were bringing in up to 30,000 queries daily for more information. A massive print advertising campaign would continue through March. "Counter cards" were being distributed to 700,000 physicians for posting in their offices, and to 150,000 pharmacies.

Fishbein's admission on the numbers surprised me, and the

time seemed ripe for someone to ask, "Hey, wait a minute, if as many persons have been affected by these pills as you claim in the class, where are they?" But Bechtle and the other judges sat in silence. All parties in the courtroom—judges and lawyers on both sides—did not want to risk unwrapping what they felt was a neat package.

Peter Zimroth of Arnold & Porter, AHP's lead man, was cautiously defensive of fen-phen. If each of the cases was litigated "fully" on the issue of whether they caused damages, "I believe that at least with people who took these drugs for less than three months, then there's absolutely no association, no increased risk for anything, and very significantly, on the issue of progressive [illness] that is, people who may have some association because of long-term use, that condition thankfully does not progress into something serious, something more serious."

Why, then, was AHP paying billions of dollars to "victims"— the vast majority of them not even known to the lawyers—who had not been harmed? Zimroth asked the question himself, and proceeded to answer it at length:

We at American Home Products have entered into a settlement which largely accommodates contrary views of the science. And you may ask, why have we done that? There's a really very simple answer . . . and it is, I know in cynical times it might sound naive, but we thought it was the responsible thing to do. We are in the pharmaceutical business. We are not in the litigation business. . . . There may be some corporations that are in the litigation business, but that's not us. . . . And we wanted to give some comfort. . . . to people who took our drugs, regardless of whether or not it could be shown in a courtroom that we were legally responsible for what they did or not.

Also, we want to have some finality to this matter. . . . We were willing and are willing to contribute a very substantial amount of money in return for finality. . . . This litigation, and except for the opt-outs, and except for certain kinds of limited categories of lung disease, if this settlement is approved and it works, we will have finality.

Zimroth turned philosophical for a few minutes. He hoped fervently that the settlement did achieve its goals—"candidly, for the legal system as a whole, because I can tell you many, many large American corporations are looking at what we have done, at what we are trying to do here, and they see that we have been willing to spend or to commit a very substantial amount of money, a very substantial amount of time. . . .

"I think that if this settlement doesn't work for some reason . . . that would be a very substantial disincentive to others, the corporations who are engaged in the tort system, to sort of hunker down and be in an entirely litigation mode and not to seek ways of compromise and settlement."

Sol Weiss was far more pessimistic about the lingering effects of fen-phen. By the estimate of plaintiff experts, he expected that 75 percent of the women aged forty to forty-nine who had taken the drugs risked incurring regurgitation. Hence they were in risk of possibly fatal infection for medical procedures "as mild as cleaning their teeth." He spoke of heart attacks, strokes, of left heart ventricles swelling so large they appear to be "bursting out of the chest."

But where were all the claimed victims? Judge Bechtle told the parties to begin distributing materials describing the proposed settlement and set a hearing for May 1 to give opposing parties a change to object. A few hurdles remained, however, that had to be cleared in the intervening weeks. One was Paul Rheingold, the New York medical specialist.

A DASHED DEAL

To the dismay of lawyers on both sides, the supposed "national settlement" quickly fell apart. Lawyers for plaintiffs who chose to opt out of the Philadelphia agreement demanded another $15 billion to settle their outstanding claims. American Home Products—by now renamed Wyeth Corporation—refused, stating that it had only $1.7 billion in cash reserves to pay an estimated 70,000 pending cases. (Wyeth/AHP had already paid about $13 billion, in individual cases and in the class action settlement; as of late 2003, the AHP Settlement Trust created to pay the latter had reduced to $2.1 billion.)

Further, many claims submitted under the Philadelphia agreement turned out to be—well, to put it politely—highly suspect. When the AHP Trust was created, lawyers anticipated that perhaps 15 percent of the claimants would have heart irregularities caused by fen-phen. But to the astonishment of Judge Harvey Bartle III (who replaced the retired Judge Bechtel) 60 to 70 percent of two batches of claimants were said to be damaged. These persons had two things in common. They were represented by the New York plaintiff firms of Napoli, Kaiser, Bern & Associates and Hariton & D'Angelo. And all had been examined by either Dr. Linda J. Crouse of Kansas City or Dr. Richard L. Mueller of New York.

According to testimony at a hearing ordered by Judge Bartle, and later incorporated into civil suits, the physicians were said to run claimants through their offices at breakneck speed. During a two-day period, Dr. Crouse was said to have signed 163 so-called green forms attesting that claimants had suffered valvular heart disease, or VHD. As many as 500 green forms came out of her office in one week. One was signed "a mere sixteen seconds after the echocardiogram ended." The civil suit alleged that Dr. Crouse's "willingness to falsify" the Green Forms made her popular with lawyers who began "traveling to Kansas City, Missouri, with claimants from all over the country or, more often, merely with echocardiogram tapes."

In the hearing, Judge Bartle heard testimony about some seventy-eight claimants who had been examined by the physicians. In an order issued later, he sharply criticized Dr. Crouse in particular, writing, "When considering the thousands of echocardiograms that Dr. Crouse interpreted during the period that she worked for the Hariton and Napoli firms, her practice resembled a mass production operation that would have been the envy of Henry Ford." He found that she "never met with the claimants, never reviewed their medical records, and largely relied on the law firms to provide the medical histories," even though the cardiologist was responsible for swearing to the accuracy of information submitted on the green forms. Instead, the judge wrote, Dr. Crouse relied on law firm employees to instruct her staff on how to interpret the echograms and "spent little time actually reviewing and approving the results."

Judge Bartle also criticized the fee arrangement under which Dr. Mueller would receive "an extra $1,500 if the claimant obtained a benefit or the claim was submitted to the trust for payment." Judge Bartle concluded, "Mueller's remuneration depended on how he interpreted the echocardiogram and on what he stated on the form. He had a financial incentive to reach a particular result." He called the arrangement a "highly questionable practice . . . [that] seems to violate a lawyer's ethical obligation not to compensate a witness on a contingent fee basis." Defending Dr. Mueller, lawyers for the firms for which he did work stated he was paid for the extra time that went into preparing the green forms.

Judge Bartle set aside claims of the seventy-eight persons whose cases were studied but gave them permission to try again with new physicians if they wished. He refused to bar the Napoli and Hariton firms from future fen-phen proceedings. And, he said, the settlement funds were for "rightful claimants who suffered from fen-phen and not as a pot of gold for lawyers, physicians and nonqualifying claimants." In the aftermath of his decision, attorneys for the AHP Trust filed civil fraud charges against both the physicians. As of this writing, those charges are unresolved.

And the turmoil had a fallout effect on the Class Action Club: rather than pocketing millions of dollars in fees immediately, the lawyers faced months, perhaps years of further litigation before reaping a payday.

FEE FEAST—OR FAMINE?

So how much money did the Class Action Club deserve for its work? The agreement had capped attorney fees at $429 million, plus expenses, but under federal rules the judge had the authority to reduce this amount. In January 2002 the plaintiff lawyers asked for the full $429 million, plus $15.9 million in costs and another $138 million in fees in cases by the opt-out plaintiffs whose lawyers benefited from discovery efforts of the class lawyers.

The 196-page brief, the handiwork of Arnold Levin and Mike Fishbein of Levin, Fishbein, Sedran & Berman, contained a bit of self-praise in detailing the work done—more than one hundred depositions, eighty-plus days of status conferences and hearings, and more than two hundred fifty proceedings before a special master. "These numbers do not tell the entire story," Levin and Fishbein wrote. The lawyers "went beyond the call of professional obligation . . . [and] approached the whole of the case with moral rigor, a zeal for excellence, and a respect for the integrity of the litigation process."

Given the ongoing turmoil over the validity of many of the claims, Judge Bartle chose to grant only interim fees totaling $150 million. The largest chunk, $51.6 million, went to the firm of Levin Fishbein, whose top partners directed work of the Plaintiffs' Management Committee.

KIP PETROFF REDUX

With the class action case headed for resolution I returned to Dallas for a final conversation with Kip Petroff. In advance I refreshed my memory by replaying a tape of our first interview, a year earlier, almost to the day. I had asked him how American Home Products could succeed in getting him off the back of its Wyeth subsidiary? I listened to his answer: "Pay me. There is talk about striking a deal. The problem is that they can't make a deal with me that says I will never take another [fen-phen] case. It's not enforceable. It would be like a gentleman's agreement, and to do that, it would have to be a whole lot of money to make it work."

With American Home Products showing no stomach for continued jury trials, Petroff had moved into settlement mode, and he was a most happy man. He beamed as he ticked off what he had been doing. "I've settled thirty-five cases since the Canton trial," he said, "eleven of them in the past week. The company finally figured it out—how many Lovetts can you try before you go broke?" (His reference was to Debbie Lovett, plaintiff in the case he tried to verdict.)

It's none of my business, I asked, but how much money have you made out of fen-phen.

Petroff shot me an indeed-it's-none-of-your-business grin and continued, "I read recently that a person who is my age, forty-one, needs $9 million to quit work and maintain their lifestyle. Let's just say that I could retire a few times."

He spoke of his own role in forcing the diet pill manufacturers to pay up in Philadelphia. "Let's be realistic," he said. "Look, you've been following litigation pretty closely—do you think for one minute that AHP would have settled the class action unless someone took them to trial and demonstrated how expensive these cases could be? We had taken eighteen depositions and obtained millions of pages of documents when the PMC was still on training wheels. We played a significant role in winning the case, we should be compensated."

So what does the fen-phen litigation say about the state of modern American law? "A good deal," Petroff stated. "Here we are, two guys down in Dallas, me and Bob Kisselburgh, who take what we've earned out of breast implants, and invested hundreds of thousands of dollars in a case from which we didn't earn a dime for eighteen months, and came out winners. Yeah, I feel pretty darned proud of what we have done. I don't hear the big-name lawyers snicker any more when they hear my name."

Over the months, Petroff realized that the physical harm caused by fen-phen was not nearly as "widespread as he had felt at the outset—that although hundreds of women suffered serious heart damage, a far greater number escaped permanent damage. And he said, in so many words, that even in the Debbie Lovett case he was "not all that strong" on the issue of causation, that is, that fen-phen hurt her heart. Nonetheless, he feels that corporate American should learn a lesson from what American Home Products brought upon itself.

Don't lie," he said. "Don't lie internally, don't lie to the FDA, don't lie to patients and doctors. 'Cause if you do, Kip Petroff and Bob Kisselburgh are going to be all over you."

5 / Lerach and Weiss: The Class Action Scourges of West and East

My letter to William S. Lerach was candid. I wrote that I had read many nasty things about him in the press, and especially in publications whose constituency is the high-tech companies of Silicon Valley—firms which had surrendered billions of dollars to him and his firm in class action securities suits over the years. I cited one particularly unkind item, a headline in *Electrosphere* that called him a "bloodsucking scumbag." That was just the headline; the text got worse. In any event, surely there must be another side of the story. Could we talk?

One meets "the most hated man in the Silicon Valley"—another trade publication's depiction—by riding an elevator to the eighteenth floor of the One America Plaza Building in downtown San Diego, hard by the harbor. Yachts and powerboats bob at anchor, backdropped by an ocean view that seemingly stretches most of the way to Asia. The electric railroad terminal is a block distant, and the clang of car bells drifts up from the street. The visitors' room at Milberg, Weiss, Bershad, Hynes & Lerach is separated from the reception area by an L-shaped tank containing dozens of garishly bright tropical fish that flash through the water.

Seeing the fish reminded me of what a defense lawyer snarled as he left the Milberg Weiss offices one evening after name-calling negotiations: "It would be a hell of a lot more appropriate if Lerach would get rid of those cute little pets and fill the tank with piranha. Or sharks."

Enter Lerach, at the hurried pace I have learned to associate with busy lawyers, his pumping arms seemingly trying to coax more speed from his feet. He was dressed . . . well, let me say it this way: Lerach was dressed unlike any big-city trial lawyer I have encountered on a workday, a study in casual white, from cotton shirt to cotton slacks, the monochrome broken only by the brown of his Topsiders. I asked later whether this was "dress-down Friday." Lerach seemed puzzled, then he laughed. "No, no," he said. "Remember, this is San Diego!" The Washington patent lawyer Bernard Meany had chuckled earlier when he told me of his first visit to Milberg Weiss as an expert witness. The receptionist, a "rather buxom woman, who stood about thirty-eight across the top," was wearing a skimpy halter.

Lerach is a stocky fellow in his midfifties, his hair (also well on the way to being white) swept up in what seems an Afro slightly modified by a barber from the styling school that developed former President Bill Clinton's distinctive tonsorial style. I had been warned to expect a man of temper, one who loses control of his tongue when talking about opposing attorneys and the high-tech executives they represent.

Stories of the temper are legion. An unfriendly adversary told me he once heard Lerach tell corporate executives during negotiations, "I don't give a fuck if I put your company into bankruptcy. I'm going to take away your beach house and your condo in Aspen by the time I'm finished with you." When he talks about high-tech executives, he tosses around vitriol such as "scumbags" and "crime in the suites." He can be combative when dealing with other lawyers. One remembers hearing Lerach storm, "Your professional life is at an end. I am going to destroy you."

But he chose to open our talk with a grin. "So," he said, "some of those guys are saying nasty things about me, eh?"

Indeed they were, for Lerach and his firm are specialists in a type of class action lawsuit that bedeviled officers and directors of publicly held companies for more than twenty years. As we shall see in due course, Lerach split away from Milberg Weiss in June 2004, taking scores of lawyers with him, to start his own firm. The feud with ranking partner Melvyn Weiss, who ran Milberg Weiss's East Coast operation from New York, was a bitter one. But when I called on Lerach, the firm was at the apex of its success, and what he felt—and said—about securities litigation remains unchanged.

Even after the firm's split, Lerach is a dominant figure in American law, arguably the lawyer who is more feared (and respected, even if grudgingly) than any other attorney in America. There was a seemingly trivial episode late in the 2004 presidential campaign that showed how the very invocation of his name can make bold men tremble. Sinclair Broadcasting, a TV chain run by go-to-hell staunch Republicans, planned to air a documentary criticizing Sen. John Kerry for antiwar comments he made after service in Vietnam. Sinclair stock dropped sharply during the ensuing controversy, even though its owners stood firm and refused to cancel the showing. Enter, then, Bill Lerach, with the threat of a suit on behalf of harmed shareholders. The very mention of his name sent Sinclair management scurrying for cover, and the documentary they had pledged to show was truncated and folded into a longer news program.

Persons familiar with Lerach's pit bull legal strategies were not surprised at the Sinclair collapse. One of the more prominent legal names in Washington, insistent on anonymity ("I don't want to get into the SOB's gun sights"), told me, "Seeing Lerach get involved in a case is tantamount to Barry Bonds coming to the plate with the bases loaded in the bottom of the ninth."

Lerach's reasoning is direct. If he feels that companies deceived investors with misleading statements, and insiders dump their stock before the truth emerges and the price drops, he sues them. More than fifteen hundred times, Milberg Weiss lawyers have marched into state and federal courts and accused executives of chicanery. And often they have marched out again with settlements or verdicts including contingency fees totaling in the billion-dollar range over the years, leaving corporate bosses seething in their wake. Since the firm's founding forty years ago, up until the 2004 schism, it claimed to have been "responsible for more than $30 billion in aggregate recoveries." Profits for the firm twice topped $100 million a year during the 1990s.

At its peak, Milberg Weiss handled more than half of all private securities litigation cases filed in the United States each year. The year 2000 was not untypical. Of the 204 shareholder class actions filed that year, 149, or 73 percent, came from Milberg Weiss, according to statistics kept by Woodruff-Sawyer & Company, an insurance broker specializing in liability policies for corporate directors and officers. In the five years ending in 2000, according to Lerach's accounting, he and his team gained almost $12 billion in court judgments and settlements. He gathered in "oh, probably $9 billion more" through the end of 2004. Most of the latter were out-of-court settlements; only about 5 percent of Milberg Weiss cases actually went to a jury trial. (According to the Federal Judicial Center, roughly the same percentage of all federal civil cases is decided by a jury.) The litigation pie is now divided between separate offices of what once was the same firm; both are prospering, with Lerach claiming a lion's share of the tangled litigation resulting from the collapse of Enron Corporation.

Before and after the split, Lerach considered himself a private regulatory policeman, doing the job that the Securities and Exchange Commission cannot or will not do. He speaks scornfully of the lackadaisical attitude the SEC has taken toward securities cheats since the Reagan administration, and continued during the era of President Clinton—a man he considered to be a friend, and for whom he raised hundreds of thousands of dollars from fellow trial lawyers.*

Lerach is even tougher on corporate financial officers. Several years before the accounting scandals that led to the collapse of Enron and numerous telecommunications companies, Lerach was warning about bookkeeping fraud. As he stated, in prescient words, financial reports are written by "insiders whose cash bonuses depend upon meeting pre-set earnings targets and whose ability to pocket millions from . . . option-related stock sales is

---

*Reflecting after I spoke with Lerach, I realized perhaps why he continued his friendship with Clinton even while deriding his attitude toward a vigorous SEC. If the SEC did its job as Lerach says it should, he and colleagues could suffer a near-terminal blow to their pocketbooks.

dependent upon meeting earnings expectations." He asserts that the figures are often juggled to present the desired result. (Lerach is not alone in his disdain for CFOs. Less than two weeks after we spoke, Arthur Levitt, Jr., then the SEC chairman, told a Wall Street group, "Increasingly, I have become concerned that the motivation to meet Wall Street earnings expectations may be overriding common-sense business practice." Levitt said that auditors are part of "a game of nods and winks" in which financial reports are "distorted" to meet analysts' expectations.)

"Let's face it," Lerach declares. "Generally Accepted Accounting Principles—GAAP—are increasingly turning into Cleverly Rigged Accounting Ploys—CRAP—by corporate insiders tempted by the huge financial gains their bonus and stock options offer."

He boasts that he has put a new word into the American language—"Lerached." He explains, "When corporate lawyers are talking to these high-tech executives who have a scheme to cook the books and make their balance sheet look better, the lawyer will warn, 'You better not do that, or sure enough, you are going to be Lerached' "—that is, be sued for making false representations.

How valid are Lerach's sweeping claims of corporate chicanery? His detractors accuse him of being a legal extortionist: a lawyer who views any blip in stock prices as the result of concealed mismanagement, rather than the marketplace at work, and who sues in the knowledge that corporations will pay him millions of dollars in settlement money rather than subject themselves to more expensive litigation. He boasts of being one of the country's top trial lawyers. Ironically, however, he was not lead counsel in a single case that went to a jury until 1987, and he lost that one.* Lerach makes money by settling out of court.

The hatred and contempt between Lerach and critics are sincere. While I was in his office, Lerach had to take several phone calls (he was hosting a fund-raising party for President Clinton at

---

*Lerach initially was lead counsel in a 1977 trial involving financier Charles Keating but turned the lead over to partner Leonard Simon in midcourse.

his home the next weekend), so I wandered around inspecting his territory and taking notes. I picked up a sheaf of press articles about his career, some friendly, others not so. At the top of the stack was a full-page story in *Newsweek* (February 26, 1996) headlined, "The Lawyer CEOs Love to Hate." The lead paragraph read, "Just how much do the high-tech folks in Silicon Valley hate Bill Lerach? They've called him 'parasite,' 'leech,' 'vermin,' 'pond scum,' and 'the lowest form of life on earth.'" When Lerach got off the phone I asked him if I could have one of the packages. He grinned and waved his hand dismissively, as if he could not care less what detractors thought of him. (A good deal of self-confidence is required of a man who accumulates and distributes dozens of negative press commentaries.)

On Lerach's side of the equation is that he has helped bring some rather notorious rogues to bay. He did the first big civil suit against Charles Keating, Jr., of savings-and-loan fraud fame. He bayed after Michael Milken, the junk-bond fraudster. He was one of several civil lawyers who got a piece of Ivan Boesky's hide. He was among the pack of lawyers who pursued the vanished billions of Bank of Credit and Commerce International (BCCI).

In many of these cases, federal regulatory lawyers amassed much of the documentary evidence that Lerach used in court. But what he recovered went to bilked investors, not the federal treasury. He also goes after persons other than stock cheats. For instance, he and partner Patrick J. Coughlin won a lawsuit filed in San Diego that forced the R. J. Reynolds Company to stop using the famed Joe Camel symbol in its advertising in the state of California. Half of one of the three floors of the San Diego office of Milberg Weiss is "the Joe Camel Room," devoted to documents, plus a trove of tobacco advertising knickknacks accumulated during the litigation. The settlement was finalized in September 1998. As Lerach explained, "If they can't use Joe Camel in California, forget it—he is dead nationwide, regardless of what Congress might eventually do." The settlement also cost RJR $15 million in cash. Joe Camel vanished.

But the majority of his prey are smaller companies, particularly high-tech outfits that work in a fast-moving, volatile business climate where products can be outdated literally within weeks after development. The attrition rate is considerable among entrepreneurs whose bright idea makes a swift transition from garage workshop to publicly traded corporation. It is these high-tech executives who view Lerach as a lurking vulture, ready to swoop down if a misestimate causes even a temporary dip in income or earnings.

Lerach views the Silicon Valley entrepreneurs as the philosophical and business descendants of the Robber Barons who dominated such industries as coal, steel, and railroads at the turn of the twentieth century. He derisively calls them "the Golden Boys" who have an exaggerated view of their own talents. Accusing them of business fraud, as he routinely does in court filings, brings shrieks of rage, which he cheerfully ignores. "Nobody likes to be called a crook or named as a defendant in a fraud case, in court or anywhere else. But what the hell—if their conduct *is* crooked, what other word are you going to use? Every man is innocent in his own mind."

Whatever the merits of their cases, business was brisk for firms such as Milberg Weiss that specialize in securities litigation. A survey in the late 1990s by the National Venture Capital Association, a trade association, provided a sampling of venture capital firms started since 1986. One in six had been sued at least once. According to the NVCA president, James F. Morgan, "On average, the companies surveyed spent 1,055 hours of management time and $692,000 per case in legal fees defending each lawsuit." Of the cases settled, an average of 39 percent of the recovery went to the plaintiffs' law firms. The average settlement was $4.5 million. According to another study, this one by the Securities Industry Association, of the some 300 securities lawsuits filed each year in the 1990s, 93 percent settled without trial, at an average of $8.6 million each. One out of two Silicon Valley companies reported being sued at one time or another.

During a period in the early 1990s lasting three years and eight months, Milberg Weiss filed 229 separate suits across the United States; 69 percent of them were filed within ten days of the alleged precipitating event. More than half the suits, 122 of

them, were in California courts. Eighty-eight individuals appeared as plaintiffs multiple times—twenty-three in three or
more cases; eleven in four or more, one in fourteen cases; another
in ten. Referring to three of these repeat plaintiffs, Rep. Christopher Cox (R., Calif.) commented tartly, "Harry Lewis, no doubt
a penniless, downtrodden widow or orphan, has appeared as lead
plaintiff in over 300 lawsuits. Rodney Shields has been in over 80
cases. William Weinberger has appeared in 90 cases as of 1990.
One judge, with a wry sense of humor, obviously, recently called
one of those professional plaintiffs 'the unluckiest investor in the
world.'"

LAWSUIT CENTRAL

Lerach's office is a study in bravado, a document-cluttered combination of work space and trophy room. The decor suggests
that it is occupied by a man who means business, and who is
good at what he does. One's eye immediately fixes on a disorderly
collection of bulging brown file folders leading out from a wall to
the side of Lerach's desk. The collection forms a blunt-tipped V
perhaps twelve feet deep and six feet across at the base. Each
folder is crammed with a foot or more of documents, and each
bears the name of a high-tech, health care, investment, or other
company which Lerach (*a*) is suing; (*b*) is thinking about suing;
or (*c*) is watching because he, a colleague, or an investor suspects
chicanery. I jotted down a dozen of the hundred or so names that
were visible, and in the following days I watched a weekly Internet listing of new securities suits maintained by the Stanford
University Law School Securities Class Action Clearinghouse.
Milberg Weiss sued four of them in a month's time.

Another display, a tidier one, represents companies that have
already been Lerached—cubes of clear plastic, perhaps two
inches square, containing miniaturized pages of settlement
agreements and verdict forms of cases that Lerach's firm won
over the years. They are stacked two and three deep on the top of
three credenzas in the corner of the office that surrounds Lerach's desk, more than thirty lineal feet of victories. I asked a sec-

retary if she had ever counted the cubes. She grinned. "Too many, and we keep putting up a new one it seems almost every day."

A question nagged me then and now. For all his success, who truly benefits from all this litigation—fleeced investors or Bill Lerach? And indeed there are some aspects of his practice that seem to bear out complaints of his critics. Although he claims to speak for the individual shareholder—the little guy being screwed by a dishonest corporation—he sometimes seems to have trouble finding anyone who has actually suffered, in terms of losing money on a stock investment. A search through court records and other documents turns up some disturbing cases. In one notorious example, one that targeted Quantum Corporation, which makes high-capacity disk drives, his two name plaintiffs admitted on deposition that they had actually *made* between 70 and 100 percent on the stock in less than a year. Lerach sued anyway, on grounds that Quantum issued falsely optimistic earnings forecasts.

John Doerr, of Kleiner, Perkins, Caufield & Byers, is arguably the most successful venture capitalist in Silicon Valley, responsible for providing initial capital for high-tech firms. He is also one of the more outspoken foes of securities suits. After being involved in three such actions, he told an SEC hearing in San Francisco, "What are the hard, specific costs? The payments to settle their cases totaled $66 million. That doesn't count the direct legal costs to defend these cases, more than $12 million. Or the direct cost of management and employee time: twenty person years. Total, over ten years, $120 million, for just three companies. And what has been realized by the shareholders, the beneficiaries of these actions? Pennies on the dollar. $120 million will employ 200 first-rate engineers for a decade, creating faster, cheaper, better products."

Even when he loses one of his suits—perhaps especially when he loses—Lerach leaves angry executives in his wake. In 1992 Lerach sued a San Diego company named Alliance Pharmaceutical Corporation after it announced a delay in trials of a new blood-substitute product. An Alliance vice president, Ted Roth, remarked to colleagues that he had met Lerach socially, at Democratic fund-raisers, and volunteered to see if he could resolve the suit without running up huge legal fees.

According to Roth, he met with Lerach and offered to let him or his associates come into the company and examine any records they wished. Roth would even put a research scientist at Lerach's disposal to guide him. "We hadn't done anything wrong," Roth said, "and I was trying to behave like a reasonable man. I thought Lerach would do the same thing. Well, I was wrong." Lerach erupted with sulfurous language that Roth did not care to repeat. The case was simply a "matter of economics," and he had already lined up an expert who would testify that shareholders had lost $100 million or more. Settle or else, Lerach told Roth.

Alliance decided to fight, Roth calling the demand "legalized extortion." A federal district judge agreed the case had no merit and threw it out. Milberg Weiss filed a notice of appeal, then dropped the matter when a panel of unsympathetic judges was assigned to hear the matter. But the downside was that Alliance Pharmaceutical still spent more than $2 million in legal fees—money that Roth said could have been used for research and development.

"Disgusting," Roth says of Lerach. "An absolutely disgusting human being, and a disgrace to the legal profession."

Bill Lerach has heard all these criticisms over the years; they no longer cause him more than flares of irritation. He settled back in a chair in his conference room, popped the lid on a diet soft drink, and got comfortably askew. "Let me tell you how it all started," he said.

FROM CORPORATE LAWYER
TO CORPORATE SCOLD

William Shannon Lerach's father graduated from the University of Pittsburgh in June 1929 and assumed responsibility for administering an inheritance left by his father. "Within months the market crashed, and by the time he had met all the margin calls he lost not only the money that was supposed to support his mother but an aunt's share as well. He had a college degree in finance, but he went to work selling shoes in a department store. Things got better later—he later sold nuts and bolts for one of the big Pittsburgh companies. But he never quite got over seeing his money vanish in a matter of weeks to people who turned out to be crooks. I wasn't born until 1946, but once I heard his story, I was suspicious of what corporations did and how it affected ordinary people such as my dad."

The elder Lerach, paradoxically, did not lose his faith in capitalism, despite the wreck that the market made of his financial life. Once he began making money again he returned to the stock market, but far more cautiously. Lerach says that he grew up in a "conventional Republican, conservative pro-business household" on the north side of Pittsburgh.

Lerach was smart, which was fortunate. His father dropped dead on a Sunday morning five days before Lerach was to graduate from high school, at age sixteen. Lerach's grades enabled him to get full scholarships at the University of Pittsburgh, both as an undergraduate and to law school. He and his mother lived in a small apartment, surviving on a social security check. Befitting the 1960s, he underwent a political transformation from Goldwater Republican to antiwar liberal Democrat. He had an activist attitude in common with many other lawyers of his generation who came out of school "determined to change the world."

Lerach had defiantly written on his law school application that he did not intend to spend his life "in a nine to five job." But he started out to do just that by his choice for his first job after his 1970 graduation, that of an associate with the big Pittsburgh firm of Reed, Smith, Shaw & McClay, which represented the cream of the town's corporate big shots, including the Mellon family and its banks, Alcoa, and U.S. Steel. He started at a "fantastic" $17,000 a year—the same salary that his father had earned after a lifetime of work. The money helped sublimate whatever misgivings the activist had about corporate work, and he learned some realities about the profession of law.

First, by Lerach's observation, many lawyers at Reed Smith cared nothing about the merits of a client's case. Even when the defendant corporation was wrong, they worked hard to get it out of trouble. He believed his fellow corporate lawyers could deflect discovery of evidence, often skirting close to flaunting the canons of ethics. Time and again he would hear colleagues joke about the strength of a plaintiff's case, and how they intended to win anyway. "I would find myself thinking, 'the poor bastard, if he only knew what he really had going for him.' Our clients knew they had done something wrong; we won by wearing them [the plaintiffs] down." A local judiciary friendly to corporate interests helped.

Thus Lerach came to realize the raw power of a firm such as Reed Smith, with its deep pockets and well paid-lawyers. "This was an important lesson to me," Lerach says. "I knew that if I ever found myself on the other side, I was going to need money— a helluva lot of money."

But Lerach learned his way around the courtroom. His unhappy speciality was what he called "worms in the can of corn cases," which he defended on behalf of a food canners association. Lerach lived in a milieu of gray flannel suits and button-down collars, and he was so good at what he did that he soon was on the path toward a partnership.

Lerach even dabbled in securities law—but on the side of corporations who came under attack by dissident shareholders. In 1972, Lerach coauthored an article in the *University of Pittsburgh Law Review* that later foes would cite with glee and accusations of hypocrisy. Lerach called class actions "procedural monstrosities" and argued in favor of requiring that pleadings be made with "great particularity" to prevent abuses by unscrupulous plaintiff attorneys. He noted that while such changes would be "a departure from the Federal principle of notice pleadings, the serious problem of the abuse of the class action justifies such innovations." Lerach went on to complain about strike suits, which he defined as "claims brought to coerce defendants into a settlement without regard for the merit of the action. Such suits are brought with the hope of obtaining large attorney's fees or private settlements with no intention of benefitting those on whose behalf the suit was theoretically brought." And, he wrote, the mere threat of a class action is useful to plaintiff attorneys "as a bargaining weapon." A decade later, defense lawyers would voice the same criticisms of Lerach suits.

Despite his success at Reed Smith, dissatisfaction tugged at Lerach. Did he really want to spend the rest of his life defending corporate pooh-bahs, many of whom he thought were incompetent businessman—and liars as well? Frequently he would feel that the very men with whom he worked knew they were helping conceal corporate wrongdoing, but seemed totally unmoved by conscience. Lerach gulped unhappily and went along with the system and enjoyed the money. Then along came a case that dramatically changed his life.

"A trust department in one of the Mellon banks had invested about $7 million in a San Diego outfit named U.S. Financial that turned out to be a scam. Now the Mellon bank had zero interest in suing anybody; their mentality was that you didn't settle differences in court. Bankers who sued other people were considered undignified. But in this case, Mellon had no choice because trust money was involved. So it told Reed Smith to go after its $7 million, as part of a class action suit on behalf of other people U.S. Financial had screwed. The firm looked around and said, 'OK, Lerach, you are the firebrand, you handle this case.' I went out to Denver for a meeting of the lawyers who were handling the case."

So one evening in 1975 Lerach rode the elevator up to the presidential suite of the storied Brown Palace Hotel for a meeting of the various lawyers. Presiding was an intense New Yorker with a dense dark beard named Melvyn Weiss, who was emerging as the dean of the small group of lawyers who specialized in suits on behalf of bilked investors. A number of plaintiffs had joined the U.S. Financial suit, and the Denver meeting was to determine who would control the class action into which all the cases were folded.

Weiss explained what the case was all about. U.S. Financial was a self-contained real estate company that "left nothing to chance. It operated its own mortgage company, title insurance company, and brokerage business. It built its own product by entering into joint ventures to build, providing all or most of the financing. It also sold most of its real estate to affiliated parties." As Weiss said, the suit "alleged that this company entered into transactions with its affiliates on the last day of every reporting period, thereby creating virtually all of the profit for the entire reporting period. In those situations, U.S. Financial was advancing the money to the buyers to make their down payments. . . . [T]he transactions had no real economic substance." The churning resulted in millions of dollars being drained from the pockets of investors.

Lerach was impressed. "Mel sat there like the complete master of the universe. He was barking orders right and left, saying which lawyer would do what, laying out the scenario for what would happen in court the next day. He was in complete charge, and all of us sat there saying, 'Yes, Mel, you're right, whatever you want.' Man, I was impressed. Mel was the smartest lawyer I had ever seen. I was used to dealing with the uptight, stuffy defense lawyers. Now I was definitely on the other side of the spectrum."

BUTCHER SHOP TO LEGAL RICHES

Mel Weiss's career was rising with the trajectory of a free-flying hot air balloon when he and Lerach met. In the courtroom or across a negotiating table, Weiss is one of the more feared lawyers in America. His black beard and intense stare make Weiss a first-glance menace. But even opposing lawyers say he is of much calmer temper than is Bill Lerach. As we talked on a December afternoon in his office high above Pennsylvania Station in midtown Manhattan, he futzed around with a golf club, bemoaning that he could not play in the winter and that critical talks concerning compensation of Holocaust victims by Swiss banks who had held Nazi money during the Second World War prevented him from taking a vacation. "People who beat on my head about being a money-hungry trial lawyer should see the amount of pro bono [nonpaid] work that is going into these cases. We [Milberg Weiss] are spending millions—right out of our own pockets." He sighed and putted a ball across the room and talked about himself.

The son of a New York auditor, Weiss spent his teen years helping his father do the books of small New York businesses, specializing in the wholesale meat district. Even after four decades the columns of figures dance through Weiss's memory, particularly the "biff sheets" for the meat vendors, adjoining columns denoting sales of beef, lamb, pork, veal, and a catch-all "provisions." Each biff sheet would typically contain thousands of digits, and verifying them required some numerical alchemy that Weiss explained to me twice, but I still don't understand. "Torturous," Weiss said. "I decided I didn't want to do auditing work."

He wasn't much of a student. He wound up at Baruch College in New York City, majoring in accounting. He was a self-described "social animal," serving as president of his fraternity and in student government. An older friend ran for the state assembly and Weiss helped on his campaign "What do you do in real life?" he asked the man one day. "I'm a lawyer," the friend said. Weiss shakes his head. "This was the first lawyer I ever knew on a personal basis. I didn't know what a lawyer was—much less law school. My degree was in accounting. I wondered, though, did I want to spent the rest of my life dealing with rows of numbers." Given Weiss's gregarious nature, and his quick mind, the friend persuaded him to try the law, which he did, entering New York University in January 1957. "I loved it from the first day. At one point I was told that I had just missed making the law review. 'What the hell is the law review?' I asked."

Weiss went to class year round, spent his few spare hours doing volunteer work for the Legal Aid Society and New York Civil

Liberties Union, and was graduated (in 1959) in two years and four months. He joined the New York firm that is now Fried, Frank, Harris, Shriver & Jacobson, and the most vivid memory of his eighteen months there concerns the financier–art philanthropist Joseph Hirshhorn, whose wife's favorite dress was ruined by a dry cleaner. "The dress became Joe Hirshhorn's biggest headache, and since Joe Hirshhorn was a valued and profitable client, the dress in turn became Mel Weiss's biggest headache." How was it resolved? Mel Weiss shakes his head, as if trying to toss away an unpleasant memory. "Jeez, I don't remember. Luckily, the army put me on active duty about that time for the Berlin Wall crisis and I didn't have to deal with it any longer."

Weiss didn't care to return to a big firm, so, after his release from active duty, he worked for a couple of small offices the next six years, learning his way around the courts, trying personal injury and real estate cases, dabbling in business investments and starting up companies that went public. Then, in 1965, he met a securities lawyer twenty-two years his senior, Larry Milberg, known as one of the more skilled courtroom litigators in New York City, and they formed the firm that eventually became Milberg, Weiss, Bershad, Hynes & Lerach.

Their timing was accidental but fortunate, for the very next year an important change was made in the rules governing federal court procedures—specifically, Rule 23, which pertains to class actions. Under the old rules, as Weiss explains, "lawyers who prosecuted lawsuits involving corporate wrongdoing focused on what are known as derivative actions—legal actions brought on behalf of corporations to recover from wrongs committed against the company, but where the company's board of directors fails or refuses to act." An investor who felt that she or he had been bilked could sue, but the amounts involved were usually so trivial that a suit made no economic sense.*

But in 1966, Rule 23 was amended to permit shareholders to

---

*An academic commissioned by a business group to do a study of securities derivative suits in New York state and federal courts from 1932 to 1944 concluded that lawyers who brought them made "the ambulance chaser by comparison a paragon of propriety."

sue as a class—in effect, lumping together thousands of claims too small to pursue individually. Nonetheless, class actions did not appeal to many attorneys who had been doing the derivative suits because court procedures required someone (usually the lawyers) to pay for notifying all investors of the action. Weiss says, "Larry Milberg and I decided that if others were unwilling to take that financial risk to pursue class actions against those who defrauded investors, it was an opportunity we would accept. As it turned out, it took many years to prove the decision worthwhile."

From the start, Larry Milberg and Weiss agreed on two principles. "First, we would never be bought off by the defense with the promise that they'd pay us a good fee if we'd just go away. Second, we would commit the resources—we'd do a job comparable to that done by the defense. Now this was tough, because when you start one of these suits, recovery might be years down the road, and you are laying out a helluva lot of money from your own pocket."

What made the early years particularly demanding, Weiss said, was that corporations and their auditors and law firms simply were not used to being sued for issuing falsely optimistic earnings estimates or using bookkeeping tricks to deceive shareholders. One of the first cases Milberg Weiss brought was against Dolly Madison Industries, a conglomerate that had made more than thirty acquisitions in a year and a half. Stock soared. Then the company wrote off a great amount of assets and its stock price collapsed. Milberg Weiss sued both Dolly Madison and Touche Ross, its accounting firm.

"As we were able to examine the work papers of Touche Ross . . . I began to enjoy accounting as I never had as a student," Weiss would say later. "I began observing that the work papers almost always have the gloss of being professionally written. The only trouble is that when you finish your review you come to realize that all too often they are superficial and completely missed the lack of economic reality in the client's results of operations.

"In the Dolly Madison case, we alleged that there were many

areas of accounting that were not being reported properly. Acquisition costs and start-up costs were improperly capitalized. Inventories were overvalued. Receivables were underreserved or not being written off when they became uncollectible. Goodwill was not being properly amortized."

To understate, Touche Ross did not enjoy being put on trial for alleged professional misconduct. "Touche Ross made their defense a vendetta against me," Weiss recalls. "They told me they were going to fight me to the last trench, and that they did." The forum was a nonjury trial before U.S. District Judge John Harmon in Philadelphia ("a blue-blood conservative of the first rank," Weiss said; "the entire Philadelphia legal and business establishment was against me"). The trial dragged on for four months, with Weiss driving down from New York each Sunday to prepare for a week of courtroom combat. In the end, Touche Ross settled for $2 million—"a huge recovery," and a significant case in establishing how class action suits could be waged. "Dolly Madison established our reputation for financial fraud cases— we were *the* firm thereafter."

The Touche Ross case, and other securities actions that Weiss brought to trial or settlement, convinced him that he and Larry Milberg had made the right choice. Weiss personally could not have been happier. He had found a niche for himself that was far more satisfying than dealing with numbers or corporate paper shuffling. As he would tell me, "Practicing law is studying little vignettes of life—how people interact with one another . . . and how they solve their problems. You make people feel good when you help them right a wrong, and you punish the person who made it happen."

GO WEST, YOUNG LAWYER

Meanwhile, Bill Lerach still toiled at Reed Smith in Pittsburgh, traveling frequently to San Diego, where the U.S. Financial case was being heard. Over the months, Lerach got to know Weiss well. Both men are brash and have an egotistical streak that neither bothers to conceal. (Few good trial lawyers are modest about their abilities.) Lerach sensed that a lawyer could earn enormous amounts of money through class action suits. The two men came to be friends, on the surface at least, and as the U.S. Financial case progressed toward a successful conclusion, Weiss said frequently, "You know, Bill, you should be working for me.'"

In March 1976 Lerach finally said yes to Mel Weiss. He had made partner at Reed Smith in what he says was record time, a tenured position that would make him financially comfortable for life. Nonetheless, "I jumped," Lerach said. "The chance to work with Mel Weiss . . . well, who could refuse him?"

There was talk of his moving to New York, then the most active venue for securities class actions. By then, however, he was smitten with San Diego, where he had been spending much time during the Lincoln case. "I told Mel I wanted to stay right here. Why? Well, you looked out of my window earlier. Who the hell would swap a place like this for New York? Ugh!" So he resigned from Reed Smith and went to Milberg Weiss for $40,000 a year.

Weiss immediately exposed Lerach to a lifestyle unknown in Pittsburgh. "I had been in San Diego only a few days when Mel called and asked if I was free the next night. Sure, what do you want? 'Grab a clean shirt and come up to Los Angeles.' I did, and I found myself going to fancy Oscar night parties and hobnobbing with big people from the movie industry. Most impressive, I must say. That was Mel Weiss."

Lerach established the Milberg Weiss beachhead on his own. "There was a guy here in San Diego named Fegen, who rented offices to kid lawyers like me and to anyone else who needed a place to work. He had floors in buildings all over town that were divided into separate offices. You would share the receptionist and the conference room, but it gave the appearance of being your own office. Guys used to call them 'Fegen suites.' Nothing fancy, but for $150 a month it was all I needed."

Lerach's timing was fortuitous. A few years after he joined Weiss, the great bull market surge got underway. Coincidentally, the Reagan administration decided to give short shrift to enforcement of the securities law. By Lerach's account, the Securities and Exchange Commission forfeited its reputation as an "eagle on the street" pledged to protecting investors. (The insider nickname for the SEC derives from the angry eagle in its seal.) In a lengthy 1982 article in the journal *Class Action Reports,* Lerach decried "reduced governmental regulation of the national securities market and less vigorous federal regulatory enforcement of the securities laws."

Under chairman John Shad, a Wall Street veteran, the SEC cut back its staff and enforcement activity and various disclosure rules. The tough-minded Stanley Sporkin, the longtime head of the enforcement division—in essence, the SEC's top cop—retired in favor of John Fedders, a onetime partner in Washington's Arnold & Porter, who had spent much of his career fighting SEC enforcement actions. Sporkin, for one, was dismayed at what happened to his old agency. He told a journalist in 1982 that when the SEC shows diminished interest in suing companies for disclosure deficiencies, "that puts a lot of pressure" on corporations' attorneys to remain mum. He continued, "When you get headlines that say, 'SEC to Limit Pursuit of Unethical Conduct,' as recently appeared in the *Washington Post,* that perception is troublesome."*

There was another drawback to SEC enforcement that works to the advantage of private securities lawyers such as Lerach and Weiss. Even when SEC enforcers prove violations of the securities laws, Lerach noted, "it has no ability to recover damages for harmed investors. . . ." Any fines levied went to the federal treasury, not to bilked investors. So an individual who was damaged, and who wanted his money back, had to resort to a private lawsuit. (Between 1992 and 1996, according to a study by the General Accounting Office, the SEC closed 534 cases against securities malefactors and collected some $215 million, all of which went to the federal government. By contrast, Milberg Weiss collected recoveries in the billions the same years.)

The early 1980s also marked a sharp increase in high-tech companies—some in San Diego, but mostly in what came to be

---

*Sporkin joined the Central Intelligence Agency in 1981 as general counsel under his old friend, the former SEC chairman William J. Casey, who served as President Reagan's first director of Central Intelligence. Sporkin then became a federal district judge in Washington, retiring in 2000.

known as Silicon Valley, the area around San Jose and Palo Alto, a fast plane ride from Lerach's office. "For the most part," Lerach told me, "the guys who started these companies didn't give a hoot in hell about the investors once they got their start-up money. Their idea of 'individuality' was that since they had the ideas, they could do what they wanted with their companies. There seemed to be a competition to see who could get the richest the fastest, in terms of stock value. With that mind-set, it was inevitable that they would play games with their books, and that the shareholders would be cheated." Choosing San Diego as a base of operations, Lerach said, "was certainly a matter of me being in the right place at the right time."

Lerach argues that the very structure of biotech and high-tech companies makes them vulnerable to lawsuits. In his view, "A small growing biotech company cannot pay its president the salary that General Motors or IBM pays their top person. In fact, a lot of the compensation for the executives is stock-option based, where the executives are going to exercise their stock options every quarter and sell the stock. This puts tremendous pressure on those executives in the short term to keep the stock price up because they know, as a matter of their ongoing compensation, that they are going to exercise options and sell stock.

"And looking at it from the most favorable light, it is just a bad matrix. The compensation system puts pressure on them to put out positive news and conceal bad news because of that."

Aligning himself with Weiss also gave Lerach something he felt essential to a successful practice. "Call it what you like, but I like the term 'fuck-you money,' which means a bankroll big enough to carry you when a suit drags for two or three years and does not provide a dime of income. Mel was doing well enough in New York, with his own stuff, that he could put up the capital I needed to get started. You can be smarter than anyone in the world, but unless you have enough money to keep a suit alive, you have nothing. You either lose, or you are forced to settle on the cheap to survive." Given the pool of capital initially supplied by Weiss, "the defense attorneys gradually learned that we were here to stay, and that they could not grind us down."

By the time we spoke, of course, Lerach had money in his own right—enough to support nearly a hundred lawyers spread over three floors of the First American Center. Weiss headed a New York office with seventy-five partners and almost a hundred associates. There were outposts in San Francisco and Florida. There were also researchers, investigators (both staff and contractors), enough computer nerds to staff a high-tech company, and specialists who did nothing else but keep track of the enormous flow of paper that sloshed around the office. (I asked Lerach how much money it cost a year to keep his operation going. He answered with a grin that said such information was none of my business. Nor would he or Mel Weiss tell me what they earned annually.)*

In 1999 litigation in Chicago (see below) however, the closely guarded figures about Milberg Weiss income came out of the closet. Here they are:

Year	Weiss	Lerach	Firm Profits (In millions)
1988	2.6	2.3	20.8
1989	7.1	6.5	35.4
1990	3.4	3.2	19.8
1991	5.8	5.8	33.4
1992	9.7	9.3	46.4
1993	14.1	13.6	85.5
1994	13.0	16.0	101.2
1995	16.1	15.0	112.3
1996	9.4	9.1	63.3
1997	7.6	7.6	61.1
1998	13.6	13.6	91.0

*Lerach made the same refusal in congressional hearings in 1995. He told Rep. Christopher Cox, "You know, my mother told me when I was growing up, the most impolite question you could ever ask another person was how much money they make. . . . I don't ask other people what they make and I don't tell other people what I make." Cox noted that since Lerach reported $255,000 in political contributions in 1994, "I guess you made more than that."

But investment in nonlawyer staff is essential to the firm's success, in Lerach's view. "Let me tell you why investigators are important," he said. "We're working on a potential case right now involving [a clothing firm on the West Coast]. At about the same time their stock began to go into the tank, the trade press carried an item saying that a forty-eight-year-old executive who had been with the company for twenty-one years had resigned 'to spend more time with his family,' which is one of the euphemisms that always catch my eye.

"So we had an investigator see what she could find out by talking to employees on the Internet. She found a chat site for people who worked for the company, and she hit pay dirt in a hurry. The owner had a . . . daughter, a high school graduate . . . [who] . . . never got out of college, and who had never had a real job. She was suddenly made the president, and she didn't have an idea of what she was doing, and other employees were mad as hell. These people in the Internet chat rooms told her the whole story. Yeah, this research is expensive, and you hit some dry holes. But you've got to scratch for information." (Sure enough, several weeks later Lerach sued the company on grounds that it had not sufficiently informed shareholders of its earnings prospects and caliber of management.)

Lerach made plain that he runs a law firm, not a training school. He does the hiring for the San Diego office, and he does not cater to just-graduated rookies. "Your slip-and-fall case, your fender bender, that's a few thousand bucks. Very little comes through the door here that isn't worth more than a million dollars. So you don't turn amateurs loose on that kind of playing field; there is too much money at stake, and investors who really need to get it back." He looks for persons with extensive trial or investigative experience, and he keeps a close eye on them through their first cases. He especially likes former federal prosecutors. One associate who left the firm told me that although he "worked my living butt off, almost three thousand hours a year," he felt the experience of working with Lerach was "incomparable." Another associate, still at the firm, complained of being

"late Friday bone-tired, and a weekend of work ahead of me."
He was looking for another job.

OPENING THE CLASS ACTION DOOR

Shareholder suits of the type that were Milberg Weiss's specialty
are brought under a section of the Securities and Exchange Act of
1934 requiring full and accurate disclosure of events that might
affect stock prices. The Securities and Exchange Commission en-
forces the act under its own rule, 10b-5. Although both the law
and the SEC are silent about intent to defraud, the U.S. Supreme
Court has held that, in a private suit, the plaintiff must prove the
defendant's "scienter," a legal term defined as a "mental state embracing intent to deceive, manipulate or defraud." Federal appeals courts have offered varying definitions of "recklessness."

A U.S. Supreme Court decision in the late 1980s also made
life easier for plaintiff lawyers. For years the courts held that in
order to recover for a securities fraud, the investor must prove
that he or she relied upon a specific fraudulent statement or
omission for which the defendant was responsible. Then the
Supreme Court made a notable change, holding that the dissem-
ination of allegedly false information to the trading markets necessarily affects the price of a security. Consequently, anyone who
subsequently traded in the stock can assert that he or she "relied"
on the information, even if in fact they never heard of it. This decision, in the view of Mark E. Lackritz, president of the Securities Industry Association, "opened the door to class actions in
which attorneys are able to allege damages on behalf of large
classes of persons." The new rule provided "a lever to coerce a
settlement by translating an amorphous fraud allegation into an
astronomical damage claim," Lackritz asserted.

Nonetheless, the core issue was—and is—the difference between deliberate fraud and the mistakes endemic in a normal
business. The rapidity with which Lerach (and other firms) bring
securities suits, the gusto with which he pursues them, the fre-
quent flashes of ego, the boasting about money, his knack of taking millions of dollars in settlement money even when the case

seems to be legally shaky—all these factors make Lerach truly the lawyer corporate executives love to hate.

Opposing lawyers, and the executives he sues, dismiss Lerach as an arrogant blowhard, and surely he provides them direct evidence that he thinks highly of himself and what he does. "They say I make too much money doing this. So I make a shitpile of money—so what?" he said in a 1995 interview. "Nothing makes me happier than crafting a terrific complaint. To me, it's like a painter painting or a sculptor sculpting." He unabashedly likes the amounts of money he hauls home from winning his cases. "We make as much as we can," he told a journalist in 1996. Although he has often claimed to be motivated by gaining justice for small investors he represents, he is candid about the commercial aspects of being an attorney. "People try to pretend the law is not a business," he told the *Wall Street Journal* in 1991. "Baloney. It's a big business."*

To these and other critics, Lerach offers a tight smile and a rejoinder, "Have any of these [several expletives deleted] ever heard of Charlie Keating? Let's start there."

THE KEATING COLLAPSE

Very soon after joining Milberg Weiss, Lerach received a phone call from a stranger who said he was an investor in something called American Continental Corporation, or ACC. The man was so mad that Lerach could imagine froth spewing from the mouth at the other end of the telephone line, and it took a few minutes to calm him down enough to coax out a coherent story. The crux of the caller's complaint was that he had invested most of his retirement funds in ACC, and the value of the bonds had suddenly dropped by about a half. The man had heard rumors

---

*For the record, these boasts were collected and circulated by high-tech executives who detest Lerach and what he does. I found them on a Web site created by Taxpayers Against Frivolous Lawsuits, Lerach's adversary in a heated 1996 California referendum on securities litigation reform. See the chapter notes for specific citations; the Web site is no longer in operation.

that ACC's chief subsidiary, Lincoln Savings & Loan, was in financial trouble. What did Lerach know? And more important, could Lerach help get his money back?

Lerach busied a research assistant with what over the years had become a stylized procedure at Milberg Weiss: a review of stock prices for the past twelve months; the company's fillings with the SEC, particularly those reporting insider trading (that is, by the company's executives and directors); and whatever media stories and other information might exist.

Bells clanged immediately. ACC had changed auditing firms a few months earlier, and the company's chief financial officer had resigned for "personal reasons," which Lerach recognized as a corporate euphemism that could cover any number of sins. As he scanned through a sheaf of computer printouts his eye recognized the name of a recently hired corporate officer.

Uh-oh, Lerach said to himself, this is trouble; the man had previously been with another company that Lerach had successfully sued for securities fraud.

Then there was ACC's president, an Arizona operator named Charles J. Keating, Jr. Lerach read about how Keating had bargained his way out of troubles with the SEC earlier by accepting what is called a consent decree. For anyone involved in securities enforcement, a consent decree is laughable. Essentially the target refuses to admit that he did anything wrong—but he won't do it again, he promises.

In this instance, Lerach felt, Keating had gone back to his old crooked ways, a suspicion confirmed in part by other SEC filings. According to these papers, ACC insiders had dumped their stock in carload lots weeks ahead of the collapse. There was no hint in required regulatory filings that the company was in trouble.

Lerach showed me how his staff puts this welter of information into comprehensible form. One of his computer wizards plots, on a multicolored graph chart, the price of a stock over a stated period, keyed to show insider sales and the public statements the company is making. Laid out in visual fashion, the chart can show an easily grasped pattern of how insiders are bailing out of a company while professing that things remain on course. Milberg Weiss first developed such charts for internal use, initially to help decide whether a particular company should be pursued. They are so effective that the firm now incorporates them into formal court filings, the notion being that the graphics can help a judge understand the critical time line of a securities fraud. And blow-ups make splendid exhibits should a jury hear the case.

On Keating, there was much more work to do: a review of detailed financial reports filed with various regulatory agencies, and of real estate records showing how pieces of property had been flipped between various subsidiaries in the Keating empire, each time with questionable increases in value. More than twenty thousand persons, chiefly small investors, had put their life savings into this investment scheme. Lerach would later estimate their losses at slightly less than $300 million.

To describe Keating's sales force as vultures insults nature's scavengers. Lincoln Savings & Loan put many of its offices outside retirement communities around Phoenix. When retirees made deposits or rolled over certificates of deposit, Keating's crowd used dishonest suasion to talk them into investing the money in debentures issued by ACC. Part of the sales pitch—a lie—was that the debentures were insured by the Federal Savings and Loan Insurance Corporation, or, alternately, were backed by the vast resources of ACC. Given Keating's prominence in Phoenix, retirees believed what they were told. On discovery, Lerach would find an ACC memo that read, "Remember the weak, the meek, and the ignorant are always good targets." This is the sort of document the Lerach realized would cause a stir in a jury box, and hard stares toward the defendants.

The bottom line, Lerach decided after several days, was that Keating was a flat-out crook. As he often does when he picks up the scent of a securities fraud, Lerach thought back to what had happened to his own father. He and his associates put together a massive class action suit on behalf of all persons who had been defrauded by Keating and filed it in federal court in Phoenix.

As Lerach and other plaintiff lawyers state at length, the class action suit levels the playing field of American law. An investor who is cheated out of a couple of thousand dollars would be economically foolish to sue a large corporation on his own, for his potential recovery wouldn't pay for more than a few hours of legal fees. Lumping thousands of persons together, in the legal form of a single plaintiff, essentially means that thousands of lawsuits can be tried as a single action. As we explored elsewhere, the lawyer chosen by the judge as lead counsel controls the case and commands the lion's share of the fees. Understandably, plaintiff lawyers often devote as much energy—and acrimony—to being designated lead counsel as they do to the trial of the actual lawsuit. Further, being able to persuade a judge to certify a case as a class action is essential to a plaintiff lawyer's success. As Lerach has stated, "Absent exceptionally persistent counsel or some other unusual circumstances, denial of class certification is fatal."

Given the number of people victimized by Keating, class certification was a snap. But what could be recovered from the rogue financier and ACC? Keating had filed for bankruptcy and was pleading poverty (nonetheless, he found money for sharp lawyers). So Lerach broadened his suit to include ACC's lawyers, accountants, and financial advisers, on the grounds that they were witting parties to the fraud.

At the trial Lerach and associates presented documentary evidence so massive, so tedious—yet so necessary, from a legal standpoint—that they risked boring the jury into inattention. But several dramatic moments snapped the jurors back to full wakefulness. First was a video of Keating making a sales presentation to the persons who were selling the worthless bonds to the retirees. At one point, his smiling face filling the screen, Keating exulted, "There's money to be made here!" and tossed thousands of dollars of cash into the air. The camera caught some of the sales people crawling around on their hands and knees, scooping up the bills.

Another emotional moment came when Lerach put onto the stand a woman in her nineties, a refugee from Russia, legally blind and deaf, who spoke in broken English. She would not be shaken. "They cheated me out of my money," she said time and again. "Somebody cheated me. I did not know what I was doing." Jurors glared at Keating—just as Lerach intended.

Nor did Keating help his own cause when he went onto the witness stand and refused to testify, pleading the Fifth Amendment against self-incrimination. Keating really had no choice; federal prosecutors were in the audience, eagerly awaiting any admissions that could be used in the criminal case they were preparing. But that Keating would offer no defense in his own words had a visible impact on the jury.

The verdict, when it came, on July 11, 1992, was stunning: three billion dollars in punitive damages, which Lerach says was, as far as he can determine, the largest such verdict in American legal history. The jurors said they "wanted to send a message." And that they did. Through posttrial negotiations, the figure was bargained down to $250 million. The swindled investors did not receive all their money back—only about sixty-five cents on the dollar—but, as Lerach has put it, "Charlie Keating didn't leave them absolutely broke."* There was other fallout for Keating's lawyers. Jones, Day, Reavis & Pogue, one of the largest law firms in the United States, on April 19, 1993, entered into an agreement with the federal government under which, although it admitted no wrongdoing, agreed to pay $30.5 million in cash and $19.1 million in notes to settle a racketeering complaint. Another big law firm, Kaye, Scholer, Fierman, Hays & Handler, was sued for $275 million by federal regulators, who also froze the firm's assets. Without admitting any wrongdoing, Kaye Scholer six days later settled for $41 million.

---

*Keating was later convicted of criminal fraud and sentenced to ten years in prison. In 1996, after he had served less than five years, an appeals court overturned the jury verdict, released him from prison, and ordered a new trial. On April 6, 1999, a frail Keating, now seventy-five years old, pleaded guilty in U.S. District Court in Los Angeles to four counts of fraud and admitted taking almost $1 million from ACC when it was financially insolvent. Under the plea agreement he was not returned to prison and would pay no more fines.

HIGH-TECHNOLOGY SUING

What galls corporate executives and attorneys who contest Lerach in securities suits is his seeming conviction that Charles Keating typifies American business in general, rather than being a crooked exception. Among these persons, the conviction is deep, and sincere, that many of his lawsuits are computer generated— that a sharp movement in stock prices alone is enough to trigger legal action.

Two such claimed victims bashed Milberg Weiss in testimony before Congress in the mid-1990s that typifies why defendants consider the firm to be a lawsuit factory.

✦   John G. Adler, president and chief executive officer of Adaptec, Inc., in Milpitas, California, did not speak English when he fled his native Hungary during the 1956 uprising against Communist rule. He worked his way through engineering school and started Adaptec in 1981 in a garage. Twelve years later, it had $311 million in annual revenues and 1,400 employees. Adaptec produces hardware and software to control the flow of data between a microcomputer and its peripherals, such as printers and disc drives. As Adler recounted, "Our company . . . had 35 consecutive quarters [of] profitability. The company . . . never lost money since it went profitable. In one quarter out of those 35 [the 23rd], we had a 15 percent revenue shortfall."

Why? The quarter coincided with Operation Desert Storm, when business nationwide slumped. Also, "the company lost a contract. We didn't know that we were going to lose it. . . . Because of the high technology nature of our product, a new product's introduction is delayed by a quarter." Adler described the situation as an example of "normal business events which companies face in the ordinary course of business every day." Despite the lost contract, Adaptec was profitable for the quarter, albeit "a little lower than we wanted. . . ." On December 10, 1990, Adaptec held a conference call with securities analysts to tell them that revenues for the quarter ending December 28 would be about 15 percent lower than the analysts had predicted in written reports. Nonetheless, Adaptec anticipated a "distinctly profitable performance" for the quarter. The next day, Adaptec stock dropped from $15 to $9.88.

On December 14, Milberg Weiss sued Adaptec, claiming that Adler and other officers knew "or should have known" of the downturn in revenues. The suit alleged misconduct dating to October 10, 1989. Adaptec eventually gave Lerach more than 1,500 boxes of documents. Lerach's firm also served subpoenas on ten of Adaptec's major suppliers and customers.

One charge was that Adler sold stock shortly before the price collapsed, making a fortune while other investors suffered. As it turned out, the sales occurred nine months before the price dropped, and were reported to the SEC. And a month before the decline, Adler purchased more stock. A federal judge threw out the case as groundless, but only after Adler had spent hundreds of thousand of dollars in legal fees and saw his business disrupted for months.

✦   Another angry executive was Richard J. Egan, chairman of EMC Corporation, of Hopkinton, Massachusetts, which builds high-performance computer storage systems, with revenues of more than $350 million and 1,600 employees.

EMC had modest origins. In 1978 Egan and partner Roger Marino pooled their savings and used their credit cards to go into business. EMC went public in 1986 and quickly became a target of suits. In 1988 a Philadelphia lawyer—not affiliated with Milberg Weiss—sued, as Egan put it, "on behalf of a fellow who I later learned was a professional investor and a partner in a money management firm." The charge was that EMC's quarterly earnings had been lower than the previous quarter. Egan's lawyer said nothing improper had been done, but that defending the case would be costly. "Because we were still a very small company, we could have been completely wiped out by an adverse court ruling. I decided, very reluctantly, that we would settle the case."

This affair had two results. Egan decided that thereafter EMC would "limit public information about . . . its progress and anticipations," releasing just enough material to satisfy SEC reporting requirements. And he would not settle another suit that he felt was baseless.

Egan's resolve was tested in 1991 when EMC announced that its quarterly results, "while increasing steadily, would show less profitability than the prior quarter." As Egan stressed, "We were not reporting an actual loss, only a decline in earnings growth." Nonetheless, EMC stock dropped from $13 to less than $7. Within twenty hours, according to Egan, Milberg Weiss sued on behalf of two persons who owned a "minute number" of shares.

The gist of the complaint was that Egan and others had concealed information "so as to artificially inflate and maintain the market price" of EMC shares. The plaintiffs claimed also that Egan and Marino, his partner, sold "hundreds of thousands of shares" of stock during the period.

But was there hard evidence of wrongdoing, or had Milberg Weiss acted on suspicion alone? In this instance, the suit dropped dead, and swiftly. A magistrate assigned to handle pretrial motions, Charles Collings, was not impressed with what he called Milberg Weiss's "broad brush approach." Magistrate Collings cited one Milberg Weiss claim in particular—"EMC was actually experiencing a deterioration in its markets as a result of weakening economic conditions which would adversely affect the company's growth rate in sales and revenues and which would cause operating income to decline."

Magistrate Collings wrote: "What is the source of this information? What is the reason for believing that it is true? What is the factual basis for stating that if true, the defendants both knew of this information and knew it to be true at the time they made the statements?" The claims were "too conclusory and amorphous," Collings wrote. Nor was he impressed with Milberg Weiss's request that it be allowed to expand the complaint. He called the case "dead on arrival."

The judge with authority over the case, Frederick Skinner, agreed, writing that the "plaintiffs apparently wish to embark on a fishing expedition at the defendants' expense." (To Egan's chagrin, he did not impose sanctions requiring Milberg Weiss to pay his legal fees.) And although Egan won, EMC spent in excess of a million dollars contesting a suit that he insisted was groundless.

Such stories were commonplace in the high-tech industry. So

what does Lerach have to say about these and other aggrieved executives?

We had been chatting for an hour or so when I asked Lerach if I could expect to hear "the alarm bell" go off that day. He arched his eyebrows quizzically. "You know," I said, "the one that rings and sets the red light to flashing whenever a stock goes down by ten percent and tells you to start writing a complaint for court." Lerach laughed. "Would that it were so simple. Be realistic. We've won billions of dollars in securities cases. We are by no means anonymous. Investors read the name Milberg Weiss in the newspapers. When their stock goes south, they pick up the phone and call—that's where our cases come from."

When examining a potential case, Lerach says he asks a number of questions: "When did he buy the stock . . . what were the circumstances, who did they talk to, what information were they given? Then you have to investigate what happened with this company. Did the stock fall precipitously on the disclosure of previously unknown bad news? Is there a reasonable basis to believe that information was known at a time when it should have been disclosed?

"And the most important thing that I look for is whether corporate inside officers have sold their stock, engaged in illegal insider trading. That to me is the single strongest indication that there has been a fraud and is something that will cause us then to go further and investigate the case more closely. And we find that frequently, perhaps in three-quarters of the cases, there has been substantial insider trading by corporate officers before we sue." One of Lerach's partners, Leonard B. Simon, says he watches for companies who explain sharp earnings drops with such vague language as "changing business conditions." To Simon, this is a "signal to us that they won't tell us what is really happening with the company."

Lerach finds it ironic—and a bit amusing—that every advance developed by high-tech companies makes it that much easier for him to sue them. His three floors of office were packed with sophisticated electronic equipment and people who know how to use it. "What a change," he said. "When we first started, we did it all by hand. If we needed closing stock prices for the last year, we'd have to go over to the public library and get back issues of the *Wall Street Journal* and write down the numbers in longhand." Collecting information on such things as insider trading was equally laborious, as was screening what companies told analysts about their earnings prospects.

No more. Lerach remarked that the Starbucks coffee chain had dropped from $65 to $28 a share, and that once an investor alerted him to the slump, he had his office start collecting material. "The Internet that these golden boys developed for us is a godsend," he said. "We have more or less immediate access to all the SEC filings, the analyst reports, and the business data base of such things as Bloomberg. My guys can put together a fairly complete package in maybe three hours tops."

Contrary to the belief of high-tech execs, Lerach insists that he does not keep running files on particular companies in the hope that they will misstep and he can sue them. Then he offered a half amendment to his disavowal. If his screening system picks up signs that a company might be in trouble, someone in the office will start clipping the papers and watching the Internet for information. Such advance preparation means that Milberg Weiss can move into court swiftly if trouble materializes.

The fastest filing of a case Lerach ever made was in one day, against a Los Angeles company named IDB Communications. "The auditors resigned. They said they could not trust management's representations. The stock fell from fourteen to seven in an instant. And it turned out that the two top stockholders had sold $405 million of their stock, every share they owned, in the prior six months. . . . We recovered $75 million in cash for the . . . investors in that case." Conversely, other cases have taken up to six months to prepare.

Milberg Weiss maintained one of the more elaborate home pages that I found during more than two years of browsing the Internet for law firm sites. The firm used the page both to disseminate and to gather information. One site was an invitation to corporate whistle-blowers. "Tell Us About Corporate Fraud," reads the headline, beneath a picture of the scales of justice. The text read, in part, "Use this form to tell us about corporate fraud. We often investigate fraud on behalf of our clients but cannot obtain enough information because the corporate officers or directors, the underwriters or the accountants try to hide the fraud. If you have specific information about fraud being committed by a publicly traded company, we would like to know." The firm requested that the information be as specific as possible, and says it can be sent in confidence. The page contained a form for whistle-blowers. Lerach says that the page "can bring in some good stuff."

Another part of the Milberg Weiss site was devoted to securities cases—those it filed as well as those brought by rival plaintiff firms. Therein lies a story. In 1996 Stanford University used Silicon Valley money—both from hi-tech companies and their lawyers—to create a securities class action clearinghouse, essentially the pleadings in every securities case filed in both federal and state courts. What burned Lerach was that it also contained an article advocating securities reform written by law professor Joseph A. Grundfest, a former SEC member. The men are not friends, to understate the matter. Lerach felt the tilt was pro-defense, so he ordered his computer people to create a rival site.

Milberg Weiss publicized new suits via the PR Newswire and media statements. The closing paragraph contained a direct sales pitch for potential clients: "If you are a member of the class described above [in the release] you may, not later than 60 days from [the date of filing], move the court to serve as lead plaintiff of the class, if you so choose. In order to serve as lead plaintiff, however, you must meet certain legal requirements. If you wish to discuss this action or have any questions concerning this notice or your rights and interests, please *contact us*." (Emphasis in the original.) The lively Milberg Weiss site contained links to information on "Biggest Recent Stock Losers" and "Stock Disaster: Are These Companies Hiding Facts?"

Yet skeptics abound who think that Lerach sees chicanery where none exists, and that Milberg Weiss is more of an extortion mill than a law office. Horror stories in the securities litigation field do abound, and especially those about boilerplate suits filed within hours of adverse earnings reports, identical down to typographical errors. An oft-cited "horrible example" involved suits against Philip Morris. On April 2, 1993, Philip Morris announced that it was reducing the price of Marlboro cigarettes by forty cents a pack. It expected operating earnings to decline as a result. Less than five hours later, at 1:25 P.M., the first of several class action lawsuits hit the courts. By the end of that business day, four more suits were filed, one of them by Milberg Weiss. Five followed the next business day. U.S. District Judge Richard Owen commented as he tossed out the suits for being without merit:

> In each of these complaints, pleaded almost entirely on "information and belief," plaintiffs accused defendants of having made fraudulent statements so as to artificially raise the price of Philip Morris's common stock. Supporting plaintiffs' conclusory allegations were a few public statements made earlier in the year with a comparison to the April 2 announcement, and the allegation that because of the differences in the announcements the defendants must have committed fraud. I note that in the few hours counsel devoted to getting the initial complaints to the courthouse, overlooked was the fact that two of them contained identical allegations, apparently lodged in counsel's computer memory of "fraud" form complaints, that the defendants here engaged in conduct "to create and prolong the illusion of [Philip Morris's] success in the *toy industry*." (Emphasis added.)

(For the record, the error about Philip Morris's "toy" products was not in the Milberg Weiss filing.)

Lerach and other securities lawyers make no apologies for engaging in what outsiders might consider a "race to the courthouse." Until changes in securities litigation laws in the late 1990s (see below) the first firm to file an action had a strong claim to being designated lead counsel, thus gaining control of the case and the largest share of the fees.

Another claimed abuse involves lawyers who make settlement

demands immediately after filing suit, then settle for a dime on the dollar, strongly suggesting the cases had no merit; of shareholders who got only four cents recovery for every dollar they claimed to have lost. The U.S. Supreme Court has recognized the perils to a defendant of fighting off a class action suit. It wrote in 1978, "Certification of a large class may so increase potential damages liability and litigation costs that he may find it economically prudent to settle and abandon a meritorious defense."

What infuriates high-tech executives is that Lerach (in their view) is so ignorant of the marketplace that he reflexively sees wrongdoing any time a stock price dips, regardless of underlying economic reasons.

GRAND JURY PROBLEMS FOR "THE NEW YORK LAW FIRM"

But did Milberg Weiss in fact go beyond ethical bounds in recruiting "token plaintiffs" in filing securities class action suits? Such long-simmering charges had been discussed for four years in legal publications relating to a federal grand jury investigation in Los Angeles. But they surged into the mainstream media in the summer of 2005 with the indictment of an ailing 78-year-old Palm Springs, California, lawyer for lending his name to scores of such suits allegedly in return for $2.4 million in kickbacks. The indictment, in the U.S. District Court for the Central District of California (#CR 05-587) named as defendants Seymour M. Lazar and his lawyer, Paul T. Selzer, also of Palm Springs. The words Milberg Weiss do not appear in the seventy-seven page indictment. But it claimed that Lazar and his family members, as part of a long-running conspiracy, served as plaintiffs "for the New York Law Firm"—identified as a "law office with principal offices in New York and California. . . . [which] represented plaintiffs in class actions and derivative actions throughout the United States."

A spokesman for Milberg Weiss, in formal statements to the

media, confirmed that it indeed was the firm referred to in the indictment. (As noted above, only months earlier Milberg Weiss
had splintered into two firms, one dominated by Mel Weiss, the
other by Bill Lerach.) The spokesman professed the firm's innocence of any wrongdoing and said Milberg Weiss had cooperated
with the U.S. Attorney's Office and turned over thousands of
documents.

Thomas Bienert, of San Clemente, California, representing
Lazar, told *The Recorder* that the Justice Department's strategy
was transparent. According to Bienert, indicting Lazar could
pressure him to give needed testimony to bring criminal charges
against the real targets, lawyers in Milberg Weiss.

As of this writing—in the autumn of 2005—whether such a
strategy exists or would succeed remains unknown. The formal
charges against Lazar and Selzer included mail fraud, money
laundering, and conspiracy to obstruct justice.

The investigation had an involved provenance. It commenced
in the late 1990s with the prosecution of a wealthy ophthalmolo-
gist, Steven G. Cooperman, who had an extensive art collection.
Cooperman fell heavily into debt, and (according to an indictment) arranged for the theft of two valuable paintings from his
own collection. He collected $17.5 million in insurance. But
when the paintings turned up in a storage warehouse he controlled, he was convicted of subscribing to a false tax return and
faced a ten-year prison term. Hoping for a reduced sentence (he
got thirty-seven months), he offered prosecutors an even grander
target: Milberg Weiss.

Just how Cooperman came to know of any arrangement
between Lazar and Milberg Weiss remains unknown. But, according to the indictment, prosecutors began gathering documents on "more than fifty" securities suits "brought by the
New York Law Firm" with Lazar as lead plaintiff dating to the
early 1980s. In return, the firm allegedly "agreed to and did
share" with Lazar "the substantial attorneys' fees" earned in
the suits, allegedly paying Lazar "millions of dollars in secret
and illegal kickbacks through various intermediary law firms

and lawyers" selected by Lazar. Other plaintiffs in the class action suits did not know of these "kickback payments," which the prosecutors claim were disguised as "referral fees." In all, according to the indictment, "The New York Law Firm" received more than $44 million in fees, of which more than $2.4 million went to Lazar.

In testimony in several of the lawsuits, Lazar denied receiving any payments for serving as the named plaintiff—in one instance, calling such questions "an absolute insult." In fact, the fees he received "substantially exceeded" any pro rata share of the settlements, according to the indictment.

Predictably, defenders of Milberg Weiss termed the case a continuation of the decades-old attacks on the plaintiff bar. They also charged political motivation, noting that in May 2005 Lerach sued Halliburton Company on charges of manipulating and falsifying financial statements between 1996 and 2001. During much of this period, Vice President Dick Cheney was Halliburton's chief executive officer. Further in 2002 and 2004, Milberg Weiss lawyers made more than $600,000 in political contributions, chiefly to Democratic candidates.

And, just as predictably, longtime foes of Milberg Weiss (and the plaintiff bar) praised the action. The *Wall Street Journal* lauded the Justice Department for "finally starting to take a hard look at some dubious legal practices, and it isn't a pretty sight." Indeed, a *Journal* editorial on July 7 (headlined "The Trial Lawyers' Enron") wished that Justice had gone a step further, observing:

"One question is why Milberg Weiss wasn't indicted given the evidence that is already public [via the indictment]. The court papers flatly state that the law firm paid these illegal kickbacks, and further say Milberg Weiss then disguised the payments in its own accounting and issued false tax returns. One answer may be that prosecutors hope the indictment causes Mr. Lazar or Mr. Selzer to cooperate with the probe and testify in detail about how Milberg Weiss operated in these lawsuits."

What will be the outcome? Even before the indictments, as we shall explore shortly, the Lazar matter was among the several factors that caused Milberg Weiss to implode into separate firms.

A GROWL FROM GINGRICH

Mark Gittenstein keeps the front section of the *Washington Post* for November 9, 1994, tucked into a bottom drawer of his desk in the Washington office of Mayer, Brown & Platt, the big Chicago firm. On a bright fall afternoon in 1998 we had been talking about the legislative battles in the mid-1990s aimed at restricting the securities litigation that had made rich men of such lawyers as Bill Lerach and Mel Weiss. Gittenstein rummaged briefly and then dropped the *Post* on the desk and waved at the headline: "Republicans Capture the Senate; Close to a Majority in the House"

"When I saw that headline," Gittenstein said, "I knew we had won. The groundwork had been done; we had all the players in place. For one of the few times in this town, we were going to beat the trial lawyers." And such happened almost a year later, when Congress overrode a last-minute veto by President Bill Clinton and passed the Private Securities Litigation Reform Act of 1995 (PSLRA). Defense lawyers derisively called it "The Let's Get Bill Lerach Act of 1995," for his perceived arrogance; the sense that he bullied innocent companies into multimillion-dollar settlements, had made him a detested figure in their eyes.

As shall be seen, President Clinton's veto came as a direct result of a threat from Lerach that, to some, was tantamount to political blackmail. The episode demonstrated the power of the plaintiff bar in national politics, even at the presidential level.

As students of politics realize, Washington is a city whose major political currency is expediency. Another constant is money. When diverse political factions feel that a temporary alliance will benefit interests that they want to help, "it's time to hold your nose and sit down and do business," as President Lyndon Johnson liked to say. Nonetheless, even by Washington standards, members of the alliance that passed the securities reform legislation were about as far apart politically as possible. It also stands as one of the more intense lobbying struggles of the 1990s. And Gittenstein was the field marshal who led the disparate forces who fought the trial lawyers, and won—on paper, at least.

In 1994 Rep. Newt Gingrich, the Georgia Republican, emerged as the intellectual leader of a resurgent Republican right. For years Gingrich had heard GOP colleagues grouse about the so-called strike suits that (*a*) hurt small high-tech businesses; (*b*) put millions of dollars into the pockets of plaintiff lawyers who (*c*) passed a good portion of the cash along to friendly Democrats in the form of campaign contributions. Thus Gingrich saw, in securities tort reform, an issue that carried multiple benefits. Gingrich's immediate interest in the subject came from a complaint from a prominent constituent, Fran Tarkenton, the former quarterback of the Minnesota Vikings. Tarkenton had been an officer of a company hit by what he considered to be frivolous litigation. Tarkenton complained to Gingrich, who listened and promised to see what he could do.

So, in the spring of 1994, when Gingrich asked legislative allies who was the central player who could help him on the subject, all fingers pointed to Gittenstein, a man whom the Republican leader had every reason to consider the political equivalent of the Antichrist.

As Gittenstein is quick to describe himself, he is the archetypical Washington liberal Democrat. He served seventeen years on the staff of the Senate Judiciary Committee, rising to chief counsel and sharing the liberal views of such Democratic powers on the committee as former chairmen Joe Biden of Delaware and Edward Kennedy of Massachusetts. Gittenstein's proudest moment was as leader of a coalition that in 1987 defeated the nomination of Judge Robert Bork to the U.S. Supreme Court. Gittenstein left the Senate Committee in 1989 and eventually joined the Washington office of Mayer Brown.

A major part of the firm's practice is corporate defense work, including fending off securities suits. Given his knowledge of how to shepherd legislation through Congress, Gittenstein was a natural for securities reform. So, on behalf of the firm's clients, Gittenstein in 1994 found himself the head of a loose lobbying alliance—high-tech companies, accounting firms that had been brought into suits, venture capital firms, and a medley of "Washington representatives." Previous reform attempts dating to 1990 had failed due to the unyielding resistance of congressional friends of plaintiff lawyers and one of their major friends in Washington, the consumer advocate Ralph Nader.

When Gingrich and Gittenstein met in Atlanta during the summer of 1994, they tacitly agreed to ignore their considerable political differences. "You know," Gingrich said, "I'm coming up with the idea for something I'm calling 'the Contract with America.' What do you think of making this [securities reform] an issue?" Gittenstein did not hesitate. He felt that plaintiff lawyers had overreached in many securities suits, to the detriment of the justice system. Gittenstein was pragmatic. Although he and Gingrich shared little political common ground, he saw the alliance as a means of getting reform legislation passed.

Gingrich's agenda was more complex. That he could help beleaguered corporations was one matter. More important, perhaps, was the political factor. In his view, Democrats in Congress and elsewhere "were in the clutches of the trial bar, and he wanted to embarrass them," Gittenstein recollected of those first talks. So securities reform went into the Contract with America, the agenda that helped the Republicans to seize control of Congress in November 1994. Gingrich was elected Speaker of the House.

Gittenstein has wry recollections of the reactions to his alliance. "My Democratic buddies were outraged," he said. "They told me, 'When the Democrats get back in, you are finished.'" Gittenstein did not flinch. Younger, more moderate Democrats were signing on in support of securities reform, while the leadership "was still enthralled with the trial lawyers. If I had waited for them [the leadership] I never would have gotten this bill passed."

So he sat down with high-tech lawyers and they crafted a bill aimed at curbing the worst excesses. Given the strong Republican majority in both houses, and the support of Democratic members who felt that plaintiff lawyers had overreached, much of the debate was over details. The legislation that emerged can be summarized briefly:

+   Plaintiff lawyers would need something more solid than their "information and belief" that a corporate had violated securities laws. No longer could they make sweeping claims, and then use the discovery process—depositions and the production of documents from company files—to find a factual basis for their allegations. The act denied plaintiff lawyers the right to continue discovery if the defense filed a motion asking that the action be summarily dismissed for lack of evidence. These changes were important because defendants faced major expenses and often chose to pay "go-away money" rather than submit to costly discovery.

+   There was an attempt to define more clearly a legal concept known as "scienter," briefly, whether the defendant had a "mental state embracing intent to deceive, manipulate, or defraud." Did a corporate officer make an honest mistake? Or did he or she deliberately deceive investors?

+   Corporations were given broader latitude in making so-called safe harbor statements in their forecasts. If a company added warning caveats to such public statements as earnings forecasts, they would be immune from suits.

+   Finally, judges would name as lead counsel the party with the highest financial stake in the litigation. No longer could a plaintiff lawyer seize control by winning an unseemly race to the courthouse or bargaining with other attorneys to divvy up control and share the fees. This change would give control of suits to investors such as public employee pension funds and brokerage houses, rather than "professional plaintiffs."

Gittenstein picked up surprising allies. Sen. Christopher Dodd (D., Ct.) was in a ticklish position. He chaired the Democratic Senatorial Campaign Committee, which depended on plaintiff lawyers for millions of dollars of contributions each election cycle. But he also represented a state, Connecticut, that is the home of insurance companies weary of paying off securities suits. After much agonizing, Dodd opted for reform, saying, "The system was no longer an avenue for aggrieved investors to seek justice and restitution, but it had become, instead, a pathway for a few enterprising attorneys to manipulate its procedures for their own personal profits, to the detriment of legitimate companies and investors all across our nation."

But even as the reform act moved through Congress, the plaintiff lawyers retained a powerful ally: President Bill Clinton. They gave him millions of dollars of campaign money; he passed himself off as their friend. During the summer and early autumn of 1995 he sent them repeated signals, *Don't worry, I'll veto it and make them come back with something you can live with. I am your friend.*

But was the president serious? The act finally passed with so-called veto-proof margins in both houses. So all sides began a tedious game of Clinton watching: Would he sign, or would he veto? What few persons appreciated was the deep, if ambivalent, relationship between Lerach and Clinton.

LERACH TO CLINTON: "VETO—OR ELSE!"

Bill Lerach and I had our first in-depth talk in September 1998, the very week that seamy details emerged of Clinton's adulterous affair with White House intern Monica Lewinsky. Lerach interrupted to take a phone call from his wife. In sotto voce murmurs he seemed to be trying to soothe some ruffled feelings.

After he hung up, he volunteered an explanation. The Lerachs were hosting a fund-raising event featuring President Clinton the following weekend. Given that Lerach has two beautiful daughters within Lewinsky's age range, the women of the house were not enthralled at entertaining a guest involved in outrageous philandering. Mrs. Lerach (the third woman to carry that title; she has since been replaced by number four, a comely younger woman who had been an associate in Lerach's office) was upset also because she had just overseen an expensive decorating job, and the Secret Service detail wanted some things moved around. But Lerach was going ahead with the fund-raiser anyway.

Lerach was typical of the Clinton supporters who during this troubling period were manually skilled enough to hold their noses and write checks at the same time. He found the president's sexual misconduct "reprehensible . . . unforgivable . . . a damned dumb thing." Without breaking verbal stride, he went on to say that he admired the president anyway because of their similar up-from-nothing rise to success in their respective fields.*

Given that he had personally donated hundreds of thousands of dollars to Clinton and other Democratic candidates over the years, and had led efforts that brought in millions more, Lerach in the autumn of 1995 was ready to demand a quid pro quo. He wanted a promise from Clinton that he would veto the PSLRA. Clinton wavered. He talked about the "veto-proof" vote. Why should he squander political capital in a losing fight? Lerach sensed that his supposed friend was wavering. And what he did can be interpreted as either (*a*) an attempt to persuade Clinton to stand by his stated intentions or (*b*) crass political extortion.

Whatever Lerach's motive, the central figure became Ralph Nader, a close friend and financial beneficiary of Lerach. Nader had long helped the plaintiff lawyers in their earlier fights against changes in securities laws. Now Nader (and Lerach) saw a means of bringing the president back in line. Along with other leftists, Nader that fall was increasingly disgusted with Clinton's centrist policies and his repeated betrayal of promises to persons who had helped him win election. Nader had already made public sounds about mounting a symbolic challenge to Clinton in the California Democratic primary the next spring. No one gave him a chance of winning. But Nader could embarrass Clinton into

---

*Mel Weiss is also a political friend of Clinton. In 1997, the *National Law Journal* surveyed White House coffee and overnight visitor lists to see how many lawyers partook of Clinton hospitality. High on the list was Mel Weiss, who gave $224,000 to the Democrats in the 1995–1996 election cycle, $200,000 of which was earmarked for the Clinton-Gore campaign.

moving left and force him to spend dollars that he preferred to save for the general election. Lerach put the threat directly to the president, either during or just after a White House dinner that fall.

Lerach absolutely refuses to discuss what passed between him and Clinton, or what he told the president. But the gist of his message was that either Clinton would veto the reform act or Lerach would give Nader enough money to make a serious run in the primary.

Clinton capitulated. He vetoed the act, citing technical objections intelligible only to securities lawyers.

Critics immediately jumped on Clinton for selling out to the plaintiffs' bar; *Forbes Magazine,* among other publications, noted that Lerach had dinner at the White House a few nights before the veto. Indeed he did, Lerach said—along with about four hundred other persons, including the chief executive of a Big Six accounting firm who supported the legislation. "Big deal, huh?" he scoffed.

The episode stands as a vivid example of the power of money in American politics, and how a rich plaintiff lawyer can bully even a president of the United States.

SKIRMISHES WON—AND LOST

To the delight of Newt Gingrich and lieutenants, the first federal judges who heard cases under the new rules behaved as if indeed Congress intended to put Lerach and colleagues out of business, and they were happy to help. Chief U.S. District Judge Jerry Buchmeyer in Dallas heard the first case to be filed under the new rules, and he delighted in making a personal attack on Milberg Weiss. The issue involved the lead counsel role in a case against a company called CellStar Corporation. Milberg Weiss was the first firm to file against CellStar, via a group of plaintiffs headed by a man named Gluck.

But Milberg Weiss was challenged for the lead counsel role by lawyers for the State of Wisconsin Investment Board (SWIB), a pension fund, whose losses were much greater than the Gluck plaintiffs—$10 million versus less than $900,000. SWIB asked that the Milwaukee firm of Grant & Eisenhofer, P.A., be named as lead counsel, and that Judge Buchmeyer impose a sliding-fee schedule that would bring lawyers far less than the 30 percent asked by Milberg Weiss.

Judge Buchmeyer agreed. He wrote, "Congress singled out the law firm representing [the Gluck plaintiffs] in this action for much of the criticism [about "repeat-players" plaintiff lawyers], stating that this firm filed 229 suits over 44 months and citing one of its partners as saying, 'I have the greatest practice of law in the world. I have no clients.'" (The words were Lerach's.)

He continued, "Wresting control of securities class actions from lawyers with nominal plaintiffs and giving the power to large investors will benefit all investors if it is done at the outset of the litigation. The best relief for the plaintiff class is not always the relief which would be sought by a 'professional plaintiff' or a plaintiff with a very small share in the defendant company . . ." Milberg Weiss thus lost the first challenge to the new rules. The firm also began losing cases on summary judgment motions, particularly in federal courts in California.

Lerach asserted that Judge Buchmeyer, as well as many other federal judges, "simply does not like plaintiff lawyers. The early adverse decisions reflected a lawyer-bashing state of mind by very conservative judges—the Reagan appointees, for the most part."

Milberg Weiss and other plaintiff firms attempted to bypass the new requirements by bringing parallel actions in both state and federal courts. Their goal was to obtain through discovery in the state proceedings, evidence needed to support a federal action. Gittenstein quickly reassembled his coalition, and Congress passed legislation that would bar such a dual-track approach.

I visited Lerach just after the bill arrived at the White House. Once again the question in the tight world of securities litigators was whether President Clinton would sign or veto.

I put the question to Lerach, What does the president intend to do? You've been working your butt off raising money for him, giving him your house, urging your friends to give him a lot of money. Is he going to stick with you, or stick it to you?

Lerach sighed and shook his head, as if sympathizing with himself. "You can't judge a president on one issue," he said. "He believes in many of the same things I do, so I am going to support him."

I read news accounts the next week of Clinton's California fund-raising trip, and his stop at what the *Washington Times* called "the Mediterranean-style mansion of lawyer William Lerach." Congress was moving toward the eventual impeachment of President Clinton, and even his closest friends were urging him to resign because of the Monica Lewinsky sodomy scandal. But Clinton heard only solace from the loyal Lerach. According to the *Washington Post,* he said, "Mr. President, don't have a broken spirit. Don't resign. . . . You stay in there, and you fight." Clinton gathered in $400,000 from Lerach's crowd, and then flew to Silicon Valley and a $25,000-a-couple dinner hosted by John Doerr—a venture capitalist who detests Lerach—and raised $650,000.

Although the bill reached the president's desk in September, he dallied as he continued to beg money from plaintiff lawyers for Democratic congressional candidates. Late the afternoon of November 3, Election Day, with all possible contributions in hand, the president signed the new reform bill.

Lerach greeted the "betrayal by my friend" with a string of expletives that he later said he preferred to keep off the record.

A BUMP IN THE ROAD

So what impact did the further changes have on securities litigation? In the following months, I monitored the securities litigation Web site maintained by Stanford University. New suits are posted weekly, with the names of the firms that file them. Milberg Weiss continued to click along at the rate of three to five cases a week.

More formal statistics bore out a judgment I made on anecdotal evidence. In the long run, the act did not hurt Milberg

Weiss's business. According to the Securities Class Action Clearinghouse, at least 235 companies were named as defendants in federal class action securities fraud suits in 1998. Professor Joseph A. Grundfest, who runs the project, said, "That litigation breaks the prior record of 227 companies sued 1994. It also indicated a litigation rate of close to 'one-a-day' for every trading day that the stock market is open." And the surge of suits continued, with 224 being filed in 2002. Of these, the Stanford clearinghouse reported, almost 60 percent were filed by Milberg Weiss. And the same trend continued in succeeding years.

Yet defense lawyers found solace in other figures. During 1998 more than half of their motions to discuss securities suits were granted, in whole or in part. Of the three cases that actually went to trial under the new rules, the defense won in each instance. One reason is that the new rules stiffened the backbone of insurance companies that previously bargained their way out of nuisance suits. Tower C. Snow, chairman of the San Francisco defense firm of Brobeck, Phleger & Harrison, said, "The insurance industry, I think, is tired of paying out very, very significant claims . . . and would like to see more cases go to trial."

One of Snow's partners, Robert Varian, won one of the three cases that went to trial, and afterward jurors were interviewed about what factors went into their decisions. Snow said, "The first was that the jurors do understand that the federal securities laws are not investor insurance, that they're there to ensure . . . full and accurate disclosure, but they are not an insurance policy for investor losses." Another factor is more human. "For jurors to find a company liable, they oftentimes have to find a large number of people, not just people within the company, but accountants, underwriters, and others . . . that they lied. And most people actually have a hard time doing that. Most people are not so cynical."

NO APOLOGIES NEEDED!

Lerach and Weiss offer no apologies for bedeviling persons whom they consider to be securities cheats or other malefactors. Weiss has heard the criticisms, and he dismisses them with a

frown that darkens his face. Weiss does have a thin skin when he
or other lawyers are criticized. The first time we met, he opened
the conversation by berating columnist William Safire of the *New
York Times* for using a Shakespeare quotation, "Let's Kill All the
Lawyers," as a headline that day. "This sort of thing doesn't
help," he said. "I've found that most people stop bitching about
lawyers when a situation comes up when they need a lawyer."

Weiss makes another point. Sure, he's made millions of dollars from securities suits. But he asserts that he's plowed much of
the money back into pro bono cases from which he received not
a dime. For instance, he was a central figure (along with class action pal Michael Hausfeld of Washington) in litigation that
forced Swiss banks to surrender millions of dollars that Holocaust victims deposited in them during the 1930s. "As a Jew, I feel
strongly about what these lousy, bloodsucking banks did to
Hitler's victims and their survivors. This is the sort of case that
needed a tough lawyer, and, by damn, say what you want about
Mel Weiss, when you hire me on, you are hiring a tough lawyer.
This is also the kind of case where a lawyer shouldn't make any
money. These people were screwed once by Hitler—they need a
break now. Now other lawyers see it differently, and there was
one group involved in the litigation who wanted to do it on the
fee-as-usual basis. No way! And why can I be so noble? Because I
made a pot of money elsewhere."

Nor is Weiss moved by criticisms of class actions. In a 1997
symposium, he challenged the perception that "a class action
lawsuit is a [money] tree growing in the lawyer's garden, and I'm
finding that that's a prevalent view with a lot of judges around
the country. But when you listen to the people who are the observers of what's really going on out there, the client population
is profoundly interested in these lawsuits, these classes of people,
and they're not only the poor.

"Now, I'm involved in these big insurance litigations, like
Prudential, where there were 10 million people who were sold
these insurance policies over a fifteen-year period, when the regulators weren't doing their job, and we're getting them relief.

"But when these cases come into a courtroom, my God, it's too complicated, it's too big, it's the lawyer's case, the lawyer is going to make too much in fees. So we're in this dilemma where we're getting bombarded as lawyers by our own profession, by our own judges, and we're being criticized for pursuing our own interest instead of social policies. . . ."

Another panel participant, Professor Linda Silberman of New York University Law School commented that the public perception is that these cases conclude with "million-dollar fees for lawyers and coupons for the class. . . ."

Weiss shot back, "You're talking about one out of two hundred cases. I mean that's ridiculous."

PROSPERING UNDER REFORM

Ironically, after a few initial bumps, Milberg Weiss thrived under the legislation that was intended to put it out of business. The firm's megamillion-dollar resources were the chief reason. Prior to passage of the PSLRA, the lawyer who "won the race to the courthouse" stood a good chance of becoming lead counsel. Even if his firm proved too small to handle the case without the help of other offices, he shared in the fees. The complaint could be very general, without alleging specific acts of wrongdoing. The plaintiff lawyer would then use discovery to find information to buttress his case.

But the PSLRA imposed a requirement that complaints had to be specific; otherwise, they would be dismissed summarily by the judge. Finding such information, of course, is a laborious and expensive process. And one tailor-made for a firm with the war chest of Milberg Weiss. Mel Weiss promptly ordered the creation of an investigative unit in the firm that ultimately numbered more than two dozen forensic accountants, damage analysts, and investigators, perhaps a dozen of the latter being former FBI agents who had specialized in economic crimes.

The PSLRA also contained a requirement that the lead counsel role go to the party that had suffered the greatest loss. The new rule rendered worthless Milberg Weiss's famed knack for being able to crank out a lawsuit within hours of a drop in stock prices. The biggest investors (and losers) in most instances were institutional—pension funds and university endowment funds, to name a few. Milberg Weiss set about courting these funds, and it soon signed up two major ones, for New York State employees, and for the University of California system. There was another benefit for Milberg Weiss: Once picked as lead counsel, its expertise and resources enabled it to proceed on its own, without bringing in other firms that previously would have shared in the fees.

The investment paid off. A study issued in early 2003 by the Securities Class Action Clearinghouse found that Milberg Weiss had been chosen as lead counsel in "almost 60 percent" of securities class actions in 2002. Further, the firm had been lead counsel "in over 50 percent of all post-Reform Act cases settled to date." The firm's dominance was continuing well into 2004.

So what did the irascible Lerach think of the unintended consequences of the PSLRA? "Just like the old saying puts it," he said, "if you shoot at the fucking king, you damned well better hit him. These fuckers took their best shot, and I'm still around. Hell, maybe I should thank them—we are making more money than ever."

STRIKE SUITS VINDICATED?

The sudden collapse of many dot.com companies at the turn of the century, and an array of other corporate scandals, notably Enron Corporation, gave Mel Weiss and Bill Lerach cause for proclaiming, "We were right all along. We told you a lot of these start-up companies consisted mainly of hot air. Now look at the mess."

Perhaps. But an attorney in a leading Silicon Valley defense firm posed what he admitted was a devil's advocate theory: "Lerach is like the little boy who kept crying out 'Wolf, wolf.' He made so much fuss over picayune stuff that when real scandals began to emerge, many people were conditioned not to believe what was going on." This lawyer hastened to add, "Don't get me wrong, by no means am I blaming Lerach for what happened. But I still think that a lot of the stuff he did in the 1990s was pure nonsense."

Predictably, Milberg Weiss moved swiftly into the financial shambles of the collapses. Lerach's most notable coup was his emergence as lead attorney for persons who saw their Enron stock become worthless overnight. He and associates set up a headquarters in a Houston hotel adjacent to the Enron offices and signed up angry ex-employees who saw their life savings vanish. And the proximity paid immediate legal and public relations dividends. A former Enron employee who had gone into her office to pick up personal belongings remarked to her husband that shredding machines were working full-time, so much so that the hallway was littered with bulging trash bags.

Hmm, the husband thought, perhaps the lawyers could use some of that stuff. At his urging, the wife returned to the building and lugged away several of the bags, which she handed over to the Lerach field office.

A surprised Lerach moved quickly to exploit the shredding. Waving thin bands of cut-up paper in the air, he went before TV cameras to denounce Enron for "destruction of evidence."

Media showmanship? To be sure. But Lerach became counsel for the University of California Board of Regents, which suffered staggering losses when Enron evaporated. In addition to suing Enron executives, he went after banking, accounting, and law firms that he termed "knowing participants in a fraud . . ." His results were staggering. In a bit more than a year's time, Lerach obtained settlements totaling $7.1 billion—"the largest class action securities settlement on record," as the *New York Times** reported. Lerach and associated firms would receive 8 percent of the first $1 billion, 9 percent of the second $1 billion, and 10 percent of recovering beyond that. As of August 2005, fees totaled about $680

---

*As the *Wall Street Journal* caustically noted in an editorial, Lerach averted his eyes from another sizable California group that benefited from some of the shady Enron deals—the California State Employees Pension Fund, or CALPERS, which with $171 billion in assets surely could have been a deep-pocketed defendant. As the *Journal* noted, CALPERS "was a direct investor in the Enron 'special purposes entities' that have Milberg Weiss's most flamboyant partner blowing steam out of his ears."

million. (Individual victims would receive pennies on the dollars.) And Lerach issued a warning to the remaining defendants: "We've said all along that those who settled earlier would do better." Lerach clearly was headed for fees above $1 billion.

THE $50 MILLION SPLIT

After about a half century as a writer and journalist, I have developed what I consider to be a fairly keen nose for sniffing out things that I feel to be true, even if I lack direct proof. For scheduling reasons, I happened to interview Bill Lerach in San Diego several months before catching up with Mel Weiss in New York. In retrospect, I could think of not a single direct statement that Lerach made that indicated any displeasure with Weiss; indeed, he sounded absolutely grateful that his partner had taken him from a dull Pittsburgh corporate life into a lively practice, and made him a multimillionaire in the process.

Nevertheless, there were enough throwaway lines and grimaces at odd moments to make me conclude, "For whatever reason, Lerach does not like Mel Weiss." And I got the same negative impressions from Weiss. Then rumblings came from both New York and San Diego about serious strains in the firm. One involved the federal grand jury investigation in Los Angeles that would result in the indictment of a lawyer accused of being a "sham plaintiff" in more than fifty Milberg Weiss suits (see pages above). Amid sounds of increasing discord, I asked a partner who was an ardent gossip, albeit an off-the-record one: "What's going on? Why are they so mad at one another?" A long pause. He mentioned the Los Angeles matter, then added, "but right now the one-word answer is Lexecon."

To anyone familiar with Milberg Weiss, Lexecon became the $50 million word. And, along with the Los Angeles indictment, it led to an explosive division of the firm in the summer of 2004.

SEEDS OF A SPLIT

Big-time litigation, at its most intense, takes on the characteristics of a parking lot brawl, with both sides attempting to destroy the other party and anyone working on their behalf. At the working level, modern law is a world devoid of the pleasantries of polite society. No longer do adversaries treat one another with feigned politeness. If winning lawsuits requires the destruction of a man and his career, so be it. But how far can an attorney go in discrediting an unfriendly witness? At what point do attacks on a person's professional reputation cross the line dividing acceptable tactics and outright slander?

It was just such a circumstance that created the fissure that eventually resulted in the dissolution of the firm of Milberg Weiss. And it began, ironically, in a case that was one of the firm's earliest big triumphs—the litigation described above concerning the financial rogue Charles Keating.

At the center of the controversy was a University of Chicago law professor (and later dean) named Daniel Fischel, a slight, diffident man with a distinguished career in conservative legal academia. In addition to overseeing what is considered one of the country's top ten law schools, Fischel, as a profitable sideline, ran an economic consulting firm in Chicago named Lexecon, Inc. The company was started in 1977 by highly respected University of Chicago professors Richard Posner, now a judge on the Seventh U.S. Circuit Court of Appeals in Chicago, and William Landes, protagonists of a conservative economics movement known popularly as the Chicago School. Free market devotees, they advanced the doctrine that economic analysis should be the basis for resolving most lawsuits, and especially those involving antitrust. Lexecon regularly hired out to defense attorneys to "help lawyers understand and analyze and present evidence about economic issues." Four persons associated with Lexecon, all Chicago School economists, are Nobel laureates.

A Cornell Law School graduate, Daniel Fischel clerked for Supreme Court Justice Potter Stewart before making his way to the University of Chicago Law School. Fischel joined Lexecon in

1980 after studying under Posner. Fischel testified frequently as a defense witness in securities suits by disgruntled shareholders, and he was a success. In 1990 he was listed as an expert defense witness against fifteen cases brought by Lerach's San Diego office, and an equal number by the New York office of Milberg Weiss. Eventually he became president of Lexecon. The *Wall Street Journal* called Lexecon "the Cadillac of firms that provide analysis and testimony for defendants in such cases," with he and three other partners earning an estimated $1.5 million each.

Fischel can be a contrarian. In a 1996 book, *Payback: The Conspiracy to Destroy Michael Milken and His Financial Revolution,* Fischel argued strongly (and often convincingly, in my view) that the 1980s, the much-defamed "decade of greed," forced corporate America into necessary changes that it would not have made on its own. Fischel's thesis was that such innovative financiers as Michael Milken and his investment banking firm, Drexel Burnham Lambert, offended old-line investment houses (who lost business) and Fortune 500 corporations (whose executives lost their jobs because of downsizing) and hence made themselves targets of the financial establishment. Having demonized Milken et al. in the media, the financial establishment encouraged federal regulators such as the SEC to pursue them. Fischel compared their "reign of terror" against Milken as being on a par with the "same anti-capitalist greed-bashing rhetoric used so successfully in Communist countries." He argued that savings-and-loan disasters resulted from market shifts and the same overzealous bureaucrats. Suffice it to say that Fischel's views on corporate America did not coincide with those of Lerach and Milberg Weiss. Even worse, from Lerach's standpoint, the professor proved a deadly defense witness in securities litigation.

In Fischel's view, his direct clash with Lerach—and, eventually, Milberg Weiss—began with a case involving Nucorp Energy, Inc., an oil and gas company whose stock soared in the early 1980s, then collapsed as the firm went into bankruptcy. Lerach sued, making his usual charges that Nucorp executives had cooked the books with the aid of high-priced outside consultants and bankers. Fischel had a different story. Although Lerach fought hard to exclude his testimony as irrelevant, Fischel told the jury that Nucorp's demise was due to turbulence in the oil market, not chicanery. Investors should have realized the risks, he said. Lerach played hard. He subjected Fischel to a biting cross-examination in an attempt to discredit his testimony. During the trial, defense lawyer Stuart Kadison would later testify, Lerach pushed his way into a crowded elevator and shouted at him, "Kadison, this case is going to bring an ignominious end to your mediocre career."

The trial, which stretched from October 1987 through the following April, was important to Lerach. It was the first Milberg Weiss case he tried before a jury from start to finish as lead counsel (he had begun the Keating matter in that role, but partner Leonard Simon took it over mid-trial). The trial was held before a hometown audience in San Diego. Lerach had already recovered $54 million in settlements from various defendants, with $8.5 million as Milberg Weiss's share, and he expected much more from Nucorp and other parties who chose to go to trial. He demanded $200 million in damages. When the deliberating jury asked for a calculator, Lerach quipped to the judge that it be given one "with at least nine places on it so they can compute a verdict above $100 million."

To Lerach's astonishment, the jury ruled for the defense.

That a prominent plaintiff lawyer had taken it on the chin in a securities case delighted Lerach's enemies. Economist Benjamin Stein wrote in *Barron's,* the business weekly, "Professor Fischel's testimony totally turned the case around . . . to almost everyone's shock, the defense won, and if there was a single pivot, it was Professor Fischel." The *Wall Street Journal* opined, "Mr. Fischel won the case. . . ."

Lerach would later argue that he paid little attention to these commentaries, which he felt were self-promoting pieces that Fischel had planted with Chicago School friends at *Barron's* and the *Journal.* He did concede, "I think my pride was probably bruised a little." Nor did he feel that Fischel's testimony was "a significant factor" in the trial, and surely not enough to start a campaign to destroy his credibility as an expert witness. Lerach testified to having taken the loss in stride. After the verdict, he and other Milberg Weiss lawyers "went to a bar by the office. We got extremely drunk."

Lerach's denials of concern notwithstanding, that defense lawyers would perceive Fischel as an effective expert witness was disturbing. Trial lawyers routinely gather information that they feel will discredit witnesses they face regularly. In politics, this strategy is called "opposition research." So Milberg Weiss quietly began putting together a dossier on Fischel and Lexecon.

If Milberg Weiss indeed wanted to end Fischel's career as an expert witness, a seemingly golden opportunity arose during the Keating litigation. As noted earlier, Keating was penniless by the time he was taken to court, so Milberg Weiss went after a coterie of accounting and law firms that had advised him during the rise of Lincoln Savings. One defendant was the accounting firm of Arthur Young & Company, (after a merger, now Ernst & Young) whose partners Lerach and Leonard Simon made a target in the suit. Early on, Young retained Lexecon. In the past, Lexecon had done much work for Keating's ACC and Lincoln S&L in the past, so Fischel and associates were familiar with how the business operated.

Someone at Milberg Weiss became suspicious. Did any of Fischel's earlier work for Keating help create the problem? Keating's enterprises had surrendered thousands of boxes of documents, and associates had spent weeks poring through them. To Len Simon's delight, tucked away in the mass of paper were four reports that Lexecon had written for Keating companies, two of them intended to dissuade federal regulators from moving against the companies. One of them stated, "We have shown that even under conservative assumptions, Lincoln is much safer than comparable thrifts and Lincoln is far safer today than it was when acquired by American Continental. . . . Our finding that Lincoln's asset portfolio is better diversified than those of comparable thrifts is not surprising. One likely reason is that . . . the use of high yield junk bonds may increase the portfolio's diversification."

Another report concerned the value of two of Lincoln's biggest assets, the Phoenician and Crescent hotels. In the later words of Judge Richard M. Bilby, of U.S. District Court in Phoenix, "Lexecon was highly critical of the appraisal methodology and conclusion of the regulators' consultants. The values reached by Lexecon allegedly assisted in preventing write-downs on Lincoln's books." There were also documents about how Lexecon helped Lincoln fend off a probe by the Federal Home Loan Bank of San Francisco in 1987. Keating's companies paid Lexecon $1,045,886 for 4,675 hours of work.

Leonard Simon happily wrote a memorandum on March 21, 1990, "We have recently discovered some work which Lexecon did for Lincoln/ACC . . . [and] we are [adding] them as defendants in the case. The information should be extremely useful in cross-examining Fischel or others from the firm."

Milberg Weiss began drafting a complaint naming Lexecon as a codefendant. As Lerach would later contend, Lexecon's reports stopped regulators from moving more quickly, resulting in losses by 23,000 Keating investors. By his reckoning, Lincoln was "$111 million underwater on its net worth requirement as of September of '86." His contention was that these losses could have been prevented were it not for the Lexecon reports.

Just how extensive was Milberg Weiss's research? Years later, no one in the firm could produce a single memorandum or other piece of paper evaluating whether the suit was warranted. Lerach would testify that any such papers were "discarded." And, as shall be seen, Milberg Weiss's complaint ignored some warnings that Lexecon made about the financial viability of Lincoln Savings.

Steve Neal, a Keating lawyer, learned what was happening, reviewed the reports, and set up a meeting so that he and Fischel could argue against their inclusion in the suit. Understandably, accounts varied sharply as to what happened.

Present for Milberg Weiss were Lerach, Simon, and associate Stephen Steinberg. According to Fischel, during a break he chatted with Steinberg in the men's room. Steinberg supposedly told him that injecting Lexecon into the suit was wrong, and that he had argued against doing so. Fischel claimed that Simon told him that Lexecon could get out of the case if he agreed to give testimony against two other defendants—Kaye, Scholer, Fierman, Hays & Handler, a law firm, and Touche Ross, an accounting firm. Milberg Weiss would prepare his testimony. As Fischel lawyer Alan Salpeter would later charge in his opening statement, "It became very clear that what Milberg Weiss was demanding was that Fischel lie under oath. . . ."

Lerach, Simon, and Steinberg denied that any such exchanges took occurred. Indeed, Lerach accused Fischel and Neal of attempting to blackmail him. Somehow Neal obtained a memo that Lerach wrote after the Nucorp trial based on interviews with jurors. To understate, it contained some very indiscreet language, especially coming from a prominent Democratic contributor who prides himself on political correctness. In the memo, Lerach asserted that women "are much more opinionated then men, less susceptible to reason and less likely to change their minds based upon the arguments of others." At another point he wrote, "An oft-repeated theory of jury selection is that heavy-set jurors tend to be good plaintiff jurors because they are happy-go-lucky types appears to be incorrect. Teachers, especially high school teachers, make good defense jurors because they are used to disciplining people, that is, saying no to them and disappointing them." He asserted that Republicans have biases that they cannot overcome.

Lerach made other disparaging remarks. "Jurors are totally oblivious as to who is trying to hide the ball from them and who is being forthcoming. . . . Jurors tend to forget at least 50 percent and perhaps as much as 85 percent of what they hear. . . ."

According to Lerach, Neal brandished the memo and said, "If you continue this lawsuit, we're going to make this jury memo public, and it's going to embarrass you, and it's going to hurt your career."

Lerach snapped in reply, by his account, "Don't threaten us!" Neal denied that any such exchange took place.

So Neal and Fischel failed in their mission to stave off the suit. Late on a Friday afternoon Milberg Weiss partner Kevin Roddy wrote the final version of a 231-page draft naming both Fischel personally and Lexecon as defendants. According to subsequent testimony, neither Simon nor Lerach had decided at that point whether to include Fischel as a named defendant, and. the evidence is that Roddy proceeded on his own. Whatever, Roddy sent the draft to no less than 101 lawyers involved in the Keating litigation, and also to the court clerk, with a request that it be filed. Circulating the document was in accordance with court procedures. But, as Fischel would complain, many of the defense firms that received the draft represented companies that were among his clients.

When Simon saw Roddy's draft on Monday morning, he ordered it withdrawn. For tactical reasons, he did not want Fischel named as a defendant, only Lexecon. So the draft was edited to remove Fischel as a named defendant. The allegations against Lexecon, however, remained intact. Simon sent a letter to other lawyers telling them to ignore the draft. He and Roddy later testified that its circulation "was simply a mistake."

Lexecon tried, and failed, to be dismissed as a defendant in the Arthur Young litigation. Judge Bilby found that material issues existed as to whether Lexecon's reports were false and misleading, and whether Lexecon knew of Lincoln's fraudulent activities. After four months of testimony in 1992 and just before the case went to the jury, Lexecon asked for a directed verdict taking it out of the case. Judge Bilby denied the motion, ruling that the jury must decide the level of Lexecon's knowledge of, and involvement in, Lincoln Savings' actions and practices.

After intense negotiations, Milberg Weiss agreed to dismiss the case against Lexecon in what the adversaries were careful to label a "resolution." The point was important. As Lexecon's lawyers stated, the company wanted to avoid the appearance that it had "settled" the case because doing so "would subject its experts to unfair cross-examination with respect to credibility and expertise" in future trials. All Lexecon was willing to admit was that its services may have been "misused" by Lincoln Savings & Loan.

In return, Milberg Weiss and the other plaintiff lawyers agreed that in future cases they would not cross-examine any Lexecon experts about a "settlement." However, the fact that a case was filed and resolved could be used on cross-examination without mention of the terms. As an appeals judge would later note, "This aspect of the resolution was included because Lexecon and Mr. Fischel were concerned that if the term 'settlement' was used, Lexecon experts would be open to in-depth cross-examination in courts across the country with consequent injury to its business."

Fischel had won what he felt was a clear vindication, even at the expense of legal bills of $3.8 million. But Milberg Weiss had by no means heard the last of the tenacious professor.

"WE ACTUALLY THINK [FISCHEL] . . . IS A CROOK"

Daniel Fischel's office at Lexecon in the 1990s was high above the Chicago Loop, with an endless view eastward over Lake Michigan. As he sat and fretted about Lerach and Milberg Weiss, he felt he heard the distinct sound of gloating coming from his adversaries concerning the "resolution" of his role in the Keating litigation.

Milberg Weiss delighted in using the Keating material to attack Fischel's credibility in other cases. The most biting comment came in pretrial proceedings in a Milberg Weiss case against Apple Computer, Inc. in which Fischel was a defense expert witness. In a hearing in the judge's chambers, partner Patrick J. Coughlin argued, "We actually think he [Fischel] is a crook . . . who let Lincoln Savings . . . carry out one of the largest frauds in the country."

After the hearing, Coughlin walked over to Fischel and said, "I apologize. I shouldn't have said that. If you want, let's strike it from the record, so that it won't be down in black and white." Fischel refused, sensing that he could put the remark to profitable use later. Any remorse Coughlin felt was short-lived, for he later declared in a written filing, "When all is said and done, Professor Fischel may well be America's leading proponent of amoral business practices and corporate lawlessness."

There was more. Milberg Weiss lawyer Eric Isaacson wrote to an attorney elsewhere a memo captioned "Dangerous Dan

Fischel—Ersatz Economist From Hell" and suggesting ways to portray him as "the reprehensible slob that he is." He asked for "additional dirt on Fischel." Among the blatant charges made by Milberg Weiss were the following:

✦　Coughlin told a San Francisco-area legal newspaper, the *Recorder,* that in his work on Lincoln Savings, Fischel made the "biggest mistake any guy made in this country."

✦　At a securities litigation conference at Stanford University in July 1991, Lerach charged that Fischel gave Keating a "clean bill of health." He refused to disavow Coughlin's tough language.

✦　Another Milberg Weiss partner, Patricia Hynes, told opposing counsel during a hearing in Chicago that Lexecon carried "too much baggage" to be an effective expert.

✦　Partner Kevin Roddy wrote a letter to the *National Law Journal* stating that Lexecon "settled" the Keating case—a word that Lexecon assiduously avoided by insisting that its departure from the case was a "resolution." Fischel was also upset that Roddy wrote that Lexecon was guilty of "wrongful activities on behalf of" a convicted felon, and "fraudulent dealings with regulators."

Finally, Dan Fischel had had enough. So one morning in October 1992 he picked up the phone and called Alan Salpeter at Mayer, Brown & Platt.

"HOW STRONG IS YOUR STOMACH?"

Alan Salpeter is a tall, balding man with the physicality of a college baseball shortstop (his position as an undergraduate at American University in Washington). The son of middle-class parents, he grew up in Philadelphia and environs and was graduated from Villanova University Law School in 1972. He immediately joined Mayer Brown, in the litigation department, which he now cochairs.

Salpeter has the competitive zeal essential to a litigator. He learned his trade fighting hostile takeovers of Mayer Brown clients. "I didn't always succeed in stopping them, but in instances where I failed I made the acquiring party pay a large premium." His next round of cases involved defending major accounting firms accused of fraud in securities. Here is where Salpeter came to detest the methods used by such firms as Milberg Weiss—their willingness to sue every conceivable defendant with the aim of forcing them to buy out of suits rather than spend millions of dollars defending them. Salpeter discovered that he enjoyed trying cases, matching his skills against other lawyer on the testing fields of a courtroom. "Lots of lawyers in big firms don't try cases; they fear they might lose." A sweep of his arms suggested he was talking about persons in his own office. "They prefer to do things on paper. They are not risk takers. When you are a litigator, what the jury says at the end of a trial tells you whether you won or you lost. I love it."

Salpeter rummaged around his memory a few moments and computed that he had tried some seventy jury trials to a verdict, winning all save five of them. "This doesn't show that I am brilliant," he said, "but that I know the ones I should get out of." To Salpeter, being a litigator "means being able to combine really good common sense with good judgment." A litigator must be able to make a cold-eyed evaluation of whether a case can be won at trial—regardless of the truth, and whether the client is right or wrong—or whether economic sense dictates that it be settled.

Salpeter keeps the obligatory "trophy headlines" about his major cases (all wins, of course) on his office wall, and he pointed to one that he especially enjoyed. ARA, the food supply chain, had a five-year contract to buy orange juice from a company named Netlog. Salpeter sued ARA for breach of contract, and ARA settled. "Then they reneged, so we sued them all over again and proved they never intended to pay." Salpeter won a jury verdict of $11.4 million in actual damages and another $5 million in punitives. During appeals, ARA bailed out for $11 million, and Salpeter says he made sure the check cleared the bank before signing off on the final papers. Mayer Brown took one-third of the settlement as its fee. Which is why lawyers such as Salpeter are a valuable commodity. All the above is a roundabout way of saying that Alan Salpeter enjoyed a considerable professional reputation when his phone rang on an October morning in 1992.

"The call came out of the blue," Salpeter said. "This voice said, 'I'm Dan Fischel at the Chicago Law School. Could you meet for lunch today?'"

"What's this all about?" Salpeter asked. He knew that Fischel taught at the law school, and was a principal in Lexecon, which Mayer Brown had used as an expert witness in litigation. Given Fischel's reputation, Salpeter realized that the request for a meeting should be taken seriously. Fischel said he would fax a draft complaint of a suit he was considering filing. He asked that Salpeter bring along associate Michele Odorizzi, who had been an editor with him on the *Chicago Law Review*.

The sixty-page complaint began coming over the Mayer Brown fax machine around eleven o'clock, and a few minutes before noon Salpeter grabbed the papers and he and Odorizzi read them as they walked the few blocks from their office on South LaSalle Street to the Chicago Club on East Van Buren.

Fischel had done his homework. When Salpeter began reviewing his background, Fischel waved him to silence. "I don't need to hear about you. I've checked you out. I think I know more about your cases than you do. I want to know what you think about this complaint." Salpeter spread out the draft complaint, which detailed the attacks Milberg Weiss lawyers had made against Fischel.

"Are the stated facts true?" he asked.

"Yes," Fischel replied.

"Then I think you'll win," Salpeter continued. "But I have two questions first."

Fischel looked across the table and nodded his head, as if saying, "Ask them."

"How strong is your stomach, and how deep is your pocketbook?" Salpeter knew that once he sued Milberg Weiss, the return attacks on Fischel would be personal, and that the firm had the money needed for protracted legal warfare.

Fischel smiled tightly. "Don't worry about either one of them," he said.

As Salpeter explained, "Fischel was deeply offended by Milberg Weiss's allegations [in the Keating pleadings] that he was a 'corrupt racketeer,' the language of a RICO complaint. [He referred to the federal Racketeer Influenced and Corrupt Organization act, aimed at organized crime figures.] He felt that malicious lies had been told about him, and he wanted the pleasure of having a jury say that he had been maligned. The money was secondary."

Fischel's suit was brought on a legal theory known as "abuse of process." As Salpeter explained, "The gist of the case was that they filed lawsuit number one—the Lincoln Savings [Keating] matter—in order to hurt Fischel and Lexecon in case numbers two, three, four, five, six, and so on. Milberg Weiss did not sue him to collect a judgment, but to hurt him. This was the abuse of process."

Such cases are rare, Salpeter continued, because most of what lawyers charge during the course of a lawsuit, in their documents and in arguments in court, are privileged—that is, immune from suit. "I can call you a wife-beating, child-molesting, deadbeat drunk, and as long as I do it in court, and not in public statements outside the courtroom, you can't do anything about it. The privilege permits you to do about anything you want to do." But in the instance of Fischel, the side comments by Milberg Weiss lawyers often came outside of court, which to Salpeter was proof of an "evil intent." Now he and Fischel had to convince a jury that they were correct.

For its defense, Milberg Weiss chose as its lead lawyer a tough litigator named Jerold K. Solovy, of Jenner & Block, of Chicago. There was a tedious round of preliminary skirmishes over whether the suit should be heard in Arizona, site of the original Keating litigation, or in Chicago, where Salpeter filed the Lexecon suit. In the end, the suit landed in Chicago, and in the court of U.S. District Judge James Zagel.

In the meanwhile, things went well for Fischel elsewhere. In January 1998, he sold his share of Lexecon for $63 million to Nextera Enterprises, a company controlled by his longtime friend Michael Milken, of junk-bond fame. Millions more went to other principals. Fischel would keep any money he won from Milberg Weiss. In the summer of 1998 he was elevated to the deanship of the University of Chicago Law School, one of the plums of legal academia.

Now he could focus on restoring the reputation that Milberg Weiss had sullied for most of a decade.

"THEIR OWN WORST ENEMIES"

To Alan Salpeter, "Once we got back to Chicago, I felt we were on a level playing field. You must realize that Milberg Weiss are powerful people who are used to having the upper hand. I also found interesting how they reacted when the traditional roles of plaintiff and defendant were reversed. Milberg Weiss didn't like being treated the way a defendant is treated.

"They went after [Fischel]—every motion, trick in the book was used. He beat them and they beat themselves. As witnesses, they were their own worst enemies—arrogant and argumentative. They made up things of whole cloth and got caught."

Milberg Weiss apparently sensed that the change of venue— Fischel trying his case in a hometown court—put it at a disadvantage. (After the trial, Mel Weiss complained bitterly to me about "favoritism" on the part of Judge Zagel.)

There was a financial problem as well. Milberg Weiss carried only about $5 million in liability insurance, a sum that rapidly melted. Just before the trial began, in April 1999, Milberg Weiss offered to settle by contributing around $10 million to the University of Chicago Law School, without admitting any misconduct. Fischel refused; he wanted his day in court. So in the spring of 1999 Alan Salpeter and Mayer Brown partners Caryn Jacobs and Terri Mazur and associates Christina Egan and Tom Nachbar sat beside Fischel in court, accompanied by Mark Hansen, a tough-talking former federal prosecutor, and Courtney Elwood, of the Washington, D.C., firm of Kellogg, Huber, Hansen, Todd & Evans.

Things went disastrously from the outset for Milberg Weiss. In pretrial rulings, Judge Zagel refused to permit evidence that the entire suit stemmed from work that Lexecon and Fischel did on behalf of the disgraced financier Charles Keating. The jury never heard the word "Keating." "The greatest perversion of justice," exclaimed an aggrieved Solovy. Hence jurors were left to divine for themselves the significance of the Lincoln Savings matter. Fischel's contention, one accepted by Judge Zagel, was that injection of the notorious Keating's name into the case would be unduly prejudicial. "Hell," Melvyn Weiss said, "Fischel hired out to him. Why not let the jury know the kind of people that the illustrious dean got into bed with?"

Nor was Solovy permitted to cross-examine Fischel about how, in his 1995 book *Payback,* he portrayed Keating as a victim of prosecutorial zealots. Salpeter struck hard at Milberg Weiss in his opening statement. "This is a case about lawyers, powerful lawyers, who misused and abused the legal system to try to destroy my client, Lexecon. . . . Revenge and money! It's about a vendetta. It's about revenge and it's about greed. It's about lawyers who abused the legal system to line their own pocketbooks."

Solovy, understandably, saw matters quite differently. Did Milberg Weiss overstep the bounds of propriety in calling Fischel reprehensible? Solovy declared, "I would call him a very neat, slick, greedy, avaricious person who ought to tend to his duties at the University of Chicago and not intrude upon the court."

He continued, "But I couldn't use such gutter language!"

So for six weeks witnesses paraded through Judge Zagel's courtroom, many of them buttressing Fischel's claims about a vendetta. There was potent testimony. For instance, Joseph Cotchett had been Milberg Weiss's cocounsel in the Lincoln Savings litigation. According to testimony, Cotchett told no less than four other lawyers that suing Lexecon was "Milberg's deal." He told each person that Lexecon had done nothing wrong and he did not want them to be sued. At trial, Cotchett denied saying any such thing. But, as Salpeter contended, "Are all four of these people lying?" One of them, Michael Hawkins, was now a U.S. district judge.

Fischel contended that the Milberg Weiss campaign hurt Lexecon's business and cost him millions of dollars. Yes, he had sold his interest in Lexecon for $63 million—but had it not been for the vendetta, it would have brought more than $100 million. Jurors saw financial statements about what Lerach, Weiss, and their firm had earned over the years—$101,295,080 in 1994 alone for Milberg Weiss, and $16 million-odd for the two principal partners. Milberg Weiss's earnings from 1988 through 1997 came to more than $618 million.*

Lerach emphatically denied any malice. Asked point-blank by Solovy why he brought Lexecon into the Lincoln Savings litigation, he said firmly, "As part of vigorously representing our clients to try to recover as much money for them as we could from everyone we thought was legally responsible."

But how credible was his story? One hotly argued point was the amount of research Len Simon and other Milberg Weiss lawyers had done about Lexecon's role before filing the amended complaint that brought Fischel and his company into the suit as a defendant. Time and again, Lerach, Simon, and other witnesses gave testimony that diverged from what they had said earlier during depositions. The turnabouts infuriated Judge Zagel, who exclaimed late in the trial:

[T]he truth of the matter is this witness had an astonishing revivification, or resuscitation, if you will, depending on whether you regard his previous memory as dead or merely moribund. But the man testifies in a 1994 deposition that he doesn't recall all this stuff, that he has no recollection. In 1999 suddenly he's got a significant recollection. Which, in and of itself would not be that important, except that it seems to fit very neatly with what the plaintiffs perceive to be the defense in this case.

*For a list of these earnings, see page 266.

Judge Zagel expressed repeated frustration when Lerach and Weiss, instead of giving direct yes or no answers, launched into long statements beyond the scope of what they were asked. The judge's anger spilled over during an exchange in which Lerach insisted that he had not "destroyed" documents relating to the Lexecon suit—that he had simply "thrown them away."

Judge Zagel did not buy this argument, saying of Lerach, "I think he's made a fool of himself on that point . . . I do not trust this witness's willingness to follow orders of the court. He refused to do it two or three times when I directly instructed him." Solovy made repeated demands for a mistrial because of the judge's remarks; none was granted.

The jurors also heard how Simon's "battle plan" memo came to light by accident. Although it had been circulated to some sixty lawyers in the firm, Milberg Weiss did not produce it when Salpeter demanded that the firm turn over, during discovery, all documents it had relating to Fischel. Salpeter learned of it in a deposition of a former associate, Greg Woodburn, who took a copy when he left the firm.

Judge Zagel, to Lerach's distress, refused to permit him to testify about numerous victories in securities cases, including his role in a $1 billion suit against NASDAQ. He was silenced when he tried to talk about his firm's representation of Holocaust survivors who sought to recover funds the Nazis stashed in Swiss banks during the war. Nor could he testify after serving on the President's Commission on the Holocaust Museum. "Stop, I said no more Holocaust!" Judge Zagel exclaimed.

During cross-examination by Mark Hansen, Lerach cheerfully acknowledged that he practices hardball law. "I have probably said to people that if necessary, we would run the defendants into bankruptcy if that's what it took to get our clients the justice they deserve."

"One of the things you try and do is make the other side afraid of you, don't you?" Hansen asked.

Lerach replied, "I certainly want them to respect me and to fear my ability to very effectively advance my client's interest, just as we fear and respect our adversaries. . . . Fear is an element of it." On one point Lerach was vehemently insistent: Contrary to what several witnesses, he had not stated that he brought Lexecon into the Lincoln Savings case as a way to "put the little fucker [Fischel] out of business." He was asked by Mark Hansen, "Is 'little fucker' a term you use?"

Lerach replied, "I've used it," but not about Fischel. He did not apologize for rough language. "At our all-hands meetings, there was profanity used, and frankly, I suspect most if not all of the defendants were at one time called that, in varying sizes." Yes, he said, Milberg Weiss gathered information about Fischel: "We certainly looked for material to use to impeach experts."

But on what came to be referred to as the "little f'er" issue, bowdlerized in the interest of courtroom decorum, Lerach was adamant: He had never directed the term against Fischel.

Then came startling testimony that completely dashed any chance Milberg Weiss had of winning.

THE "PERRY MASON MOMENT"

During a trial with many millions of dollars at stake, lawyers and principals for both sides more or less surrender any thought of normal life. The key figures from Milberg Weiss—Lerach, Weiss, and Simon—moved into a Chicago hotel. Many nights Salpeter and Hansen slept in the Mayer Brown office, showering and changing clothes for court. And Salpeter was working away the evening of Sunday, April 1, as the trial entered what would be the final week of testimony.

The telephone call came in late evening, when Salpeter was settling in for an all-night stint. It was from a Los Angeles friend, Mike Zypren, of the firm Altschuler, Grossman, Stein & Kahan, LLP. "Hey," Zypren said, "do you remember Mike Sherman? He knows something about your case." Zypren related the following:

Michael A. Sherman, a partner in Alschuler, Grossman, Stein & Kahan in San Diego, read in the April 5 issue of the *National Law Journal* about Lerach denying the "little fucker" remark. He remarked to a partner that the Lerach comment "rang a bell." Several years earlier, Sherman had been with the San Diego office of Barrack, Rodos & Bacine, which shared space with Milberg Weiss. He attended a Milberg Weiss party after Lerach won a $100 million verdict. Fischel had been a major witness for the defendant company. Several Milberg Weiss partners, Lerach among them, repeatedly said that 'that little fucker is dead, and he'll never testify again.'" Sherman told the story to several lawyers, and it eventually reached Zypren.

"Would this help you?" Zypren asked Salpeter.

"Are you kidding?" Salpeter replied. As he related, "For six weeks the Milberg Weiss people have been saying, 'Fischel is no big deal, expert witnesses wash each other out.'" He telephoned Sherman, now practicing in Los Angeles, and asked if what Zypren told him was accurate. Indeed it was, Sherman said, adding more detail. The Milberg Weiss lawyers were sipping champagne and exchanging high-five handslaps as they celebrated the demise of a man they repeatedly called "that little fucker" and said "he is dead as a witness."

The account staggered Salpeter. "This was unbelievable. I was going to win anyway—or so I thought—but this would nail it." Then he ran into an unexpected problem. Would Sherman come to Chicago, accept a subpoena, and testify? Under federal rules, Sherman could not be compelled to appear because he lived more than one hundred miles from the court.

"No way," Sherman responded. "I work with these people [Milberg Weiss]. My firm gets referrals from them." He was angered that Zypren had told Salpeter about what he felt was a private conversation.

Now commenced negotiations that lasted several days, Salpeter calling Los Angeles during breaks and after court adjourned in the afternoon. With testimony rapidly coming to a close, Salpeter had to be persuasive, and in a hurry. He offered several alternatives. What if he sent Sherman a letter asking him to come to Chicago to testify?

"I am not coming to Chicago, period," Sherman said. "I don't want to be involved. Zypren should never have told you this story." Salpeter appealed to Sherman as a lawyer—did he want to see Milberg Weiss's denials of animosity toward Fischel go unchallenged when Sherman knew otherwise? Sherman yielded. He would give a videotaped deposition provided Salpeter sent someone to Los Angeles, and yes, he would tell the same story that he had related to Zypren, although he would also state that he was an unwilling witness.

Caryn Jacobs flew to Los Angeles and took the deposition on April 7 and immediately returned to Chicago, videotape in hand. Judge Zagel held a hearing at 7:00 A.M. on April 8 to hear Milberg Weiss lawyers object strenuously to the eleventh-hour evidence. Solovy charged that Salpeter had known of Sherman all the while and orchestrated his late appearance. "I wish I was as clever as they say I am," Salpeter stated.

Judge Zagel ruled that the video could be used, and Salpeter prepared for what he called "a true Perry Mason moment." He said, "Your Honor, we now would like to call a rebuttal witness. Can we douse the lights?" Milberg Weiss lawyers seethed as four large TV monitors were positioned before the jurors. The tape had been edited down to about twenty minutes, and jurors sat on the edge of their chairs as Sherman related the "the little fucker is dead" story. (Some later told Salpeter that they found Sherman's testimony "very powerful.")

The Sherman tape was the last evidence the jurors saw before beginning deliberations. And any chance that Milberg Weiss had of winning the case vanished in the flickering lights of the videotape players.

"IF LERACH WAS PINOCCHIO"

Alan Salpeter did not mince words in his closing argument. "This is not the way honest and honorable lawyers behave," he said. "Honest lawyers investigate carefully and file proper claims. . . . These rich and powerful Milberg lawyers have manipulated the legal system in this case to ruin this man and his firm. . . . They did it to line their own pockets with literally million and millions and millions of dollars." If the case became a chapter in a book, it should be entitled "Lawyers Above the

Law." He quoted a line from Mario Puzo's novel *The Godfather:* "One lawyer with a briefcase can cause more damage than a hundred men with guns." He continued, "Now, we're not saying that Milberg Weiss tried to shoot Dan Fischel with bullets, but they did try to silence him with a stroke of a pen. . . ."

At his deposition in 1994 Lerach could not remember what investigation he had done before filing the complaint against Lexecon. "But," as Salpeter pointed out in his closing argument, "in 1999, just in time for this trial, he . . . had this miraculous recovery of memory. He even remembered talking to an expert named Manny Siden about the Lexecon reports. Of course, he had never told us before about Manny Siden, never said he talked to him about this case." So, where is Siden? How could he be deposed. "Well, that's going to be difficult," Lerach said, "because he's dead." Salpeter got scornful: "How convenient. How convenient! We can sure videotape a deposition in Los Angeles, but it's pretty hard to take a deposition where Mr. Siden is now located."

Salpeter ridiculed Lerach's testimony, calling him "clearly the most slippery of all the defendants. He didn't know what the word 'dirt' meant. He didn't destroy documents, he just 'threw them away.' As though there's a difference. . . ."

Raising his hand to touch his nose, Salpeter said, "Now, if Lerach was Pinocchio I think we know what would have happened. This would have happened many times while he was testifying. But he also had a way of revealing himself. His face would get very red when he wasn't telling the truth. And you could observe that. And you could observe that like a red light." Salpeter asked for $209 million damages, representing lost business, the diminished price Fischel received when he sold his share of Lexecon, and legal fees.

Rebutting, Solovy said, "One economist with a briefcase in this matter caused $250 million worth of damage to the 23,000 victims of what Mr. Salpeter admitted in his opening statement was a fraud, fraud, fraud, scandal, scandal, scandal." He derided Fischel as a "professional witness. . . . No matter what the situation, when he's at the defense table, there's never any damages."

Final arguments came on Friday, April 9. Judge Zagel instructed jurors that they had to agree that Salpeter and Hansen had proved several elements to sustain an abuse of process case: That Milberg Weiss's primary motive in suing Lexecon was to accomplish a purpose "outside the Lincoln Savings case," and that the motive was ulterior; that the Lincoln Savings allegations were actually used outside that case; and that Lexecon suffered harm as a result. The only proper purpose of suing Lexecon would be to recover money for their clients in the Lincoln Savings case. "The law prohibits lawyers from bringing a lawsuit, even a valid lawsuit, if the lawyers' purpose . . . is primarily to accomplish some purposes or purposes other than recovering for their clients."

At 3:00 P.M. on Monday, the jury returned with a verdict: $45 million in actual damages against Milberg Weiss. For one of the few times during the six weeks, Fischel permitted himself a small smile. But there were no happy faces on the Milberg Weiss side of the courtroom, where Lerach, Pat Hynes, and Len Simon shook their heads in dismay. Judge Zagel ordered a hearing the next morning on the separate issue of what, if any, punitive damages should be assessed against Milberg Weiss and the individual defendants. Salpeter told the judge that he would call only three witnesses—Weiss, Lerach, and Simon—and these only for fifteen minutes each. All he wished was to affirm their personal financial statements, and those of the firm, which were already in the trial record. Then he would make his closing argument.

HEAVY CASH, IN A HURRY

During the trial there had been perfunctory talks about an out-of-court settlement. According to Salpeter, Milberg early on offered a $10 million contribution to the University of Chicago Law School, but no admission of wrongdoing, a proposal that Fischel rejected. He turned down a later offer of around $20 million—again, because Milberg Weiss would not admit misconduct.

At the outset, Salpeter decided that he and Hansen would not concern themselves with any settlement talks. One reason is psychological: "You can't talk peace while you're preparing for war."

Robert Helman, a retired Mayer Brown chairman, did off-and-on settlement negotiations with Milberg Weiss "but no figure was ever heard that remotely satisfied what Fischel wanted."

So Salpeter and Hansen buckled down for more work, bent on winning millions more in punitive damages. They sensed that what lawyers call a "boxcar verdict"—one in the high millions—was in the offing. He related, "Mark and I were in this office about two o'clock on Tuesday morning, preparing our closing arguments, when we began hearing scuttlebutt about settlement being possible. We ignored it. We did not want to be distracted. When you 'think settlement' it distracts from the business at hand." As these talks went on, Salpeter drafted the argument for punitive damages. (As events turned out, Salpeter did not have to deliver it. He saved his outline and gave me a copy.)

His words were tough. He would ask for "up to another $45 million." He wrote, "These Milberg people are people who understand only one language—money. . . . Please send them a message to Milberg Weiss that is so loud and clear that they can hear it in both their New York and San Diego offices at the same time. . . . Tell Milberg Weiss, by your punitive damages verdict, that what they did was wrong. It was nasty. It was dirty. It was immoral. It was unethical and unprofessional. . . . Please tell Milberg Weiss, by your verdict, that lawyers are not above the law. Tell them that they give lawyers a bad name."

When Salpeter and Hansen arrived in court around 8:45 A.M., Patricia Hynes walked over. "She looked awful, like she's been up all night." She addressed Hansen, a fellow former federal prosecutor. "Can I talk with you, Mark?" she asked. When Saltpeter glanced up from his papers she quickly added, "You can come, too, if you want to." Salpeter shook his head. "No, you go ahead, that's all right."

Hansen was beaming when he returned. "Alan," he said, "it's all over—they want to settle. They are willing to pay $50 million"—the $45 million already won, plus another $5 million in punitive damages.

Salpeter laid down firm rules. Fischel and Mayer Brown would write the settlement agreement, and Milberg Weiss must accept it without change. Further, Milberg Weiss must pay $50 million cash, by wire, into a Mayer Brown escrow account by the close of business that day—5:00 P.M., eight or so hours away. When one of the Milberg Weiss people showed signs of argument, Fischel waved his hands in dismissive disgust. "Let's start the hearing now," he said.

So the deal was struck. Milberg Weiss was permitted to deny that the $50 million payment was a concession that the jury verdict was correct. Lexecon specifically reserved the right to state otherwise. Further, there were no confidentiality restrictions. Judge Zagel accepted the settlement, but warned that if the money was not in Mayer Brown's accounts by 5:00 P.M. he would treble the punitive damages. The case was over.

At midday the wire transfers began flowing into Chicago, six of them in all—four from various Milberg Weiss accounts, one from a Lerach account in San Diego, another from an account in the name of Lerach and his wife. By 3:30 P.M. the $50 million was in hand, and Lexecon and Salpeter had won the largest-ever abuse-of-process verdict in American legal history.

Salpeter and other lawyers interviewed six of the nine jurors. The consensus they found was that "suing Fischel personally showed Milberg Weiss's evil intent, because his name was not on any of the reports" concerning Lincoln Savings & Loan. These jurors thought that Lerach and Simon "were liars." Simon had what seemed to be a perpetual smirk on his face; he would seemingly smile during tough cross-examination by Hansen, who asked him at one point, in effect, "Is there something funny, Mr. Simon, about suing a professor for a billion dollars for racketeering?"

One lawyer in Milberg Weiss—a person whose name does not appear in this book—offered me some "background reasons" for the settlement. Had the punitive phase gone before the jury, Lerach, Weiss, and Simon would have had to reveal their net worth, and that of the firm; all that had come out at trial were their annual earnings. Weiss is an entrepreneur as well as a lawyer, one who has profited handsomely from venture capital investments. Few, if any, persons in his firm know exactly what Weiss is worth. "But hearing the amount," my lawyer source suggested, "well might have encouraged a ruinous verdict. It's like the country song goes: 'You got to know when to hold 'em, and know when to fold 'em.' "

A "HOME-COURT" ADVANTAGE?

Several weeks after the trial, I asked Weiss why things went so awfully wrong for his firm. "The one-word answer," he said, "is 'Chicago.' " Weiss groused at the impossibility of outsiders getting justice in a court permeated with graduates of the University of Chicago Law School. "A lousy situation" he said. "Here is a judge hearing the case who went to the University of Chicago, you have the dean of the law school as the plaintiff—a job he got a couple of months before the trial. Look up to the appeals court and you have a former Chicago law professor, [Richard] Posner, the guy who started Lexecon, and another judge, Easterbrook, who writes books and articles with Fischel."

I first dismissed Weiss's gripes as sour grapes. The next time I was in New York, I made myself comfortable in a conference room at Milberg Weiss and rummaged through umpteen file boxes of trial transcripts. After several hours, I ran across something that supported, somewhat, Weiss's complaint. The exchange came when one of Fischel's lawyers, Mark Hansen, tried to stress the strong relationship between Lexecon and the University of Chicago. Solovy objected to the relevance.

JUDGE ZAGEL: You don't intend to attack the University of Chicago?
SOLOVY: I would.
JUDGE ZAGEL: In this courtroom?
SOLOVY: I would. Why? You like the University of Chicago?
JUDGE ZAGEL: I have two degrees from the University of Chicago.
SOLOVY: Well, then, we may be in the wrong courtroom, Your Honor.
JUDGE ZAGEL:. . . [E]ighteen members of my family graduated from the University of Chicago, a fine university.

Weiss said he was confident that had Milberg Weiss chosen to appeal, the case was replete with reversible error. "But to appeal, we'd have to post 150 percent of the compensatory damages, and then risk ruinous punitive damages in a court that was out of control. We couldn't run the risk. Pay it off, get it behind us. A hard decision, but one that had to be made." Weiss claimed hypocrisy on the part of Fischel. "We constantly hear conservatives such as Fischel and his University of Chicago crowd complaining about 'abuse of the legal system' by plaintiff lawyers, and then they turn around and pull this kind of travesty of justice."

Weiss was also miffed that his earnings, as well as those of Lerach and their firm, were given to the jury. "But," he said, "Zagel ruled irrelevant any testimony about all the pro bono work I do on behalf of Holocaust survivors. Why? That might make me look good, rather than like a greedy, rich trial lawyer."

I asked Weiss the obvious question. Was Milberg Weiss going to survive the verdict? "Oh, hell, yes," he said, "as far as I am concerned it's old news now. But I am still mad as hell. And we're going to keep going after the security cheats."

Salpeter did not accept Weiss's argument about Fischel having a home-court advantage. "Look," he told me, "they have as their counsel Jenner & Block, the premier litigation firm in Chicago. The judge has the reputation of being one of the smartest ones on the Chicago federal bench. He is well regarded by lawyers, other judges, the appellate court. He is easily one of the top three district judges in town."

So what was the lesson to be learned from the Lexecon litigation? Just as Weiss told me, the financial damage to the firm was fleeting. Within a month of paying the $50 million cash penalty, it recouped that amount in a single securities case. According to my monitoring of the Stanford University securities litigation Web site, Milberg Weiss showed no slackening of new suits.

On the flight back to Washington for my Chicago interviews, I pulled out the notes that Salpeter had written for the argument he had planned to make to the jury during the punitive damages phase of the case. As he had told me earlier, "What I was going to say shows why I think this sort of suit is important–not only for Dan Fischel, but for our legal system as a whole." Salpeter had written the notes during the heat of legal combat, and even after his victory he continued to have strong feelings about the suit, and he made no apologies for the strong language that he had intended to address to the jury.

Salpeter had written, "These are people who have no respect for the very legal system that pays them millions and millions of dollars. They don't respect judges, they don't respect juries, they don't respect their clients. All they respect is money." Lerach, he wrote, "likes the idea of using fear to get results. He says it's good to be irrational. He's threatened to drive companies into bankruptcy as a litigation tactic. . . . He compares himself to a bounty hunter. Can you imagine that, a lawyer who compares himself to somebody who hunts people down for money? He likened himself to a snake.*

"No wonder lawyers have a bad name in our society."

FROM FRIENDSHIP TO DIVORCE COURT

From Mel Weiss's perspective, his partner Lerach was responsible for the Lexecon debacle. That he was forced to pay part of the $50 million settlement rankled him no end; so, also, was the forced disclosure of firm finances that he would have preferred to remain secret. Persons then in the firm recall several rancorous exchanges between the two men. One man in the San Diego office said he detected signs that Weiss acted jealous because Lerach commanded far more media attention—even if a good part of it was negative. That Lerach divorced his wife and married a shapely younger associate in his office also miffed Weiss, a strong proponent of family values.

---

*The reference was to Lerach's oft-quoted quip likening himself to the mythical snake who, when cut in two, regenerates into two snakes.

There were business strains as well. One episode in May 2003 infuriated Weiss—and also showed the stresses resulting from the firm operating major operations on both coasts. This dispute, a major one, involved a case concerning WorldCom, the big communications company that was in financial free fall. Litigation proliferated, with lawyers all over the country scrambling to find clients on whose behalf they could sue. In the midst of all this legal turmoil, Lerach dispatched a stern letter to Alan G. Hevesi, the New York State controller, who was pursuing a case against WorldCom. Lerach threatened to sue private attorneys representing Hevesi if their case undermined class action claims that he was pursuing.

What Lerach apparently did not realize (and even his detractors give him the benefit of the doubt) was that the New York office of Milberg Weiss represented Hevesi on other matters. Indeed, Weiss considered Hevesi to be one of the firm's most important clients, because he had the ex officio authority to steer litigation to it.

No one is prepared to give details of the telephone call that ensued between Weiss and San Diego, although one attorney formerly in the firm suggested, "If the call went over land lines, they would have melted."

Weiss told Lerach, in so many words, "Bill, what we have just isn't going to work anymore. It's time we went our separate ways." Lerach could not disagree. So the announcement was made: In due course Lerach would spin off the San Diego office, while Weiss would dominate the East Coast operations. The firm had myriad details to sort through—who would get what clients, how would income from existing business be divided, which lawyers would go where. Both Weiss and Lerach treated the divorce as driven by business considerations, and neither man would go on the record with criticisms of the other. "Differing interests" was a frequently used phrase.

But persons in the firm—partisans of both Weiss and of Lerach—knew better. To San Diego partners, Lerach constantly pointed to Lexecon as the precipitating event, saying, "It cost

Mel a potfull of money, and the Lexecon lawyers brought out some personal financial information that he did not want to make public." To which Weiss replied, in essence, "If Lerach wants to put it that way, I won't argue with him."

So in June 2004 the divorce became official. Milberg Weiss became Milberg, Weiss, Bershad & Shulman. Lerach created a firm (based in San Diego) that became Lerach, Coughlin, Stoia & Robbins.

A firm that had recovered more than $3 billion for investors and other persons since its founding in 1965 no longer existed.

6 / Cadwalader, Wickersham & Taft: Metamorphosis of a White-Shoe Law Firm

Donald A. Glascoff's normally ruddy cheeks flushed even redder with emotion on a winter evening in 1992 as he gazed out over a banquet room at the Waldorf-Astoria Hotel in New York. Before him were some of the grander stars of Wall Street law—the partners and associates of Cadwalader, Wickersham & Taft, assembled with spouses and various escorts to celebrate the firm's two hundredth birthday. George Washington had just been elected to his second term as president of the United States in 1792 when a lawyer named Johns Wells began practicing law in Manhattan in service to the nation's fledgling financial houses. Wells's one-man practice over the years evolved into the firm that in lawyer verbal shorthand today is simply Cadwalader, a fixture as prominent on Wall Street as is the New York Stock Exchange.*

Hence Glascoff felt it a signal honor to be chosen as master of ceremonies of the celebration, and he decided to do something special. He tapped a spoon on his water glass to hush the audience, and he tugged up his tuxedo jacket and put his hands

---

*The name partners were John L. Cadwalader, a former assistant secretary of state who joined Wells & Strong in 1878; George W. Wickersham, a corporate defense lawyer who joined in 1883 (and left briefly to serve as attorney general under President William Howard Taft); and Henry W. Taft, the president's brother, another corporate attorney, 1889. The firm became Cadwalader, Taft & Wickersham in 1914.

on either side of the podium. *What a proud moment, both for Don Glascoff and for Cadwalader, Wickersham & Taft.*

Glascoff would describe his spotlight moment later when recounting why he said what he did. He related, "It was really the complete firm from New York and from all the offices, and to me it seemed to be a very appropriate time to remind all of us and ourselves about the pledge in the partnership agreement that the partners made to themselves and to each other to support their professional activities and in the development of their businesses. So I included a verbatim reading of that paragraph at the tail end of my speech." Here is what Glascoff read:

> The parties to this Agreement mutually pledge to each other their best efforts to aid each other's professional success and advancement during the continuance of this Partnership, so that each party shall receive from the others a fair opportunity to use his best talents and faculties to the common benefit, and shall have an approximate if not complete or perfect compensation for his industry and abilities out of the Partnership funds.

Glascoff's audience arose as he finished reading, and the clink of touching wineglasses resonated across the room. Cadwalader partners. A band of brothers. All for one, one for all. In sickness or in health. For better or for worse.

A Cadwalader lawyer who heard Glascoff's slow reading of the core of the partnership agreement told me some time later, "Don's reading was very dramatic, but a lot of us were mentally shaking our heads. In a nutshell, Cadwalader was a fucked-up firm, and he knew it—and it must have known that some blood was going to be splattered on the floor if things were to be straightened out."

The partner's misgivings proved prescient, for in the following years Cadwalader was rent by one of the nastiest brawls ever to sully a Wall Street law firm. In a euphemistically named purge called Project Rightsize, the firm shed 17 of its 105 partners. In a separate but related action, it also closed its fifteen-lawyer office in Palm Beach. Two of the ousted lawyers sued—Steven A.

Ruskin, a New York tax partner, and James W. Beasley, Jr., a Palm Beach litigator—and Cadwalader not only endured the humiliation of having its internal affairs aired in court, it also was ordered to pay $5 million in judgments. Persons involved in the litigation estimate that Cadwalader paid many times that amount in its unsuccessful defense of the suits.

The episode was all the more startling because Cadwalader, as is true of other white-shoe law offices, frowns upon publicity of any sort, much less acrimony among its own lawyers. Corporations regularly pay hundreds of thousands of dollars to Cadwalader to keep them out of such messes

The Cadwalader melee was more than an intramural dispute among highly paid lawyers. What happened there was significant in the evolution of modern law because it was an object lesson in the changing nature of law partnerships—of how many first-class firms have become dollar-driven, with concepts of collegiality, honor, and trust pushed aside.

The lawyers who run Cadwalader, and who engineered the purge, use different words to describe what happened—that plunging profitability threatened the firm's existence, and that partners whom they considered to be deadwood had to be jettisoned, regardless of their years and quality of service. A Florida judge rejected those arguments, as did a New York jury; both found that Cadwalader improperly expelled its partners, and that they deserved damages.

When I was writing this chapter, and discussing it with friends, several persons asked, in essence, "Hey, what's the big deal—corporations were downsizing during the 1990s. Why should law firms not do the same thing?" Judge Jack C. Cook, of Palm Beach County Court, who tried one of the Cadwalader dismissal cases, disposed of this argument by quoting Benjamin Cardozo, chief judge of the of the New York Court of Appeals:

> Co-partners . . . owe to one another, while the enterprise continues, the duty of the finest loyalty. Many forms of conduct permissible in a workaday world for those acting at arm's length, are forbidden

to those bound by fiduciary ties. A trustee is bound to something
stricter than the morals of the market place. Not honesty alone,
but the punctilio of an honor the most sensitive, is then the standard of behavior. As to this, there has developed a tradition that is
unbending and inveterate. . . . It will not be consciously lowered by
any judgement of this court.

The Cadwalader metamorphosis exemplifies an important
change in the practice of law in recent decades. In a bygone era,
lawyers typically joined large firms with the intent of spending
their professional lives there. To be sure, not all achieved partnership status, and many had to seek jobs elsewhere in due course.
But for those who made the grade, partnership status was the
equivalent of academic tenure.

Another major change was driven by law firm economics—
the realization that firms had to offer full services to major
clients. A corporate firm specializing in securities work found
clients demanding that it also handle real estate leases, human resources problems, taxes, the full gamut of legal work. Rather
than grow through a hire at a time, firms found it expedient to expand by merging with another office, or luring away a "practice
group" of dozens of lawyers. Lawyers' attitude is not unlike that
of baseball players since free agency: "Follow the green"—that
is, if another firm offers you more money, take it and leave. Of
the top one hundred firms on the *American Lawyer*'s list for
2003, no fewer than forty-seven had taken over all or parts of another practice since 2000.

There is another reason that the rupture was significant. A
man familiar with Cadwalader told me that the turmoil there left
him "stunned with man's inhumanity to man, lawyers' perfidy in
the face of greed, their shortsightedness, the evil that can pervade
the good." Lawyers should set higher standards for themselves
than the rest of society, in this man's view, because "then, now,
and in the future . . . lawyers literally act in the crevices of government, political, social, economic, and philosophic life in most
civilized countries. If sufficient numbers of them are oblivious to

such sensitive responsibility, there is a reaction that affects us all."

In the end, Cadwalader scrambled back to its feet, noting far higher per-partner profits the years after the turmoil and with a talent roster that lawyers in the firm contend make it a far more productive office. But the bitterness lingers. So do the questions of fairness and legality. Did Cadwalader act properly (and legally) in the partnership purge? Are law firms the equivalent of shoe outlet chain stores, or house siding sales operations?

AUTHOR'S NOTE

I first read about the Cadwalader problem in publications such as the *Wall Street Journal* and the *American Lawyer*. I wrote James Beasley in Palm Beach and Steven Ruskin in Dallas asking for interviews. "We'll put the file boxes out for you," Beasley told me, and he did, a dozen or so of them. Ruskin was cautious. He wanted a more concise definition of my mission. He did not intend to "cooperate" for any stories that approved of what Cadwalader had done to his life. A *Wall Street Journal* article praising Cadwalader for having the yuppie-economic wisdom to shed seventeen partners had galled Ruskin. Was I writing another puff piece about the wisdom of law firms tossing out partners of two decades standing?

"Steve," I said, "I am sixty-four years old."

"Come on down to Dallas," Ruskin said. "Let me tell you how my partners did me in."

I read what Beasley and Ruskin had in their files, and I eventually received rebuttal materials from Cadwalader, Wickersham & Taft—a documentary base more than three feet thick. What follows is a case study of how a major Wall Street law firm addressed a crisis, and the conflicting obligations of partnership and profitability.

PARADISE LOST IN FLORIDA

Let us begin the Cadwalader story many miles distant from Wall Street, in Palm Beach, Florida, and a partner named James W. Beasley. What happened to Beasley typifies the manner with which Cadwalader cast off partners in the name of profit. Beasley's pre-Cadwalader career is given to show that Cadwalader was not dealing with a police-court lawyer when it decided to toss him into the street.

Beasley has the open face and South Florida drawl that I have come to associate with trial lawyers who work below the Mason-Dixon Line. Do not be fooled. The easy exterior shields an incisive Harvard law graduate who was known as one of the grander rainmakers—that is, a business getter—in Florida law even before he joined Cadwalader. (His last full year as a Cadwalader partner, 1993, he made $584,000.)

When Beasley testified in his suit against Cadwalader on July 9, 1996, he was a week shy of his fifty-third birthday. He attended Davidson College, then transferred to Harvard, graduating from its college in 1965 and its law school in 1968. He worked briefly at Sullivan & Cromwell on Wall Street, then entered the army as an intelligence officer, spending most of his two years in the Pentagon. "I liked Washington, so I stayed there, with Wilmer, Cutler & Pickering. Then my parents moved down to the Miami area, so I went there so I could be close to them."

Armed with a strong recommendation from Wilmer Cutler he joined a Miami firm and worked for such clients as the *Miami Herald* and Miami Dolphins. "This was what was then considered a medium-size firm with twelve lawyers, about half of them graduates of Harvard Law. I had gotten very lucky. I made partner in 1975, then there were some political undercurrents that ultimately ended in the firm dissolving. By that time, fortunately, I was out of there. I had developed my own clients, and I opened the offices of James W. Beasley in a windowless office, One Biscayne Tower."

Expansion was swift, and Beasley soon had a profitable array of deep-pocket clients. Arvida, the largest real estate firm in

Florida, now part of the Disney empire. Tropicana, the juice company. Peat Marwick. Banks. Developers. "Within ten years, I had a thirteen-lawyer firm. It got national attention as a very fine small law firm." *American Lawyer* named it one of the top twenty small law firms in the country in 1980.

"A couple of the younger partners felt we were missing the boat by not being part of a larger firm. Bigness is not necessarily best, but the more lawyers you have on board, the more you can do for clients. If you stick to litigation, for instance, the client goes elsewhere when he has a tax problem. Put a tax lawyer in the firm, and you keep that business." Several offices made merger invitations, including Holland & Knight of Tampa, arguably Florida's premier firm. But the most attractive came from Tom Tew, an old courtroom buddy of Beasley who had a seventy-partner practice. "I initially resisted; I was happy. Then Tom made us a very attractive proposal." In 1988 Beasley merged with the sixty-five-lawyer firm of Tew, Jordan & Schulte, adding his name as a partner. The partnership lasted a year, and he made about $425,000, plus $25,000 in a "basically nonaccountable expense account. I was very comfortable, sitting there in a corner office overlooking Biscayne Bay."

But Miami had lost much of its appeal. "The turning point was the Mariel boatlift, when Fidel Castro essentially flushed the toilet and dumped his human garbage into Miami. Put a hundred thousand crazies into any city, and it ain't fun no more." Beasley also remarried in the period; his wife, Libby, who studied urban planning at Princeton University, had come to Miami to help the Rouse Company develop the downtown Bayside harbor complex.

"So one day in June 1989 I got a call from a headhunter . . . who told me he represented a large, very well respected Wall Street law firm that had an office in Palm Beach. . . . They were looking for someone to create a litigation practice there and would I be interested in doing that." Depends on what firm you are talking about, Beasley said. "He told me the firm was Cadwalader, Wickersham & Taft." Hearing the name, Beasley shifted in his chair and said, "Hmm, tell me more." Cadwalader had offered him a summer job in 1967, when he was at Harvard Law. He did not know anyone personally at Cadwalader, but "it was, I knew, the oldest law firm on Wall Street and maybe in North America, and the firm's reputation was one of being a very gentlemanly but very high-quality practice."

Beasley saw several advantages to Cadwalader. "It was a way of leaving Miami without moving a thousand miles away. It was the chance to get back to a premier Wall Street law firm, an icon. And I also realized I'd been doing a lot of work in Palm Beach County, chiefly litigation for Arvida. I knew the top lawyers and the judges."

Beasley went to Palm Beach and met local managing partner Frank Chopin and Martin A. "Skip" Purcell, another partner. Purcell did most of the talking. Palm Beach had been specializing in trusts and estate work, catering to superrich retirees and coupon clippers. Cadwalader wanted someone who could help build "an all-purpose firm," including litigation. Beasley replied that he was generating about $3 million a year in business, much of which he could bring with him. Further, he had a proven track record in building up firms.

What Beasley calls "the courting process" lasted several months. Cadwalader gave him financial statements for 1987 and 1988 showing what he would later describe as "terrific years. . . . They had earned about ninety thousand dollars a share in those two years." But 1989 did not portend to be as good, so they settled on a guarantee of $300,000 a year, matching Beasley's draw from his Miami firm.

Beasley recognized the risks. "The assumption was that I was going to build the litigation practice starting with my own clients. There was no anticipation that any large amount of business would flow from the other offices of Cadwalader to me in Palm Beach." He accepted the partnership offer in September 1989. At no time did Beasley make any inquiries as to how Cadwalader treated partners, although he heard nothing to diminish its reputation as "being a very gentlemanly place to practice law."

Beasley also learned how Cadwalader divvies up its profits. For accounting purposes, in 1989 Cadwalader had 438.50 shares, which were allocated among partners on the basis of hours billed, income brought into the firm, and responsibility for clients. Beasley's initial allocation was five shares. To maintain a working capital fund, partners were obligated to meet a "capital requirement" amounting to $35,000 a share, meaning that Beasley put $175,000 into Cadwalader (paid via a 10 percent deduction from his gross income each month). He and other partners drew annual interest at the prime rate plus 3 percent, calculated monthly. Under the firm agreement, "you basically got your capital back whenever you left the firm."

Concerning income, Cadwalader made distributions, "basically what they made the preceding month, so a partner's income would fluctuate by manifold times. . . . There were times when I got a distribution [of] . . . nothing for a month, and there were times when I got a distribution of a hundred and twenty or thirty thousand dollars. I was concerned that I had to have some . . . assurance of a reasonably steady income because, if they had happened to have had a couple [of] bad months when I first came up here, that would not have been a very good thing."

Beasley realized he faced a start-from-scratch situation. Trucks dumped six hundred file boxes from his old practice in the Cadwalader offices at 440 Royal Palm Way, the downtown boulevard that dead-ends into the Atlantic. "All of a sudden I found myself as a sole practitioner basically because there was no other litigation help in the office. . . . they had a very fine library for tax material, but they had virtually nothing that was useful or required for me in my litigation practice." So he bought one. He hired paralegals and associates, and in three months the expanded office was up to speed. "Business was very good. Cadwalader had given substantial publicity to my joining the firm. They had a press person down here and in New York. . . . I didn't really go out actively prospecting or that sort of thing. I rarely do that. Simply, business just came as a result of people realizing that I had moved, who knew I was now with Cadwalader."

But soon Beasley realized that he had not foreseen a major problem in the Palm Beach office: the ranking resident partner, L. Frank Chopin.

THE FEUDING PARTNERS

Frank Chopin did not like Jim Beasley in 1989, and he did not like him a decade later, when we talked in his office on Royal Palm Way—the same suite, ironically, that he had occupied while at Cadwalader. Chopin did not want to talk about the Cadwalader litigation, and when he started discussing it anyway, he gestured for me to turn off my recorder.

In essence, Chopin feels that Beasley came to Cadwalader with an inflated reputation and a penchant for stretching the truth about how much money he had been making in Miami—something, he claimed, that Cadwalader did not realize for years. Beasley even had to borrow money from the firm to pay back taxes, Chopin said. The point was that if Cadwalader had known the full story, Beasley might not have been hired.

Chopin can be charming. He has an aquiline face, stylish blond hair, and the casually correct attire that appeals to Palm Beach males. Stretching out his arms to ensure that his cuffs were straight, he told me about his life. Chopin was left fatherless in New Orleans at an early age, and his mother's brother, a Catholic priest, had some advice. The kid must grow up around men who will paddle hell out of him when he misbehaves. So Chopin had scholarships to Catholic schools and then to Loyola law school of New Orleans and to Oxford University for graduate school. Chopin wrote a dissertation on European taxation systems. He knows tax law, and he is not reticent about his coups. He gave me an example: He spent an air flight to Canada reading a lengthy brief that another firm had written for a client. He spotted an omission of a salient point, he got on the phone and set matters straight, and he saved the client more than $30 million.

Chopin taught briefly at Drake University Law School, then joined Cadwalader in New York. The firm soon sent him to Palm Beach to tend to the affairs of the wealthy. The bulk of his work was taxes and trusts and estates, and he earned an enormous amount of money, both for himself and Cadwalader. And he also busied himself in Palm Beach's hyperactive social life.

Chopin and Beasley were a mismatch from the start. By

Beasley's account, Chopin considered Palm Beach to be his "isolated office," and he did not welcome an outsider who had come in with a mandate to turn it into a litigation practice. After two, perhaps three days, Beasley told Chopin that he foresaw problems. "I told him that I knew that he had [been] . . . basically running it as the main partner for ten years and that it was going to be difficult to adjust to other people coming into the office. That was only natural. . . ."

Beasley soon wondered whether he erred in joining Cadwalader. "I found out that Frank Chopin was not interested in trying to turn the firm here into a full-service office. And that was rather startling news, since that's the reason I had come up here. But that was the idea of the people in New York. And so I think from the very beginning Mr. Chopin was happy with the firm as a three- or four- or five-lawyer office."

According to his testimony, Beasley also saw the flip side to Chopin's charm. "It happened from time to time that Frank lost his temper, and when he did—I don't believe that it was intentional, but when he did, he erupted throughout the whole office. I mean, he would yell and scream at people. It may have happened two or three times a year. But it was unpredictable and nobody knew when it was going to get set off. . . ." The office layout was such that the men worked on opposite corners of the Cadwalader floor. "Basically we decided to stay out of each other's way. . . . It was a truce, and it worked, for a while."

Beasley subtly let New York partners know that Chopin's tirades caused tension. There was periodic talk of bringing Chopin to New York, where tighter reins could be kept on his conduct. But in the interim, "I was under direct orders from New York that I had to get along with Frank. . . . They told me that Frank was great, and it was up to me to get along with him."

Despite the tension, Beasley prospered. In his full four years, between 1990 and 1993, he averaged earnings of $535,000 a year. He made lateral hires and recruited bright young lawyers and soon had the original five lawyers up to seventeen. Nonetheless, he was unhappy, and he wondered if he wished to spend the rest of his career at Cadwalader.

TROUBLES IN NEW YORK

Even as Beasley prospered, grave unrest beset the Wall Street office, driven by unhappiness over how money was divided. Depositions and internal Cadwalader memoranda tell of fears by younger partners that the firm was on the verge of implosion. Criticisms eventually centered on a group of older partners, and especially the management committee chairman, Rodney S. Dayan.

Even persons who became his critics could not fault Rod Dayan for his contribution to the growth of the modern Cadwalader. He had a reputation for being perhaps the best lawyer on Wall Street in the arcane speciality of securitization of debt for financial clients; he earned millions of dollars for the firm.

But as Dayan aged, younger men felt he rested on his laurels. One document that junior partners read with anger noted that Dayan billed direct clients only thirty-six hours during 1993. "Any associate in the place had that many hours by Wednesday noon of any given week," one of the disgruntled men told me. But the same document credited him with $17 million of client business that he had brought in over the years, and compensation is based on that factor as well as hours actually worked. He also spent about two thousand hours on business development, income from which enriched every lawyer in the firm. Finally, he managed day-to-day operations of the firm.

Nonetheless, some younger men were upset when the final Cadwalader financial statement for 1993 showed Dayan with a net income of $1,130,740. The next highest earners were Robert Eller, with $824,303 and Mitchell I. Sonkin, $718,710. Eight partners were in the $600,000 range; another eighteen, in the $500,000 range.*

---

*Long after Project Rightsize, Dayan was nonapologetic when he spoke with Vera Titunik of the *American Lawyer*. He acknowledged not billing many hours but said he would "swoop in on" major deals when needed, and built the firm's practice through lateral hires and by introducing younger partners to clients. He told Titunik, "If you're going to be available to clients . . . you cannot be the guy who spends two hundred hours on a transaction, twelve hours a day, because it makes you unavailable to other clients or the same client on another project."

Internal documents suggested that some partners were coasting. A January 1994 memorandum by litigator Jeffrey Smith, a member of the management committee, noted that of 95 partners in the firm in 1993, "an astonishing 40 of them, or 43 percent, billed fewer than 1,500 hours. Twenty-three partners billed fewer than 1,300 hours, 9 less than a thousand." The Wall Street standard was around 1,900 hours. Smith wrote, "I would be surprised to find that *any* other major firm has such an abysmal record." (Smith's emphasis) He was disturbed that 60 of the 95 partners billed fewer hours in 1993 than in 1992. "If 1993 is any indication, we are clearly heading in the wrong direction at an alarming rate."

There was another financial worry—the firm's office building at 100 Maiden Lane, in the center of the financial district. In 1984 Cadwalader paid $72 million to purchase and convert three separate buildings into a twenty-four-story tower. The result was a spiffy building, with 292,000 square feet of floor space, a nine-story atrium in the core, and row after row of offices with outside views. Traditionalists insisted on bringing along handsome mahogany doors from the old office. Portraits of the founding lawyers adorned the wood-paneled reception area.

But the project required Cadwalader to take a $60 million mortgage, $57 million of which remained unpaid at the end of 1993. The finances concerned Beasley. He had friends who had been partners in the Finley Kumble firm, which toppled into spectacular bankruptcy earlier in the 1980s, leaving them liable for a share of its debts. By becoming a Cadwalader partner, "I assumed joint and several liability for the entire fifty-eight or fifty-nine million dollars" remaining on the mortgage. Beasley was assured that the firm was financially sound.

But other major firms were moving to more convenient offices uptown, away from Wall Street's congestion. "An awful decision, to spend so much money and lock yourself into an outdated location," a lawyer from another firm commented. A memo to partners in 1993 stated, "It was assumed that the value of the building would appreciate substantially in 15–18 years." The reverse occurred. The crash of the New York real estate market in the early 1990s knocked the building's value down to between $30 million and $40 million. The partners had to cough up $2 million a year for a decade to contribute to a building reserve fund. If the firm should dissolve, partners would be left with the liability for paying off the difference between what the building would bring on the market and the mortgage—millions of dollars. These concerns caused some nervous lawyers to bail out of the firm.

Beasley cited one seemingly minor item that he said typified loose management. By coincidence, he received in the same mail one day the annual report of Harvard Law School and the Cadwalader financial statement. "I went to the managing partner and said, 'Do you realize that Cadwalader spends as much money on its law library as does Harvard Law School?' He basically said, 'Yeah, I've been trying to do something about that for years, but everybody gets the books they want, and that is the way we do it.'"

EMERGENCE OF THE YOUNG TURKS

Concerns of younger firm members took concrete form during the winter of 1993. The prime movers were Robert O. Link, Jr., a real estate partner who was a Phi Beta Kappa at the University of Tennessee, and Karsten P. Giesecke, a Dayan protégé described in firm material as "one of the foremost authorities on securitization in the nation." Both men were in their early forties—and ironically, as subsequent events showed, Dayan had brought both men into Cadwalader only four years earlier. Just before Christmas, in the first document produced by what came to be known as "the Young Turks," Giesecke wrote a memo to Link and Holland West, a corporate partner, which suggested tossing out partners. Giesecke derided the management committee as an "oversized, overpaid group of managers in semiretirement from a law practice [who were overseeing] a large group of unproductive partners." He sketched a scheme whereby about forty partners he labeled "the Good Guys" would seize control of the firm, purge the management committee of partners who were "overpaid [and] unproductive," and replace them with persons willing "to lead by example." The goal was to rid Cadwalader of about one-fifth of its partnership, twenty lawyers, and give more than $1 million in bonuses to twenty partners considered to be deserving of more money. Giesecke put his partners into various categories including "the Old Guard," "Upstarts," and "Moderate." Giesecke was bold enough even to take aim at John "Jack" Fritts, then a powerful figure on the management committee. Fritts would lose that position if the plan worked. "Treat him as unfortunate victim of upheaval, that removal is not a negative reflection on him personally," he wrote.

So the Young Turks discussed drastic measures. Giesecke recounted, "The first conversation was a fairly small gathering at which there were discussions to the effect that the firm had a serious problem with underproductive partners, that recent compensation adjustments were not adequate to deal with that problem, and that steps needed to be taken to see that a certain number of partners left the firm." Attending were Giesecke, Link, Jordan Schwartz, Gary Barnett, and Mike Gambro. There was also talk between sweat-soaked partners after squash matches at the Downtown Athletic Club.

The initial request, in their view, was modest: infuse the management committee with younger men who wanted to change the direction of the firm. Dayan listened politely, and then put forth a slate of partners considered to be standpatters satisfied with the way things were being run.

Stung, the Young Turks put up candidates of their own, a break with the tradition that the management committee made the nominations. And when votes were cast in January 1994, the discontent proved deeper than many persons realized. Not only did eight of their candidates win, including Giesecke, the partners also voted not to keep Dayan on the management committee. (Fifteen months later, in April 1995, Dayan retired to California at the age of sixty-two.)

Years later, Beasley found it ironic that he and other Palm Beach partners voted unanimously for the new management committee that would within months cast them out of the firm. Indeed, he shared the Young Turks' contention that Cadwalader had stagnated. "It was backward, overly seniority driven, and very, very poorly managed, from a business standpoint. There was a pattern of senior partners . . . getting a very disproportionate amount of compensation. If the pie is big enough, you can cut a couple of big slices and everybody else gets little bitty slices. Even in a marginally profitable firm, a couple of guys can make off with a great deal of money. . . ."

But the election of the new management committee did not calm fears of the Young Turks. Indeed, fear turned to anger in July when younger partners and associates learned from the annual compensation review that firm profits had dropped sharply, with per-share payouts slumping by almost $15,000. While compensation of many younger members was increased, they were not satisfied. Link and others said openly that unless compensation increased, they would leave. As Link stated in a deposition, the review "left a good number of our productive partners unhappy." The "real issue," Link stated, was the "inequality and imbalance" that he and others felt should be corrected.

The Young Turks could not help but quake as they saw other distinguished Wall Street firms in trouble. In January 1994 the remaining members of the once-prestigious office of Shea & Gould dissolved their partnership, the coup de grâce being a decision of a group of highly productive partners to leave the firm. As the *National Law Journal* reported, "The restless lawyers have a total of $20 million in business—not enough to have sunk the firm economically but enough to set it back emotionally, which it did." Another prestigious firm, Lord, Day, Lord, Barrett & Smith—the only firm in the city older than Cadwalader—headed for dissolution because of what was called a "failure to adapt to the new legal market." So, too, with Mudge, Rose, Guthrie, Alexander & Ferndon (former home of President Richard Nixon and Attorney General John Mitchell), which collapsed in 1995.

But how valid were fears that Cadwalader was in trouble? When final figures for 1994 were toted up, the firm still ranked fortieth in the country in profits per partner, with an average of $425,000. This sum put the firm's profits above those of many other prestigious offices, in New York and elsewhere. Further, Cadwalader's gross revenues in 1994 actually proved to be higher than previous years. Steven Ruskin, later fired from his tax partnership, would contend in legal papers that the dip in per-partner profits was due to nonrecurring events, which he believed would ultimately generate profits: the purchase of new computer systems, and the hiring of a large number of lateral partners and associates who were not yet generating the profits the firm felt they would ultimately bring in.

Regardless of the fairness—or legality—of their conduct later, several of the Young Turks seemed sincere when describing their fears for the future of Cadwalader. W. Christopher White, a real estate partner since 1987, movingly pictured his conception of the firm.

[Earlier in my career] I was at a law firm that . . . slid slowly into oblivion, and the factors that were evident in Cadwalader in 1993 and 1994 were the same factors that I saw played out at Breed, Abbott [and Morgan] and it was clear to me that, if something was not done to stem the tide, that the firm, whether it would be quick like Shea, Gould and Mudge, Rose, or whether it would be slow, the firm would decline to the point where it was nowhere near the firm that it was when I joined it. . . .

[T]he smell of death that was creeping into Cadwalader was the same smell that I smelled at Breed, Abbott, and maybe I was a little slow in picking that up, and maybe the head of my department was a lot smarter about that back at Breed, Abbott, but it is the same thing.

What happens . . . is not that the weakest partners leave. . . . [T]he best partners leave, and, when the best partners leave, the firm's existence is at stake. That was beginning to happen at Cadwalader. . . . Once it starts, you can't stop it because, once one or two very productive partners leave, other partners psychologically lose their commitment to the firm and start to look elsewhere. . . . [I]t may not happen in two months or three months, but it happens, and you just have to look at what happened to Breed, Abbott over the last ten years. . . .

The compensation review prompted a new round of secret meetings among the Young Turks, and with a renewed flurry of alarmed memos from Karsten Giesecke. He put onto paper the ideas he and other Young Turks discussed in their covert meetings. He wrote one partner, "Our current goal is not compensation for performing partners but rather identifying weaker partners." He had ideas on how to single out partners he felt were weak and whose "continued viability . . . comes into question." He resorted to baseball jargon in describing his scheme. He would create a "Mendoza line" below which partners fell at their peril. (The reference was to Mario Mendoza, a shortstop for the Pittsburgh Pirates, Seattle Mariners, and Texas Rangers whose lifetime batting average was .215. In baseball, an infielder whose average falls "below the Mendoza line" begins to think seriously about another occupation.) Giesecke did not cite a dollar figure that was the equivalent of the Mendoza line, but his intent was clear. And one of the men who Giesecke would target for removal was tax partner Steven Ruskin—a man who, paradoxically, seemed well above any such arbitrary line, based on his 1994 compensation.

A TARGETED PARTNER

Steve Ruskin was fifty years old the summer of 1994, toiling happily in the tax department at Cadwalader, which he had joined in 1972. A native of Long Island, he was graduated magna cum laude from Princeton University and went on to Columbia Law School and then got a master's degree in taxation from New York University Law School. A quiet, compact man, he worked as an associate for five years and in 1977 became a partner.

In his own words, Ruskin was a service provider who worked chiefly on deals brought in by copartners and institutional clients—transactional taxes, mergers and acquisitions, issuance of debt or equity, real estate deals, trusts and estates, charitable organizations. To some outsiders, tax law is arcane and boring, the sort of detail work that drives many persons batty. But

Ruskin loved shaping a deal to the maximum financial advantage of clients and having corporations and institutions ask for him by name when they had a deal underway.

Ruskin produced. During the five years ending in 1993 he ranked first among Cadwalader's eight New York tax partners in productivity, client contact receipts, and supervising receipts; he was second in billable hours and total hours. For the years 1989, 1990, and 1991, respectively, Ruskin's billable hours ranked sixth, fourteenth, and seventh among all of Cadwalader's approximately one hundred lawyers. His productivity, as measured by the management committee, was fifth, fifteenth, and twenty-first, respectively, among all partners.

Ruskin also did an enormous amount of in-house work, including helping on annual tax returns. When Cadwalader decided to face up to its office-building crisis in 1993, Ruskin spent more than a thousand hours trying to straighten out what could have been a costly debacle. Indeed, the financial drain of the building was largely responsible for a dip in firm income during those years. "I kept the situation from being a heckuva lot worse," Ruskin told me. One of the committee members wrote to Glascoff in August 1994 describing Ruskin's work as "masterful." Nonetheless, the in-house work meant that the hours he billed to clients dropped precipitously that year. But his loyalty to the firm remained undiminished. He voted to admit numerous new tax partners to Cadwalader, including one as late as January 1994. He voted as well in favor of some of the lateral transfers who would later turn against him and drive him from his firm.

During the 1994 compensation review, Ruskin cheerfully accepted a half-share cut in his partnership allotment, to 5.5 shares, the same cut given the chairman of the tax department. Business volume had dipped, and Ruskin felt that the decrease was justified. Other partners whose work had fallen significantly took deeper cuts. Even so, his 5.5 shares put him in the top third of all partners. He was confident that the firm would shake out of its slump and that he would continue making from $500,000 to $600,000 annually.

But his partners had a different view of Steve Ruskin. In one brief they called him "the very epitome of what was wrong at Cadwalader." They depicted him as a fussy man who "over-lawyered" issues, running up unnecessary fees that irked clients. Further, Ruskin was said to have "never brought a single client of any significance to the firm in his seventeen years at Cadwalader."

Ruskin disputes these accusations. Yes, he is methodical; an error by a tax lawyer can be devastatingly expensive to a client. He had developed well in excess of $1 million of pure tax work from existing and new clients, only to have billing credit stripped from him during the planning for Project Rightsize. And he pointed to his previous hours, and the amount of work he did to solve Cadwalader's real estate crisis, as ample rebuttal to the "nonproductive" charge.

What he saw at Cadwalader, Ruskin said, was a change of culture. He liked working at Cadwalader during his early years. The firm was run in democratic fashion, with monthly partner meetings. When a significant issue arose, documents were circulated in advance, and everyone had a chance to speak his or her mind. As the number of partners increased, the management committee tended to make more of the decisions. But Cadwalader tradition was that every partner was equal.

Ruskin has old-fashioned values. He can use words such as "integrity," "loyalty," and "collegiality" without sounding preachy. He was a Cadwalader man who had read the partnership agreement, and he believed in the precepts it stated. His faith in his partners would prove unwarranted.

THE YOUNG TURK SOLUTION

One way to give the younger partners more money was by increasing their shares in the firm's income. But doing so by simply issuing shares would dilute the value of existing shares, something that Giesecke would not tolerate. He wrote, "We must recognize that significant departures and cuts are in order to avoid dilution. . . ." of profits per share. He wanted "zero dilution." Hence the "significant raises" for "stellar partners"—including, of course, the Young Turks—would be achieved by seizing shares of the partners marked for the purge.

Giesecke had the common sense to worry about the impact his purge would have on Cadwalader's reputation. Another major Wall Street firm, Milbank, Tweed, Hadley & McCloy, had recently dumped a number of partners, but gave them acceptable severance agreements and avoided lawsuits. Nonetheless, Giesecke wondered in a memo: "Publicity—Does this move mean trouble? By saying that all the Milbanks are perceived to be stronger for all the fuss, are we engaged in wishful thinking?"

Giesecke's memo flow was so steady that an outsider could wonder how much attention he paid to his practice. He fretted about many things. Eventually he wrote a memo for specific action, noting: "Key to solution—elimination of the underproductive partners" that would be followed by the firm. The key portion of his scenario read, "Consider alternatives of high-profile firing of 20 or more partners, or more low-key, but not delayed, approach (i.e., still tell people by September 1, but with different departure schedules, and without major announcement, so the impact is softer)." Giesecke realized the downsizing would cause controversy, so he suggested: "Consider handling of publicity both inside and outside the firm, *particularly in light of the origins of this movement being outside the Management Committee.*" (Emphasis added.)

Under "Results," Giesecke wrote: "Long-term improvement in profitability" would result in the "opportunity to bring in good lateral partners in top fields, and to recruit law students. . . ." With the scenario in hand, Giesecke compiled a list of lawyers to be driven out of Cadwalader. He directed that David Strumeyer, Cadwalader's manager of accounting operations, do a "productivity analysis" of all partners based on billable hours, client contact fees, and supervising fees. The process contained overwhelming circumstantial evidence that the Young Turks wanted to shed Steve Ruskin, his performance notwithstanding. By the testimony of Strumeyer, the first set of figures did not produce the result Giesecke wanted. By his figures, Ruskin was given $1,297,842 in client contact credit for 1994, placing him

29th out of 97 partners. When all three of Giesecke's criteria were considered, Ruskin ranked 41st in the firm, far above Giesecke's "Mendoza line." Ruskin's rank was higher than that of the chairman of the tax department, David W. Feeney, and very close to firm cochairman Don Glascoff. Giesecke was not deterred. Strumeyer described what happened:

> Mr. Giesecke asked me if I could modify a few of the partners' figures as—the numbers attributable to the 94 partners might not necessarily reflect accurately if origination credit, client contact fees, really belonged to certain partners. . . .
>
> He asked me to take a piece of client contact credit that's attributable to Ruskin, and assign it to another partner. Then, if I did such, where would Mr. Ruskin fall within the rankings.

The billings stripped from Ruskin went to Mike Ryan, a member of the management committee. Many of them pertained to what Ruskin would describe as "one of the firm's most important institutional clients . . . and among the top Cadwalader clients in collections." Ruskin said he had done all the tax work, often billing more than $1 million a year, and was responsible for the client for years. When the partner who did other work for the client left Cadwalader, Ruskin introduced Ryan as his successor, and thereafter they split client contact credit fifty-fifty. During the 1993 compensation review, those billings had been credited to Ruskin. No one told Ruskin that they were being taken from him. Cadwalader challenged Ruskin's claim that the corporation was "his" client, saying he had inherited the account.

Giesecke kept confidential the fact that Strumeyer was doing such a survey. Giesecke said it was his decision "to keep it a secret, or as secret as I possibly could from the other partners." In Giesecke's view it "would not be appropriate to disseminate this data beyond the management committee." Nonetheless, he shared the material with other Young Turks. And it was Strumeyer who came up with the term "rightsizing," which the Young Turks agreed sounded better than "downsizing."

Strumeyer eventually did models based on ten to thirty departing partners (at one time, according to Glascoff, as many as thirty-five names were bandied about for departure or reduced compensation). Glascoff told Strumeyer to assure, as the basis of his calculations, "that these . . . partners would be out of the firm, period, as of a certain date." A smaller grouping would be continued with reduced compensation.

Giesecke was satisfied with Strumeyer's new results. He wrote a memo on July 29 stating that with "20 fewer partners . . . profitability per partner and per share still goes up dramatically. . . ." He next asked Strumeyer to do another analysis assuming that Cadwalader added productive new partners "to replace the departing ones."

The group recognized right away that they faced a basic problem: The Cadwalader partnership agreement did not provide any procedure for removing partners (other than for a partner who experienced "sudden and total disability"). But the management committee had the authority to set compensation, which some of the Young Turks saw as an opening—to cut partners' compensation to a point where they would leave voluntarily.

Giesecke was asked later whether, if a targeted partner did not leave, the last step would be not to pay them anything.

"Yeah," he said.

Despite its doubts, the management committee decided to use the compensation ploy, according to Giesecke. There were "comments to the effect that there was explicit authority to set compensation and that the safer course to follow in connection with the partners under discussion at the time would be reduction in compensation and encouragement for voluntary departure rather than to terminate."

Was using this method legal under New York partnership laws? "I did give thought to whether firing partners would violate the firm agreement," Giesecke said. "My understanding of the agreement is that the authority to set compensation would include authority to set compensation at zero. That, coupled with the other provisions, I would view as giving the authority to terminate. . . . I'm not aware of any express statement to the effect that the management committee has the authority to terminate a partner."

Why did not the management committee amend the partnership agreement to include a provision for expulsion? Given that the various "hit lists" contained names of as many as thirty-five partners, out of a total of slightly more than a hundred, the committee realized it could never receive the 75 percent vote required to amend the agreement.

Surprisingly, few management committee members bothered to read the agreement. As shall be seen, when their use of the compensation gambit was challenged by Beasley and Ruskin, the firm's story did an abrupt about-face, with committee members insisting for the purposes of the litigations that the compensation cuts were not in fact designed to drive partners from the firm.

CALAMITY AT THE BRAZILIAN COURT

Meanwhile, problems of another sort entirely had disrupted Cadwalader's Palm Beach office.

The Christmas season of 1993 was an awful time for Frank Chopin. Earlier in the year, he underwent major abdominal surgery at the Mayo Clinic, an ordeal from which he was slow to recover. In a protracted legal fight, he helped Kathy Ford, widow of Henry Ford II, fight off a challenge by the auto tycoon's children for the $250 million that he left to her. The Chopin marriage had broken up.

Given these strains, Chopin was not in the best of moods the December evening when the Cadwalader office held its holiday party at the Brazilian Court Hotel. As some fifty or sixty persons milled around during cocktails, Beasley was amused to see Chopin was rearranging place cards to insure that he sat next to some of the younger, more attractive women, including Beasley's secretary, Dianne Bishop. "He . . . somehow fancied himself as a ladies' man of sorts," Beasley told me.

As related by Beasley and other persons present, Chopin arose during dinner and started an impromptu speech. He made the obligatory greetings, and then turned to Ms. Bishop, who was across the table from her husband, an athlete and professional model. The exact words he used differ from memory to memory, but the gist was that he had enjoyed being close to Ms. Bishop during dinner, that he wished he could get even closer to her, and that if he did, he would prove a better partner than her husband. To many present, Chopin's comments carried clear sexual implications.

Chopin was almost incoherent, contended Beasley, who felt that he had had far too much to drink. Whatever the cause, what Beasley called "very disparaging remarks about my secretary and her husband just drew gasps from the audience. . . ." Beasley felt close to Ms. Bishop, who had worked for his wife for two years before coming to Cadwalader.

Chopin was not finished. He turned and waved to retired partner Roy A. Povell, who stood and bowed, obviously expecting holiday compliments. He did not get them. Chopin said he realized that some of the things he was saying could be considered sexual discrimination but "we are lucky here to have with us tonight the king of sexual discrimination, Roy Povell!" (When deposed in the Beasley litigation, Chopin blamed his conduct on medication he was taking after major surgery.)

Tears swelled in Ms. Bishop's eyes as she and her husband rushed to Beasley. She had been humiliated before coworkers and friends. How could such conduct be tolerated? The husband said he was giving serious consideration to punching Chopin in the nose. Ms. Bishop filed a sexual harassment complaint against Cadwalader, claiming $250,000 in damages. She continued working for Beasley but kept her distance from Chopin.

Don Glascoff, who, as noted, served on the management committee, would recount that Chopin was sent a "formal letter expressing our severe displeasure and condemnation of his actions" and that "we intended to fine him $5,000, and that was subsequently taken out of his partnership distribution." Beasley was not satisfied. Cadwalader was discussing a settlement under which Ms. Bishop would be paid $75,000 but would also be required to leave the firm. The decision disgusted Beasley. "The perpetrator gets off with a slap on the wrist and the victim has to leave her job. It wasn't fair at all," he told me.

As Beasley found later, during the course of discovery for his lawsuit, New York had heard reports for several years about Chopin's disruptive behavior. Indeed, he said that a member of the management committee in 1992 sent Chopin a letter that said, in effect, one more episode would force him out of the firm.

If New York was so distressed with Chopin, I asked Beasley, why didn't they toss him out the door?

Beasley laughed at my naïveté. "Very simple," he said. "Frank produced two or three million dollars a year of business." The episode was an example of "the guys in New York . . . getting the financial benefits of the profits from Frank's practice, but they didn't have to put up with him from day to day, so it was OK with them."

The managers did realize that the episode meant that the Palm Beach office needed closer scrutiny. They decided that Glascoff, Jack Fritts, and Jonathan Wainwright, a partner who had a good relationship with Chopin, would go to Palm Beach to see, in Glascoff's words, if they could "deal with what we perceived to be behavioral problems with a partner who was extraordinarily talented, extraordinarily good with clients, extraordinarily profitable, but at the same time extraordinarily hard on people and quite often difficult to deal with."

Glascoff said in a deposition, "We perhaps naively thought that the three of us, all of whom believed that Mr. Chopin was a talent, could spend time with him and enforce the view of the management committee that he had to change his behavioral patterns and, also, enforce in his mind the view that the firm valued him as a partner and valued the Palm Beach office and that the Palm Beach office could not go on if he was going to continue to behave in the fashion he had. . . ."

The confrontation stretched over a day and a half in a hotel room, not the firm office, so that it would not "crank up the rumor mill which we believed was already operating at full tilt . . . after the Bishop incident. . . . Part of our efforts with Mr. Chopin were to convince him that his behavior was a little bit beyond the pale. . . . [W]e asked him as gently as we could whether he'd considered that perhaps he should do something of a professional nature that might temper his behavior a little bit." According to Glascoff, Chopin said he was "under treatment for stress," that he had sought professional help to stop smoking, that he had undergone "rather serious abdominal surgery at the Mayo Clinic in September or October of 1993. He was still not fully recovered. . . . Indeed, I think the surgery and the abdominal nature of it contributed to the Bishop incident when combined with the fact that he'd had something to drink at that Christmas party. But we tried to be gentle with him; at the same time we tried to be firm with him. We tried to point out that the firm valued him, the firm wanted to retain him, but the firm wanted him to mend his ways."

The outcome of the meeting did not satisfy Beasley, who told New York partners emphatically that he was "on his way out of the firm" if Chopin remained; Chopin's personality "was so embedded that there was little hope of changing his behavior in a way which would be conductive" to peace. If Beasley left, "the office would self-destruct."

Soon after this confrontation, Jack Fritts returned to Palm Beach, several New York partners in tow. They met Beasley and local partner James Bertles in The Meadows, an upscale restaurant, for dinner. By Beasley's account, the restaurant was crowded and so noisy that normal conversation was difficult. Nonetheless, Fritts "drank at least two bottles of wine" before saying, "We came down here to talk about these problems. What do you think?"

Beasley shook his head in dismay. "If you want to know what I think about all this," he said, "let's have a business meeting where we can talk about it—not in a crowded restaurant with a bunch of people around and [when] everyone has had too much to eat and drink." The requested meeting never occurred. Glascoff came down several weeks later for compensation meetings. Beasley said, "I felt we had good relations. . . . There was a good conversation about the office. . . . I now know that for several weeks they had been running figures on closing the office. . . ."

Two major things came out of the compensation meetings. First, Beasley got an increase in shares, to seven, and Chopin was knocked down by two, to five. Chopin got the message. As he told me, he let Cadwalader know then that he did not intend to stay with the firm, although he set no firm departure date. Beasley interpreted his increase as a signal that the management committee was satisfied with his work.

Unbeknownst to either Beasley or Chopin, the management committee was already discussing whether to close Palm Beach. Bertles learned of this during a visit to New York in March. Four scenarios were discussed: to close the office altogether, to continue without Chopin, to continue without Beasley, or to continue without either man. Bertles was sworn to secrecy. He could not tell men with whom he worked daily that their jobs were at risk. Bertles felt the Beasley-Chopin split was so severe that much of his time was "spent being what amounted to a referee in a prizefight."

By midsummer Beasley heard rumors that the office might be closed. Beasley took these reports seriously, and he talked with a former associate, Steve Katzman, about forming their own practice. Cadwalader had refused partnership to Katzman the previous year, chiefly because of opposition from Chopin. Over breakfasts and lunches, Beasley sounded out three associates on the idea of joining a new firm. Beasley would insist at trial that he had no firm plans to resign from Cadwalader, that he made the overtures to the younger men to reassure them they would not be left jobless if the Cadwalader office closed.

What Beasley did not realize is that the decision had already been made to do just that.

THE CLEANSING PLOT

By midsummer Project Rightsize was so far along that the plotting partners turned to veteran Wall Street lawyer Francis H. Musselman for advice on how to proceed. Musselman had spent forty years doing corporate work for Milbank, Tweed, Hadley & McCloy, a major New York firm. In retirement, he did consulting work for the Hildebrandt legal consulting organization. When Fritts first contacted him, Musselman thought that Cadwalader was considering a merger. He soon learned differently. What Cadwalader had in mind, Fritts told him, was what he called a "rightsizing" of the firm.

Musselman immediately saw through the euphemistic language. "What they call rightsizing," he would testify, "is really a downsizing." Musselman was told at the outset that the decision had already been made to downsize the firm and to close the Palm Beach office. This statement is subject to two interpretations. One is that the Palm Beach closing was not part of "Operation Rightsize," as Fritts and other partners would later insist. Another is that the management committee simply was not candid with Beasley and others when it later contended that the formal closing was not decided until late August.

What was wanted from Musselman was advice on how to cut down the New York, Washington, and Los Angeles offices as efficiently as possible. He spoke with some of the Young Turks and reported on their views in words that were recorded by managing committee member Raymond Banoun. Referring to Link, Gambro, and Schwartz, Musselman stated:

> [L]ike many Young Turks they are interested in instant gratification. They don't want the job done in two or three stages. They want to see more money for them and less for others. Firms like CWT can't carry too many partners. People should be paid what they are worth. They don't believe in anything at all for past performance, only for present performance. They will not accept ten points for Dayan. They want something definitive for each of the people on the list. I think you can do this in a caring, compassionate way that will satisfy them.

Later, during the Beasley trial against Cadwalader in Florida, Musselman testified that he felt that Robert Link had come to the firm "for money."

Musselman had made no study of the firm's situation when, on July 29, he wrote Fritts memorandum on how the management committee could carry out a downsizing. He warned that Cadwalader was headed for rough waters regardless of what it did: "A decision by the leadership in any law firm, especially a firm which is and which views itself to be collegial and caring, to force out one or more partners by early retirement or otherwise can have a traumatic effect on the entire firm for years to come if badly handled. By the same token, failure to make and implement such a decision can have equal and greater unhappy consequences. . . ."

One thing that Musselman urged should not be done was to create a hit list of lawyers to be discarded. When such lists are compiled, "Other partners resent it and not just the partners who are on one or more hit lists. . . . When you do things badly, the firm can go down the tube because you did it badly." Regardless of security, contents of hit lists "are some of the poorest kept secrets in a law firm."

Even as he talked with the management committee, Musselman was not sure that Cadwalader actually intended to discard partners. "In a downsizing," he said, "you can have partners retire, retire early, take less compensation, go on a part-time basis. . . . I did not anticipate or did not expect necessarily that partners would be terminated, would no longer work with the firm other than in those categories." But he concluded that the firm was out of balance, writing, "A major law firm in New York cannot compete efficiently with a ratio of associates to partners of less than two to one. Cadwalader, Wickersham & Taft has too many partners for its size, client base. . . ."

AN AUGUST SUNDAY AT THE MARRIOTT

By early August, the Young Turks were ready to take the purge a step farther by putting their plan before the full management committee. They chose to meet on the first Sunday of the month at the Marriott Hotel, many blocks uptown from 100 Maiden Lane. Even in the dead of a New York summer, the Cadwalader office is chock-full of busy associates, so a meeting there would be certain to stir gossip.

The meeting droned for some ten hours—lawyers discussing the fate of more than a dozen of their partners. In the end the committee made the decision: It would cut salaries drastically, even to zero, to force out unwanted lawyers. Palm Beach would definitely be closed. There would be later haggling over details, to be addressed at another committee meeting on September 24. But the die was cast.

Why was not the downsizing discussed at a partnership meeting before the committee put the plan into motion? "Because it wouldn't have made sense," said partner Grant B. Hering. "If we had done that, then the whole world would have known, and the damage would be incalculable. So even I was not in favor of doing that." He did speak "with maybe a dozen" partners in New York, and some in Washington as well, about what was afoot. He would not call the meetings clandestine. "Everybody in the firm knew about it. . . . You had to be living in Timbuktu—I mean, even being in Washington, I knew this was going on, and, believe me, you generally don't hear a lot that's going on."

Both in his deposition and his trial testimony, Fritts was questioned about why the committee chose such a Draconian course. He made no apologies: "I've been in the business of getting lawyers out of Cadwalader for a long time. I ran the associates for a long time and part of that job was to get people who were not performing up to expectations to another position outside of Cadwalader and to do it efficiently and effectively. And what you do is you have to get the people running very hard to find another job. . . . The topic is to get the person out there in the market, because at the stage when the decision has been made by the firm that the person doesn't belong at the firm, that the person [should] get somewhere else and not dither at Cadwalader, and historically they dithered."

Several years earlier, Fritts said, Cadwalader used the cut-salary method to rid itself of an unwanted partner in New York and of a woman partner in the Washington office.* He said,

---

*Names of these persons, as well as other lawyers dismissed through Project Rightsize, are in court papers. I do not repeat all of them because I am not convinced of the validity of the judgments made on them by Cadwalader partners who were determined to remove them from of the firm.

"The first decision on [the New York partner] was to give him a year to . . . get himself to be productive. And nothing happened. And the same thing happened with the associates. When I was first doing this business . . . there had been a guy who had been told to leave the firm nine or ten months before I became a partner and they were saying he's still here and spending his time reading the *Times* and *Wall Street Journal*. . . ."

Word of the pending cabal circulated through Cadwalader. The secrecy disturbed some partners. Why should not firm business be discussed openly? Why should Cadwalader rules be ignored? These concerns materialized in a memorandum that went to Fritts in midsummer. It was unsigned, and Fritts said on deposition that he could not name the source. (Lawyers for Steven Ruskin would comment tartly, "Fear was so rampant at Cadwalader that the author of this memorandum was afraid to disclose his identity.") The memo stated:

Section 42 of the Partnership Law requires the rendition on demand of true and full information of all things affecting the partnership. At the next firm meeting, you should tell about the partners who are making demands regarding their own compensation and the dispatch, termination, or expulsion of some group of other partners. Also, you should explain what has been said regarding threats to leave in the event these demands are not met.

In the event that you do not disclose this information on the basis that the demand does not identify by name of any partner making this demand, then please read this aloud and ask if any partner joins in the demand. I expect that you will indeed find some substantial number of your partners who are interested in learning the identity of those partners who are breaching their fiduciary duties through cabal and violation of the Firm Agreement.

The significance of the memorandum went beyond its admonition against secrecy. Someone had taken the trouble to review New York State law on partnerships, and the firm's partnership agreement, and concluded that what was happening violated the law. He so notified Jack Fritts, the management committee chair. The record shows that the warning memo was not acted on.

Management committee member Raymond Banoun also had qualms, he was to claim later. He had just finished going through the compensation review, "a very exhaustive and exhausting process. . . . I wasn't happy to have to start all over again. . . . [M]y view is that we . . . would sort of look foolish having spent so much time, having issued a report—having issued a list of shares." He suggested "taking points away from everybody and putting them in a pool and then paying bonuses to those who had really outstanding years as an alternative."

Banoun's suggestion died quickly. As Jonathan W. Johnson, an attorney for Ruskin, would write later, this tactic "would have required that all of the partners contribute to the cost of rewarding the 'stellar' ones. It was more enticing for this committee to choose a select group of partners for departure and to use a portion of the money derived from the seizure of their shares for the bonus pool." Another partner, Jeff Smith, protested to Banoun that the "process had no integrity and was precipitous action due to pressure from people who didn't understand the firm."

PLANNING FOR A PURGE

Meanwhile, Frank Musselman, the outside consultant, continued working on the mechanics of discarding the unwanted partners. One of his concerns was that Cadwalader put a "positive spin" on the purge. He wrote:

> The implementation of a program to retire, retire early, reduce status, outplace and terminate for whatever reason a large number of partners had many dangers and can be disastrous if not done very well—It is not a simple matter. It is very complex. You are dealing with a whole bunch of individuals and families of individuals. One needs to make sure that the implementation of the program goes down well with the partners, the staff, the clients, the media & the outside world. . . .

Musselman suggested that partners near retirement should be given "of counsel" status because it would "lend a certain amount of class" to Project Rightsize and "helps them keep their self-respect, dignity—not castoffs." He wrote that this "class" could be attained at a nominal expense, chiefly "an office and shared secretarial service." The younger partners should not mind because, as he wrote, "most of the Young Turks are really interested in money anyhow."

At the Marriott meeting in August, each of the twelve members of the management committee was asked, in the words of Grant Hering, "to submit a list of who they . . . viewed as unproductive partners" to be used as a basis for discussion. Seven members "refused to respond." Five did, however, and Glascoff drew up a compilation showing "the number of times that each person appeared on each of the five individuals' lists."

It fell to Fritts to assemble the recommendations into a final list, which he typed personally on his computer on August 22, to avoid secretarial gossip. He headed his memo: "Subject: Rightsizing." It dealt with twenty-nine partners. The last item, of a total of twenty-one, read, "Florida office—Close 12/31/94. Bertles considering relocation to NY."

That Palm Beach was listed on a memo headed "Rightsizing" would throw into question Cadwalader's later claim that the closing was done independently of what happened in New York. In June 1999 Robert Link, by then the firm's managing partner, argued to me that this was in fact the case—that Palm Beach was included on the list only so that its financial numbers could be considered along with other "Rightsizing" changes. The Florida judge who heard Beasley's suit disagreed with the firm's argument; he ruled that the closing was part of Rightsize.

Essentially, Link said, the firm was "fed up" with the turmoil between Beasley and Frank Chopin, and with the problems created by the sexual harassment charge against the latter. Beasley had angered New York by permitting a client (a friend) to run up a legal fee in the million-dollar range. Beasley was essentially running a litigation operation that did not mesh with Cadwalader's corporate practice.

In any event, the first name on Fritts's list was a lawyer who had been a partner for nineteen years, and who was seven years short of retirement. He earned $388,889 in 1993. For retirement purposes, he would be paid a "lump sum upon departure . . . to avoid burden on future partners of periodic benefits." The list continued with Steven Ruskin ($543,706): "Leave on points; depart 12/31/94; departure benefit and severance payment calculated in same manner as [the first person named]." On and on rolled the roster, listing salaries and departure dates. The list would undergo many mutations during August and September; at one time more than thirty partners were named as persons who should either be forced out of the firm or given reduced compensation. The final run showed seventeen departing partners.

In another memo, Fritts sketched out a game plan: "Management committee final decision by 9/2/94. Fritts and Glascoff meet with each affected partner individually between 9/6 and 9/13; no formal announcement to partners but discussion anticipated at firm meeting.

"Publicity: None; response to press inquiries to be prepared.

"Outside counsel: To be retained in anticipation of litigation . . ."

The jettisoning of the New York partners would await a partners' meeting in September. At the Marriott meeting, the committee had authorized Glascoff to move against the Palm Beach office with no further ado. Although no public announcement would be made, he expected news of the action to reach the press. To help contain what was expected to be a nasty backlash, Cadwalader hired the public relations firm of Burson-Marsteller. On August 29 Fritts wrote a memo, "Subject: Response to Palm Beach Inquiries." He cited the changed nature of the Cadwalader practice and the firm's "ongoing efforts to position the firm to concentrate on its strongest practice areas. . . ." He also cited "economic and competitive factors" and "increasing potential conflicts of interest" between the firm's national client base and Palm Beach.

The memo addressed another worry: "As a precaution, due to the extent of the rumors now prevalent . . . we have made arrangements . . . for an unobtrusive security service to provide security [at the Palm Beach office] over the weekend—make sure that no unhappy staff person . . . engages in acts of vandalism, etc."

BEASLEY BATTLES BACK

Jim Beasley spent Tuesday, August 30, meeting a client in Miami. His secretary reported that Don Glascoff had phoned several times but they did not make contact until around five P.M., when Beasley returned to Palm Beach. He later testified, "I had no reason to suspect what he was going to say or talk about other than routine client matters. . . . Mr. Glascoff told me that he was sorry to have to be the one to tell me that the management committee had decided the night before to close the Palm Beach office as of December 31, 1994. . . .

"It was a complete surprise to me. . . . I had not been consulted or advised or had any discussion with anyone about the possibility that the office might be closed or what we might be able to do in order to solve whatever problems that somebody thought there were at the office. I was absolutely stunned."

Glascoff said he would come to Palm Beach to discuss the severance pay of Beasley and other partners. Associates would be offered six weeks' salary as severance, in addition to their annual draw and bonus. The latter, however, would be cut to two-thirds of "your regular bonus."

Almost five years later, Beasley still seethed at Cadwalader's conduct. He told me, "Had they come to us and said, 'Look, for various reasons, we've decided not to emphasize Florida, or whatever. What do you guys want to do? Take six months to a year to figure it out.' That would have been fine."

The appearance of a uniformed security guard, armed with a holstered pistol, in the office early the next morning disturbed the staff and offended Beasley. "Here was this person with a Sam Browne belt and a Smokey the Bear hat, standing around a law office. This did not go well with people." (A management committee member contended that Musselman, the consultant, recommended the guard to prevent a disgruntled employee from trashing the computer system.)

Beasley made a close reading of the partnership agreement, and he knew that Cadwalader was on very thin legal ice. He and Chopin decided that their price was going to be far more than a quarter of their annual draw.

On September 22, he and Chopin fired the first salvo back at New York. They sent Cadwalader an opinion by professor Robert W. Hillman of the University on California Davis Law School ("the nation's leading authority of law firm law and law firm breakups," they called him) that contended that the expulsions were illegal. Because the Cadwalader partnership agreement contained no expulsion clause, it did not have the authority to toss out partners. As Beasley and Chopin wrote, "Our wrongful expulsion triggers automatic dissolution of the firm. . . . Our wrongful expulsion gives us the right to a judicial dissolution of the firm, its liquidation, and to payment of our percentage interests in the firm plus damages."

The next Beasley heard from New York was a letter addressed to him and Chopin from Fritts and Glascoff on September 23. They rejected the Hillman memorandum. They also tacked on a sentence that Beasley felt outrageously inaccurate: "At this time, you continue to be partners in the firm. We reiterate and *confirm the continuance of our proposal that you relocate to New York.*" (Emphasis added.)

The sentence puzzled Beasley. In fact, this was a "longstanding proposal in Frank's case." But Cadwalader had never discussed moving Beasley to New York. "It couldn't be serious. I have no clients in New York. . . . At that point, we had learned they were firing or contemplating firing a bunch of partners in New York who didn't have any business, so why would I go to New York when I didn't have any New York business?" He had spent most of his professional life building a client base in Florida, clients who could not use him if he moved. He had not practiced in New York for twenty-five years.

Conditions in Palm Beach deteriorated rapidly. As Beasley

said, "I had a very active practice at that point. I had one major case involving twenty-five million dollars that was originally set for trial in November, and I was involved in extensive discovery and depositions and hearings on a regular basis to prepare for that case, and I had a number of other matters going as well. I was probably spending more time on that particular case than anything else. . . ." Chopin was winding down the office, "starting to interview for jobs and things like that, but I was in the office every day, most weekends, continuing to try to take care of my clients' business and the firm's business the best I could under the circumstances."

Associates quickly bailed out for other jobs. In an attempt to get out from under the heavy rent burden, Cadwalader struck a deal with the landlord to pay off half the lease and let him start converting space on December 1. "So you had basically a construction site with a lot of people already gone and people going out the door every day. It was a fairly critical situation," Beasley related.

"The people in New York were dismissing me as just another Florida lawyer," Beasley said. "They didn't take me seriously; they felt they could shove me around." He called John Pickering, a founding partner of the Washington firm of Wilmer, Cutler & Pickering, where he had worked after coming out of the army. "John was indignant at the way I was being treated." Pickering talked with Samuel Butler, managing partner of Cravath, Swaine & Moore, his office's correspondent firm in New York, who agreed to help. Beasley related, "I said to them, 'You guys talk to Cadwalader, whatever you recommend that I should take, I will take.'"

By any measure, Pickering and Butler are deans of the American bar. Pickering had the appearance that central casting would love should it have a role for a senator—a burly man with flowing white hair and a trademark black bow tie. He and Butler had worked together on complex matters for decades. But even these emissaries got nowhere. They went to 100 Maiden Lane for a scheduled meeting. They sat cooling their heels in the reception area for more than an hour. As Beasley said, "The people running things at Cadwalader wouldn't even talk with them . . . it was incomprensible behavior." Pickering and Butler asked for $900,000 each for Chopin and Beasley. As Pickering pointed out, Chopin had earned $4.2 million in profits for the firm between 1990 and 1993, and Beasley $3 million. Further, some of the partners were getting retirement benefits—$216,000 for one of the ousted lawyers, for instance, and $115,000 for Steve Ruskin.

Cadwalader countered by offering them $120,000 each, less distributions already made that year. "We tried to pound some sense into those dummies," Pickering told me months later. "They should have listened. Eventually, being dummies cost them four times, or more, what they could have paid."

At this stage Beasley began to realize that Cadwalader intended to squeeze him out on terms as unfavorable as possible. He talked with his former Miami partner, Tom Tew, about representing him. They drafted a complaint charging that Cadwalader illegally terminated him, "I was hoping that we wouldn't need it, that New York would listen to reason." Word came that the remaking of the firm would be finalized at a partners' meeting on November 9.

Beasley wondered whether partners who were not on the management committee had any idea of the questionable legality of the firings. Over the weekend of November 4 he and Chopin wrote a lengthy memorandum restating Professor Hillman's argument that the firings were not permitted under the partnership agreement, and making the case that Palm Beach was profitable. As a matter of courtesy, they sent a draft to Glascoff and Fritts, stating that they would assert their right to put it before the full partnership meeting if agreement was not reached before November 9. The memo should be distributed "so that the partners can decide whether the firm should settle or litigate," Beasley concluded.

If he was to be shoved out, he argued, he should take a decent severance package with him. "In the past," he wrote, "when the firm has seen it to be in its economic interest, it has not hesitated to make substantial payments to partners who have voluntarily departed, without laying any claims against the firm. For example, Tom Russo left to take a job with Lehman Brothers in early 1993 and received $500,000. A relatively junior partner, Jeff Quinn, left earlier this year for Merrill Lynch and received $125,000. These payments were undoubtedly inducements for these gentlemen to send future business to the firm and they have done so. A junior partner in the Palm Beach office, Chuck Senatore, who had only been a partner with the firm for two years, left earlier this year to join the Securities and Exchange Commission and received a payment of $250K. Again, we stress that these payments were voluntary on the firm's part, since these partners had no legal claim on the firm."

Included in the package were copies of various Project Right-size documents, which friends had bootlegged to Beasley—including some of the original lists of partners who had been discussed as targets. For the first time, many persons learned that their futures had been at risk. That Beasley revealed what Fritts and others considered to be confidential information infuriated the management committee.

Late the afternoon of November 7, Chopin came into Beasley's office and reported that he had reached a satisfactory settlement, and that his name should not be on the memorandum. (In subsequent court papers, Cadwalader listed the amount as $528,000. Chopin declined to tell me a specific dollar amount but said he was "most satisfied.") Beasley decided to proceed on his own. He gave copies of the memo to Sam Butler and John Pickering to distribute to partners in New York and Washington, respectively.

Early the morning of November 9, Beasley was driving from Miami to Palm Beach when his office called on the car phone and said New York partner Tim Rogers was trying to reach him. Beasley pulled off the highway and called Rogers. "He informed me that the management committee had been confiscating from right off partners' desks or even right out of their hands the memorandum that I had sent to all the partners which had been delivered in New York early, very early, seven or eight on the morning of November 9." A few minutes later Beasley received a similar report from Washington: The memos were being confiscated, rather than distributed to partners to whom they were addressed. (Cadwalader would maintain that Beasley's memo unfairly revealed the names of partners whose removal from the firm had been discussed, then rejected.)

The partners' meeting was to have been over lunch. "When I learned that they had confiscated the memoranda and prevented me from communicating with the partners, I don't believe I even came back to the office. . . . I had the complaint in my briefcase. I went straight to the courthouse and filed the lawsuit."

The suit, filed in Palm Beach Circuit Court, charged Cadwalader was "attempting to appropriate millions of dollars in Florida-generated revenue in an effort to help solve the firm's financial problems." Cadwalader had no authority to force him out of the firm, and the suggestion that he transfer his practice to New York was a sham. He asked that the court liquidate Cadwalader and give him a fair share of the proceeds. He also demanded his share of 1994 income and an unspecified sum in punitive damages.

A few hours later, Beasley and other out-of-New York partners "attended" the lunchtime meeting by conference calls. He said, "At the end, somebody raised the question about what was going to happen with me and I . . . got on the speakerphone." Once again he told about the Hillman memo, and he announced he had just sued the firm for unlawful discharge. "The partnership meeting ended and I went back to my office and went to work."

As a matter of courtesy, Beasley faxed a copy of his complaint of New York. When Jack Fritts read through the document, one name jumped out: Tom Tew. For months, Cadwalader had been defending its role in the collapse of an organization named Premium Sales, located in the Miami suburbs. The Securities and Exchange Commission moved against Premium, charging that it was largely a Ponzi scheme. A court-appointed trustee, Harley Tropin, sued law firms and accountants who had worked for Premium in an attempt to recoup some of the $250 million lost by defrauded investors. One of the firms targeted by Tropin was Cadwalader, and one of the lawyers involved in his effort was none other than Tew—the man now involved in suing the firm on behalf of a disgruntled partner who had been marked for dismissal. In May Tew had threatened a $30 million securities fraud and legal malpractice suit against Cadwalader.*

To the management committee, what Beasley had just done was tantamount to professional treason. As would be argued by West Palm Beach lawyer Sidney Stubbs, who ultimately defended Cadwalader in court, Beasley's complaint charged his partners with "fraud, bad faith, breach of fiduciary duty. . . ." Stubbs asked, "How in the world could a law firm talk to clients with a person sitting in the office who has filed a public complaint . . . using the kind of language that is used in the complaint . . . ?"

Beasley came into the office on November 11, Veterans Day, and found a fax from Fritts that had arrived late the previous day. Fritts wrote, "We believe your actions in suing the firm, retaining Thomas Tew and his law firm to represent you, communicating with persons outside the firm about private firm business, and circulating to all partners preliminary and internal management committee communications constitute breaches of your fiduciary duties to the firm and its partners, breaches of contract, and actionable torts against the firm and its partners." He must be out of the firm at five P.M. that day, and he must not take any files with him.

Michael Dolan, an administrative partner from New York, had flown into Palm Beach the previous night. He appeared in the Cadwalader office "first thing that Friday morning. He . . . basically told me he was there to enforce the November 10 letter

---

*In October 1995 Cadwalader settled the suit for $10 million. The firm's insurance carrier paid the sum. John K. Aurell, a Tallahassee lawyer who defended Cadwalader in the action, said, "Every lawsuit, particularly where a jury is involved, has risk. A combination of litigation risk, very substantial costs, and the desire of the firm's insurers to settle led to this settlement."

and by that time they had hired another security guard so they had one there during office hours as well. . . . They changed the locks, asked me to turn in my key, and Mr. Dolan told me that notwithstanding this reprieve that I had received . . . they did not want me to sign my name to any letters on the firm stationery from that point forward unless he personally approved it. So, all during the day I would run back and forth from my office to the office Mr. Dolan was occupying saying, 'Is it okay if I send this?' Well, most of them were bills to clients to pay money to Cadwalader. So, of course, he had no major objection to that."

COMPENSATION OR TERMINATION?

Although he had no way of knowing it at the time, Beasley's protests caused the Young Turks to rethink their scheme to use reduced compensation to drive out unwanted partners. Beasley's memo from law professor Robert W. Hillman stating that what Cadwalader was doing violated the agreement sent ripples through the New York office, and resulted in hurried changes in the scenario for Project Rightsize.

The first "script" written to orchestrate the September 29 partnership meeting had referred to two categories of targeted partners: "I: Departing Partners," and "II: Compensation Adjustments." The memo said that the "departing partners" (Ruskin was so named) would be "advised . . . that compensation may be further reduced (perhaps to $0) at December 31 or June 30, as applicable, without regard to billable hours put in prior to that date . . . [and] that departure is highly recommended."

But receipt of the Hillman memo, and its charge that the firm was acting illegally, caused significant editing. A revised version dated September 23 changed "Departing Partners" to "Reduced Partners." The category on "Compensation Adjustments" became "Additional Compensation Adjustments." The phrase, "departure is highly recommended," was altered to "departure should seriously be considered."

There was another worrisome factor. In August firm cochairman Glascoff had asked an associate to do a memo addressing the question "How can the partnership force a partner to leave the firm in the absence of a termination provision in the partnership agreement?" The question arose from a man who had left the firm, moved to Colorado, and then threatened to sue for wrongful discharge.

The associate's answer: "The partners may amend the partnership agreement to include a termination provision and then exercise that termination provision to expel a recalcitrant partner." The associate went on to warn that a targeted partner "could argue that . . . he was constructively terminated by being asked to leave and having his compensation reduced."

Glascoff did not like this conclusion at all. He called in the associate and—in his words—"focused him" on the conclusion that he desired, that is, management in fact could use the compensation power to force a partner from the firm. Associates do not argue with firm managers; Glascoff got the memo he wanted.

STEVE RUSKIN IS AXED

As had everyone else, Steve Ruskin heard the swirl of rumors about what was simmering. He did not worry. The praise he had received in the compensation review seemed assurance enough that he would not be on any hit list. Too, he considered himself to be close enough to Jack Fritts that he would have been warned if his career was in peril. They were friends, of sorts. Fritts's wife ran a summer camp for girls in Maine, and for nine straight years Ruskin and his wife had gone there with their daughter for parents' day.

Shortly after noon on Tuesday, September 27, Fritts called Ruskin and asked if he "could come to my office to speak to me." Puzzled, Ruskin said yes, and Fritts added that he'd like to bring Don Glascoff with him.

As his two partners entered the office, Glascoff turned and shoved the door closed. Ruskin said, "This looks very ominous."

"We have some very heavy things to discuss with you," Fritts said, omitting any amenities. "The management committee would like you to seriously consider leaving the firm."

Ruskin's heart pounded, blood rushed to his head. "I could not believe what I was hearing," he told me. "I tried hard to keep control of myself. I was afraid to take a drink of water; my hands were shaking so badly. All I could ask was 'Why is this happening? This firm was my life.' It was like being told by your wife that she is leaving you."

Fritts showed no sign of recognizing his partner's distress. He had a yellow pad before him, and he continued reading what he had prepared in advance. "Effective October 1, three days later, your points will be eliminated and you will be on a salary of $225,000 a year until December 31, and if you are still at the firm on January 1, your compensation will be reduced further. As an inducement to you to leave the firm, we will pay you one quarter of your 1994 compensation." He then recited pension benefits that Cadwalader would offer—numbers that were meaningless to the stunned Ruskin.

Ruskin began literally pleading for his professional life. "Have I done something wrong?" he asked.

Fritts shook his head. "No, you are a fine lawyer. We have an institutional problem in the tax department. We have too many tax partners, and too few tax associates."

Ruskin sensed an opening. "Well, this sounds to me like a compensation issue. What if I were to take a reduced compensation for some period of time, at the end of which I could recover my points and become a full partner again?"

Again, Fritts shook his head. "That would not be appropriate."

Ruskin tried again. He had done trusts and estates work in the past; if necessary, he would transfer to the T&E department. "No," Fritts said, "that would not be acceptable." Nor would the management committee consider letting him work three days a week out of Washington.

The management committee's refusal to let Ruskin shift to Washington suggested that Fritts and others were determined to get him out of Cadwalader regardless. Michael Ryan of the management committee would later admit that "the tax practice in the Washington office was in fact booming, and there was too much work for the tax partners in Washington to handle and supervise." Tax lawyers there were "overwhelmed," he said. A new tax partner had been hired directly in Washington in early 1994, and another transferred down from New York. Glascoff conceded that Cadwalader had "a fairly significant history of partners relocating between our offices." Peculiarly, at the same time Cadwalader was offering two tax partners in the Palm Beach office the opportunity to relocate to New York—even though the firm was claiming that tax work there had diminished so much that Ruskin was not needed. Neither of these partners accepted the New York offer. Ruskin told me these offered transfers were "litigation posturing" that no one took seriously.

"You mean I have no choice but to leave the firm?" Ruskin asked. "Yes, that's correct," Fritts replied. Anger began to overcome Ruskin's shock. He felt the offered compensation package was outrageous.

"You are converting me from a percentage of profits to a fixed salary October 1, and you know that a substantial percentage of the profits of the firm come in in October, November, and especially December, so by cutting me off percentage you are in effect reducing my compensation that I have earned."

Fritts gave no answer. If Ruskin wanted to discuss the pension further, he was willing. He would be given a severance payment—but only if he left Cadwalader by the end of December.

Ruskin shook his head in slow disbelief. Could men with whom he had worked as partners for nearly two decades end his career in such unfeeling, cavalier fashion? Their work done, Fritts and Glascoff arose and started for the door.

"You can find a job if you try," Fritts called back. He said that placement counselor Francis Musselman would be contacting him to "assist you in finding a job." They left.

Ruskin stared at the closed door a few minutes. All he could think of doing was picking up the phone and calling his wife. "Honey," he said, "I've just been fired."

"You're kidding!" she exclaimed, trying to laugh at what surely must be an attempt at humor.

"No, it is true—I am no longer a partner at Cadwalader," Ruskin said.

Francis Musselman came in the next morning. "I want to be your friend," he said by way of greeting. (The following is based on Ruskin's trial testimony.)

"Well," Ruskin replied, "I think I could use a friend right about now, but aren't you a paid adviser to Cadwalader? Aren't you responsible for this happening to me?"

"That's not the right attitude," Musselman protested. He mentioned the Hildebrandt organization and urged that Ruskin prepare a resume within twenty-four hours so that it could be reviewed. Musselman continued that Ruskin "should leave the firm as soon as possible or you'll become . . . a pariah, which is like a leper."

Ruskin was still curious as to the provenance of his firing. He knew that Musselman had worked with the management committee. Perhaps he had the answer. "Why did this happen?" he asked directly.

"Well, it was brought to you I believe by Bob Link and his gang," Musselman said.

"Who is in this gang?" Ruskin asked.

"Well, all those corporate types that work with Bob Link. But the decision was made with respect to you before I was hired. I wasn't responsible for the decision. I was hired after the decision." Then Musselman suggested, "You should hire a lawyer."

Ruskin demurred. "The last thing I want to do is hire a lawyer and get into a confrontation with my partners. I'm sure I can work this out."

Musselman stared at him. He repeated, "Hire a lawyer," and walked out.

Fritts and Glascoff made their rounds throughout the day, delivering the news to other targeted partners—your compensation is being cut, and we want you out of here. Fritts wanted them "running very hard to find another job."

Ruskin had a right to appeal the management committee decision to the full partnership. But when he came into the lunchtime meeting on September 28 he found that partners had been given a package of financial data projecting what Project Rightsize would mean in terms of individual profits. Income per share would increase by $14,600 in 1995; $26,000 in 1996; and $30,600 in 1997. Tossing out the targeted partners would eliminate 88.7 shares, leaving the remaining partners with 348.8 shares. Consequently, the surviving partners would find their pool increased by $5,162,340 in 1995; $9,068,800 in 1996, and $10,672,280 in 1997—or a total of $24,904,320 for the first three years alone.

Ruskin recited those figures to me much later as we sat in his new law office in Dallas. "The meter is still running," he said. "This money was wrongfully taken from me and other partners; it was illegally confiscated. What they continue to earn today comes out of my pocket."

But once Ruskin saw his partners going through the figures, and mentally computing how much more money they would receive if he and others were ejected, he knew that his career at Cadwalader was over.

The purging of Ruskin and others brought sharp dissent. One of the angrier persons was Terry Gilheany, a partner since 1973. He wrote a blistering memo to Fritts. "The proposal will impose from the top down rigid and, for most partners, impossible to meet standards, which will then be perceived, whether justifiably or not, as designed to favor a small and select group of partners."

Changes might be necessary, Gilheany conceded, but was Cadwalader doing so in proper fashion? He wrote, "Jack, do we really want to commit this to writing? I understand that a lot of the lunatics think we ought to be taking a hard second look at L.A. [Los Angeles] and for once I don't think I disagree with them." By "lunatics," he said he referred to "the group of partners who, after the distribution of points at midyear in 1994, had come to the management committee and basically said that more action needed to be taken." When deposed by Palm Beach attorney Robert Montgomery, who represented Beasley in his litigation, Gilheany singled out Robert Link as "one of the group that I . . . referred to with that phrase."

Ruskin made one more try at preserving his career. For procedural reasons, a formal vote on accepting the management committee's recommendations would not come until October. So Ruskin wrote a memo on October 10 addressed "To My Partners." He conceded that on the surface his billable hours did show a sharp decline, from 2,108 in 1991 to 995 in 1993. Fees derived from client contacts dropped from $1,901,921 in 1991 to $945,417; nonetheless, he had continued to "supervise" business that brought Cadwalader from $1.6 million (in 1992) to $802,286 (in 1993). But he also explained in detail the large amount of work he did for the firm, including the building situation and "tough legal hours spent working on the Firm's tax matters," as he put it. He worked 1,054 hours for the firm in 1993 alone, giving him a total of 2,049 hours for that year. He wrote:

As you can imagine, I was shocked and dismayed to be told that I must find employment elsewhere. Cadwalader has been my home for almost a quarter of a century, and I had expected to be a partner of the Firm for the balance of my career. My anger regarding the terms of my forced departure was quickly mixed with concern for the well-being of the Firm, since the Cadwalader I grew up in and helped to build was a family of professionals who understood the deeper meaning of the concept of partnership.

I have done nothing, to my knowledge, to deserve to be terminated as a partner. I have received accolades every year for my professional work, industry and loyalty to the Firm. This is reflected in my compensation, which ranks in the top half of all partners. Even in the meeting in which I was told to find employment elsewhere, my skill as a lawyer was praised.

I have been a productive, loyal, hardworking member of this firm. If this can happen to me, it can happen to you.

The basic premise of this partnership is stated in . . . the Firm Agreement. We have pledged to each other our best efforts to aid each other's professional success and enhancement so that each of us shall receive from the others a fair opportunity to use his or her best talents and faculties to the common benefit. In times of prosperity it is easy to fulfill that pledge. It is in hard times that our pledge has true meaning and the willingness of the partners to fulfill their responsibility to each other is tested. If the partners live up to their pledge to each other, the Firm will work its way through hard times. I am prepared to do my part and to live up to my pledge, and I ask each of you to do the same.

Jack Fritts and Don Glascoff responded on October 26 with a brush-off letter. As members of the management committee, they "must . . . look to the future of the Firm. We find ourselves in a position where we have too many tax lawyers for the amount of tax work we have. There appears to be no prospects for you to be fully utilized in the future . . . and that significant cuts in compensation would naturally ensue."

In the meanwhile, Ruskin became a pariah. One partner, a man he considered a friend, told Ruskin he would not provide him any work his remaining weeks and that he doubted that anyone else would either. Another partner told him, "What do you really want? Your partnership is over."

In a deposition, Fritts sought to justify axing his partner: "[N]o work was coming to him. It wasn't a matter of occupying tax partners. It was a matter that people didn't want to use Steve Ruskin to do their work. . . . Anacomp didn't want to use him, the Palmieri people didn't want to use him. No clients, nobody—he brought nothing in and nobody in the firm took him any business except doing the building, and that was because . . . he didn't have any other work." Ruskin told me, "That is nonsense, and Jack Fritts knows that it is nonsense. What he said is absolutely false. Why did he say such things? Because we were in litigation, and he had to justify his actions somehow."

Incredibly, Ray Banoun would insist during the Beasley litigation in Florida that Ruskin had "voluntarily withdrawn" from Cadwalader, the mass of contradictory documents notwithstanding.* Further, he claimed that Ruskin made a big "mistake" because, had he remained, "I think he would be doing very well today."

Banoun continued, "I like Steve a lot."

THE BITTER AFTERMATH

Cadwalader succeeded in creating an unsightly mess in its own office, and protests were vehement, both from partners who were "rightsized" and those who remained. Jerome Shelby, a former management committee cochairman, wrote a memo to all partners on September 29 stating that "by creating a long list of partners we would not miss, we destroy the loyalty of all personnel of the firm." He cited the rumors of a "list of 35" circulating in the firm (an accurate rumor, in fact) and commented, "Now that 18 [actually 17] terminations and three drastic moves to downgrade status have been publicly announced, the statement that there are no further lists may well be doubted by the remaining 14 and the rest of the firm." Concerning Ruskin, Shelby wrote: "Steve Ruskin is a partner who is always willing to be useful and work very hard. . . . [I]t seems to be very harsh to boot the man on whom the firm relied so much for noncollectible work for it in connection with the building, mortgage and the amendment to the partnership agreement and who has been asked to analyze the new limited liability company law."

Another partner who complained bitterly was one of only two blacks to reach partner rank. He circulated a memo noting that he had supervised a major Cadwalader effort to mobilize community support against drugs; he directed a guidebook on the subject that was published on the firm's two hundredth anniversary. "Now," the man complained, "partners are terminated without any regard for their recent performance." He was told

---

*In fact, Ruskin would testify during a subsequent trial that he never received a formal notice that he should leave. But the circumstances made plain he had no choice but to leave.

his income would be reduced to $100,000 a year, a substantial cut. He left.

The protests of the ousted partners, many of which got into the court record during the Ruskin litigation, are poignant protests against perceived betrayal. "The management committee . . . has now, in effect, shown me the door," one man wrote. Another said that the decision "is not what I would have expected from my partners. . . . The extreme action is unfair and unwarranted. This action may be illegal. . . . At the very least, partners should be accorded a more dignified exit. . . . I will need to do a lot of explaining to salvage my career as news circulates, as it already has, about these actions."

The partner was prescient. Word of the upheaval spread quickly to legal journals, which used language from Cadwalader sources (without naming them) referring to "deadwood, unproductive partners, and underproductive partners." Robert Link was quoted in one newspaper as saying some of the departing partners were so out of touch with their practice areas that "they still made hula hoops." Ruskin and another ousted partner were identified by name. As Ruskin would tell me, "When I read in the *New York Law Journal* that I was deadwood, I knew my career as a lawyer in my hometown was over. I knew I had to vindicate myself. I had no choice but to sue."

There was more. On October 14, administrative partner Michael G. Dolan circulated a draft of a proposed "letter to clients" giving Cadwalader's version of what had happened. It was a masterful example of obfuscation. It referred to "some changes at Cadwalader, changes that we regard as very beneficial to the firm's ability to better serve your needs and the needs of all of our clients." It stated that "we have taken steps to reshape the Firm to meet the changing needs of the marketplace," and that this was being done to match "*the best attorneys* [emphasis added] and their expertise with the needs of our clients."

The draft outraged Ruskin, who was still demanding that the firm reverse its decision concerning his career. He told Glascoff and Fritts that the "best attorneys" reference was inappropriate and injurious to him. Further, "compensation adjustments"—

the euphemism still used by Cadwalader, in stubborn opposition to reality—had never before caused such a letter of explanation to clients.

Ruskin would struggle on for weeks, attempting to force the entire partnership to vote up or down on Project Rightsize. Fritts used parliamentary wiggles to prevent him from doing so. Cadwalader tried to buy him off by offering him a better severance package and a June 30, 1995, departure date. The firm's former chairman, Rod Dayan, told partners at a firm meeting on October 26 that the meager size of the severance package offered to Ruskin was "obscene," in view of what he had done for Cadwalader.

Ruskin finally got his vote on November 9. His motion to reverse Project Rightsize failed, 52–24. He began clearing out of his office at the end of the year. A client for whom he was doing a refinancing deal asked him to finish it, so he did not formally leave until January 20.

As Ruskin feared, landing a new job was nigh impossible. The nature of his practice at Cadwalader was one factor. "My clients were institutional, businesses that needed a full-service law firm, not a sole tax lawyer. So my business was not portable," Ruskin told me. What remained unfathomable was whether clients were interested in doing business with a lawyer whose own firm had not considered him among "the best attorneys." And there was continued publicity. In November the *National Law Journal* had an article mentioning him by name as a "victim" of the Cadwalader purge.

He picked up an odd case or two, handling them from his home in Armonk, New York. And he also followed the advice given him by Frank Musselman, the consultant: He hired the hard-nosed plaintiff firm of Kreindler & Kreindler, and he sued Cadwalader for breach of the partnership agreement. And after two painful years as a solo practitioner, he moved to Dallas, to join a large law firm, which he knew because it represented his wife's employer, a real estate investment trust listed on the New York Stock Exchange.

In contrast to Ruskin, Jim Beasley did have clients who were "portable," and he managed to reestablish a practice almost immediately, in West Palm Beach. Nonetheless, his ouster from Cadwalader took a toll. His half-million-dollar income in 1993 plummeted to about half that amount. And, as did Steve Ruskin, he incurred enormous legal fees in preparing to take Cadwalader to court.

CADWALADER IN COURT

Beasley's case was heard without a jury before Judge Jack C. Cook of Palm Beach County Court. Beasley won a number of pretrial scuffles over admissibility of evidence. Cook ordered Cadwalader to surrender internal documents about firm finances and scores of pages of memoranda about Project Rightsize. And in a ruling crucial to the case, he ruled that Cadwalader violated the partnership agreement by expelling him.

Cadwalader, meanwhile, tossed some things back at Beasley. Working though West Palm Beach lawyer Sidney Stubbs (who by coincidence is in the same building as Beasley's current office, several floors down) Cadwalader filed a countersuit claiming that Beasley lied about the amount of money he earned before joining Cadwalader and was so broke that the firm had to pay his back income taxes. He was also accused of causing dissension in the Palm Beach office, and of letting a client run up a $1 million tab, in violation of Cadwalader policy that bills must be kept current. Beasley countered he got behind on taxes because Cadwalader paid him less than promised his first two years, and that the firm's billing administrator was aware of the $1 million bill and did not object.

The discovery lasted for more than a year, with depositions producing thousand of pages of testimony in addition to a voluminous file of documents. (Much of the foregoing material is drawn from these papers.) Beasley hired Palm Beach litigator Robert Montgomery, famed for his role in tobacco litigation. Montgomery wisely chose to work in tandem with Ruskin's counsel, Lee and James Kreindler, and their associate Jonathan Johnson. Given his decades in Cadwalader's New York office,

Ruskin knew the filing system, the sort of documents that are generated by the firm, and where they were apt to be hidden. What he and the Kreindlers found was shared with Beasley and Montgomery.

One of the most striking moments came when Jack Fritts spoke eloquently during his deposition about the new phenomenon of firm hopping among lawyers who saw more money elsewhere. The crux of the problem, he argued, is that Cadwalader feared losing "a bunch of extraordinarily productive partners" unless they got more money. He continued:

> And life is not made up of love, it's made up of fear and greed and money—how much you get paid, in large measure. Unless we didn't get Cadwalader's profitability to where it was with our competitors' firms, my great fear was that people were going to be leaving and that we would then not be able to sustain ourselves. . . .

Fritts continued, "What we want to have is a Cadwalader that is here for the next 200 years, as strong as it's been in the first 200 years, and that's what we are trying to do. You keep saying trying to get money in more people's hands. There's lot of things involved in that." He and other Cadwalader witnesses maintained that the firm did not expel Beasley—it simply closed the Palm Beach office and offered to move him to New York, and he refused.

Cadwalader lost, and in doing so it drew brutal criticism from Judge Cook. In July 1996 he awarded Beasley $1,987,502 in actual damages, $500,000 in punitive damages, and $1,075,749 for legal fees. He wrote, "Apparently for the sake of expediency, Cadwalader bent to the will of the disgruntled partners by expelling others to whom they owed a fiduciary duty. Such duty cannot said to be honorable, much less to comport with 'the punctilio of an honor.'* It was a gross breach of fiduciary duty for some partners to throw others overboard for the expediency of increased profits. Cadwalader's conduct was so reckless as to

*This phrase referred to the opinion of Judge Cardozo quoted earlier.

amount to a conscious disregard to the rights of Beasley and the other expelled partners. . . . It is . . . clear that the management committee did not have the right to expel a partner. . . . The ouster of Beasley and the other partners was done for the express purpose of producing greater profits for the remaining partners. . . ."

Nor did Cook attach much importance to Cadwalader's accusation that Beasley had lied about his finances when he joined the firm, and that he was secretly forming a new firm the summer of 1994, just before he left.

Cook wrote, "If Beasley had dirt under his fingernails, Cadwalader, Wickersham & Taft was up to its elbows in the dung heap."

An appeals court later affirmed Cadwalader's liability. It did reverse the award of legal fees, and refused Beasley's claim of $935,261 in "lost profits," leaving his total recovery at $1,603,502 plus interest. Nonetheless, Beasley considered his case a signal victory. "I take considerable satisfaction in the fact that they spent $3 or $4 million defending the case, on top of what they had to pay me. It was a very expensive and stupid decision on their part. Had they treated people reasonably at the outside, none of this would have been a problem."*

Several years after the fact, Robert Link of Cadwalader still found Judge Cook's decision incomprehensible and contradictory. Contrary to what Beasley insisted, Cook ruled that he indeed had planned to leave Cadwalader at the end of 1994 and start his own firm. Why, then, should he receive damages for a period when he would not even be with Cadwalader? And Judge Cook also ruled that Cadwalader had the right under the partnership agreement to close the Palm Beach office. Why, then, could Beasley claim unlawful discharge?

Link offered an explanation. Before becoming a judge, Cook

---

*Beasley's practice revived quickly. He took in two new partners, David Leacock and Robert J. Hauser, and set up offices in West Palm Beach. A week or so after we spoke, he wrote with the excited news that he and Bob Montgomery had won a $22.8 million verdict in a wrongful discharge case involving two physicians and a local hospital.

had worked in a small office, one of two, perhaps three lawyers. So he had not the slightest notion of how a major firm operated, and how it must be on a sound business footing or perish. "Beasley sued because he wanted the money. That's it, pure and simple," Link said.

Next came Steve Ruskin's turn, in a trial before a jury in a New York State court. Day after day Ruskin listened to his former partners—his onetime friends—try to discredit him as a has-been. And day after day Jim Kreindler threw documents back in their faces—the work Ruskin had done on trying to save the partnership from going bankrupt because of the botched deal on 100 Maiden Lane, his earnings over the years, the favorable reviews he received during the compensation review only months before he was cast out.

Jurors gave many long and nasty looks at the Cadwalader people. After a weeklong trial, it took the eleven men and women less than an hour to agree unanimously on a $3 million judgment. "The hour included a lunch break." Ruskin smiled. Cadwalader did not appeal.

The first time we talked, Ruskin was practicing from a skyscraper office in the heart of downtown Dallas. Was he happy there? He shrugged. He liked the firm, but he is a New Yorker, and I was not surprised, a few months later, to receive an announcement that he had become a partner in the New York office of the San Francisco megafirm Morrison & Foerster. The main thing he accomplished, Ruskin said, was "I stood up to them and showed them that what they had done was wrong." The courtroom victory did much to restore his morale.

BOOTY FOR THE YOUNG TURKS

In a deposition for the Beasley litigation, Young Turk Bob Link was asked whether he felt Project Rightsize succeeded. "Yes. We were right on the nose," he replied. The firm treated itself to considerable media boasting. A long article in the *American Lawyer* months later said that Cadwalader's "leaders crow about the result: average profits per partner rose 33 percent last year to a record high of $565,000, according to Karsten Giesecke." Fritts ("ruddy-faced . . . rumpled") was quoted as saying, "We had to get there quickly." Fritts said that what happened was the "style of the next generation of lawyers," and that the alternative is to "fade into obsolescence." Cadwalader opened offices in London and Charlotte, North Carolina. And the Young Turks and their allies took immediate profits from Rightsize.

	1994 Bonuses	1995 Bonuses
Robert O. Link, Jr.	$250,000	$350,000
W. Christopher White	150,000	200,000
M. Holland West	100,000	150,000
Jordan M. Schwartz	100,000	75,000
Michael S. Gambro	75,000	
Robert A. Rudnick	75,000	150,000
Richard A. Weiner	75,000	
Peter G. Bergmann	75,000	
Gary Barnett	35,000	
John E. McDermot	35,000	
Jeffrey Q. Smith	35,000	75,000
Mitchell I. Sonkin		300,000
John A. Fritts		50,000

But the publicity was not universally favorable. In an editorial headlined "Generation Gap," the *National Law Journal* commented: "In a way, recent upheavals reflect a resumption of the 1960s war between the generations. The Young Turks, who were reared in the competitive cauldron of the 1980s, know little of the way it used to be. Giving little thought to who will help support *them* in their old age, they stress the importance of such youthful traits as energy and physical stamina over the mellower virtues of wisdom and judgment." Older men make firms cautious in taking on shady clients and "ethically unquestionable matters." Because of their need for instant gratification, Young

Turks "eventually will face a chastening." An opinion article in the same paper bore the headline, "Some Partners See a 'Cad' in Cadwalader."

So how did the surviving Cadwalader partners feel five years later? On a June morning I sat in a conference room at the firm, across the table from a smiling Robert O. Link, Jr., now the Cadwalader managing partner, and Grant B. Hering, his de facto chief of staff.* Both wore sports shirts. At Cadwalader, what started as dress-down Fridays evolved into dress-down summers, and the lack of formality in what was known as an extraordinarily stuffy Wall Street firm takes a moment of mental adjustment. I thought back to the formal portraits in the reception area downstairs of the firm's founding lawyers—Wells, Cadwalader, Wickersham, and Taft, men of somber mien and stiff collars.

No matter. Cadwalader was concerned more with its future than its past, and Link looked back at Rightsize as unpleasant but necessary business. A few weeks earlier, the partners had enjoyed their annual retreat in Bermuda, and Link shoved a sheaf of papers across the table, the slides he had used to illustrate the firm's growth.

Impressive. From 286 lawyers in 1995, Cadwalader had grown to 460. "Let me tell you something about that figure," Link said. "We have not grown by merging with other firms; when you do that, there is a certain loss of quality control, for you must take the good with the not-so-good. We are not 'growing for the sake of growth.' We are finding people who fit into what we are doing." As an example, he mentioned Dennis Block, with twenty-seven years at Weil, Gotshal & Manges, who defected to Cadwalader in May 1998. "That is the sort of lateral

---

*My request to Link for an interview drew a response from Marsha Horowitz, of the Howard Rubenstein public relations juggernaut in Manhattan. She was curious that I was writing about "changes" in the legal profession, and asked what I had in mind. "Well, Marsha," I replied, "when I asked Clark Clifford for an interview in 1971, he returned the call in person. Now I get a call from a press agent." My pejorative term did not cause any offense, and I got the interview.

hire that a firm would die for, and that he chose Cadwalader says much about how far we have come."

Link flipped to another page, and a chart showing profits per partner (PPP). Here Cadwalader has exceeded its strategic planning goals for five years in a row. For instance, for 1995 the projected PPP was $472,000; the actual figure turned out to be $565,000. The 1999 projection was $725,000; at midyear the firm was on track for $925,000. Both partners and associates were working longer hours. In 1994, the average billable hours for partners was 1,541, for associates, 1,738. In 1999, these hours were up to 1,885 and 1,960 respectively, with a goal of 2,000 for each.

More important than the numbers, Link contends, is that Cadwalader had undergone a total change in culture. "The problem is that the firm had been asleep for twenty years," he said. "We are a business, and we must compete in a competitive environment. It's as simple as that."

Given that much of Cadwalader's business is linked directly to what happens on Wall Street, the fear of a stock market dive was never far from Link's mind. Hence the firm's strategic plan called for an emphasis on countercyclical practices such as bankruptcy and insurance/reinsurance—areas that tend to roll along regardless of what the market is doing. There was also rainy day planning. One slide read, "As an institution, we must be prepared for both good times and bad." There was a "bad times" slide, which, after some hurried consultation, Link and Hering decided not to let me have. I peeked. If the stock market did collapse, one worst case scenario showed that up to sixty associates could be out of Cadwalader within thirty days. (When the market tanked months later, Cadwalader reduced its associate ranks by some thirty-five lawyers, calling the cuts "normal attribution.")

After an hour or so, our business was done, and Grant Hering walked me down to the street. We paused on one level of the atrium while he told me of how the architect had essentially merged three separate buildings into one, and made artistic use of what had been an air shaft. A spiral staircase curves around the nine levels of the atrium. He gestured to the reception area at ground level. "We have the firm holiday party there," he said, "and at some point the Cadwalader Chorus performs. Yes, we have our own choir. And it is most impressive, to look at the winding stairs and see lawyers and staff and their spouses and children looking down and listening to the music."

At such moments, Hering seemed to be suggesting, Cadwalader, Taft & Wickersham was once again a family, rather than a law firm transformed into a bottom-line business. But the brutality with which Cadwalader threw out such men as Steve Ruskin and Jim Beasley is eloquent commentary on the profit-driven realities of big-time law.

Conclusion:
What's to Be Done?

Susan P. Koniak, who teaches law at Boston University, is one of the more thoughtful legal ethicists in the country. Her writings show that she is a woman of consistent wisdom, capable of juggling the often countering forces of rage and common sense. Suffice it to say that the corporate scandals that rocked the financial world the past several years really ticked her off. As she commented:

> The dirty secret of the mess is that without lawyers, few scandals would exist, and fewer still would last long enough to cause any real harm. Lawyers need to be regulated. No other legal reform enacted will do any good as long as there are no consequences to lawyers who bless anything a manager wants to do.

As a quasi libertarian, my hackles instinctively rise at the sight of the word "regulate." Yet Professor Koniak states a truth that extends far beyond the corporate scandals that were her immediate subject. Consider something as outwardly bland as those ubiquitous sweepstakes mailings that numerous state attorneys general have accused of bilking the unwitting elderly out of hundreds of thousands of dollars. The fine-print disclaimers stuffed into the envelopes surely came from the pen of a lawyer clever enough to skate on the thin ice separating acceptable behavior from criminality. Or recall the lawyers who were the intellectual craftsmen of a shameful deception that concealed the dangers of cigarettes for generations.

But would regulation make any significant difference in how law is practiced? I think not, and for a very basic reason: Lawyers would write and enforce any reform laws, and I doubt that the legal profession has any driving interest in putting its house in order. Consider the "securities reform legislation" of 1995 (discussed in chapter 5). Although the new law put needed curbs on securities "strike suits" of the type beloved by William Lerach and Melvyn Weiss, it also put a more or less impenetrable shield around the lawyers who help corporate executives craft some rather smelly business deals (witness Enron, for instance, or Tyco).

Several possibilities exist for making some sense out of the legal profession. The first four, in order, are Congress, through reform of the tort system; the organized bar, at the state and national level; the courts, by curbing excessive awards by runaway juries; and the law schools, by producing graduates who adhere to the traditional (if now unpopular) concept that the law should be something more noble than contriving new and interesting ways of suing other persons. I shall leave the fifth possibility unnamed for the moment.

Tort Reform Enacted by Congress?
Three bulging file cases in my basement testify to the futility of the U.S. Congress achieving any legislation of consequence. Hearings, manifestos by interest groups on both sides, countless journal articles—an ongoing sound and fury that has accomplished nothing. Former Rep. Newt Gingrich, when Speaker of the House, included tort reform among his famed "ten points" agenda for remaking the United States when his Republican Party gained control of both houses of Congress in the 1994 elections. Seemingly unbalanced by his accession to power, Speaker Gingrich promptly shot himself in the foot with a number of ethical gaffes and then took care to pick off his remaining toes, one by one. The Judicial Conference of the United States, the body that speaks for the federal judiciary, has pleaded with

Congress for almost two decades to pass legislation dealing with the asbestos mess. So, too, has the U.S. Supreme Court, in a number of opinions. Nothing has happened.

Curbs by the Courts?

Here there are scattered signs of sense. One of the more promising was a 2002 ruling by the Supreme Court that reversed a $145 million punitive damages award against State Farm Insurance for egregious misconduct in the handling of an auto accident death claim. State Farm could have settled the case by paying its policy limit of $50,000. In the face of strong evidence that its client, a man named Campbell, was at fault, State Farm refused to pay and insisted on going to trial. A jury returned damages of almost $200,000. The lawyer whom State Farm had hired for Campbell shrugged and said, "You may want to put a for sale sign" on Campbell's house, because the insurance company was not going to pay the amount in excess of its policy.

Whereupon Campbell sued State Farm and won a jury award of $1 million actual damages and $145 million in punitive damages. Although the Supreme Court sharply criticized State Farm's conduct, Justice Anthony Kennedy wrote, "A defendant should be punished for the conduct that harmed the plaintiff, not for being an unsavory individual or business. . . . [T]he wealth of a defendant cannot justify an otherwise unconstitutional punitive damage award." Although State Farm's handling of the claim "merits no praise," nonetheless there should have been a "more modest punishment for this reprehensible conduct." The court held that the ratio of punitive damages to compensatory damages may not exceed a single digit—9 to 1, in other words, save in rare instances. And the 145 to 1 in the State Farm case was excessive.

The court's ruling was a sane step toward restoring justice to the justice system, and stopped the "send the bastards a message" verdicts coaxed out of outraged jurors who succumb to the inflammatory arguments of plaintiff lawyers. What will be the lasting effect? There were earlier restrictive rulings on so-called boxcar verdicts that exceeded the bounds of reason, hence there seems little hope for confidence that the ruling will have any immediate impact on excessive awards.

How About Bar Self-Policing?

Here let me reveal one of the dirtier little secrets of modern American law. On a daily basis, lawyers pay about as little attention to bar associations as they do, say, to the Book-of-the-Month Club. Many lawyers say they join the bar and pay dues only because most states require membership before they can be "admitted to the bar"—in less formal terms, pay a licensing fee to practice. Solo practitioners and small-firm lawyers express little interest in what the bar does. Those who join the so-called speciality sections of the American Bar Association (antitrust, intellectual property, tax, etc.) do so to have the chance to tinker with laws and regulations governing their practice, usually for their own financial benefit.

At one time the ABA was given much weight in determining whether nominees for the federal bench would be approved. Such a courtesy vanished when the ABA's judiciary committee issued highly partisan appraisals of nominees during the Reagan and Bush I years. President George W. Bush and Senate Republican leaders who deal with nominees recognized the ABA for what it is: a liberal special interest group with its own agenda, regardless of who occupies the White House. Such a recognition seeped into the public consciousness, to the further detriment of the ABA and other bars.

The state of California is by no means typical of America, but the state bar there does epitomize what has gone wrong with the system. What happened in California suggests that the organized bar can lose touch with reality. Bar bureaucrats and a subgroup called the Conference of Delegates consistently took political positions anathema to many—perhaps even a majority—of its 156,000 members. Among the issues it advocated were same-sex marriages, reduced penalties for narcotics dealers, and special rights for transvestites and transsexuals. To be sure, valid pro and con arguments exist on both sides of these issues. But as critics asked, "What do they have to do, in practical terms, with the practice of law?" Most of these proposals came from the Conference of Delegates, composed chiefly of activists who used the bar to push for their political agendas. Working lawyers simply did not have the time, energy, or interest to squabble over such matters, giving the activists clear political sailing.

There was also much opposition what the bar calls mandatory continuing legal education, that is, bar-run courses that lawyers are required to take (and pay for) every several years to retain their license to practice law. The logic behind such MCLE courses is simple: Make sure that lawyers stay abreast of court decisions and changes of the law in their areas of expertise, so that they can offer competent representation.

But oh, what nonsense can be performed in the name of logic. George Kraw, who practices in San Jose, has a connoisseur's delight in collecting titles of MCLE courses that have been offered through the California bar over the years. One series in which he took particular delight involved so-called substance abuse. Cocaine and vodka, perhaps? Nope. Courses in the series—for six hours credit—included "Strategies for Handling Cravings: Pizza, Potato Chips, Nuts, Ice Cream and Candy" and "Compulsive Overeating, Emotional Acting and Food Addictions." (Perhaps I am a cynic, but I would not knowingly retain a lawyer who had to go to class to develop proper eating habits.)

Other Kraw favorites are offered through the Nyingma Institute, a meditation center in Berkeley. As Kraw writes, "Among other things, the institute classes teach the use of Tibetan 'Kum Nye' exercises to relax. Kum Nye theory is based on bringing 'the energies of the mind and body' together. It seeks to integrate 'the physical and psychological,' claiming that this results in a deeper/more profound effect on the lawyer-initiate than just addressing the mind or body alone." OK, if you say so. Kraw comments tartly, "Who knows, the hard chargers of the Nyingma may end up reshaping our profession."

Dissident members finally sought to call a halt to bar nonsense. The precipitating event was to protest the use of their mandatory dues to pay for lobbyists who worked for stringent gun control laws and a nuclear weapons freeze. The California Supreme Court agreed that this constituted illegal lobbying and ordered it stopped.

But the bar persisted on pushing issues that offended many members. A bar committee tried to block the appointment of Janice Rogers Brown to the California Supreme Court in 1996 on grounds that she was unqualified. The true reason, many lawyers felt, was that she was a conservative. And then the bar took the side of plaintiff lawyers and supported a bill that would have overridden reform of the state's chaotic medical malpractice system.

So Governor Pete Wilson struck back. San Diego attorney Mark S. Pulliam, who wrote about the dues issues for the *California Political Review* and the *Wall Street Journal,* commented, "Like monopolists everywhere, the bar began to believe it was invulnerable and behaved accordingly—to the irritation of its members and the state legislature, which must authorize the mandatory dues." The bar long relied on state law to require any person who practiced in California to join the bar and pay mandatory dues. The rationale for the state's role was that the bar ran the disciplinary and certification systems. But by 1997, dues had soared to $478, by far the highest in the nation, and indeed more than twice the average in the other states. The annual budget was $66 million, which supported a staff of more than 750 full-time employees. Wilson recognized an attractive political issue and he vetoed a bill extending the bar's authority to mandate dues, called the bar and its staff "bloated, arrogant, oblivious and unresponsive." Columnist William Safire of the *New York Times* applauded the action, writing, "Here was a legal lobbying juggernaut with a staff of 750, in the pocket of the trial lawyers, supporting political correctness and knee-jerkily rating judicial nominees as unqualified."

The bar responded by cutting dues by $10 a year and protesting that it spent only sixteen cents of every dues dollar on lobbying. (Members who protested the use of their dues money for lobbying on behalf of issues they opposed received a one-dollar refund, a payment many considered insulting.) And it made the peculiar (and stupid, as matters worked out) decision to give a no-bid $900,000 contract to a former bar employee to lobby for continuance of the mandatory dues. The man was promised a $75,000 bonus if he succeeded. Since such contingency fees are illegal, he had to pay a $2,000 fine when the deal was revealed.

Bar leaders continued to insist that the majority of California lawyers agreed with how the association was being run. But the evidence is to the contrary. What happened was a damning referendum on what California lawyers actually thought about their bar association: When the bar asked that members continue paying dues, despite Governor Wilson's veto, only 25 percent coughed up the full amount. The *Los Angeles Daily Journal* found that a majority of the state's lawyers agreed with Wilson's harsh veto language, and more than three-quarters felt their dues were excessive. And Wilson told California journalists that the veto was one of his most popular acts as governor—"especially among lawyers."

On the national level, the leftist bias of the American Bar Association became so pronounced that both President George H. W. Bush and his son George W. no longer give the bar veto power over nominations for the federal bench. Alberto Gonzales, while White House counsel (he is now U.S. attorney general) called the ABA "just another special interest group" undeserving of special attention.

So, How About Law Schools?

A laughable venue for any "solution." Despite high-minded blather from law school deans and professors about teaching "standards of an honored profession," what is offered on campus after campus is the stuff of trade schools. Lawyers are taught how to craft a brief and how to research the arcane inner recesses of, say, the federal tax code.

Courses on ethics? To be sure, they are offered, but time and again I found myself reading law review articles that seemed to seek ways to shortcut ethical standards and solve a client's problems by any means possible.

And, for the most part, law faculties are stacked strongly in favor of the plaintiff bar. Indeed the stimulus for many of the oddball suits plaguing our nation had their origins in law school.

Consider all the noise about blaming fast-food purveyors for obesity in America. Such suits are the brainchild of Professor John F. Banzhaf III of the George Washington University Law School in Washington. (Oddly, for the commander of an anti-fat crusade, Banzhaf is a comfortably portly fellow.) So far as I can make out, Banzhaf thinks that the way to slim down America is to sue McDonald's and other fast-food chains and force them to pay such hefty damages that they will stop selling stuff that makes people fat. In pursuit of this cause Banzhaf makes good use of his tenured position as a law professor. He writes op-ed pieces for friendly newspapers. He joins with plaintiff lawyers to stage conferences on how to bring class action suits against fast-food chains. His concept of what law is all about is reflected in the vanity license plate for his car, SUETHEBASTARDS. He has produced a veritable generation of young lawyers infused with this concept of what law is all about.

Thus let us look to a fifth solution:

Persons should begin to take individual responsibility for some of the things that go awry in their lives and not foist off blame (and expenses) on others.

Consider the forementioned Banzhaf and his fast-food suits, which are a sort of paradigm for what I contend is wrong with American law. Not much sense is required to figure out that if a person stuffs his or her gut with outlandish servings of hamburgers and french fries and milk shakes, some weight gain might result. McDonald's and other fast-food chains began making available information on the calorie content of its servings years ago; pass through the Golden Arches anywhere and you are going to find brochures giving details about any item on the menu.

As of this writing, despite the considerable publicity generated by Banzhaf and his friends in the media, the fast-food suits have fizzled. What was billed as a landmark suit by a group of teen fatsos in Brooklyn was tossed out by a federal district judge who wondered from the bench whether parents should not bear some of the blame for letting their kids bloat up.*

For Americans to stop looking reflexively to the courts to "make right" any conceivable situation that disrupts their lives is going to require a change in national attitudes that I doubt will occur in my lifetime. Consider the driver who gets drunk in the local saloon and tries to drive home down the wrong side of the freeway. Blooey. The lawyer for his widow argues that the manufacturer could have, should have, whatever, installed stronger seat restraints that might have kept the drunk from catapulting through the windshield.

Modern law has produced a legal system that is a de facto welfare state, with all of us compelled to pay (though higher prices) for whatever woes befall other persons. Socially acceptable? Perhaps. But so long as lawyers keep the public convinced that "someone must pay" regardless of blame, the system is not about to change.

*An appeal was pending as of late September 2005.

Notes

Chapter 1: David Boies: The New Superlawyer

p. 4 "Everybody's in the winning business": Boies interview, *Charlie Rose Show,* PBS, November 9, 1999.

p. 5 He suffered from dyslexia: Thomas Fields-Meyer, Eve Heyn, Barbara Benham, Glenn Garelik, and Susan Garland, "Making His Case," *People,* November 22, 1999.

p. 6 "He was No. 1": David Margolick, "The Man Who Ate Microsoft," *Vanity Fair,* March 2000. Some of the biographical details of Boies's early life are gleaned from the Margolick article.

p. 7 "It's like having a pack of Dobermans": Renata Adler, *Reckless Disregard: Westmoreland v. CBS et al., Sharon v. Time* (New York: Alfred A. Knopf, 1986).

p. 12 "After the first day": Bob Brewin and Sydney Shaw, *Vietnam on Trial: Westmoreland v. CBS* (New York: Atheneum, 1987). In terms of presenting a chronology of the trial, and offering a contemporaneous description of the courtroom atmosphere, the book by this husband-wife team is invaluable. Unlike Renata Adler in *Reckless Disregard,* they give considerable credence to the CBS documentary. I found Adler's skepticism the more convincing, but the merits of the Westmoreland case are beyond the scope of this book.

p. 14 "He looked every inch": Connie Bruck, "The Soldier Takes the Stand," *American Lawyer,* January–February 1985.

p. 19 "David wanted to run": Phone interviews with two Cravath partners by author, October 2000.

p. 21 Discussing the episode: Amy Singer, "Boies Will Be Boies," *American Lawyer,* June 1997.

p. 29 The ultimate hired gun: In addition to my own reporting, I used two other major sources for background on the Microsoft case. Most valuable was a fifty-page article by John Heilemann, "The Truth, the Whole Truth, and Nothing but the Truth: The Untold Story of the Microsoft Antitrust Case and What It Means for the Future of Bill Gates and His Company," *Wired,* November 2000. Joel Brinkley and Steve Lohr covered the case for the *New York Times* and edited their reportage into *U.S. v. Microsoft: The Inside Story of the Landmark Case* (New York: McGraw Hill, 2000).

p. 31 "David would read": Mark S. Popofsky, interview by author, October 11, 2000.

p. 31 "Microslop": *Wall Street Journal,* May 19, 1998.

p. 31 "transatlantic ambulance chaser": Robert D. Novak, "Vendetta Against Microsoft," *Washington Post,* September 23, 1999.

p. 33 That Gates came across: Gates's depositions, and those of other witnesses, are on a Microsoft Web site maintained by the Justice Department's Antitrust Division. The site also contained more motions and briefs than you care to read.

p. 37 It "takes a good ten minutes": Joseph Nocera, "The Empire Strikes Back," *Fortune,* January 11, 1999. (Nocera covered the trial in diary fashion, with his major comments on Boies contained in this article.)

p. 38 "has seemed to be": David Ignatius, "Now for Some Real Courtroom Drama," *Washington Post,* February 17, 1999.

p. 39 After the trial: Karen Donovan, " 'Perry Mason Moment' in Microsoft Case." *Recorder,* February 4, 1999.

p. 39 "The documents were never": *U.S. v. Corn Products Refining Company,* 234 F. 964 (1916).

p. 41 "He cross-examines": Steve Lohr, "Microsoft Trying to Rebuild Tarnished Case in Antitrust Trial," *New York Times,* February 8, 1999.

p. 41 The real story of the trial: Jared Sandberg, "Microsoft's Tormentor," *Newsweek,* March 1, 1999.

p. 42 "Boies had led": David Segal, "The Thorn in Microsoft's Side," *Washington Post,* October 19, 1998.

p. 42 "successfully defended IBM": Rajiv Chandbasekaran, "Microsoft Trial Set to Open," *Washington Post,* October 19, 1998.

p. 42 "the unpredictable maverick": John R. Wilke, "Microsoft Trial Promises Stars, Impact, Legal Fireworks," *Wall Street Journal,* October 16, 1998.

p. 43 Unbeknown to lawyers: The resultant books were Joel Brinkley and Steve Lorh, *U.S. v. Microsoft: The Inside Story of the Landmark Case* (New York: McGraw Hill, 2000); and Ken Auletta, *World War 3.0: Microsoft and Its Enemies* (New York: Random House, 2001).

p. 47 Should Napster be considered a loss?: Lee Gomes, "Napster Is Ordered to Stop the Music," *Wall Street Journal;* and James V. Grimaldi, "Napster Ordered to Shut Down," *Washington Post,* July 27, 2000.

p. 47 "We see Boies": Richard L. Berke, "Beyond Courtroom, Duels Continue on Other Fronts," *New York Times,* December 4, 2000.

p. 48 "worked pro bono": Kevin Sacks, "In Desperate Florida Fight, Gore's Hard Strategic Calls," *New York Times,* December 15, 2000.

p. 48 "the cult of Boies": James V. Grimaldi, "For David Boies, Working for Gore in Florida Caps a Year of High-Profile Cases," both in the *Washington Post,* December 25, 2000.

p. 49 "the finest lawyer": David Barstow and Dexter Filkins, "For the Gore Team, a Moment of High Drama," *New York Times,* December 4, 2000.

p. 49 "many round-heeled journalists": George F. Will, "Truth Optional," *Washington Post,* December 12, 2000.

p. 50 "It was a *schadenfreudian* joy": Tony Blankley, "Judgment Day for Gore," *Washington Times,* December 6, 2000.

p. 54 Although Boies's publicity flood: Jenny Anderson, "Greenberg and A.I.G. Agree to End Relationship," *New York Times,* March 29, 2005.

Chapter 2: Thomas Hale Boggs, Jr., Washington Superlobbyist

p. 59 "I kind of wish it was": Thomas H. Boggs, interview by author, September 8, 2000. Boggs quotes in this chapter are drawn from this interview unless otherwise noted.

p. 60 "an overdressed shark": David Segal, "Washington Hearsay," *Washington Post,* September 13, 1999. Noting Patton Boggs's creation of a Web site, Segal facetiously suggested that it picture "a smoldering cigar, or a rare steak from Morton's," the Georgetown steakhouse frequented by big-shot lawyer lobbyists. The firm decided upon an opening screen displaying a piercing eye and the slogan "Where others see problems, we see opportunities."

p. 60 Boggs is "the archetype": Louis Jacobson, "Makeover on M Street," *National Journal,* October 31, 1998.

p. 60 "He has refashioned the town": Carl Bernstein, "King of the Hill," *Vanity Fair,* March 1998. Two Patton Boggs partners laughed at this article as "Tommy's puff piece."

p. 62 Several years ago Boggs gave an interview: Jacqui S. Porth, "How Lobbyists Influence Foreign Policy," United States Information Agency, undated, circa late 1990s.

p. 64 "I was very close": Thomas Hale Boggs, Sr., Oral History Interview with T. H. Baker, Lyndon Baines Johnson Library, March 13 and 17, 1969.

p. 68 "I'll be curious to know": James Patton, interview by author, Washington, D.C.

p. 80 The investigation of Hales Boggs: Relations between Boggs and the FBI are in FBI File Number 94-37804, Subject: Thomas Hale Boggs. Available under the Freedom of Information Act in the Reading Room at FBI headquarters in the J. Edgar Hoover Building in Washington. Documents quoted in this section are from that file. In the interest of conciseness, I am not citing each piece of paper.

p. 81 "Boggs is an old drunk": Material in this section is from FBI File Number 94-37804, Subject: Thomas Hale Boggs. The "old drunk" quotation is in a Hoover memorandum of April 25, 1971, reporting to subordinates on a phone conversation with Rep. Samuel L. Devine.

p. 86 "Attending fund-raising activities": John L. Zorack, "The Lobbying Handbook," Washington, Professional Lobbying and Consulting Center, 1990.

p. 86 "Just letting them know": John Reistrup, telephone interview by author, March 13, 2000.

p. 87 "There's a catchphrase": Mark Cowan, interview by author, May 17, 2000.

p. 95 "Baby Doc was strictly": Carl Bernstein, "King of the Hill," *Vanity Fair,* March 1998.

p. 97 "I had gone": Jeffrey T. Smith, interview by author, Washington, D.C., August 4, 2000.

p. 101 "Scrimshaw from a whale": Mark Savit, interview by author, Washington, D.C., June 22, 2000.

Chapter 3: Breast Implants: The $10 Billion Rush to Judgment

p. 115 "There is no convincing evidence": Institute of Medicine, "Safety of Silicone Breast Implants," National Academy Press, Washington, 1999.

p. 116 "It felt just like": Mimi Schwartz, "Silicone City," *Texas Monthly,* August 1995.

p. 119 "We had a dickens of a time": Nancy Hersh, interview by author, San Francisco, January 18, 1999. Material from the Stern case is drawn from this interview. Also useful was Michael Castleman, "Woman's Warrior; Enemy Within," *California Lawyer,* March 1993.

p. 122 The most damning documents: These documents came to light in the Stern litigation and later in other implant cases; manufacturers grudgingly gave others to the FDA after losing a court battle concerning their confidentiality. The most accessible compilation is in "Is the FDA Protecting Patients From the Dangers of Silicone Breast Implants?" Hearings, Human Resources and Intergovernmental Affairs Subcommittee of the House Committee on Government Operations, December 1990. Summaries are contained in a staff report by the same subcommittee, "The FDA's Regulations of Silicone Breast Implants," December 1992.

p. 125 Dow Corning took the position: Dan Bolton, interview by author, San Francisco, January 19, 1999.

p. 127 The Mariann Hopkins Case: A bare-bones outline of the proceeding is in the opinion of the Ninth U.S. Circuit Court of Appeals, *Hopkins v. Dow Corning Corporation,* 33 F.3d 1116 (1994). But lawyers who have defended implant cases assert the opinion is "more political than legal or scientific," in the words of one of them.

p. 129–130 A researcher for Dr. Angell: Dr. Marcia Angell, *Science on Trial: The Clash of Medical Evidence and the Law in the Breast Implant Case* (New York: W. W. Norton, 1996).

p. 132 Included in the Dow Corning materials: The Dow Corning report, and the FDA's comment, are summarized in a staff report of the Intergovernmental Relations Subcommittee of the House Committee on Government Operations, "The FDA's

Regulation of Silicone Breast Implants," December 1992, p. 8. This report is blatantly one-sided, in essence a brief for the prosecution in breast implant litigation.

p. 132 fibrosarcoma "occurs in rodents": Jack W. Snyder, "Silicone Breast Implants: Can Emerging Medical, Legal and Scientific Concepts Be Reconciled?" 18 *Journal of Legal Medicine* 13 (1997), as summarized in David E. Bernstein, "The Breast Implant Fiasco," 87 *California Law Review* 2 (March 1999), pp. 465–466.

p. 133 The incidence of breast carcinoma: Dr. Angelo Cammarata, Dr. John Georgiou, Dr. Ernesto Cruz, Virginia Birnbach, B.A., and Dr. Robert E. Rothenberg, "Inflammatory Carcinoma in a Patient With a Breast Implant," *Breast: Diseases of the Breast,* 10, no. 3 (1984).

p. 133 "If anything": Institute of Medicine, *Safety of Silicone Breast Implants* (Washington, D.C.: National Academy Press, 1999), p. 187.

p. 133 Wolfe served on a panel: Dr. Jack Fisher, interview by author, San Diego, September 21, 1998.

p. 133 "Public Citizen's nascent crusade": Bernstein, "Breast Implant Fiasco," id., p. 467.

p. 134 Chung called silicone gel: Transcript of *Face to Face With Connie Chung,* December 10, 1990. Burrelle's Transcripts, Livingston, New Jersey.

p. 136 "we needed to get": Quoted in Bernstein, id., p. 469.

p. 138 But how valid: "An Evaluation by Plastic Surgeons of the 90 Documents Alleged by Commissioner David Kessler to Justify Moratorium on the Use of Silicone Gel Implants," prepared by the Silicone Implant Research Committee, Plastic Surgery Educational Foundation, February 1992, files of Dr. Jack C. Fisher, University of California Medical School San Diego.

p. 139 The most devastating indictment: The exchange between Angell and Kessler are reproduced in articles in the *New England Journal of Medicine* in 1992, at pp. 1695–96 and 1713–1715. Other commentary by Angell is taken from her *Science on Trial,* id.

p. 141 A juxtaposition of medical research: For an understanding of why Houston women loved implants, and how implants became a cash cow for lawyers, I cite with admiration the skilled reporting of Mimi Schwartz, "Silicone City," *Texas Monthly,* August 1995.

p. 144 a farmer whose prize bull: Paul Burka, "Taking the Law into His Own Hands," *Texas Monthly,* September 1994.

p. 146 He would later argue: Angell, *Science on Trial,* p. 139.

p. 147 woman named Mary Klager: Max Boot, "A Tale of Silicone City," *Wall Street Journal,* November 29, 1995.

p. 150 What was the first of many: Dr. Gabriel's study was printed as Gabriel et al., "Risk of Connective Tissue Diseases and Other Disorders After Breast Implants," *New England Journal of Medicine* 326 (1993), pp. 1713–1715; it is summarized in Angell, *Science on Trial,* pp. 100–102; and reprinted in "House FDA Regulation," pp. 35–39. The quotes from Dr. Gabriel concerning the attacks on her objectivity are from Gina Kolata, "Study Finds No Implant-Disease Links," *New York Times,* June 16,

1994. Additional quotations from Dr. Gabriel concerning her study are in her testimony, "House FDA Regulation," p. 123.

p. 152 Chesley . . . had been involved: Chesley listed thirty-two class action cases in a letter to Judge Louis C. Bechtle of U.S. District Court in Philadelphia on January 19, 1998, in asking to be named to the Plaintiffs' Management Committee in fen-phen litigation.

p. 155 "I worked out": Joseph Nocera, "Dow Corning Succumbs," *Fortune,* October 30, 1995.

p. 156 "Frankly it may not be": Matt Schwa, "Plaintiffs Happy With $29 Million; Implant Manufacturers Vow to Appeal Jury's Verdict," *Houston Post,* March 4, 1994.

p. 157 "rough-and-tumble": Nocera, "Dow Corning Succumbs," id.

p. 158 Kirkland & Ellis dropped the young lawyer: Bernick's major cases are summarized in an untitled, undated booklet compiled by his office. Many of them were also discussed by Bernick in an interview by author, Chicago, July 29, 1999.

p. 159 "He stands out": "Forty-five Under Forty-five," *American Lawyer,* December 1995.

p. 161 A Houston physician Dr. Andrew W. Campbell Bernick's cross-examination of Campbell, and his citation of exhibits and deposition testimony, are in *Turner v. Dow Corning Corporation et al.,* Civil Action #92-CV-150, District Court for the City and County of Denver, Colorado, May 24, 1993.

p. 164 Disparaging remarks about Ms. Turner-McCartney's lifestyle: Chuck Van-Devander, "Silicone-trial Verdict Correct, Says Juror," *Rocky Mountain News,* June 18, 1993.

p. 165 Bernick went to Houston: The cases at issue were *Glady J. Laas et al v. Dow Corning Corporation et al,* Cause #93-04273, and *Jennifer H. Land et al v. Dow Corning Corporation et al,* Cause #94-19485, both in the 157th Judicial District Court in Houston. The final arguments in the case can be found at http://implants.clic.net/tony/Corner/E/0197.html. In addition to lengthy interviews in Chicago and Washington, David Bernick supplied the author with a hefty file of documents containing testimony and various exhibits in the case. The trial concluded in February 1995. A good journalistic overview of the events leading up to the trial of the case, and the aftermath, is in Joseph Nocera, "Fatal Litigation," *Fortune,* October 30, 1995

p. 171 The person who was wrong: Kessler testimony, hearings, "Is the FDA protecting patients?," Subcomiimittee on Human Resources and Intergovernmental Relations, House Committee on Government Reform and Oversight, December 1990.

p. 171 "I don't like": Hersh, interview by author, San Francisco, January 18, 1999.

Chapter 4: The Diet Pill Wars: Meet the Class Action Club

p. 175 "withdrawal, from a financial standpoint": FDA memorandum, "Record of Telephone Conversation/Meeting," March 23–26, 1994, Dr. Lisa Stockbridge.

p. 176 "that boy": Stanley Chesley, interview by author, Washington, D.C., November 5, 1999.

p. 177 "at the heart of it": Rheingold, interview by author, New York, January 19, 2000.

p. 178 "the startling results of which": Dr. Michael Weintraub, "Long-Term Weight Control Study," *Clinical Pharmacology and Therapeutics* (May 1992).

p. 178 "While Weintraub and his colleagues": David Terry, "Litigating Fen-Phen Cases," conference sponsored by Association of Trial Lawyers of America, October 16, 1998, Las Vegas, Nevada. (Referred to hereafter as "ATLA Fen-Phen Conference.")

p. 180 Fen-phen's fall from grace: Pam Ruff, telephone interview by author, January 25, 2000; also, John MacDonald, "Tech's Hunch Exposes Diet Drugs," Associated Press, July 22, 1997.

p. 189 As Petroff would later complain: Petroff summarized the discovery findings in our first interview in April 1999, and in more detail at the ATLA Fen-Phen Conference in October 1998. Quotations in this section are drawn from these sources, as well as copies of the cited documents. I consulted tape recordings of the ATLA session as well as various backup materials supplied to participants.

p. 196 Petroff elicited the story: Deposition of Dr. JoAlene Dolan, January 15, 1999.

p. 203 "Predictably, an attorney who is granted": John Coffee, Jr., "Class Action Accountability: Reconciling Exit, Voice, and Loyalty in Representative Litigation," *Columbia Law Review,* 100, no. 2 (March 2000).

p. 206 Nor did the group include: Richard B. Schmitt, "Trial Lawyers Rush to Turn Diet-Pill Ills into Money in the Bank," *Wall Street Journal,* October 24, 1997.

p. 210 "I do not know": Virginia G. Drachman, *Sisters in Law: Women Lawyers in Modern American History* (Cambridge, Mass.: Harvard University Press, 1998). The Strong quote is from the same book.

p. 213 still wary of graduates of Rutgers: Lisa Berman, "Rutgers Investment in Women Reaps Big Dividends in the 1990s," *National Law Journal,* April 13, 1998.

p. 214 Kohn never talked: Connie Bruck, "Harold Kohn Against the World," *American Lawyer,* January 1982.

p. 221 Months after the "beauty contest" hearing: Rheingold, interview by author, New York, December 17, 1998. Rheingold also provided me with the draft copy of an article he wrote concerning the state-federal split on fen-phen litigation.

p. 228 cherry picking: Lawyers for AHP, both in-house and otherwise, frequently gave me insights into their thinking, and that of the corporation, as the litigation progressed. None would do so for the record, however, to my regret. Hence the anonymous quotations in this section.

p. 230 Petroff kept the case simple: Petroff, interview by author, Dallas, April 26, 2000. Summaries of the testimony are in closing arguments for both sides on August 4,

1999, which Petroff provided to me. The case was formally styled *Mark Armstrong, plaintiff; Debbie Lovett, intervenor, v. Wyeth-Ayerst Laboratories Division of American Home Products, Inc., et al.,* Case No. 97-665.

p. 231 "Three people who worked": Kathryn Culver, "Three Jurors in Fen-Phen Case Certain," *Tyler Morning Telegraph,* August 8, 1999.

p. 232 We had to send a message: Allison Hoard, "Jurors Say They Were Sending a Message to Diet Drug Makers," *Van Zandt News,* August 9, 1999.

p. 233 "I was taking": Sol Weiss, interview by author, Philadelphia, January 28, 2000.

p. 235 The U.S. Supreme Court: *Ortiz v. Fibreboard Corporation,* 119 S.Ct. 2295 (1999).

p. 236 News accounts differed: Richard B. Schmidt and Robert Langreth, "AHP to Pay \$3.75 Billion in Diet Suits," *Wall Street Journal,* October 8, 1999; and David J. Morrow, "Fen-Phen Maker to Pay Billions in Settlement of Diet-Injury Cases," *New York Times,* October 8, 1999.

p. 238 "We at American Home Products": Quoted on AHP Web site, statement posted December 21, 1999.

p. 240 According to testimony: The dispute over the validity of examining physicians' reports is spelled out in an opinion issued by Judge Bartle in January 2003 in Re: Diet Drug Litigation. Media coverage was by Shannon P. Duffy in the *Legal Intelligencer,* September 9, October 3, and November 19, 2002; and October 22 and November 17, 2003.

Chapter 5: Lerach and Weiss: The Class Action Scourges of West and East

At the outset, I must commend the generosity of Melvyn Weiss and William Lerach, who gave interviews even when they sensed they were dealing with a writer who was skeptical about their securities class action practices. Weiss's openness continued even after his firm was on the losing end of a \$50 million settlement of a suit in Chicago, to the point that he gave me access to firm files about the litigation and saw to it that someone in his office fed the copy machine for me.

When I commenced work on this book, Congress was considering tightening the laws on securities class action suits. Such legislation had been in the works for years, and was the subject of hearings, which are a treasure trove of information on the subject. I put these to ample use. They are:

"Hearings, Private Litigation Under the Federal Securities Laws," 1993 (hereafter cited as "Senate One")

"Hearings, Securities Litigation Reform Proposals," 1995 (hereafter cited as "Senate Two")

Both hearings were conducted before the Senate Committee on Banking, Housing, and Urban Affairs, Subcommittee on Securities.

The third set of hearings was:

"Hearings, Common Sense Legal Reform," 1995 (hereafter cited as "House Common Sense")

The latter hearings were conducted by the Subcommittee on Telecommunications and Technology, House Commerce Committee. Both the Senate and the House committees were under the control of Republicans hostile to class actions, but both sides, in my estimate, were given their say.

p. 245 "bloodsucking scumbag": *Wired,* June 4–11, 1996.

p. 251 A survey in the late 1990s: Both studies are reported in "Senate Two."

p. 251 According to another study: Marc E. Lackritz, president, Securities Industry Association, prepared statement, March 2, 1995. Senate, p. 23. The same figure was reported by Vincent O'Brien, "The Class Action Shake Down Racket," *Wall Street Journal,* September 10, 1991.

p. 252 "Harry Lewis, no doubt a penniless": "House Common Sense."

p. 253 "What are the hard": Doerr testimony, "Senate Two."

p. 256 Lerach coauthored an article: Walter T. McGough and William S. Lerach, "Termination of Class Actions: The Judicial Role," 33 *University of Pittsburgh Law Review* 445 (1972).

p. 260 An academic commissioned: The Wood Report, Chamber of Commerce for the State of New York. F. Wood, "Survey and Report Regarding Stockholders' Derivative Suits" (1944). Cited in Coffey, CLR at n. 10 and elsewhere.

p. 261 Milberg Weiss sued both Dolly Madison: Weiss outlined this litigation in an interview, then remembered he had written a paper on the subject, which he found for me: Melvyn I. Weiss, "Why Auditors Have Failed to Fulfill Their Necessary Professional Responsibilities—and What to Do About It," Abraham J. Briloff Lecture Series on Accounting and Society, School of Management, Binghamton University, State University of New York, 1992.

p. 263 The Securities and Exchange Commission forfeited its reputation: "Levitt Decries Financial Report Abuses," *Washington Post,* September 29, 1988. A good account of the SEC during the Reagan years is in David A. Vise and Steve Coll, *Eagle on the Street* (New York: Scribner's, 1991).

p. 264 In a lengthy 1982 article: William Lerach, "Life After Huddleston: Streamlining and Simplification of the Securities Class Action," *Class Action Reports,* November–December 1982.

p. 264 Between 1992 and 1996: Report, "Money Penalties: Securities and Futures Regulators Collect Many Fines But Need to Better Use Industrywide Data," the General Accounting Office, #GAO/GGD-99-8, November 2, 1998.

p. 269 "They say I make too much": *Buzz,* November 1995.

p. 269 Very soon after joining Milberg Weiss: A good journalistic account of the rise and collapse of Keating is in Michael Binstein and Charles Bowden, *Trust Me: Charles Keating and the Missing Billions* (New York: Random House, 1993). Further details concerning Keating are in a series of court rulings arising from the Lexecon litigation discussed below.

p. 274 Two such claimed victims: The accounts by John Adler and Richard Egan are in "Senate Two." [24] A federal magistrate also issued a finding on the Egan matter, *Tapogna et al. v. Egan et al.*, 96-636 Federal Securities Law Report.

p. 278 The fastest filing: Lerach testimony, "House Common Sense."

p. 280 An oft-cited "horrible example": *In Re: Philip Morris Securities Litigation*, 93 Civ. 2131 (1995).

p. 281 "Certification of a large": *Coopers & Lybrand v. Livesay*, 437 US 463 (1978).

p. 290 To the delight of Newt Gingrich: *Sidney Gluck et al. v. CellStar Corp. et al.*, USDC ND-Texas, C 3.96-CV-1353-R., Opinion by Chief Judge Jerry Buchmeyer, August 19, 1997.

p. 292 News accounts the next week: The *Washington Times* and *Washington Post* accounts appeared September 27, 1998.

p. 298 The $50 Million Split: The bulk of the section pertaining to the Lexecon litigation is drawn from the record in *Lexecon v. Milberg Weiss*, #96-C 7255, in the United States District Court for the Eastern District of Illinois. As is true of such hotly contested litigation, the documentary base is enormous. Defense lawyer Jerold Solovy, representing Milberg Weiss, exaggerated only slightly when he said that his client had surrendered "hundreds of thousands of boxes" of documents during discovery, a pile that "would fill this courtroom." Mel Weiss was gracious in defeat, even if unhappily so. Although he made plain he wished I would ignore the Lexecon matter in this book, he gave me comfortable space in a conference room in his New York office and detailed an aide to bring me whatever documents I requested—trial transcripts, depositions, exhibits. He also answered my questions. His victorious opponent, Alan Salpeter, understandably, was equally kind when I visited him, providing not only hours of interview time, but also hefty stacks of papers he felt to be important elements of his case. For space considerations, I am forgoing citations of specific documents; the origin of most statements should be obvious from the text.

The Keating litigation—wellspring of the Lexecon suit—consumed the attention of trial and appellate courts for years. The best overall summary is in *In Re American Continental Corporation/Lincoln Savings & Loan Securities Litigation*, MDL No. 834, 794 F. Supp 1424 (Eastern District of Arizona, 1992). The cases pertaining to jurisdiction over the Lexecon litigation are in *In Re American Continental/Lincoln Savings & Loan Securities Litigation; Lexecon, Inc., and Daniel R. Fischel, v. Milberg Weiss Bershad Hynes and Lerach*, 845 F. Supp. 1733 (1993) and 884 F. Supp. 1388 (1995), both in the Eastern District of Arizona.

Details of the Arizona phase of the Fischel litigation are derived from *In Re American Continental Corporation/Lincoln Savings & Loan Securities Litigation*, 794 F.

Supp. 1424 (D. Ariz., 1992); 845 F. Supp. 1377 (D. Ariz., 1993); and 854 F. Supp. 1888 (D. Ariz., 1995). Keating's last court appearance was in 1999. His earlier convictions had been overturned on appeal, and he pleaded guilty to other counts in return for being credited with time he had already served in prison. See Christian Berthelsen, "Keating Pleads Guilty to Four Counts of Fraud," *New York Times,* April 7, 1999.

p. 300 The Cadillac of firms: Edward Felsenthal, "What Happens When Legal Heavyweights Are in a Grudge Match," *Wall Street Journal,* November 7, 1997.

p. 301 Totally turned the case around: Benjamin Stein, "The New Defense in Shareholder Suits," *Barron's,* June 6, 1988.

p. 301 "Mr. Fischel won": "The Efficient Markets Jury," *Wall Street Journal,* May 2, 1988.

Chapter 6: Cadwalader, Wickersham & Taft: Metamorphosis of a White-Shoe Law Firm

A byproduct of fiercely litigated lawsuits is a plethora of documentary material, and especially depositions in which both sides describe, in their own words, the conduct at issue. Hence the primary source for this chapter is the voluminous record in two suits: *Steven A. Ruskin v. Cadwalader, Wickersham & Taft,* Supreme Court of the State of New York, County of New York, Index No. 95-100954; and *James W. Beasley, Jr., v. Cadwalader, Wickersham & Taft,* Circuit Court for Palm Beach County, Cases Nos. 96-3818 and 97-146 (consolidated). An early draft of this chapter cited an evidentiary source for each quotation—a process that increased the length by almost a quarter. Hence I decided upon this omnibus citation, with sufficient description in the text to tell from whence a quotation came.

Beasley gave me free range of dozens of file boxes containing depositions, documentary exhibits, and various pleadings. Because his lawyers shared information with those of Ruskin, there was a considerable overlap between the two cases. Kristen K. Brennan of Beasley's office gave me expert guidance through the material and directed photocopying of more pages than I care to count. She was a good hostess. I am thankful to Beasley, David Leacock, and Robert J. Hauser both for interviews and for the courtesies given me during four days at the firm of Beasley, Leacock & Hauser in West Palm Beach. Frank Chopin consented to an interview but decided to speak off-the-record for the most part concerning his relations with Beasley and Cadwalader. Judge Jack H. Cook, of the 15th Judicial District Circuit Court, Palm Beach County, provided me with a copy of his decision in the Beasley matter, as well as that of the decision by the 4th District Court of Appeal.

In Dallas, Steven Ruskin provided me not only with an interview, but also with copies of the motions for summary judgment that laid out his case. We spoke later after he returned to a New York practice.

Grant B. Hering of Cadwalader supplied me with copies of summary judgment motions in both cases. I also benefited from interviews with Robert O. Link, Jr., and Hering, as well as with several other persons in the firm who declined to be identified.

Background on the development of Cadwalader is from Deborah S. Gardner, *Cadwalader, Wickersham and Taft: A Bicentennial History 1792–1992,* printed by the firm in 1994.

John Pickering, of Wilmer, Cutler & Pickering, Washington, described his futile efforts to negotiate a settlement of the Beasley matter.

p. 329 Co-partners . . . owe: *Meinhard v. Salmon,* 249 NY 458, 164 NE 545 (N.Y. 1928).

p. 338 Dayan was nonapologetic: Vera Titunik, "The Rising Suns," *American Lawyer,* March 1996.

p. 342 The Young Turks: "Curtain Drops on Shea & Gould," *National Law Journal,* February 7, 1994.

p. 342 "failure to adapt": "Oldest Law Firm Is Courtly, Loyal, and Defunct," *New York Times,* October 2, 1994.

p. 344 create a "Mendoza line": Paul A. Dickson, *The New Dickson Baseball Dictionary* (New York: Harcourt Brace, 1999), pp. 322–23.

p. 384 "Generation Gap": Editorial, *National Law Journal,* November 11, 1994.

Conclusion: What's to Be Done?

p. 388 "The Dirty Secret." Susan P. Koniak, "Who Gave Lawyers a Pass?" *Forbes Magazine,* August 12, 2002.

p. 392 But oh, what nonsense. George Kraw, "Classroom Capers: Once Again, Our MCLE Providers Push the Envelope of Legal Education." *San Francisco Daily Journal,* January 7, 1997.

p. 393 "But do bar groups reflect." Mark S. Pulliam, "Last Call for the California Bar," *Wall Street Journal,* May 11, 1998.

p. 393 "Legal lobbying juggernaut." William Safire, "Not-So-Silent Cal," *New York Times,* May 14, 1998.

Acknowledgments

Uncountable persons helped me explore various nooks and crannies of law. In addition to those formally cited in the text of the book, here are some other people to whom I am grateful for help.

In Washington, D.C.: Dr. Mary McGrath, John Greenya, David A. Jewell, Bernard Meany, Peter Bleakley and Dixie LaBrake of Arnold & Porter; Norah Lucey Mailer; office of Rep. Henry Waxman; Rep. Henry Hyde; Joseph McDonald, House Judiciary Committee; Meryl Vlatas, Senate Judiciary Committee; Arthur J. Bryant, Theresa D. Henige, Trial Lawyers for Public Justice; Dr. James Benson, Health Industry Manufacturers Association; Thomas H. Henderson, Jr., Nicholas S. Ricci, Carlton Carl, Eileen C. Moseley, Association of Trial Lawyers of America; Mark H. Gitenstein, Mayer, Platt & Brown; Tim Wells, managing editor, the *Washington Lawyer;* Thomas Nordby of the District of Columbia Bar; Richard J. Medalie; James Wilderotter, Jones, Day, Reavis & Pogue; Brian Wolfman of Public Citizen; Jerry McCoy; George E. Whittle, Senate Committee on Banking, Housing and Urban Affairs; James Srodes; Cecile Srodes; Martin Lobel, of Lobel, Novins & Lamont; Bryce A. Arrowood, LawCorps; Richard Levick, John Hellerman, Helen Whitely, and Jamie Fargus of Levick Strategic Communications; Thomas Hale Boggs, Jr., James Patton, Mark Cowan, Ted Delaney, Edward Newberry, Mark Savit, Linda Walker, Elaine Stephanos, Timothy J. May, Carolyn Pomponio, Terry Gunn, Patton Boggs LLP; Ralph Savarese; Victor Schwartz, Crowell Morin; Sheila Jackson, Freedom of Information Reading Room, FBI; Robert Bork, Jr., Bork & Associates; Milton Friedman, Arnold & Porter; Ernest Brooks, D.C. Court of Appeals; Carol Threlkeld and Sherry L. Hamilton of the Board of Professional Responsibility of the D.C. Court of Appeals; Jack Lahr and Howard Fogt, Foley & Lardner; and Veronique Rodman, Robert W. Hahn, and Kumber A. Husain of the American Enterprise Institute.

In Virginia: John Toothman, Elizabeth McGee, and John White of The Devil's Advocate, Alexandria.

In Texas: Scott Baldwin, Sr., Scott Baldwin, Jr., Jack Baldwin, Jean Hiser, Bill Lewis, all of Marshall; Judge Donald Ross, Court of Appeals for the 6th Circuit,

Texarkana; William F. Alexander, Steven Ruskin, Carmen George, Frederick Baron, Kip Petroff, Dallas; Jon Optel of Citizens Against Lawsuit Abuse, Houston; Kenneth B. and Susan Livingston, College Station; Judge Robert A. Parker of the U.S. Fifth Circuit Court of Appeals, Tyler; and Richard Pena and Sharon Ley of the Texas State Bar.

In California: Boris Feldman, John Wilson, Bruce Vanyo, Larry Sonsini, Alan Austin, Lisa Gomes, Diane Brown, Ashley Heinze of Wilson Sonsini Goodrich and Rosati, Palo Alto; Nancy Hersh of Hersh & Hersh; Dan Bolton, Reed R. Kathrein of Milberg Weiss, San Francisco. In Berkeley: Larry Schonbrun. In Torrance: Valerie L. Goodman, DecisionQuest. In San Diego: Dr. Jack C. Fisher, William Lerach, Patrick Coughlin, and "KL" of Milberg Weiss.

In Oregon: Jeff Sapiro and Peggy Miller, Oregon State Bar; Judge Frank L. Bearden of Multoman County Court; U.S. District Judge Robert Jones, Carolyn Wells, and Dave Howard.

In Florida: Dr. Mutaz B. Habal of Tampa; Judge Jack C. Cook; Polly Earl; James Beasley, David Leacock, Robert J. Hauser and Kristen K. Brennan, of Beasley, Leacock & Hauser; L. Frank Chopin, Robert Montgomery, Sue Chopin; Polly Earl and Kirk Friedland, all of West Palm Beach; Richard and Charlotte Barnett, Naples; Angela Parsons, the Florida State Bar.

In Maryland: Nancy B. Currie, FTI Consulting, Annapolis; Peter Angelos, Baltimore.

In New York: Chief Judge Judith Kaye; Denise M. Dunleavy and Serena G. Brown, Weitz & Luxenberg; Melvyn Weiss. Lois Silverman of Milberg Weiss; Gregory Little of Philip Morris Company; Professor Lester Brickman of Hofstra Law School; Paul Rheingold of Rheingold, Valet, Rheingold, Shkolnik & McCartney, LLP: D. Scott Wise, Davis Polk & Wardwell; Christopher Duca of Reliance National; Robert O. Link, Jr., and Grant Hering of Cadwalader, Wickersham & Taft; Stephan Berg of Stephen Berg Public Relations, Inc.

In Wisconsin: Jim Haney and Donna O'Connell of The Office of The Attorney General.

In Minnesota: Brian N. Freeman, Faegre & Benson, Minneapolis

In Pennsylvania: Mary McKenna, Sheila Jeffers, Aida Ayala, and Sharon and Nicole, of the Office of the Clerk of the United States District Court for the Eastern Division of Pennsylvania; Sol Weiss, Bernard Smalley, and William B. Collins.

And, finally, thanks to some persons who transformed an idea into the book you are now holding: Carl D. Brandt, of Brandt & Hochman, best of friends and a superb agent for four decades and fifteen books; Kenneth J. Silver and Amelie Littell of St. Martin's Press; and Laura Plattner of Truman Talley Books.

Index